Beyond Sacred and Secular

Beyond Sacred and Secular

Politics of Religion in Israel and Turkey

Sultan Tepe

STANFORD UNIVERSITY PRESS

STANFORD, CALIFORNIA

Stanford University Press
Stanford, California
© 2008 by the Board of Trustees of the
Leland Stanford Junior University.
All rights reserved.

Printed in the United States of America on acid-free, archival-quality paper

Library of Congress Cataloging-in-Publication Data

Tepe, Sultan, 1969-
Beyond sacred and secular: politics of religion in Israel and
Turkey / Sultan Tepe.
p. cm.
Includes bibliographical references and index.
ISBN 978-0-8047-5864-2 (cloth: alk. paper)
1. Religion and politics. 2. Judaism and politics—Israel. 3. Democracy—
Israel. 4. Political parties—Israel. 5. Islam and politics—Turkey.
6. Democracy—Turkey. 7. Political parties—Turkey. I. Title.
BL65.P7T46 2008
324.2561'082—dc22
2008007822

Typeset by Westchester Book Group in 10/12 Sabon

To my father—my first, best, and continuing teacher

Contents

List of Tables   ix

List of Figures   xi

Acknowledgments   xiii

Introduction
Beyond Sacred and Secular:
A Comparative Analysis of Religious Politics
in Israel and Turkey   *1*

PART I
Paradox of Modernity?
The Conundrum of Religion in Politics

1. Politics of Religion:
Competing and Coalescing Conceptualizations   *33*

2. Religion in the Making of the Israeli
and Turkish Nation-States:
Incomplete Debates and Continuing Institutional Reformations   *65*

PART II
Ideologues or Pragmatists?
The Ideas and Ideologies of Religious Politics

3. Representing the Sacred in Mundane Politics:
The Ideologies and Leaders of Mafdal and Shas   *103*

4. Representing Islam in Secular Politics:
The Ideologies and Leaders of the Nationalist Action,
the National View, and the Justice and Development Parties *159*

PART III
The Popular Roots of Religious Parties

5. Between Zionism and Judaism?
Religious Party Supporters in Israel *229*

6. Between Laicism and Islam?
Religious Party Supporters in Turkey *283*

Conclusion
Sacro-Secular Encounters:
A Comparative Model of Religious Parties *343*

Notes *371*

Index *407*

List of Tables

2.1 Turning points in the incorporation of religion into the state structure 82

3.1 A comparison of the ideological premises of Mafdal and Shas 155

4.1 A comparison of the ideological premises of NAP, the Prosperity Party, and JDP 224

5.1 Main determinants of party choice in Israel 261

5.2 Most salient issues for religious party constituencies in Israel 263

5.3 A multinomial logit model of Shas and Mafdal support 268

5.4 A logit model of Shas support 274

5.5 Assessment of Shas's performance by its supporters 276

6.1 Religious practices and religious party support in Turkey 311

6.2 The state of political trust in Turkish politics 320

6.3 Salient issues for NAP, Prosperity, and JDP supporters 323

6.4 A multinomial logit model of religious party support in Turkey 329

C.1 A typology of religious parties 366

List of Figures

2.1   An ideological map of the prestate movements and the genealogy parties in Israel   *80*

2.2   An ideological map of the selected major movements and the parties in Turkey   *87*

4.1   Genealogy of National View parties   *188*

5.1   Vote shares of party blocs and nonparticipants in Israel   *230*

5.2   Religious self-identification of Israeli citizens   *250*

5.3   Birthplaces and self-defined ethnic identities in Israel   *256*

5.4   Political positioning of parties on two ideological dimensions   *279*

6.1   Vote share by party blocs and nonparticipants in Turkey   *284*

6.2   Support for laicism and religiosity   *306*

6.3   Endorsement of Islamic (Sharia) rule   *308*

6.4   Dispersion of religiosity and party support in Turkey   *310*

6.5   Sources of primary identifications and party choice in Turkey   *313*

6.6   Political positioning of parties and leaders on the Left-Right spectrum, 2005   *318*

Acknowledgments

The following pages are the product of a long journey, which has been enormously rewarding and challenging. I am grateful to all of my colleagues, friends, and students who are intrigued by the question of "why not" as much as "why" and were not confined to the comfort zone of their immediate intellectual neighborhoods.

I could not have braved it through this journey if not for Konuralp Pamukçu's clear vision and relentless support. Special thanks to Roni Baum, Michal Shamir, Frank Tachau, Aryeh Schmulewitz, Bob Luskin, Müge Göçek and Rabbi Avidani, who contributed to this project in so many different but substantial ways. The University of Texas at Austin, the University of Illinois at Chicago, and the U.S. Institute of Peace were all very generous in their endorsement of my research. I am also grateful to Kate Wahl and the feedback of the reviewers for proving that publishing a book can be an enjoyable process despite all the horror stories. I was lucky to have Matt Powers, Elisabeth Muhlenberg, and Heidi Lawson as research assistants; their meticulous work deserves much praise. Had not my dear parents, sisters, and friends in Istanbul, Jerusalem, Ankara, Tel Aviv, Austin, and Chicago constantly reminded me of why the arduous journey was worthwhile, I could not be writing these sentences.

Beyond Sacred and Secular

Beyond Sacred and Secular

A Comparative Analysis of Religious Politics in Israel and Turkey

> Some religions are the harbingers of democracy and progress, whereas others are not. It may be argued that in a number of countries neither capitalism nor democracy could develop because the beliefs associated with the religions that dominated there were incompatible with an autonomous and progressive civil society.[1]

Politics based on the sacred is often seen as antithetical to liberal democracy. Even scholars such as Tocqueville, who saw religion as an asset to democracy, warned, "When ... any religion has struck its roots deep into a democracy, beware that you do not disturb it; but rather watch it carefully, as the most precious bequest of aristocratic ages."[2] This concern is based on the idea that private beliefs have distinctive public consequences. Being a good believer and a good democrat may pull individuals in opposite directions: Being a faithful believer means often deciding today's social issues in accordance with a prophesied future, taking some religious ideas as unquestionable facts, and basing public decisions on the exercise of beliefs rather than reasoning based on contesting positions. Being a good member of a democracy, on the other hand, requires a skeptical mind, the belief that today's decision shapes an open-ended future, the willingness to negotiate on important, even religious, issues, and the compliance to consent to the majority's ideas in order to secure the community's overall well-being. Attending to these crosscurrents, even scholars who valued religion's potential also questioned whether the greater role of religion in today's societies made them more susceptible to authoritarian forces, especially when they lacked free and vibrant civil milieus.[3] Others have argued that to the extent that religion has made inroads into politics and effectively commands unqualified loyalty and obedience from larger groups, it becomes a major liability and a dangerous force for democracy. Obedience, in essence, entails acting "at the bidding of some external authority," and such action "would have no place in a state where the government is vested in the whole people."[4] Democracy's promise—and also its premise—involves a fundamental paradox: it protects free will only for as long as the people *exercise* free will. In a democracy "people would remain free, as long as the laws were done not on external authority, but their own free consent."[5]

A short historical survey shows why these ideas left a permanent impression on our inquiries into religion. At first the fear of religion's impact on politics seemed to have dissipated in many ways. At the abstract level, more people supported the idea that democracy's real value is to find a place even for those who question its fundamental principles. But more importantly, the recent triumph of liberal democracy seemed to seal the fate of religion and eased anxiety over its political role. Since the early 1970s, religion seemed to have lost both its interest in world politics and its ability to command significant authority in an increasingly pluralistic and secularized world. In the aftermath of the cold war, world politics reached an unprecedented normative consensus: the political survival of polities seemed to depend on their ability to maintain their public sphere as an open marketplace of ideas where both secular and sacred ideas count only as different opinions or ideological positions and nothing more. Under such a system, no ideas or beliefs are given immunity from democratic scrutiny or political challenges. Nor are they permitted to claim inherent final authority. The quickly growing number of democracies and the decline of the public quests based on religion seemed to indicate that the heyday of religion's popular role in the public sphere was over.

The recent, sudden rise of religious political parties, which brought old ideas and new institutions together, unexpectedly disturbed this clear picture. Since the early 1980s, religious parties have established themselves as pivotal actors in one country after another, ranging from advanced to transitional democracies. Among many other parties, Japan's Komeito, India's Bharatia Janata Party, Sri Lanka's Jathika Hela Urumaya party, Indonesia's Prosperous Justice Party, Lebanon's Hizbullah, and Palestine's Hamas have achieved stunning successes despite their short histories and weakly professed ideologies. The proliferation of religious groups has reached such a level that it is hard to find a country where religious symbols and beliefs have *not* become a critical component of the political landscape. This remarkable capacity of religion to maintain its influence in the national and international political spheres at a time when the conditions would seem to be the most inimical constitutes one of the most puzzling aspects of world politics today. Scholars in many subfields of the social sciences and beyond attend in one way or another to the pervasive questions of (1) why religion assumed a pivotal role in so many countries where secularization has seemed to have consolidated its roots and (2) how religion's growing political power will affect world politics. For political scientists the riddle of religious parties pertains to the tide of authoritative religious movements in many countries which are also marked by a powerful rise of liberal democracies.[6] This enigmatic return of religion poses some daunting questions: Are religious parties the new contrivance of liberal democracies that blend instrumental logic and faith into an unconventional couple? Or are they new demons of liberalism that both capitalize on and undercut the liberties that democracy secures? Furthermore, are we witnessing a religiously-driven expansion of democracy and liberalism or a religiously-rooted threat to democracy and world peace? Alternatively, are religious parties in some societies manifestations of homegrown democratic ideas, and thus a blessing in disguise to world politics? What, if anything, do different religious movements subsumed under the global rise of religion have in common? Do we misidentify sui generis religious movements by classifying them under the title of global return of religion? Are religious movements products of global secular conditions and can they be seen as unconventional agents that ultimately enhance global integration and the promises of modernity?

These questions lie at the heart of the following chapters. Our analysis builds on the idea that the politics of Judaism and Islam, two areas that are often segregated analytically, when examined together, offer a unique perspective on the politics of religion. Despite their popular description as exceptional cases, not only did the global wave of religion sweep over the political forces in both Israel and Turkey, but religious parties rose to prominence in each country in remarkably similar ways. The stunning salience of religious issues and the political victories of religious parties since the mid-1980s have generated an almost experimental setting for closely examining the global and local aspects of religious parties. Comparing the politics of Judaism and Islam or the politics of religion Israeli and Turkish religious politics might appear to some like comparing apples and oranges. Not only the received wisdom but also the prevailing scholarly accounts tell us that there are vast differences between Judaism and Islam, thus a comparison of the parties embedded in these doctrines is an exercise in analytical stretching, ultimately amounting to a futile academic endeavor. Scholarly studies perpetuate this idea by carefully separating Judaic and Islamic parties and treating them as different genres. Our analysis questions precisely this conviction and shows that the pervasive assumption—that religious parties of distinctive doctrines are incommensurable—creates a critical gulf in our understanding of religious parties. Unless we approach various manifestations of political religion through the same conceptual matrix without oversimplifying them, our explanations become self-fulfilling prophecies.

Crossing the boundaries between the politics of Judaism and Islam affords us a view of religion from beyond the boundaries of a specific religious doctrine. Our expanded horizon permits us to both engage in a critical dialogue with and to benefit from a range of studies that fall into narrowly defined research areas (e.g., those that explain why a religious movement is successful in a certain country) to those that tackle broad research conundrums (e.g., those that delve into why religious groups became critical contenders for power not only in new but also in old democracies in an era when we expect to see them least). Therefore, the following analysis deliberately seeks to transcend the conventional boundaries of various disciplines. Our inquiries engage with and across various research fields, starting at the most detailed level of discussion, typically contributed by experts on a certain region or electoral politics, and moving to a much broader level, one most often frequented by social theorists. One might argue that the absence of detailed studies and the limitations of existing research need to be weighed against the recent metamorphosis of world politics. In fact, by all accounts the terrain of world politics has been drastically transformed over the last two decades and remains in a state of flux. Scholars in general and students of political science in particular search for continuities in the midst of radical transformations and face the challenge of developing a clear view of the future from a chaotic picture of the present. The products of the intellectual anxiety over the unanticipated and powerful role of religion have been mixed. On the one hand, it has served as the catalyst in the exponentially growing number of accounts on such popular themes as the threat or lack thereof of religion to domestic and global peace. On the other hand, these accounts often come without a commensurate effort at collecting empirical data or holding intense conceptual debates that can build bridges between different approaches.

Attesting to the shift in world politics and widespread audience interest, between 1980 and 1990, seven hundred books on the impact of religion on politics were entered into the Library of Congress. Mirroring the escalating attention, this number rapidly rose to three thousand in the following decade. As the overall quantity grew, the studies increasingly fell within the boundaries of narrowly defined research communities whose interest lay in specific issues, ranging from the violent actions or reactions triggered by religion to religion's ability to provide new political skills to urban marginals. The urge to analyze the pressing questions posed by what seems to be the inexorable rise of religion has been impaired by some major obstacles, especially in political science. Speaking to the star-tling lacuna that exists today and to the intellectual stumbling blocks that prevent an improved level of knowledge, an overall assessment of the state of political science in 2006 concluded that "apart from economics and geography, it is hard to find a social science that has given less attention to religion than political science."[7] Wald and Wilcox attributed this bleak picture to the fact that the religious factors "fit neither the legal institu-tional framework that dominated the early years of the discipline nor its later positivist turn to behavioralism and empiricism." While religion is an acknowledged conundrum, its analysis does not easily lend itself to the dominant methodological and theoretical preferences, such as those pre-sented by rational-choice or institutionalist approaches. In some cases "the sheer complexity and the challenges of measuring" political aspects of religion "constitute a barrier to entry" for religion as a research topic.[8]

In an effort to address this theoretical and empirical void, the follow-ing chapters incorporate and engage with the arguments of scholars working in a variety of research areas, from specialized area studies with context specific puzzles—such as why the election shares of certain par-ties have increased—to overarching theoretical ones that grapple with cross-spatial and temporal conundrums—such as how democracies pro-tect individual differences and liberties against homogenizing but impor-tant claims for group rights. Among others, these broad queries ask whether a new form of parties, religious democratic parties, is in the mak-ing; whether religious parties are a menace to liberal democracy; or whether they give new meaning to, or serve as unconventional carriers of, liberal democratic ideals. The answers offered indicate that a "view from nowhere," without paradigmatic lenses, is hard to achieve for any social issue—especially the politics of religion. More importantly, generating empirically well-informed analyses in an area that has long been neg-lected by scholars cannot be commensurate to the growing interest unless the limits of our inquiries are carefully defined, conventional research tools are recalibrated, and outcomes are made relevant to the understand-ing of other cases.[9] To more clearly depict the debates that this analysis both draws on and is critical of, we can, at the risk of simplification, iden-tify two sets of approaches: the *convergence* and *confrontation* frame-works on religious politics and *the modernity* and *multiple modernities* debate on the broader role of religion and liberalism. Each approach to religion and politics filters its complexity and explains why religion resur-faced as a political force and how it affects the ongoing reconfiguration of world politics. More importantly, each offers us an ultimate direction that is likely to emerge from the current political flux.

The convergence approach to the politics of religion contends that liberal democracy differs from other modes of governance in that it strikes a unique balance between individual autonomy, economic welfare, and political stability. History, especially the cold war era, has confirmed that regimes that suppress rival ideologies are eventually doomed to fail. Only political systems that treat their polities as a marketplace of ideas prevent their own demise. It is therefore inevitable that narrow and limited forms of government will deteriorate and converge on the merits of liberal democracy. This prediction makes the pluralism of the public sphere and the recognition of other views not a choice, but a political imperative for political survival. Therefore, religion can only maintain its public presence through a secularization process that enables it to recognize multiple centers of political power and normative values and to accept the decline of its political and moral authority in the public sphere.

Studies informed by the convergence framework contentedly declared victory in the mid-1980s and early 1990s, when the number of full-fledged democracies increased at an unprecedented rate from fifty-three to eighty-eight countries.[10] The global tide of democratization appeared to be pulling many countries along and securing not only the hegemony of liberal democracy but also one of its premises and products—the secularization of world politics. Yet critics of this paradigmatic dominance labeled it a premature celebration that distracted scholars from urgent trends. The wave of global democracy masked some strong opposing currents that have the potential for altering the entire landscape of world politics. Transitions to democracy seem to have halted in countries where free elections did not generate fair political competitions or where democratically elected governments used electoral politics in service to their authoritarian policies. Instead of participating in a global community of liberal democracies rooted in the protection of individual rights and liberties, many countries appear to be languishing in a gray zone of illiberal democratic regimes. These hybrid regimes have stalled at the difficult point of transition, have infringed on the rights of the political opposition and of ethnic or cultural minorities, and have undermined the autonomy of individuals, all while still enjoying international recognition as democracies.[11]

Among those who believed in the ultimate convergence of competing regimes under liberalism, the responses to liberalism's potentially powerful undercurrents and to the democratic balance sheet of expanding religious groups have been diverse. Firm believers in convergence view the return of religion not as a sign of decline, but as a powerful validation of the penetration of liberal democracy. In their view, religion's current political presence is its last gasp and final backlash before its assured demise. Others turn to structural, cultural, or economic reasons to explain the tenacity of religious movements. As a result the entrapment of religion by failed processes surfaces as an explanation to the delays in and impediments to the global march toward democracy. As many observers refrain from questioning liberal democracy and convergence as the ultimate destination, they contend that many countries are in a transitional phase and cannot yet be assigned to a specific regime. In this view, religious parties need to be seen as ephemeral forces with a limited capacity to delay democratization efforts. Accordingly, many labels have been created that would have been considered a contradiction in terms only three decades ago, such as "illiberal democracies" or "transnational oppositional progressive religious movements." Collier and Levitsky have identified more than a hundred qualifications of the term *democracy*, from pseudo and façade to delayed, tarnished, or unruly.[12]

Skeptics, on the other hand, ask whether some countries are mired permanently in the precarious gray area between full-fledged democracy and outright theocratic dictatorship. For this group, inventing qualifiers for the concept of democracy only serves to mitigate the fear that global liberalization could fail. By introducing hybrid regimes and unconventional political movements as oddities of transitional politics or as reactionary and thus evanescent forces, these paradoxical phenomena become normalized, thereby hindering our understanding of new political groups, ideas, and processes. If this is indeed the case, the convergence model only marginalizes the role of religion and fails to understand its ever-increasing political role except as a deviation and a surmountable obstacle on the global march to liberal democracy. It also glosses over the fact that during this global wave of democracy, religious movements asserted their power not only in new but also in established democracies, and that the impacts and social networks of these movements transcended national boundaries. The Christian Right Movement in the United States, the Free Theological Movement in Latin America, the Islamic Brotherhood Movement in North Africa, the Catholic Movement in Eastern Europe, the Orthodox Movement in the former Soviet Union countries, and the Hindu Nationalist Movement in India all became main contenders for political power, indicating that religion's relationship to democracy is more complicated than many have anticipated.

While the convergence supporters grapple with the question of how religion can be incorporated into the global liberal world and the reasons for the lack of integration, the trajectory of changes provided by the confrontation model leaves us with a less optimistic picture. Unlike the convergence model, the confrontation model assigns a central role to religion and singles out religion as one of the most resilient and salient sources of difference among and within political communities. From the lenses of the confrontation approach, with the demise of other ideologies religion emerged as the main cause of conflict in post–cold world war politics at both the local and international levels. Religion claims to be the ultimate source of social order and the final authority on many controversial issues that have bearing on not only those who endorse, but also those who question these beliefs. Therefore, ideologies rooted in religion clash with the premises of liberal democracy, which rests on the autonomy of individuals, the diversity of values, and the superiority of reason to belief.[13] It is important to note that from the confrontational perspective, distinct religious traditions do not necessarily form a coherent, monolithic bloc. Quite the contrary, the increasing interactions among communities and ideas grounded in different religious traditions sharpen their contrasts and bring to the fore their contradictory theological convictions. Therefore, not only the confrontation between religion and secularism, but also the rivalry between different religious communities is inevitable.[14] The rise of religious parties attests to this unavoidable pluralization of the marketplace of ideas and to the increasing awareness of inherent differences among religious and secular groups.

The confrontation paradigm leaves some room for an affirmative role for religion, albeit in an ironical fashion. Echoing the projection of the convergence approach, some scholars argue that religious beliefs could become part of a liberal project by relinquishing some authority over social norms and political order. After all, even in a Tocquevillian world that readily assigns democratic values to religious association, it is believed that "religion, being free and powerful within its own sphere and *content with the position reserved for it*, realizes that its sway is all the better established because it relies only on its own powers without external support" (emphases added).[15] Yet doing so would undermine the claim of omniscience that is inherent within sacred and fundamental ideas of religion. Since such a process of self-negation is unlikely to happen, a clash between religious and other political forces is a more probable scenario. The widespread appearance of local and transnational religious movements is taken not only as a sign of the tenacity of religion in general but also as a mounting reaction to the diminished role of religion under liberal democracy. The driving force behind religious parties, therefore, is the irreconcilable difference between ideologies embedded in religion and secularization that are amplified in political contexts imprinted by liberal democracy. The increasingly popular metaphor of "a new kind of cold war" between religion and liberal democracy captures the antagonistic nature of this politics. For many scholars this new cold war is "no less obstructive of a peaceful international order than the old one was." After all, "no satisfactory compromise between the religious vision of the national state and that of liberal democracy is possible."[16]

A review of convergence and confrontation frameworks to religious parties reveals that, behind their differences, they both share and perpetuate some deeply rooted foundational concepts. In both, the term *religion* encompasses monotheistic and other belief systems, but within the realm of monotheistic religions, Judeo-Christian traditions and Islamic traditions have been carefully separated. The few and weak attempts that have been made to defy this strict separation by using the term of *Judeo-Islamic* have not been successful.[17] Underlying this distinction is the idea that the communities and institutions of Judeo-Christian traditions either had limited claims to political authority (captured by "Render unto Caesar the things which are Caesar's") or underwent a gradual historical process of secularization that led them to limit their social and political claims. Islam's distinctive historical evolution (or lack of it) and doctrinal differences set Islam apart from other religions. Islam has never been secularized in countries with majority Muslim populations and has never ceased to be the most significant source of state legitimacy and, therefore, a main force in politics. While scholars have delved into the question of whether Islamic traditions and democracy are compatible from very different perspectives, the notion of Islamic exceptionalism emerged as a shared, implicit understanding, glossing over Islam's complex, multifaceted doctrines.[18]

While many of the existing analyses can be seen as different articulations of the confrontation and convergence models, the debate can also be approached at a higher level of abstraction in order to better understand our paradigmatic windows. For social theorists, the preoccupation with the vexing question of whether religious parties can be instrumental in creating or strangling liberal democracy reflects a deeper issue that often escapes the interests of scholars who study the form and appearance of religious parties: Can modernity take multiple forms? Put differently, can the promises of liberalism be fulfilled in traditional settings and by what appear to be authoritarian agents?[19] Beneath the ongoing debates lies the idea that modernity is rooted in the Enlightenment-humanist rejection of tradition and authority in favor of reason and natural science.[20] Some take this origin to the extreme and conclude that modernity is the triumph of reason over belief, and more importantly, an essentially Western product that emerged from the intellectual debates, political conflicts, and social transformations of Western Europe. Therefore, liberal democracy, as a political product of modernity, may fail to take root in culturally and historically alien territories. Having their roots in the modernity thesis, it is not surprising that neither the convergence nor the confrontation model questions this normalized conclusion. For this reason, even the accounts of those with a less skeptical view of religion are imprinted with the Western experience. For instance, some scholars acknowledge that instead of challenging democracy, religious parties can play and have played an instrumental role in the demise of authoritarian regimes, as they did first in Europe (1970s) and then in Latin America (1990s), gradually evolving into mass parties without completely relinquishing the ideas that make them religious.[21] However, implicit in these conclusions is the belief that Christian-Democratic movements and parties ultimately benefited from the Judeo-Christian tradition of accepting multiple sources of political authority and of challenging authoritarianism without trying to dominate politics. Many of the new religious parties of today are embedded in ideas from non–Judeo-Christian traditions, a circumstance that appears to make them especially threatening to the stability of world politics. These parties' political experiences have not been those of secularization through which the boundaries between religious authorities and others are contested and negotiated. To become a reliable player in the game of democracy, religious parties need to be exposed to such a process or adopt its outcomes. Some observers are especially alarmed by their awareness that in Islamic countries, religious parties have established themselves as critical actors at a time when their respective democracies are still weak, thus making these democracies susceptible to totalitarian tendencies and clashes, both locally and globally.

While this ubiquitous, yet mostly implicit, conflation of Westernization and modernity continues to sharply imprint efforts to understand new religious parties, it has also led some to speak of the possibility of multiple modernities.[22] Recognizing that modernity can be conceived of as plural invites us to resist conventional wisdom and normalized assumptions. This pluralistic incision directs our attention to the need to loosen the tight grip of deductive and deterministic accounts on our efforts to understand how the contribution of religious movements and parties can unfold in different directions—including toward democracy. Such adjustment requires a deep shift in our thinking to allow us to acknowledge that the ideas of modernity (e.g., autonomy of individual, free will, an understanding of history as an open-ended project) can take root in unexpected places, practices, and traditions. Although deductive approaches suggest otherwise, the possibility that religious doctrines are capable of accommodating autonomy, and that a strong religious community can coexist with independent agents, needs to be part of our inquiries. After all, at its core modernity entails the breakdown of all traditional legitimizations of the political order. However, it does not and cannot preclude multiple ways of constructing a new order.[23] Therefore, tradition does not necessarily disappear in modernity. Instead, it is reinterpreted in critical ways.[24] Each community can produce the principles of modernity according to its habitus, its life patterns, shared sets of meanings, and structures of response. Reinterpretations of different traditions under conditions of modernity could give way to a variety of sociopolitical arrangements that may or may not involve religion. The understanding that modernity does not replace existing traditions, and that traditions can accommodate modern ideas, has given us terms such as the *vernacularization* or *indigenization* of democracy. These concepts indicate that communities can and are likely to produce their own modernity. For example, Judaic or Islamic parties can generate modern political ideas on their own terms and in their own unique ways. Accepting that universality of modernity does not need to manifest itself as a homogenizing force, provides us with a perspective where religious parties could serve as unusual agents of local articulations of democracy, and not necessarily a threat to liberalism.

From the perspective of the multiple modernities debates, the convergence and confrontation models are hamstrung by their overt and tacit assumptions about religion, which express themselves best in the overall suspicion of new religious political groups. Both approaches express anxiety over the ability of religious parties to harbor antidemocratic traits under the guise of political parties: although they act under the façade of a new institution, religious parties are likely to act as sect-like ideologies and mirror the fundamental ideas of their respective doctrines. Their political leadership and their political agenda are expected to be submissive to their religious leadership. Religious parties ultimately have the potential of moving politics in an authoritarian direction by imposing their religious ideology. The convergence model, in part due to the positive role that Judeo-Christian parties have played in world politics, seems to offer a more favorable, but still wary, assessment of these parties. The cautious optimism of the convergence model suggests that, when allowed to compete politically, religious groups are forced to become less programmatic, more ideologically distinct, and more heterogeneous. Therefore, religious parties can and have become agents of democracy through bargaining, strategic action, or external forces and not through internal, self-enforcing, ideological commitments. Underlying this conclusion is not a different view on religion, but a widely shared faith, especially among political scientists, in the transformative power of democratic competition: against all odds, democracy can take root without democrats, and democratic ideologies are often not the main ingredient but a by-product of democratic electoral competitions.[25] All participants in a democracy, once they are engaged in the electoral competition, change and come to accept not only the procedures but also the principles of democracy.

Against this backdrop of contested and overlapping understandings of and prospects for the interactions between religion and liberal democracy, the following chapters first introduce us to a set of implicit and explicit abstract postulations, the limits and potential of the primary data, and the ways in which we use empirical evidence to analyze religious politics. Given the dearth of theoretically and empirically grounded studies, our analysis responds to the calls that urge us to integrate primary empirical evidence into our explanations. Due to the complexity of religious ideas and the reluctance of religious leaders and partisans to participate in studies, any effort to draw on the primary analysis of religious ideas and their carriers poses some challenges. The integration of primary observations and empirical evidence ipso facto cannot illuminate the nature of religious movements. Our analysis therefore includes frequent reminders of the argument that theory-neutral analyses of empirical data cannot exist. Unless we keep our instruments in perspective and remember their limitations and promises in assessing the compiled empirical evidence, they might permanently blur our vision. More significantly, given the long history of religion in social life and its marginalization by scholars, it is especially important to remember, as Dryzek put it, that with frequent applications of its instruments, a theory can fade from awareness, "so the method can yield seemingly direct access to observed phenomena. In reading a thermometer one does not need to be aware of how Boyle's law is applying." As the instrument can become like a permanent window through which a room is viewed, "the observer can let the instrument slip from awareness."[26] In an effort to ensure that we are not treating the view from our window as the only universe that exists and presumably encompasses the nature of the politics of religion, the subsequent analysis also calls into question the roots of our postulations and how we substantiate and test the deductive explanations that follow from the convergence and confrontation theories.

Our comparative inquiry into politics of Judaism and Islam positions itself first in the existing frameworks and then seeks to carve out a new analytical space that eventually moves beyond their boundaries by blending primary data and conceptual debates. A systematic comparison of the theoretical premises, units of analysis, and teleological frameworks of both convergence and confrontation models indicates that each concentrates on different aspects of the puzzling appeal of political religious groups. They privilege either the characteristics of religious doctrines (ideas) or the social or the political context in which these parties are embedded (structure), or center on their adherents, namely the leadership and their partisans (agents). Religion's interaction with liberal democracy is seen in binary terms as either acceptance or rejection (e.g., modernity thesis) or is presented as an unprecedented new path to local and global coexistence and enlightenment (multiple modernization thesis). Seldom do studies penetrate the nexus of religious ideas, the capacities of religious agents and the unique political settings they are part of without subsuming them under teleological expectations. The prevailing analyses assume that ideologies per se cannot be used as explanatory variables unless the comparison is made across different religions or denominations. After all, common wisdom tells us that ideologies derived from the same religion generate more or less the same ideas, thus molding all religious parties it informs similarly. In cases where the ideological differences between religious parties based on the same religion are too significant to ignore, observers have used the competition for power among religious leaders to explain the divergences among them. Even in cases where observers have taken the ideologies of religious parties seriously, the ideas contained in those ideologies have been played down. After all it is not its specific content, they presume, but the overall role played by ideology that matters most.

The angst over the sudden appearance and unanticipated nature of religious parties manifests itself best in the proliferation of accounts that either offer very thick descriptions of one religious community, movement, or leader, or very thin analyses that simply juxtapose various cases without seeking analytical commonalities. The broad and institutional study of political parties has been losing its once dominant role in social science and has become increasingly narrow and confined more and more to analyses of survey data. In fact, political scientists have been urged to refocus their attention on big theoretical issues, to treat the organizational and ideological aspects of parties holistically, and to question their broad roles in social and political processes by developing macro-level and panoramic analyses of the broader political process.[27] Missing in the studies of the politics of religion and parties are conceptually or empirically more-elaborated and well-defined accounts that can generate new ideas and test the validity of existing approaches. The shortage of these studies is especially critical given that macro-level structural accounts tend to depict the supporters of religious parties as socially reactive and culturally displaced masses or as religious conservatives who turn to religious parties in order to voice their political dissent.

Alternative studies are grounded in ethnographic descriptions of selected communities or are rich in anecdotal evidence in order to illuminate the worldview of religious partisans. These studies direct our attention to how individuals or communities cope with their changing social and economic environment by imbuing their religious beliefs with new ideas and values. In these studies, we often find analytically expedient illustrations of how seemingly outdated traditional practices become the foundation of social capital in newly emerging, alienated urban settings and succeed in enhancing accountability and mutual trust. The individual-level thick descriptions are especially helpful for us to grasp the ways in which religious parties and their followers understand politics and how they become major players in global political interactions, and thus assets for the establishment of democracy in their respective countries. Notwithstanding their contributions, these studies often describe religion's new social role in a political vacuum, and religious parties are treated as black boxes. Regardless of their individual contributions, when viewed together, existing analyses and scholarly accomplishments have created isolated explanations that are marred by a persistent disconnect between deductive and inductive approaches, between theoretical a priori assumptions and empirically grounded accounts. Thus, overall, we are faced with a decisively limited supply of systematic, primary observations pertaining to the structure of religious parties, their elites, or their supporters; furthermore, our understanding is limited by the inclination of a wide range of scholars to treat Islam as a sui generis case and give scarce attention to the political implication of politics of religion in the Jewish world.

The comparative design central to this study was inspired by the remarkable parallel electoral successes of religious parties and the development of comparable public discourses on religion in Israel and Turkey. In both democracies, once-marginal religious parties have steadily broadened their electoral support and established themselves as pivotal political actors and main contenders for political power. For instance, despite its ultra-Orthodox outlook, Shas (*Hit'akhdut ha-Sephardim ha-Olamit Shomrey Torah*, International Organization of Torah-observant Sephardic Jews) won seventeen seats in the May 1999 election and became the third largest bloc of votes in the Knesset, the Israeli parliament. In the watershed 2003 local election, in which the political bases of many other parties were severely eroded, the Shas Party held on to its eleven Knesset seats and 160 council memberships, surprising all those who had anticipated its demise.[28] In the most recent 2006 election, which resulted in a metamorphosis of Israeli politics, Shas proved that its ability to maintain its power is not a fluke. The party not only held on to its seats, but gained an additional mandate, proving that it is a permanent and pivotal force in Israeli politics. While Shas, a party popularly described as an ultra-Orthodox ethnic party, expanded its popular appeal, support for Israel's moderate Mafdal (*Miflaga Datit Le'umit*, the National Religious Party) has been declining. Although the party continues to enjoy disproportionate power in Israeli politics, its role as an indispensable bridge between secular and religious groups has been weakening. The overall increase in religious votes and the shift of support from moderate to ultra-Orthodox religious parties constitutes one of the most critical aspects of Israeli politics. Yet the research around these parties suffers from the theoretical and empirical limitations faced by studies of religious parties everywhere.

In Turkey, the December 1995 elections represented a turning point. A party publicly adhering to Islam, the Welfare Party (*Refah Partisi*), gained a plurality of the votes (21 percent). No other openly religious party in the country's history had ever before attracted such a high percentage of the electorate. When the Welfare Party seemed to be faltering and its discourse was under scrutiny, another party, the Justice and Development Party (JDP, *Adalet ve Kalkınma Partisi*), achieved an even more stunning success in the November 2002 elections. The party captured 34.31 percent of the total vote, giving it a large margin over the other parties. Its landslide success occurred despite, or perhaps because of, the fact that just prior to the election, the JDP's leader was banned from holding public office as a result of his divisive religious views, and the party's future depended on a constitutional court decision regarding its legal status. The election results proved that despite Turkey's secular ideology, which bans parties that run on a religious platform, pro-Islamic parties are major political actors in Turkish politics and continue to expand their power in spite of opposition. In the post–cold war era, Turkey also witnessed an increased Islamization of its nationalist parties, especially the Nationalist Action Party (NAP, *Milliyetçi, Hareket Partisi*), whose support has fluctuated yet significantly grown. After its Islamization, the NAP also performed electoral miracles, reaching the highest level of support it had achieved in its history in 1999 with 19.1 percent of the total vote. A comparative look at the last five election results in Turkey shows that Islam, and political ideas drawn from it, constitutes one of the main defining political forces in the country, despite the country's official commitment to *laïcité*, an areligious public sphere.

The remarkably similar transformation of religious politics in Israel and Turkey poses some intriguing conceptual and empirical questions and offers an ideal setting that allows us to both include and control for the role of a large set of factors. Deepening our understanding of these two countries, both critical to world politics, is a significant exercise in its own right. The main promise of this comparison, however, lies in its ability to place us in an exceptionally advantageous analytical position from which we can address both specific, practical political questions and big, general theoretical questions. Among others we ask: Are the parallel fortunes of religious parties in Israel and Turkey a mere coincidence? What do the politics of Judaism in Israel and the politics of Islam in Turkey have in common? Are there common factors and processes in place that can explain their similar manifestations of religious politics? Do more Israeli and Turkish voters support religious parties because of short-term considerations, or is the electorate experiencing enduring changes in its ideological commitments? Do we find more evidence for the convergence model than for the confrontation model or vice versa? Can we find one definite answer to the question of whether the rise of religious politics represents a decline of secularism, a shift to illiberal democracies? Does the rise of religious politics in both countries reflect the expansion of democratic principles to religious actors in these countries? Are the politics of Judaism and Islam in fact dissimilar, as the general wisdom suggests? Are religious parties and democracy strange bedfellows? Do religious parties promote democracy under new global conditions? What can we learn from the Israeli and Turkish experiences that will help us to demystify religion's resurgence elsewhere?

Even a cursory look at the history of Israeli and Turkish politics illustrates that the these countries share more than a popular image of being "exceptional cases" in the Middle East and world politics, and they offer an excellent ground to delve into the politics of religion. The nationalisms, state structures, and party systems of both countries are rooted in comparable conflicts and challenges, and have sometimes developed analogous solutions. Both countries emerged from the ashes of the Ottoman Empire during the wave of nationalism that swept through the empire in the early twentieth century. The constitutive elite of the two nation-states shared intellectual ties during their formative years. Along with Turkey's state elite, a significant number of Israel's initial leaders, including Ben-Gurion, Israel's first prime minister, were educated in Ottoman schools, were active in the Ottoman parliament, and were exposed to the ideas that shaped the empire's unique political system—most important its *millet* system, which consisted of autonomous religious communities and sought to prevent the empire's disintegration along sectarian lines.

The principles of nationalism in both countries were imprinted with the ideals of modernity. For the state-founding leaders in each country, nationalism was a prerequisite for a stable and enduring polity. Ironically, despite their skepticism of the role of religion, the elites in both countries relied on religion as the unifying force for keeping different cultural groups together in one nation. Yet at the same time, they aimed to reform the public role of religion to make it more compatible with a modern nation-state. Thus, religion acquired an ambivalent role in both polities: on the one hand, it sustained the nationalist ideology and was one of the sources of legitimacy for the nascent regimes; on the other hand, the nationalist elite challenged and restricted religion's claim to political authority out of a fear of its capacity to undermine the foundations of their modern state. As a result, each country created a complex web of institutions around the public role of religion that cannot be adequately represented through a Western form of secularism or understood within a simplified model of the separation of church and state.

The early years of the two new nations Israel and Turkey saw the establishment of secular nationalist parties, Mapai and the Republican People's Party, respectively, as the countries' dominant political parties. Their state-centric and somewhat exclusive policies sparked massive opposition that paved the way for the formation of a range of conservative opposition parties. In both countries, a two-party dominant political system gradually evolved into a multiparty system in which religious parties have finally now established themselves as major players. Since the mid-1980s, the transformations of Israeli and Turkish politics have continued to unfold in a surprisingly analogous way. Not only have both countries witnessed a remarkable growth of support for religious parties, they have also seen religious parties evolve into competing political camps. The presence of rival religious parties enhances the analytical purchase provided by an examination of these countries by facilitating a multilayered design that compares and contrasts religion's role both within and across Turkey and Israel. In Israel, the Shas Party and the Mafdal compete with each other, as do the Nationalist Action Party, Prosperity Party, and the Justice and Development Party and its predecessors in Turkey.[29] The parties show how the same religious doctrine can affect politics differently and how the different religious doctrines can encompass parties that subscribe to similar positions. Put differently, variations within Jewish and Islamic politics help us tease out why and how the political ideologies of religious parties embedded in the same religion differ, and whether their divergence displays similar patterns across religions. Situating the ideologies of these parties, their elite structure, and the socioeconomic-political positioning of their supporters first in their domestic environment, and then in a broader comparative setting, promises to reveal both their doctrine-specific, context-bound particularities and their universal traits.[30]

The ideological richness of religious parties in Israel and Turkey, and a two-level comparison both within and across religious doctrines, also helps us to discuss why the existing basic concepts do not allow us to finely tune our analysis and detect decisive nuances. For instance, studies that attribute political capacity to the main characteristics of religious doctrines fail to capture that the way in which religious ideas are used by agents actually matters more than the overall features of a given doctrine. Honing our conceptual tools and analytical insight cannot happen only through vertically deepening studies (i.e., studies of the same doctrine or cases from the same political context), but requires broadening our horizon by viewing comparable and contrasting experiences at the same time.

Our concepts need to grasp first and foremost how religion is experienced, appropriated, and positioned vis-à-vis other ideas and institutions within a given polity. Such conceptual recalibration is especially critical in light of the existing and sometimes deliberate elusiveness of some religious ideologies and actors.

Some of this conceptual fuzziness surrounding the politics of religion marks even the very basic terms. Perhaps the most striking is the very term *religious parties*. Although religious parties and the politics of religion have become part of the daily political parlance, their characteristics are not always conceptually straightforward. The role of religion and its manifestation in the form of political parties in a given society is a function of a complicated set of factors, including such diverse elements as the rules of electoral competition and the presence (or absence) of politically salient issues significant to religious doctrine. Institutional context is especially important to understanding specific manifestations of religious politics. For instance, although no scholar would question the fact that religious parties exist in Turkey, no party leader would refer to Islamic ideas in the public sphere overtly because any such mention would disqualify the party from political competition. Constitutional restrictions prevent even genuinely religious parties from using religion unequivocally in their official rhetoric. The situation is further complicated by the fact that, as religion becomes the main currency of politics, many secular parties refer to religious values and ideas in one way or another to enhance their own public appeal. In many regards, the perplexing terrain of religious politics in Turkey is not exceptional, but only amplifies issues that exist in other polities. The challenge for analysts is to clearly differentiate religious parties from others, particularly since a broad range of parties integrate religious beliefs and values into their rhetoric. They vie for the support of voters with variant levels of religiosity, and seek to justify their issue positions via the legitimizing power of religion. This study defines religious parties as those that *consistently* refer to religious ideas and values in the formation and implementation of their core policies and in their proposed solutions to major controversial issues.

A thorough, scholarly assessment of the politics of religion faces not only the challenge of identifying which parties are religious parties but also of ensuring that the term does not limit but serves as the initial step of our engagement with them. Once they have been identified, the public rhetoric of religious parties, the most opaque aspect of their appeal, poses perhaps an even greater and more serious challenge to analysts. Party leaders often use an intertwined rhetoric: one designed to appeal to their hard-core constituency and the other meant to address the general public. An understanding of both, especially the former, requires a careful study of the ideational world of these parties and an unpacking of the symbols derived from religious doctrines. Furthermore, some policy positions are justified by advancing nonreligious reasoning instead of a rationale informed by religious ideas and norms. Therefore, before venturing into the appeal of religious parties and understanding their policies, one must first unravel their sometimes idiosyncratic ideological vocabulary. Only after penetrating their façade and peeling off the outer layer of their discourse can we offer a detailed analysis of the political positions of these parties.

By using the global rise of religion and the politics of Judaism and Islam as a springboard, this book seeks to integrate some disconnected debates and contribute to analytical endeavors in some loosely linked communities. Given its ultimate objectives, this study, first and foremost, does not celebrate religious parties as unfairly treated agents of modernity—an approach favored mostly by analyses that treat any vernacularization and sign of proactive political participation as a step toward modernity; nor does it readily assign them to potentially antidemocratic forces in the guise of modern parties—a view supported by some convergence or confrontation theories. Without taking an a priori normative position or trying to present a predictive model, this study seeks to see what lies beyond the anomalous appearance of religious parties. We ask questions inquiring into how these parties have been able to establish themselves as main contenders for political power despite the fact that their success has tended to be overshadowed by suspicion of their radical political goals. For instance, how have their political messages made themselves attractive to different groups despite the mounting opposition of the secular public (e.g., in India, Indonesia, and Israel)? How have their networks sailed them through tumultuous electoral processes given the adverse reactions of the state affiliated institutions (e.g., in Egypt, Algeria, and Turkey) and the international community (e.g., in Lebanon)? Who are the supporters of these religious parties? Why do they turn to religious parties? If religious parties progressively increase their electoral support, where does their new support come from? Which ideas constitute the backbone of these parties' ideologies? How do they perceive secular institutions and ideas? Who are the religious party elites? Are they pragmatists who capitalize on religion's appeal among masses? Are they ideologues from distinct backgrounds? Does the religious elite offer new policy positions or capitalize on politics of resentment? Do religious parties pose a threat to democracy by obstructing rational dialogue and fruitful democratic negotiations? Are they able to overcome the epidemic of political apathy and carve out a new political arena, thereby broadening the boundaries of democracy in their countries?

Second, the book's approach brings together context (structure), agents, and ideology—the three elements of the politics of religion. We probe the political views and positions of religious elites and partisans by locating them in their political settings and identifying the multiple actors with whom they interact. Religious ideologies can be seen as articulations that agents refer to in order to have an impact on their political environment, and this setting imprints them in return. The interdependency between institutional and individual aspects in the formation of these meanings necessitates conceptualizations that approach the ideologies of religious parties without limiting them to the specific myths and beliefs of their religious doctrines, locate them in relation to their settings, and include the role of agents. This study treats religion as a symbolic system with multiple, changing meanings. Emphasized in such abstraction is both the latent, fixed ideational capital of religious doctrines as well as their continuing multiple interpretations. The conception of religion as a symbolic sphere emphasizes the role of the agents as users and interpreters of these symbols and as articulators and modifiers of the repertoire of religion's symbolic capital. It also emphasizes that individuals do not have a limitless array of options to use their religious vocabulary or define its meanings. On the contrary, it draws our attention to the interplay between the specifics of the doctrine, as well as the historical institutional settings. It is this intersection that shows how each restricts or opens up the latitude for interpretation.

When we move beyond the simplistic understanding that assumes that the politics of religion simply mirrors religious doctrinal beliefs and promotes the religious public interest in the political system, we are able to recognize that analyzing the political relevance of religion requires an understanding of (1) the interactions among the agents (especially among users, or interpreters), (2) the religious vocabulary or symbolic system, (3) the constraints introduced by the given institutional and ideational context, and (4) the political positions and alternative vocabulary of other actors. It is not any single component but the reciprocal relationship among them that makes analyses of religious politics especially intriguing and challenging. As a result, this analysis focuses neither on a macro-level structural and institutional analysis, nor on a micro-level, individual behavioral or ethnographic one. It moves back and forth between the two, while its focus lies at the juncture of the complex interface between these levels and the underlying, mutually transformative processes.

Third, the following chapters seek to bring to the fore the analytical costs of a parochial, religion-specific, and context-bound analysis and highlight the long-term implications of incurring those costs. The comparative inquiry by no means assumes the politics of religion in Israel and Turkey to be essentially similar, but draws on them as a fecund analytical platform for elaborating on a set of existing questions, always allowing for the possibility of new answers. In our multilayered and multipronged comparison we try to understand (1) whether the simultaneous rise of these parties shares deeper traits other than their electoral successes, (2) what common and unique domestic, regional, and structural factors can be found at the root of their ascendancy, and (3) how the ideas of their respective religions reveal themselves in the ideologies of these parties. The comparative design of this study, its simultaneous inquiries into the politics of Judaism and Islam, and its attention to variations within each prevent us from falling into the trap of essentialism that marks prevailing accounts. In other words, the study's comparative setting enables us to explain the popular appeal of religious parties within and across these countries without attributing their traits entirely either to their unique contexts or to the ideas that are perceived to be intrinsic to their respective religious doctrine.

Fourth, the book analyzes party elites and partisan views on their own terms to avoid the fallacies of idiosyncratic, myopic, or sweeping generalizations about religious politics, and more importantly, to prevent self-confirmatory conclusions. The arguments presented throughout this analysis are gleaned from primary sources, ranging from participant observations to the content analysis of party documents gathered during field research in Israel and Turkey between May 1998 and May 2007. The main threads of the arguments are derived from in-depth interviews with a large set of the members of religious party elites, including party representatives in the Knesset and the Turkish Parliament, as well as party consultants and activists. These interviews were conducted using a comparable format to explore how religious party elites adopt religious symbols and traditions in defining their ideal political order. The interviews open up the ideational world of religious party leaders and uncover the multiplicity of ways in which religious party leaderships accommodate and challenge the concept of a secular nation, redefine the role of individuals and community, reassess political and economic opportunities, and evaluate the implications of changing global politics for their constituencies. By the same token, to understand the popular foundation of religious parties, the question of who turns to religious parties and what factors determine their support is analyzed by drawing on the Israeli and Turkish national election surveys from 1988 to 2005.[31] In order to broaden and deepen the findings of the existing studies, two representative national surveys were specifically designed for this analysis. Both surveys sought to tap into an unexplored reservoir of information about religious parties and partisans. Relying heavily on primary sources produced by the leaders and supporters when available and accessible, this analysis tries to offer an inside-out assessment of religious parties and explores their positions on a range of issues vis-à-vis democracy through an inductive approach.

The subsequent discussion is organized to reflect the rationale and ultimate goals of the comparison discussed above. The following chapter, Chapter One, "Politics of Religion: Competing and Coalescing Conceptualizations," retraces how different schools of thought grapple with the role of religion in the public sphere. Revisiting the arguments put forth by a wide range of scholars, including Emile Durkheim, Max Weber, Peter Berger, Steven Bruce, and Oliver Roy, this chapter lays out the intellectual foundation the analysis rests on and the reasoning behind its conceptual language. Our terminology refrains from referring to concepts that reify the religious and the secular as contradictory forces. Instead, the terms presented here try to highlight and capture how the religious and secular spheres coexist and continuously shape each other. In order to better grasp the agendas of religious parties, their policies and motivations, our inquiry at all levels seeks to move past conflict- and compromise-based analyses to probe into the mutually transformative interactions between the secular and religious. We identify how the public's repertoire of "religious" beliefs has increasingly been appropriated and shaped by the "secular" and vice versa by paying attention to the interrelationship of ideas rather than accepting their assumed antagonism or inevitable synthesis. Recognizing the permeability of the religious and secular spheres opens up a new analytical space and a new set of questions: What are the ways in which the religious and the secular mold each other? Is it a random process? Are there any processes that capture the transmutation of beliefs and ideas assigned to the secular and the religious? How can we analyze the sacred beliefs and symbols carried by religious parties if they are altered by the secular? Establishing the mutual permeability of secular and religious beliefs does not take us to relativism or nihilism, or force us to conclude that these beliefs no longer matter. Instead, understanding their permeability can help us explore how religious parties form their ideologies in multiple ways. In order to tease out the shape and direction of this transformative process, it is important to highlight the gray areas masked by the dichotomous terms of the confrontation and convergence models by using more accommodating terms, such as *adaptive transformation* or *compliant dissension*.

The current political role of religion, regardless of country or religion, has evolved from a set of conflicts and compromises. Even so-called socially engineered changes and top-to-bottom policies cannot be understood when they are divorced from their historical institutional settings. Israel and Turkey are no exception to this pattern. In both countries, religion plays a crucial role in forming national identities and serving as a source of social values. Both countries have crafted highly complex institutional arrangements whose structure and boundaries have continuously been contested. Chapter Two, "Religion in the Making of the Israeli and Turkish Nation-States," details the ideas, agreements, and shifts that have marked the broader settings of religious politics in Israel and Turkey. The semiautonomous structure of the religious bloc in Israel is contrasted with Turkey's strict secularism. A fine-tuned assessment of Judaic and Islamic politics demonstrates that, regardless of their doctrinal content, both religions represented comparable conundrums for the newly emerging nation-states. The ways in which the political role of religion was, and continues to be, negotiated and the processes by which compromises were reached affected the institutions that developed in each polity and the roots of current pressing issues. Half a century after the establishment of the Israeli state, Israelis continue to debate vigorously how to untangle Israel's religious character from its national character, or whether and to what extent Israel's lenient policies toward the religious bloc undermine its dedication to pluralistic democracy. Debates often center on how to protect the role of religion without infringing on the rights of secular groups and undermining the legitimacy of the state. Likewise, one of the most divisive issues in the Turkish polity involves figuring out how to include Islam and Muslim groups in the public sphere without ceding total control over it to religion. Interestingly, recent changes adopted in both countries appear to signal an ironical convergence of their institutional configurations. Israel's electoral law has been changed to prohibit the use of religious symbols in politics, indicating the way in which Israel tries to further limit the role of religion and the concessions made to the religious public. On the other hand, the political practices in Turkish politics seem to be adopting an approach more favorable to religious groups and symbols in the public sphere, in striking contrast to its early years of strict secularism. The historical background of the political milieus of Israel and Turkey and their religious parties further indicates that their analysis is not merely an academic exercise but a critical venue to understand how the political power of religion is Janus-faced, pervasive, and contested. Analyses bereft of such historical context not only fail to capture the interplay of institutional frameworks, the ideas derived from the doctrines, and the capacities and limits of the agents, they also miss out on an evaluation of the nature of political negotiations.

Central to Chapters Three and Four is the question of whether the ideologies and elites of religious parties can be better described as "Ideologues or Pragmatists?" and what constitutes their political paradigm. While the religious party elites in both countries form competing groups and differ significantly from nonreligious parties, they exhibit similar profiles across countries. Their commonalities become more pronounced when we ask how religious movements expand their reach in each country. None of the religious leaders are insular local religious scholars who are antagonistic toward the state. On the contrary, their political ideas were often formed only once they left their insular communities, occupied state positions, and encountered the world beyond their religious origins. Shared and similarly compartmentalized traits suggest that we can speak of an engaged, inventive, locally grounded, and internationally well-connected elite, rather than insular, passive recipients or reactive leaderships whose political responses were imprinted by opposition to existing political forces. The blurred boundaries between religious and secular elites are a function of shifting interrelationships among their ideas.

Mapping out how religious party elites are formed, what constitutes their policies and religious ideas, and how they mold their decisions is crucial for an overall assessment of these parties. The ways in which religious party leaderships approach religious tradition and values reveal the presence of two underlying processes. We call these processes *sacralization* (i.e., assigning religious meanings to secular ideas and institutions and treating them as beyond question, as sacred) or *internal secularization* (i.e., accommodating secular practices as religiously acceptable). The following chapters elaborate on these latent processes and better position us to determine whether and how these parties are able to develop a strategic rhetoric that remains beyond the reach of secular parties. More significantly, putting the religious parties under the prism of sacralization and internal secularization exposes contradictions in religious party ideologies that are not easily discerned and encourages us to revisit some prevalent notions, such as the concepts of moderate and radical religious parties. Parties that adopt the sacralizing strategy may appear more moderate than those that adopt internal secularization when, in fact, they are more receptive to authoritarian policies. Likewise, the pluralism of parties that sacralize the state turns out to be more tenuous. Paradoxically, parties that appear confrontational and seek to create parallel religious discourses are more inclined to engage in a process of internal secularization and are more likely to transform religious ideas from within. Irrespective of their short-term radical rhetoric, in the long run their efforts to create parallels better positions them toward accommodating both ideologically and practically some of the premises of a pluralistic democratic society. The visible and paradoxical short-term positions and more latent long-term inclinations further caution us against selective interpretations and holistic conclusions—especially against those that label religious parties as threatening or minimize them as unconventional flag carriers of democracy and *indigenizers* of modernity.

The questions of who the religious partisans are and why they support religious parties are central to Chapters Five and Six, which share the common theme of "Popular Roots of Religious Parties." Each chapter evaluates the validity of prevalent explanations of religious party support as informed by variants of the confrontation and convergence approaches. More specifically, eliciting our arguments mostly from rarely used survey data, we ask whether we can attribute the expansion of religious party support to *conflict* (i.e., to individuals' reaction to secularist values), *crisis* (i.e., response to ongoing socioeconomic crises), *political alienation* (i.e., individuals' declining trust in politics and parties), or *mobilization* (i.e., the effectiveness of party apparatus or the charismatic attraction of the party leadership). These models attribute the electoral fortunes of religious parties to (1) the inevitable conflict between secular and religious values being inevitable, (2) the presence of politically alienated groups who are drawn to parties due to their anti-systemic nature or their welfare programs and eventually vote for religious parties to oust the ruling parties, or (3) the assumption that religious partisans come disproportionately from the urban poor, swayed by the party leaders' charismatic appeal or the parties' political machines.

Although the existing Israeli and Turkish national election surveys provide us with invaluable tools for distinguishing religious party supporters from others and for delving into their common political beliefs and socioeconomic positions, they are also susceptible to some shortcomings. In the first section of each chapter we define the shortcomings and promises of the existing survey data used in order to better take advantage of the wealth of information generated by them. Ironically, addressing some of the limitations of the survey data overall contributes to our discussions of religious party supporters and assists our efforts to sharpen our empirical means to study religious groups by bringing to the fore less visible aspects of religious party support. For instance, the underrepresentation of some religious party supporters in the existing studies prompts us to think more deeply about whether this lacuna is a question of party identification, sampling bias, or disproportionately high nonresponse rates among religious partisans. Addressing the shortcomings of the survey as a tool and probing into the underlying reasons for its limitations in studying religious communities illuminates the characteristics of religious party supporters as much as the surveys do themselves. The inadequacies turn our attention to more specialized surveys that include more finely tuned questions on religious ideas and focus on the permeability of religious and secular views without restricting them to the binaries of religious/secular, democratic/antidemocratic. The two specialized representative national surveys conducted for this comparative study provide us with more revealing data than the routine surveys. They also control the validity of some of our findings through a more detailed questionnaire and a higher participation of religious partisans.[32] The 2003 Israeli survey oversampled Shas supporters to analyze the political beliefs of this group, while the 2005 Turkish Religious Party survey included open-ended questions about laicism and detailed questions regarding religious beliefs that allowed respondents to state their opinions without constraints. In the subsequent chapters we report some of the findings directly, while many others have been integrated into the overall analysis and inform the discussion indirectly.

The surveys of self-reported perceptions of religious partisans reveal that the demographic traits and socioeconomic positions of religious party supporters defy the popular image of them as atavistic, risk-averse, and economically marginalized masses. Neither do they necessarily belong to specific ethnicities, maintain an identifiable socioeconomic status, or define themselves as either strictly religious or antireligious. The nuanced depiction of religious constituencies helps us to address more complex and crucial questions, for example, why voters choose religious parties over others, given highly competitive political environments that offer dozens of electoral choices. A finely tuned approach to religious party supporters brings ideology back into the picture. Including the ideology of religious parties and asking how they position themselves vis-à-vis other parties helps us to explain why many seemingly unlikely supporters of religious parties vote for religious parties rather than secular ones. A spatial analysis of the data from public opinion surveys, which asked respondents to assess the positions of the parties, affords us a multidimensional picture of electoral competition. The respondents' perceptions of the parties indicate that voters do not view religious parties to be at the fringes of the political space. Rather, they seem to occupy a strategic position in areas left vacant by the major political parties. The overall competition and the fulcrum of each country's political center have been changing, and the roles of religious parties need to be seen within this shifting political environment.

The final chapter, "Beyond Laicism and Islam?" reminds us of the importance of comparative inquiries in solving the puzzle of the global return of religion. While the idiosyncratic religious beliefs of Judaism and Islam, such as messianic ideas and *ummah*, respectively, equip religious parties with different political and symbolic tools, agendas, and capacities, these parties are members of the same genus and face the same dilemmas. To understand this new genre of agents in world politics, the term *religious party* needs to be incorporated into our conceptual world without homogenizing these parties. Such conceptual identification is also important to prevent treating them as a residual category or continuing to label them as antisecular, antiglobal, or popular protest movements. Only then can we recognize that religious parties are not simply a by-product of rapid political transformation and reactive movements, but are products of their domestic and global environments and engage in politics in an attempt to determine the course of the changes unfolding in their respective countries and in the outside world. Within the family of religious parties very few exist (e.g., United Torah Judaism in Israel) that do not seek to become mass parties. Overall, the success of religious parties in expanding their appeal depends on their ability to take unconventional political positions by imbuing religious symbols with secular ideas and vice versa, forge national institutional networks to disseminate old-new ideas, change the praxis of politics from bottom to top, and form new nationwide and international communities. They gain strength not as intransigent or quiescent groups, but as active agents and driving forces of political change. They mobilize supporters by positioning themselves strategically in their respective polities. More significantly, they use a locally embedded and nationally integrated party organization that couples a modern party structure with a traditional interpersonal and communal fabric. With their ability to present themselves as strategic choices not affected by the epidemic of political impasse that afflicts major parties, the intricate and contradictory nature of some of their positions amount to both the most precarious and the most promising agents of change in their respective political environments.

Religious parties blend religious and secular beliefs under new conditions and create novel positions that span from traditional authoritarian to modern liberal. We cannot be freed from taking a closer look at their praxis by simply acknowledging the hurdles posed by efforts to grasp the intricacies of religious ideologies. In fact, that makes it difficult for us to see religious parties as new parties without assigning them to liberal or antiliberal practices or subsuming them under teleological models. The normalization of religious parties requires a reclaiming of the neglected obvious point that religious parties at the end of the day are political parties, and their analysis requires treating them as such. Their organizations and strategies cannot be trivialized as sect-like structures, and their goals cannot be viewed as simply the desecularization of politics. Just like other parties, they try to maximize their appeal and they need to be approached in the same way as other political parties. Their supporters turn to them not necessarily out of (selfless) binding beliefs, but as a political choice. It is important to build our research on how their ideology presents a hybrid vocabulary and how their supporters engage in delicate calculations. Thus, to determine the important factors for their supporters' choice of religious parties over their competition, we need to probe into the social imaginary and ideological visions wrapped up in these parties' ideologies and processes. Judaism and Islam serve as spiritual capital in both countries, in which religious and secular beliefs and symbols interact with each other in new forms.

To conclude, the findings presented in the subsequent chapters indicate that sparse comparative analyses of religious politics are symptomatic of the deeply ingrained assumptions that guide research communities, as well as the inherent obstacles to constructing an empirically and theoretically sound comparative research design. Such a gap is especially alarming as cross-doctrinal and cross-regional comparisons provide an indispensable venue to understanding the global rise of religion. The Israeli and Turkish cases open a window on the complexities of religious parties, indicating that, regardless of doctrinal differences, religious parties are capable of assuming contradictory roles in both the short and long term. Understanding these parties' relations to liberal democracy cannot be accomplished through deductive accounts or selective readings of a single aspect of these movements. Given the diversity of religious movements across religious doctrines, the universal and dichotomizing question of whether religious parties challenge or impede democracy needs to be questioned itself. These conundrums cannot be answered without understanding to what extent a given religious party's views and praxis embody democratic ideas in different areas. Not only are the religious parties' democratic balance sheets mixed in general, but the same party often has a varied record across policy areas. Parties that are internal secularizers, for instance, successfully advance an agenda toward the recognition of group or communal and cultural rights, regardless of religious doctrine. Yet this ability does not always translate into the enhancement of individual rights and liberties. Given the intricacies of religious parties, our comparative inquiry into the politics of Judaism and Islam and the typology of religious parties developed in this study is intended to serve as a heuristic device for further inquiries. Only typologies that overcome the oppose/accept dichotomy and understand that religious parties challenge, incorporate, and alter the ideas of secular institutions enable us to look beyond blanket statements that obscure the overall positioning of religious parties in their democracies and world politics.

A review of the literature on religious parties in general, and religion and democracy in particular, concludes that we still know too little about these new-old actors in politics and their role in, and impact on, democracies, despite the ever-expanding presence of religious parties in world politics. More and more observers agree that "the prospects of 'inter-civilization,'" of comparisons of religious politics, are both a promising avenue of future research in comparative politics and a daunting challenge to the "scientific aspiration of political science as a discipline."[33] Such analyses not only face the host of research barriers mentioned above, but must also deal with negative reactions to "comparing apples and oranges." In the following chapters, we try to face this challenge by answering very simple, yet crucial, questions about what religious parties stand for, who supports them, and how their electoral power affects their respective democracies. Placing these parties under the same analytical lenses ipso facto calls into question our common a priori assumptions or tendency to treat them as sui generis. We also discuss more complex questions, such as where the boundaries of these parties' ideal polities are and what they mean to their respective democracies. In our engagement we pay special attention to *how* we try to answer these questions and what questions and alternative answers are left out.

Political scientists in general adhere to a methodological consensus that midrange analyses and especially those with a comparative framework are more conducive to generating new ideas and bypassing the traps of a macroanalysis of structural conditions or a microanalysis of specific groups. This methodological solution, however, ignores other divisions in the fields. Such midrange exercises need to be accompanied by approaches that move beyond a strictly doctrinal separation that attributes the essential ideological core of religious parties to religious traditions.[34] Therefore, it is important to note that conducting midrange inquiries is not only a question of adjusting scale or scope or juxtaposing different movements. Instead such attempts demand a careful blending of otherwise separated regional, doctrinal boundaries—empirical knowledge and conceptual perspectives—not only to discover causal links but to build analytically informative inferences. Reaping the benefits of such midrange models necessitate inclusion of untapped comparative analyses as the sine qua non of their successful development.

The pervasiveness of empirically unsubstantiated arguments regarding the politics of Judaism and Islam especially warns us that if we continue to approach religious parties in the Middle East as exceptional cases or if we treat the success of religious parties as democratic accidents, the product of ideological extremism, or the beneficiaries of economic failures, they will continue to be trivialized as sui generis movements, performers of electoral miracles, theoretical anomalies, and democratic puzzles. More importantly, unless we close the gap between analytically, conceptually, and empirically isolated explanations, many accounts of religious parties will become ascriptive approaches or self-fulfilling prophecies, thereby preventing us from escaping the vicious cycle of insight deficit that deplete inquiries into these parties. The following chapters are an effort toward building bridges between analytical islands of our own creation, as well as islands formed by the old-new religious parties themselves.

PART ONE

Paradox of Modernity? The Conundrum
of Religion in Politics

Politics of Religion

Competing and Coalescing Conceptualizations

Religion does not require a belief in God but only a belief taken seriously without reservation.[1]

A person can have a religion and not know it because, unknown to the person, his or her life philosophies might actually qualify as religion.[2]

The interface of religion and politics may have inspired some of the most intriguing social science puzzles and theories. In *Euthyphro,* Socrates captured the perpetual dilemma that lies at the nexus of religion and politics by asking a deceptively simple question: Is the right action right because it is required by the divine, or is it intrinsically right? In the answer lies the paradox that reverberates among theorists and ordinary people alike: if the divine approves the right actions only because they are already right, there must be a nondivine source of values, which human beings can come to know independently of the divine via their reason. As a corollary to that, creating a moral order for a political community would therefore not require a religious foundation. However, if only the divine defines the right and just, then religion is the only venue through which we can learn them, and religion must be the sine qua non of a just social system.

Conflicting answers to the question of how we can create a stable, just political system have taken the central role in many debates that continue today. In other words, how can we define just, fair, and right? Can they be defined only within a religious paradigm? What happens if different secular and religious values claim authority over the same areas? How can we resolve their conflicts? Can people contribute to democracy if they come to the public sphere with staunch religious beliefs? Put differently, can democracy accommodate actors with uncompromising positions? Is the increasingly popular expression, *religious political parties* an oxymoron? Why have religious parties made a comeback over the last two decades, after liberal democracy and its secular values had already gained global hegemony?

These questions span two vaguely delineated areas with contested definitions: politics and religion. Politics is often defined as what pertains to the city (polis), or the art of governance, and citizenship. Plato believed that that the formation of a polis, namely people gathering in communities, was an imperative for the achievement of common goals. Yet this universal imperative prompts the need to enforce laws, resolve disagreements among citizens, and make decisions about public policy. In fact, gathering under a polis or state generates both collective power to be distributed and obligations to be shared. Accordingly, some have defined politics as the use of this accumulated power to allocate limited resources. If, as in Harold D. Lasswell's words, politics is a process that constantly defines "who gets what, when, and how," it involves making decisions that sometimes bind citizens against their will. Only in reference to an ideal society can we decide who can get what, when, and how in a polity.[3] This very understanding of politics then, first and foremost, requires an idealized just society to answer these questions: What is the best way to distribute collective power? What are the criteria for filling the positions of authority? What are the rights of those being ruled? Who decides on the social division of labor?

In the face of these questions, David Easton coined one of the most popular albeit elusive definitions of politics. In striking contrast to his efforts to promote a value-free political science, Easton defined politics as "an authoritative allocation of *values* in society" (emphasis added).[4] This textbook description did not answer "whose and what values?" but the discussion among political scientists lauded democracy and eventually declared it the best platform for politics. Ironically, when Aristotle was searching for the best embodiment of politics, democracy, rule by many, did not emerge as an ideal type. On the contrary, he felt that the instrumental approach of common citizens to political activity—pursuit of their own interests—would degrade politics, which has an intrinsic and independent value in the pursuit of common good. Nevertheless, applying the same instrumental logic he was critical of, Aristotle concluded that democracy was the *ideal nonideal* regime because even in its deteriorated form, it would be able to correct its failures while posing the least amount of harm to its citizens. Regardless of or perhaps due to the continuing questions and unsettled answers, discussion on politics generated a belief that only in a democracy would all citizens have their values protected and have a chance to weigh in on the rules of the game without giving up their right to disobey when facing authoritarian tendencies. These discussions culminated in a prophecy that politics in a liberal democracy, given its ability to balance individual autonomy and freedom with social justice and welfare, would surpass the rival models and become a hegemonic paradigm.

Religion is, on the other hand, another multifaceted social phenomenon which, according to Benavides, is impossible to capture with a single definition.[5] What makes religion different from other belief systems is that it often describes an ideal society, thus subscribing to a certain set of power relationships. Religions, however, do not contain one static model for social and political interactions and order.[6] On the contrary, they harbor a variety of ideas, which often constitute a battlefield for different groups not only across but also within the same religion. Therefore, studying the interface of religion and politics does not mean bringing two independent worlds together. Instead, the questions posed about politics or by politics often find their answers in religious doctrines. Religion, along with other systems, provides answers for how to create a political system that distributes power justly and ultimately eliminates conflicts.

The secularization process seemed to have resolved the conflict over the form and spirit of a good society once and for all. The gradual decline of religion and its authority in the public sphere was seen as a forceful and an unavoidable process in tandem with the advancement of science and the consolidation of modern societies. Morally and intellectually independent people were expected to be increasingly disenchanted with transcendental facts and values. Reasoning and contestation, as opposed to belief and acceptance, would emerge as the sole foundation of a just society.[7] However, the ascendancy of religious groups since the mid-1980s shows that the secularization paradigm was tenuous at best. Religion has maintained and, to a certain extent, expanded its claim that it can offer a superior understanding of social reality, justice, order, and stability.

In fact, given the long-lasting secularization process, the recent rise of political religion has been one of the most striking and unexpected elements of post–cold war global politics. One of the leading scholars of secularization, Peter Berger, declared the end of religion in the public sphere in the 1970s, only to reverse his conclusion in the mid-1980s. This sudden puzzling *de-secularization* of world politics has generated broad interest and various explanations since the 1980s. A cursory look at the skyrocketing numbers of studies on religion and politics shows, however, that (1) at the conceptual level these studies treat the secular and the religious as separate and competing sources of values; (2) at the analytical level they study religious parties only in relation to secular institutions, where a loose understanding of the term *secular* (e.g., anything not overtly religious) is adopted; (3) in their efforts to explain the "return of religion," they focus on either macro-level trends that seem to trigger religious reactions or on leaders, whose charisma sways the masses; and (4) the newly emerging multiple modernities approach celebrates the assumed role of religion in world politics as a step forward in imbuing traditional ideas with modern values, or in creating a local understanding of modern ideas. Many of these studies present the return of religion to the public sphere as a theoretical puzzle. A common thread throughout is the uncertainty as to whether this trend will result in a dethronement of liberal democracy and a desecularization of the world, a global dominance of "traditional reactionary," or "hybrid publics."[8]

RELIGION AND POLITICS: COMPETING AND COALESCING CONCEPTUALIZATIONS

More often than not, religious beliefs are associated with authoritarian systems and undemocratic societies. Hence, it is not surprising that studies of religion under democratic systems are often marginalized as the study of tradition. This basic, yet pervasive, understanding of religion explains the difficulties encountered by political scientists grappling with the role of religion in pluralistic democratic societies. Going back to the studies of Max Weber and Emile Durkheim, we can identify two relevant conceptualizations of political religion that continue to guide the current understanding of religious politics, albeit often in simplified forms.

Weber laid the groundwork for the conceptualization of the social meaning and implications of religion by drawing on one of the most comprehensive explorations of world religions to date. The legacy of the wealth of arguments he offered has been mixed, however. His observations paved the way for contesting accounts that promote a strictly static, binary understanding of religion and secularization, as well as dynamic ones that capture religion's ability to adopt paradoxical roles. For instance, in Weber's analysis of traditional society, religion serves as a source for hierarchical and authoritarian political structures, but it is also expected to evolve subsequently into a more rational system. After all, these societies are susceptible to broader transformations as "[e]very increase of rationalism in empirical science increasingly pushes religion from the rational into the irrational realm; but only today does religion become the irrational or antirational suprahuman power."[9] As charismatic leadership in these societies legitimizes itself through beliefs and faith, as opposed to reason, traditional societies arc inherently unstable in their approach to the transfer of power.[10]

In the Weberian world, the ways that religion changes its social environment and the forms in which the tension between politics and religion is expressed are more complicated than a linear evolution or the confrontation model would suggest. For instance, the section that scholars often quote to declare the end of religion based on the advance of reason continues with a less frequently noted section:

The extent of consciousness or of consistency in the experience of this contrast, however, *varies widely*. Because of this apparently irreconcilable tension, prophetic as well as priestly religions have repeatedly stood in intimate relation with rational intellectualism. The less magic or merely contemplative mysticism and the more "doctrine" a religion contains, the greater is its need of rational apologetics (emphases added).[11]

In similar statements, Weber tells us that religion's relationship to rationalism is not a mutually exclusive one and that religious reactions are not always directed at the secular world. The complex role of religion becomes apparent when Weber discusses how the tensions between religion and politics erupted for the first time when local religions defended the then-existing political systems against the advance of universal religions, that is, "when the barriers of locality, tribe and polity were shattered by universalistic religions."[12] More importantly, Weber's inquiry into the social role of religion showed that religion is not necessarily only a force for stability. In contrast, it is also capable of facilitating the most revolutionary social changes. Despite modernization's dictum, some of the most massive changes did not come at the expense of religion but via religion. Calvinism as a "this-worldly" religious doctrine instigated not the stagnation of social forces but the rise of capitalism, proving that religious ideas have the capacity to transform the social and economic orders, albeit, in some cases, as an unintended consequence.[13] Thus Weber's inquiry warned us that our understanding of the role of religion needs to be enhanced by including *value-rationalism*, where individuals act rationally to achieve goals defined by values and are not driven by their self-interest alone. This perspective allows for the possibility that rationalism does not necessarily conflict with religion but can serve it and be served by it to create new social practices.

Alternatively, in Durkheim's approach to religion we can find the traces of ideas nested in convergence theories. His explorations culminated in the argument that "even the most barbarous and the most fantastic rites and the strangest myths translate *some human need, some aspect of life, either individual or social*" (emphases added). Therefore, "the reasons with which the faithful justify them [religious values] may be, and generally are, erroneous"; but the true reasons, Durkheim contended, "do not cease to exist," and it is the duty of science to discover them.[14] To study religion we must free the mind of all preconceived ideas of religion, he wrote, and see how they separate the sacred from the profane. Religion is

less an indivisible whole than a complex system of parts consisting of *rites* (determined modes of action) and *beliefs* (collective representations). Religion is thus a mode of action, but also a mode of thought—one not different in kind from that exercised by science. Like science, for example, religion reflects on nature, man, and society, and attempts to classify things. Advances in science can diminish religion as a mode of thought. However, as a mode of *action* religion will endure, albeit under unforeseen forms.[15]

In Durkheim's world, we face a constant duality where the individual and the social are separate, yet also interdependent: "We lead an existence which is simultaneously both individual and social."[16] Parallel to Weber's analysis, Durkheim views "organic" societies, where increasing the division of labor brings individuals together, as replacing traditional, "mechanical" societies, where the shared, common practices surrounding religion keep individuals together. This transition is marked by a quest to "discover the rational substitutes for these religious notions that for a long time have served as the vehicle for the most essential moral ideas."[17] Ironically, the first empirical research conducted by Durkheim probing into the reasons of suicide indicated the importance of religion: when the need for cohesion was left unattended, the incongruity between individuals and society could lead to self-destructive decisions. Religion appears as an important force even in modern societies by shielding the community against anomie, the absence of shared values.[18] Religion, after all, is one of many meaning systems and creates an internal, shared community that transcends the tension between sacred and secular (profane). Therefore, Durkheim did not rule out the possibility that religion could cohabit the same social space with its opponents once society had advanced to the point where the sacred had limited power. This shift from the perspective that the religious and the rational are in constant tension and seek to dominate each other to the understanding that they can inhabit societies side by side presaged the idea that religion can acquire multiple roles and can coexist with alternative worldviews in a pluralistic modern society, posing the question of how.[19]

A review of subsequent studies of social change shows that the belief in the inevitability of a replacement of religion's social role with rationality has prevailed—notwithstanding Weber's and Durkheim's repeated acknowledgments of religion's contradictory and complex roles. Various philosophical and theoretical approaches, perhaps best labeled as *secularization theories*, promoted the idea that religion requires particularistic and affective relationships and thus serves as the foundation of traditional communities or quiescent, insular communities if it maintains its relevance in a modern context.[20] Various secularization theses prophesize that some social transformations are not only inevitable but irreversible, as they challenge the role of religion by replacing personal ties with rule-governed contractual relations. When secularization establishes itself, the social system operates without reference to religious institutions or the religious orientation of individuals.

The reductionist descriptions of social transformation seem to present an unavoidable dilemma for religion. To maintain its presence in the modern world, religion must accommodate itself to the forces of rationalization. Such accommodations, however, undermine the critical self-perceptions that define religion. Challenged by the social transformation of modern societies, religion faces the option of adjustment or rejection. Despite the profound imprint of the deterministic view of secularization on the studies of religious politics, there have been various attempts to posit the survival of religion in modern societies. Talcott Parsons, for example, argued that religion acquires a new function in a pluralistic society and continues to be one of the most important components of the social order. According to Parsons, religion's core function is "the regulation of the balance of the motivational commitments of the individual to the values of the society." Religion serves as the medium of ultimate balance and sense of justice.[21] In the same vein, Peter Berger argues that in a pluralistic society, religion preserves itself through a "plausibility structure"—a set of institutions and social networks that keep religious beliefs acceptable.[22] In the modern world, most nation-states embrace a diversity of religions and plausibility structures. Instead of an all-encompassing "sacred canopy," however, religion maintains its presence as a part of a pluralistic society. In these societies religion becomes a *choice* instead of a *given*.[23]

A review of the treatment of religion in the social sciences demonstrates that the concept of choice in the studies of religion is a relatively new phenomenon. In many popular accounts, members of religious groups have often been characterized as lacking the ability to choose and consider alternative belief systems. The very etymological root of the word *heretic*, in effect, epitomizes the basic idea that religion negates one's ability to choose. The word stems from the Greek *hairetikos,* which literally means "able to choose." The word implies that one's ability to choose becomes possible only if one can distance oneself from the religious order or reject it completely.

Likewise, only recently has the concept of "religious voluntarism" emerged in reference to the idea that an increasing number of individuals choose their religious belief system without the constraints of denominational loyalties and customs.[24] The "rational choice" approach is a model of human behavior in which individuals act rationally, weighing the costs and benefits of potential actions and choosing those actions that maximize their net benefits. According to rational choice models, people choose not only their faith, but also a level of commitment, not because of some dogmatic belief, but in light of cost-benefit calculations.[25] Applying the framework of rational choice, for example, Stark and Bainbridge redefine religion as a system of general compensators (attainable rewards) based on supernaturalist assumptions.[26]

Choice-centric frameworks help us to engage with different secularization theses and offer not only abstract but also empirically grounded critiques. The premise that an individual has the ability to decide focuses attention on the idea that religion can continue to exist in a secular and modern society as the choice of rational actors. Including choice in our accounts also reintroduces the principle of methodological individualism to the studies of religion and politics.[27] Illuminating the individual roots of religious politics is especially critical in light of the absence of individuals, seen most noticeably in the deterministic formulations of the secularization theses. Despite the fact that societies or groups often serve as a natural unit of analysis, attending to the multiplicity of ideas within society, and sometimes even within the same person, suggests that we can understand some decisions only by centering our analytical efforts on individuals. In other words, in contrast to the ubiquitous trend of reducing religion's role to one common function at the group level, choice-centered views uncover some missing components of religious politics. Choice-centered models claim the common legacy of Weber and Durkheim when they emphasize that religious groups and individuals can host contradictory ideas, take different forms, assume proactive roles, and serve as agents of change while also being capable of expressing reactions to the ongoing change in modern societies.

Different points of entry into the world of religion and politics draw our attention to the challenges of providing an overarching explanation for the new public role assumed by religion in global politics. In the ongoing debates on the global return, contesting views cluster around three different causal explanations or modes: *the conflict (inherent tension) model, the crisis model,* and *the choice model.* These models explain why religion has returned to politics and propose reasons for the religious parties' remarkable electoral victories. However, their success in overcoming the limits of the analytical and conceptual hurdles we laid out varies. It is important to note that our classifications are by no means exhaustive and that our analysis refers to them (1) to indicate the multiplicity of explanations for the ascendancy of religious parties and the sets of assumptions that guide them and (2) to point out the analytical implications of existing and newly emerging deterministic perspectives of different research communities. These models amount to neither coherent research communities nor mutually exclusive paradigms. Rather, they offer a set of prevailing research premises shared by a diverse group of researchers and observers. They enable us to delineate and question what is left beyond the main contours of the confounding analytical frameworks. The section below provides a brief clarification of each model and directs attention to their tendency to obscure the nexus of individuals and their institutional political environment, as well as the symbolic world of religion. We lay the groundwork for explaining the choice-centered terminology and broad heuristic model adopted in this study.

The Conflict Model

The first model—the conflict, or normative contention, model—constitutes one of the most prominent and most challenged approaches in studies of religion and politics. The model is rooted in the assumption that reason and religion have contradictory views of and engagements with the world and, therefore, cannot coexist and blend.[28] The inherent tension between them presumably explains political conflicts in countries where religious institutions and elites continue to retain significant power. Only the disappearance of views with religious or secular foundations from the public sphere can prevent such conflicts. Other proponents of the view that secular and religious beliefs host irreconcilable values argue, however, that it is not religious values per se, but religion's tendency to single-handedly define the political order and monopolize social authority that makes its resurgence a problem. Modernity, by increasing education, urbanization, technology, and scientific advancement, as well as the prevalence of individually based social organizations, unavoidably engenders pluralism and a differentiation of political and social values and beliefs. In such plurality, religion's claim to be a self-sustaining and overarching foundation to all practices loses its weight.

Efforts to find room for religion in this pluralistic view presume, at best, that people accommodate secular and religious values for different aspects of their life through diversification (or compartmentalization).[29]

Religion remains an individual concern and satisfies a person's moral needs in the private sphere, while the public sphere remains modern and rational. Thus, as religion evolves into an *individualized* belief and serves merely as a matter of personal conscience, it can continue to be part of modern society. According to this rationale, religion can maintain its presence in an individual's consciousness only by losing its capacity to act as the sole map and mobilizing force for sociopolitical change. However, the shifting of the social and political position of religion and the decline in its authority often induces a reaction, that is, a return to religious traditions. Thus, modernization includes a decline of the social authority of religious values in the public sphere, as well as the resistance of religious groups to this decline and to the relegation of religion to an individual belief.[30]

The conflict model is particularly prevalent in explaining politics in newly emerging nation-states, as it elucidates the contradictory role of religion in formation and proliferation of nationalist sentiments. While nationalism takes different forms and often seeks to replace religious ties, it also can establish itself via religion. Nevertheless, many nationalist ideologies (e.g., voluntary or cultural nationalism) foster the principles of individualism and self-governance and see the collective will of people as a source of public decision making.[31] These national identities cannot be consolidated unless there is a comprehensive subordination of all atavistic ties, including religious ones.[32] While nationalists in many countries seek to forge modern identities with universal referents, their opponents attempt to revive religion to prevent this fundamental transformation of the traditional order from taking place, thereby consolidating the relevance of religion in politics.

Adherents of the conflict model contend that religious politics are more visible in countries where the secularization process is part of an official state policy rather than the result of a gradual historical process. The religious masses reject modernist and secularist policies and the relegation of religion to the private sphere with the consequent diminishment of its public authority. Regardless of their immediate goal, these parties are established to articulate these reactions by selectively adopting the principles of democracy (e.g., they endorse elections at the national level but oppose them in their party organizations). Although they seem like a modern political apparatus, the parties are instrumentalist in the sense that they use the modern conduits of political participation to reverse secularist policies. This is why, for example, religious political parties are neither organized interest groups nor purely religious sects, according to Roy. Instead, they lie somewhere in between, with the sole goal of maintaining their religious community while simultaneously resisting the secularization of society as a whole.[33] The leaders of religious parties are commonly charismatic figures who oftentimes define the stances of their parties by deriving their discourses exclusively from religious doctrines. Their members profess an unquestioning allegiance to their leaders and the party's policies.[34] Accordingly, whatever the façade and the immediate function of the religious movement, they are in perpetual conflict with and emerge as a reaction to modern secularist values.

The Crisis Model

According to the crisis theory, it is not the decline of religion and the process of modernization but the ways in which modernization policies unfold that creates religious reactions. Growing disillusionment with secular nationalism and problems of legitimacy in the existing regimes, along with the differential effects of economic and political liberalization, often initiate social reactions that prompt people to resort to religious doctrines for their expressions. Drastic social and economic transformations have produced groups of people who could not cope with the rapid changes, especially in countries experiencing the third wave of democratization.[35] These globally challenged groups, as losers in the global economy, react to modernity by asserting tradition.[36] Religion acts only as a tool of opposition for the masses against the radical elitist-secular policies that aim to restructure society.[37] In other words, the exclusive policies of the secular elite, together with the intertwined processes of secularization as a social project and political economic liberalization, often result in multifaceted crises that enhance the political purchase of religion as a venue to protest and claim order.

Thus, it is both the advancement of modernization and the unequal distribution of its benefits, rather than the inevitable tension between the religious and secular, that prepare the ground for the emergence of religious parties. The differential effects of socioeconomic and cultural modernizing policies create a fertile milieu for the return to religion. While the secularist elite effectively incorporate the ideal of an egalitarian society into their rhetoric, their policies fail to transform resistant traditional economic and cultural structures. The resulting economic deprivation, social exclusion, and political underrepresentation of the masses reintroduce the idea of a religious society as an alternative stable social system and the return to religion as a panacea for resolving existing problems. Socially displaced individuals, with limited education and restricted access to venues of mobilization, do not feel fully incorporated into the political and economic system.[38] As a result, the masses view modernization and Westernization not as forces of progress but as policies that exacerbate economic dependency and further erode the living conditions of all but a small elite. According to the crisis model, the political appeal of religion must therefore be seen as a corollary to the quest for political, economic, and cultural development and stability. Religious politics functions as a politics of resentment, a familiar venue to express political angst and protest appealing to the socially disadvantaged citizens. The implicit assumption is that, if successful, modernizing and secularizing policies would alter the role of religion in the society and prevent the resurgence of religion.

The conflict and crisis models continue to permeate today's analyses despite the challenges to their premises posed by the strengthening of religious movements in multiple forms. The first model isolates religion as a set of (uncompromising) values, and the second reduces it to the foundation of a tightly bound society, or a distinctive political lexis for political and economic survival. However, conflict and resilience do not cover all possible ways in which religious and secular values interact. Rather than being replaced by new secular norms, traditional religions and religious institutions persist and prove to be capable of adjusting to the terms of political and economic modernization. Disengagement of religion from politics and the privatization of religion do not seem to be universal imperatives, and they do not go hand in hand. On the contrary, religion and politics coexist in an intertwined and complicated relationship that remains unrepresented by linear modernization theses.

The Choice-Centric Models

The critiques directed at macro-level explanations have prompted a new research agenda in which what some have called "a new paradigm" accentuates the necessity of seeing religious movements and support for religious parties as individuals' choices.[39] Most of the new paradigm studies began with examinations of the so-called anomalous American experience, which has defied the secularization thesis with the strong and persistent presence of religion since the country's inception. This new approach strives to understand diversity and the voluntary aspects of politics, as opposed to the old paradigm's emphasis on monolithic religious doctrines, authoritarian religious institutions, and reactionary religious movements. In this approach, "religion (churches) can no longer take for granted the loyalty of adherents. Their ideas, which previously could be authoritatively imposed, *now must be marketed. . . .* Religion has long been disestablished, pluralistic, structurally adaptable, and empowering" (emphases added).[40]

In the same vein, this new genre of studies brings to the fore the *individual* foundations of the resurgence of religion. The model presumes that an individual's decision to participate in religious movements or to support religious parties is a rational choice like any other decision. Individuals support those parties that appeal to their immediate interests. All of these approaches emphasize the voluntary nature of individual choices and turn away from deterministic macro-level analyses. Religious parties are not the result of the tension between two worldviews, secular versus religious, or the destabilizing effect of socioeconomic crises. Instead, individuals *choose* to support religious parties.[41] Thus, religious parties, like other parties, are vote maximizers and compete for votes by capitalizing on religious beliefs.[42]

What differentiates choice-centered models from others is not their unified analytical framework but their point of entry to the world of religion and politics. For instance, the Resource Mobilization Model (RMM) is one of the choice-centric models that exemplifies their dominant rationale and adds a new dimension: the organizational capacity of religious movements. The central question in this approach is how religious movements and parties *mobilize* people and how they do so more effectively than others. This very question shatters the common assumption that religious party support is a by-product of the ever present appeal of religious values or of the movements' reactionary nature. From the perspective of RMM, religious politics needs to be understood through the creation and distribution of a range of political resources, such as leadership, communications networks, resources for recruitment purposes, funds, beliefs, ideologies, economic and social status, and the like. Religious groups that have been politically dormant become strategically active by using the organizational and ideational resources at their disposal. Thus, it is the resources and incentives accessible to a religious group and the ability of the religious elite to tap into them that define the political capital and the nature of religious groups and parties. Religious party supporters become politically active with the attraction of rewards that religious mobilization offers.

When viewed in its entirety, the RMM normalizes or finds rationality in religious mobilization by relabeling participants of religious politics as actors who seek political power by using the resources available to them. Resources are defined in a broad sense, and organizational resources are not necessarily limited to religious sources. Instead of being insular oppositional forces, religious groups are embedded in a broader network of interactions and engage with others in a complex way. When they are treated as mobilizers in a broader albeit still limited pool of resources, various forms of rivalry, co-optation, and cooperation surface. For instance, some of the resources that religious groups attempt to garner might be provided by secular groups wishing to gain political leverage against their opponents.[43] It is not rare to find examples of secular leaders seeking to gain the support of religious groups by incorporating their demands into their agenda and securing more resources for them (for example, state-financed religious schools or tax-relief policies that allow religious groups to allocate more funds toward voter mobilization efforts).

Overall, variants of choice-centered models play a key role in directing our attention to individuals—a neglected aspect of the politics of religion—and their engagement in their political environment. The models aptly unlock what are often perceived to be the stagnant immediate decision-making milieus of religious agents and their reflexive decision-making processes. Nevertheless, the focus on the individual and the immediate environment can come at the expense of minimizing the broader social and political context of the movements. Although the analytical strength of these models lies in their ability to explain the host of resources used by religious activists and the intricate rationale of the participants, they are typically applied to groups only after they gain public recognition, thereby allowing their accounts to be filtered by the outcomes at the expense of initial, broader resources and agents. As choice takes a central role under these models, they are able to successfully incorporate informal and noninstitutional aspects of politics. Nevertheless, unless its various tenets are carefully balanced this much-needed inclusion does not close the doors on the reductionist understanding of religious parties, which views these parties as mere by-products of or as dependent upon the networks formed by successfully mobilized religious publics. Absent in the various applications are (1) structural and ideational factors that affect individuals' choices beyond their immediate environment, (2) other mobilization options available to them, (3) internal competition, and (4) the ways in which the networks are created and reproduced. Perhaps more importantly, missing in these analyses is the recognition that networks can be rather fragile and dependent on the parties for their survival; therefore, their presence and organization need to be seen as a variant and important component—not a constant or cause—of various manifestation of religious politics.

With their recovery of midrange structures and individuals, choice-centered analyses help us to capture the diversity of religious beliefs and the political implications of how religious identity and the choice to support religious groups and parties are not simply given and static, but rather, are highly malleable, bitterly contested, and responsive to political opportunities. Accordingly, they establish how probing into how the choices are formed and expressed in political religion is inevitably a multidimensional task. Such undertakings not only require a thorough description of the context and resources of the secular and religious spheres but also an analysis of the ways in which individuals make decisions in an environment impacted and imprinted by both. Such approaches prove most helpful when the process of mobilization does not overshadow the central role of individuals and their choices. They aptly illustrate how social-religious networks, close-knit interactions among individuals mobilized by religious groups, cannot be viewed as an effortless chain of interactions and autonomous social systems that have an ample supply of resources (such as traditional values and the readiness of religious people to participate once the resource mobilization is achieved effectively). In contrast, just like other social constructs, religious networks seek to be relevant by communicating recursively and coordinating the redistribution of resources. Their internal structures embody the intricate nature of the politics of religion. Therefore, to keep the analytical incisiveness of choice-centered models clear, we need to approach religious values, as well as the coherency and decisions of groups, neither as constants nor as outputs of individuals' decisions and the mobilization network, but as pivotal components in relation to others.

Politics of Religion in Israel and Turkey

The frequent descriptions of religious resurgence in the Israeli and Turkish public spheres as "unexpected developments," "political enigmas," and "political surprises" captures the leitmotif of many prevailing accounts that view religious parties as anachronism in the age of liberalization. Echoing the premises of the normative contention and crisis models, many accounts of the politics of religion attribute the root cause of religious outbursts to the masses' resentment of their socioeconomic conditions and their expressions of defiance against elitist-secular policies.[44] Even some of the more elaborate accounts reveal imprints of these postulates. For instance, the rise of the Shas party is often explained thus:

These new arrivals met a dominant and seemingly impregnable Ashkenazi [read dominant elite] establishment bent on shaping a "new" Jew, who would be secular and Western in outlook. In the process, the country's leaders ignored the cultural mores and traditions of these Sephardi Jews. Also, many of them were sent to far-flung, undeveloped regions of the country, like the Negev, where they were housed in transit camps and where infrastructure was thin and jobs scarce. Social dislocation soon followed as the family structure began to disintegrate and a growing number of young Sephardi men got caught up in crime.[45]

Likewise, the "political earthquakes" set loose by pro-Islamic parties prompted many to ask, "How is it that in the last decade, while the reconstruction of Turkish modernization took important strides forward, the economy was radically liberalized, and a smooth transition to a postcoup democratic regime almost thoroughly accomplished, that Islam also emerged as an important political variable in Turkish politics?"[46] The description of religious parties as anomalies, however, generated another literature; by referring to the same causal factors, these accounts declare religious parties to be representative of genuine mass movements whose electoral victories heal their respective countries' authoritarianism and promote democratization.

Tackling the ubiquitous conundrum of persistent support for religious parties, many scholars turn to the constitutive year of these democracies and contend that the masses react to their marginalization and the top-to-bottom nature of state-sponsored nationalist and secularist policies by resorting to the traditional values and practices.[47] In Israel, Zionist nationalism is often presented with its opposing desire to simultaneously maintain and modernize religious blocs by incorporating secular principles into the state's ideology and by establishing parallel religious and secular educational systems. In Turkey, for instance, Kemalist nationalism is seen as a radical project marked by reforms such as the abolition of the caliphate and the introduction of a secular civil code.

In their search to find the root cause of religion's untimely return, other scholars turn to the existence of an unequal pattern of development and assign the religious parties' political capital to rampant unemployment and underemployment, a continued trend of rural–urban migration, and the growth of shantytowns around the major metropolitan centers.[48] Socially and economically disadvantaged groups, in this picture, turned to religious parties to change the status quo. Thus, the inadequacies of the secular modernization projects imposed by the state elites, coupled with the deterioration of economic conditions, paved the way for the resurgence of religion in politics. Religious parties gained strength as challengers of policies that seek to define Judaism and Islam primarily as cultural constructs, rather than as the source of social reality. The economic deprivation of the traditional masses only increases the intensity of their opposition and antisystemic sentiments, according to this view. The ascendancy of religious party support reflects the quest to reform the existing state system in favor of the traditional mass public.

It is not surprising, therefore, that many analyses of Israeli and Turkish religious politics exhibit a tendency to ignore the pluralism of religious groups. In Israel, the term "religious bloc" encompasses three separate and competing religious parties, namely Mafdal, Shas, and the United Torah Judaism. In Turkey, until recently, the National View movement was regarded as the sole representative of political Islam. Instead of questioning how religious supporters distributed their votes among these parties and why their support continued to expand, analyses focused on external factors and "triggering" or "critical" events (e.g., the miraculous victory in the 1967 war, the enforced Turkification of Islamic rituals). Religious party supporters are presented as individuals who simply mirror the charismatic party elites' opinions and/or have clearly defined religious ideologies. Such categorical assumptions have always been questioned by well-established findings that show that religious party members are neither ideologues with extensive religious knowledge nor unquestioning party loyalists. A growing discrepancy between the conceptualization of religious politics and its practice continues to puzzle us and raise the question of what brings an increasing number of people together in support of religious parties. More importantly, how can we explain the growing lure of religious parties in their respective democracies without reducing it to the ability of religion to offer a stable social shelter within a changing society and to an eternal fight against what traditional people perceive as heretic antireligious authorities?

In short, the description of religious parties as agents of the ideological conflict between the religious and the secular in Israel and Turkey fails to recognize the complicated, reciprocal effects of secularist policies and religious publics. Even a cursory look at the Israeli and Turkish states indicates that although they have controlled religion through a secular educational system, they have also relaxed their strict secularism to meet the demands of religious publics. In the current context, the assumed strict boundaries between the modern and the religious, between the national and the ecumenical, are highly ambiguous. In many areas, religiously observant publics are given preferential treatment, for example, an exemption from military service in Israel. In Turkey, one of the highest budget allocations goes to the Directorate of Religious Affairs. In both societies, religion plays multiple roles, serving as both the foundation of the political regime and its main contestant.

Therefore, it is especially important to move beyond the myths of the separation of church and state or the official map of institutions to understand religious politics in Israel and Turkey. Furthermore, within pluralistic parliamentary systems, secular ideologies incorporate elements of religious doctrine in order to appeal to a wider electorate. Religious parties increasingly focus on secular-nationalist issues by addressing the national community as opposed to the religious one. The existing studies pay scant attention to the fact that religious partisans (1) are not necessarily monolithic groups of ideologues who devoutly follow their spiritual convictions, (2) come from different and oftentimes clashing socioeconomic backgrounds, (3) subscribe to diverse and competing religious ideas and (4) find certain religious ideologies appealing for various reasons. As a result, left beyond the scope of many accounts are a number of unanswered questions, such as how do religious parties distinguish themselves from other parties? Why do an increasing number of people turn to religious parties despite the efforts of other parties to gain their support? Why do some people, marginalized by economic social policies, choose to support religious parties, while others do not? Are religious parties Trojan horses that seek to undermine democracy? Are religious parties novel hybrid agents of liberal democracy? Is democracy adopting a new form in these countries? Is the Middle Eastern experience an exception, as many argue? Configuring the less visible components of the relationship between the context of individuals' choices and their actual selections allows us to identify the underlying reasons individuals choose to support religious parties.

In order to address these questions, this study adopts a conceptual lens that seeks to expand the limits of the nondeterministic, choice-centric models. To begin with, we need to clarify the terms of the analysis this study will use.

BASIC TERMS REVISITED

This study is not guided by a single theoretical model. Instead, it brings together a distinct set of concepts that emphasize both the voluntary and intentional aspects of religious party support and the importance of individuals' choices for their identification with religious movements. We contend, however, that these individuals' choices can be better understood only when we delve into the symbolic world of religion. It is these symbols that often constitute the core of the ideologies of religious parties, not the sheer presence of conducive structural conditions. Our analysis seeks to offer a heuristic model that accommodates the significance of the institutional and political context of political action. It incorporates the constraints on the rational calculations of religious partisans and the political use of religious ideas. Instead of treating religion as external to its model, it also looks at the symbolic sphere of religious doctrine and questions how these symbols are used for political ends. Our analysis does not reduce religious ideologies to a set of ideas mirroring their respective religious doctrines or to an array of mere instruments used by religious groups to achieve their goals. On the contrary, the ideas of religious movements are brought into the center of our analysis to show how religious and secular ideas are porous and enable these movements to take novel positions beyond the reach of other parties. Many political questions are derived from religious doctrine. More questions are posed by contemporary politics where religious parties successfully blend traditional views and new ideas. The idea of fundamentalism, seen as a complete isolation from the political context and a refusal to consider any ideas beyond religious doctrine, is rare among religious parties. In reality, they function in and accept the modern world; the question is how they do so, in what forms, and with what implications.

The following section introduces the central concepts that subtly and explicitly form the basis of this analysis, namely religion, secularism, and religious politics, and briefly sketches how a broadly defined institutionalism informs this study. Through the idea of the nexus of decision making, the study discusses how these concepts are related and, when considered together, how they highlight individual aspects of religious politics. Focusing upon this nexus, instead of the individual components of the politics of religion, shows how the reasoning of individuals is informed by religious as well as secular beliefs; this focal point also pays special attention to the supply side of ideas, or in other words, the set of ideas formed by social and historical processes. The overarching theme of this section is that one cannot provide a full picture of current religious parties unless one reveals secularism's multilayered process and incorporates a definition of religion that allows for a broad array of religious ideas. The relationship between religion and the secular is more complicated than simple rejection or acceptance can express. More importantly, we cannot study religious politics in a vacuum. Nor can we include the structure randomly or selectively in our models. Whether and how we can systematically evaluate the context of religious politics poses another challenge not addressed by many studies. Therefore, a complete model must systematically address the perceptions of religious parties among the voters, the context of religious party politics, the structure of the religious parties, and the options available to individual voters.

Religion

This study defines *religion* as a symbolic system that can convey multiple meanings and inform diverse positions. In fact, the continuing debate on the roots of the term traces it back to "rereading" (relegio) or "related to gathering" (res-legere) and reveals that the term did not originate to imply a fixed set of rules inspired by a deity. Rather, it emphasized the attempt to understand and the power to unite. The definition emphasizes that religions are not static and absolute doctrines but rather they constitute a symbolic universe that can be used in multiple ways. Individuals constantly reproduce and interpret the religious doctrines with which they associate.[49] In this regard, this study benefits from approaches to religion first proposed by Durkheim and later elaborated on by others, such Clifford Geertz:

A religion *is a system* of symbols which acts to establish powerful, pervasive, and long-lasting moods and motivations by men by formulating conceptions of a general order of existence and clothing these conceptions with aura of factuality that the motivations seem uniquely realistic. (emphases added)[50]

Viewing religion not as a fixed meaning system, but as a symbolic domain capable of generating manifold meaning systems, however, does not suggest that symbols are inconsequential or that religion inspires only subjective meanings. On the contrary, religious symbols and the meanings attached to them carry certain core ideas, and their interpretations are bounded by certain rules, shared knowledge, and acknowledged practices. More often than not, novel interpretations tend to follow detailed discussions of various meanings. Accounts of political religion mostly focus on the easily discernible and fairly static sides of the doctrine (the codes for behavior, normative rules, institutions endorsed in the religious texts or by religious leaders) at the expense of examining the users. Beneath what appear to be their static parts, religious doctrines are full of metaphors, broad rules, suggestions of voluntary practices, and questions. None of them benefit from a large set of clear and undisputed rules. In a pluralistic, modern context, religious doctrines and their texts provide only the blueprints from which people selectively adopt the norms with which they regulate different parts of their social life.[51]

Behind this conceptualization of religion is the idea that religion in itself cannot become a political force. This study is therefore based on the assumption that the way religion regulates behavior depends on how individuals use, produce, and interpret the doctrine. The doctrine defines the domain of the symbolic world. How individuals use its political potential makes it political. For instance, in Sri Lanka, Buddhism, "a religion stressing peace, non-violence, rationality and friendship," has become part of the ongoing political conflict and violence by serving as "a cultural matrix for the majority of the Sinhalese."[52] Therefore, the content of religion per se cannot be excluded from our studies, but it cannot be taken as definitive either. First and foremost, we need to understand the nexus of religious politics and probe into under what conditions and how individuals give meanings to religious symbols. In the case of Sri Lanka, the political positioning of Buddhism as the main source of identity for the majority of the population made it susceptible to conflict-supporting interpretations. This process culminated in the formation of a political party, which contradicts the religious ideas inherent in Buddhism.

In this sense, Islam and Judaism are not homogeneous belief systems, but include variant conceptions and practices, sometimes making differences within the same religious community more noticeable than differences across religious communities. Consequently, religion refers to the symbols and meanings available to people through Judaism and Islam, and not to any specific Judaic or Islamic doctrine. The understanding of religious political movements needs to include a pluralistic understanding of the religious doctrine, the complexity of its context, and the multiple and sometimes contradictory ideas it contains. Indeed, according to Berger, from a sociological and sociopsychological point of view, religion can be defined as a cognitive and normative structure that makes it possible for individuals to feel "at home" in the universe by availing themselves of an overarching worldview.[53]

Increasing pluralization changes the political and social context of such interpretations. With the growing normative dominance of liberalism, different sectors of social life now come to be governed by widely discrepant meanings and meaning systems. As a result, it becomes increasingly difficult for religious traditions and institutions not to respond to the demands of modern needs. Hotly debated issues within religious communities are often questions of how to incorporate new ideas into the doctrine rather than how to reinvent religious beliefs in isolation. Inquiries into the relationship between religion and politics need to attend to this mutually transformative interaction. They should thus not start by asking whether an individual accepts a religious or a secular doctrine, thereby reinforcing the analytically depleting dichotomization that isolates the sacred from the secular. What is crucial instead is *how* individuals construct their belief systems and *how* religious ideas and values affect individuals' choices. In this modern context, the simple distinction between the secular and the religious becomes blurred, and the meanings attached to a religious doctrine diversify more than ever. How individuals interpret existing religious doctrine is not always apparent, and religious ideologies often present dual and complicated discourses. For students of politics and religion, the challenge lies in understanding these meaning systems and including them in their analyses.

Secularism

Secularism is a central term for explaining the emergence of religious parties. The common perception treats secularism as an ambiguous set of beliefs with one shared trait—they are not religious. This binary thinking and the elusive definition only limits our understanding of religion's role in societies in general and religious politics in particular. Therefore, only by demystifying the secular and the secularization process and its multifaceted influence on religion is it possible to understand how the complex structure of secularism plays a part in the support for religious parties.

Simplified conclusions from the Weberian idea that secularization reflects an increasing disenchantment with religious worlds and from the Durkheimian dichotomization of sacred and profane have limited analytical expediency for understanding the current rise of religious politics.[54] The last two decades have made it clear that we need to understand the rise of religious movements not *against* but *in* an increasingly secularized world. Rather than viewing the secular as a progressive force contradicting religion, following Dobbeleare and Chaves, our discussion is informed by a multidimensional conceptualization of secularism, and treats it as constituted by three intertwined processes: (1) individual, (2) institutional, and (3) ideational.[55] Accordingly, secularization is best understood by focusing on three distinct dimensions: *laicization, internal secularization,* and *religious disinvolvement.*[56]

In common usage, secularism has been equated with the institutional decline of religion. However, laicization, which refers to the process of differentiation by which political and other public institutions gain autonomy from religious ones and vice versa, is one of the most visible, if limited, aspects of secularization. Internal secularization is the process by which religious organizations internally appropriate the values, ideas, and institutions of the secular world and vice versa. Religious disinvolvement is the decline of religious beliefs and practices among individuals.[57] This disaggregation of secularism shows that the secularization of a society is not a monolithic process; the three aspects of secularism might follow different trajectories. With laicization, religion becomes just one institutional sphere among many, enjoying no primary status. A confinement of religious institutions in the public sphere (laicization), for example, may not necessarily result in a vast cognitive secularization (religious disinvolvement) among individuals. To the contrary, it might increase religious involvement at different levels.

This book focuses on the less visible aspect of secularization, namely internal secularization, to show the interaction between secular and religious values. Religion not only incorporates but also transforms secular values and vice versa. When the pervasive nature of internal secularization is taken into account, it becomes clear that the desecularization thesis, simply understood as the reestablishment of religion's dominant role in society, is highly misleading. The current ascendance of religion's political appeal does not exhibit a simple "return of religion," but also includes an intensive internal secularization process. Rather than assuming a relationship of dominance and control, we need to identify the multiple ways in which the religious and the secular interact. For instance, according to Heilman, such interaction can take the form of *adaptation and transformation* (the conversion of religious practices into secular national loyalties and vice versa), *bivalence* (inhabiting two divergent, contradictory cultures simultaneously) as well as *counter-acculturation* (deliberate isolation from the secular world).[58]

This study offers another typology, which further elaborates on the relationship between religious and secular. Taking the sacred as our foundation, we identify two processes: internal secularization of the religious and sacralization of the secular. *Sacralization of the secular* includes assigning religious meanings to secular ideas, thereby treating them as sacred. *Secularization of the sacred* (or internal secularization) shows how religious terms can be redefined to accommodate secular ideas.

It is important to note that sacralization is a process, not an instantaneous change in commitments. Neither is the object of it (i.e., what is sacralized) random. Rather, the direction and the object of sacralization emerge from the important question or questions affecting the political context. The process does not create an absolute taboo, an area beyond any scrutiny that commands ultimate loyalty. On the contrary, it assigns a religious mission to the underlying idea and the ultimate role of the secular institution, not to the *declared* role or expressed reasons for the real embodiment of the institution itself. In other words, religious ideas that justify sacralization are of prime importance, not the institution. Therefore, a sacralized state does not become an ultimate source of authority as in fascism, but merely an institution to serve a religious cause. In contrast, the sacralized is not only revered, it also becomes the object of religious expectations, scrutiny, and sacrifices (when the institutions fulfill their religious mission or need to be placed in the right trajectory of action). For instance, when the state is sacralized due to its redemptive role, the state is revered to the extent it complies with its redemptive role.

Likewise, internal secularization is not an invasion of the religious by the secular, but a reimagining of religious terms and ideas through the use of modern references. This process thus explores particular secular ideas in a given religious context and merges them together. Compared to Weber's value-rationality, or rational actions that pursue values or serve ultimate meanings (i.e., dedication to religious ideas rationally), internal secularization represents something of its polar opposite, a pursuit of religious ideas to achieve secular goals. For example, the Medina Contract, a document of purely religious significance signed by the prophet, guides behavior to achieve "coexistence" and "plurality," very secular terms and pillars of liberal democracy. Likewise, the Sephardi's religious movement, *teshuvah* (return to religion), is important in the creation of a more encompassing identity in modern Israel where coherent ethnic-religious identities continue to have important political leverage through their control and autonomy in selected policy areas, thereby resulting in the construction of a pillarized political system. Paradoxically, Israel's multilayered system both perpetuates and contains some social and political differences, thus bestowing Shas' policies with a distinctive role in both expanding and transforming the shared public space—a promise of secular nationalism.

These approaches are not mutually exclusive. They may be adopted for a variety of reasons, ranging from the historical tradition that the movement is embedded in to political. Regardless of their raison d'être, they highlight a distinctive interaction between the different forms of transformation of religious and secular ideas. What makes the approach intriguing is that through this disaggregation, we can identify the coexistence of conflicting trends. For instance, an application of these processes in understanding the ideologies of religious parties indicates that they often fuse what appear, to outside observers, to be contradictory positions. Likewise, some parties that are popularly defined as moderate can and often do accept secular structures (for example, a secular state, military system, and education), yet their acceptance can remain conditional on expected (or uncontrolled) transformations of the institutions. Therefore, these parties cannot be decisively described as inclusive or prodemocratic. More importantly, they might challenge some secular democratic principles in their ideologies, such as religious pluralism within a national community, more fervently than other "radical parties." At the individual level, an increasing involvement of individuals in religion does not necessarily translate into increasing support for religious parties. People can also pursue religious rituals that reinforce some of the ideas espoused by ethnic secularity.

Religious Politics

As we observe the increasing presence of religious groups and parties in world politics, we can identify the various terms used to describe this ongoing process. Many of them are meant to show how religion and politics are often fused. Among many others, we can find terms such as *theopolitics* or *religiopolitics*. Arjomand, in his book *The Political Dimension of Religion*, explains why naming the current role of religion in world politics is rather problematic. To be appropriate, the term needs to span various interactions between religion and politics, "from the disjunction between 'political action' and 'religious action' to complete mutual independence." Arjomand captures the range of relationships with terms like *politically relevant religious action, religiously conditioned political action, religiously relevant political action,* and *politically conditioned religious action.*[59] Although this study agrees with Arjomand's concerns, we see a detailed categorization of the interaction between the religious and politics as counterproductive. First, such detailed naming presumes that a distinction exists between the political and the religious, and second, the classifications reduce the relationship to various potentially meaningless combinations and interactions.

What makes the role of religion in politics so intriguing is that some of the demands citizens raise in the public sphere are rooted in religion or justified by it. Therefore, this study focuses on public expressions of religion that seek to attain political power. *Religious politics* or *politics of religion*, then, describes all political activities that express themselves by drawing on religious texts, symbols, and institutions. The term is intentionally broad, as it seeks to explore various manifestations of religion in the political sphere without subsuming them under a certain typology. In other words, by defining religious politics as all public expressions of religion by which political power is sought, we describe the domain of our inquiry without having a priori assumptions regarding the nature of these expressions.

Such a broad description can open ways to further categorizations. For instance, we can explain the relevance of religious ideologies and institutions to politics by pointing out their capacity to (1) provide the groundwork for framing certain issues, (2) enhance the resonance of issue positions, (3) generate social legitimacy and grounds for mobilization, and (4) supply symbols that provide a rationale for action and a foundation for collective identities. In fact, religion carries a significant capacity to influence political beliefs and participation, given its symbolic system, organizational structure, and the power to affect the public imagination with historically entrenched allegories. The religious symbolic sphere differs from others in how it includes five important ideational and behavioral constructs directly affecting politics: *order, commitment, ritual, common allegories,* and *the sense of history.*

Taken together, religion's capacity to define and create these five constructs can legitimize the foundations of multiple political systems. Order, as one of the main promises of modern politics, is also promised by religion. Any religion, in the end, offers a blueprint for a harmonious society. The promise of a stable society that is less vulnerable to contradictions, exceptions, and contingencies than the one entrusted to political processes is one of the most salient features of religious practices and beliefs. The idea of an enduring order becomes more powerful when coupled with the notion that it can withstand the impact of massive temporal dislocations. It is not a coincidence that, one way or another, a harmonious and stable society serves as the main promise of religious parties. The second aspect of religion pertinent to politics is its capacity to foster commitments to certain ideas and values. For example, commitments to various ideals such as divine redemption or establishment of *ummah,* global Muslim community, become significant determinants of individuals' political ideas and choices.[60] Rituals that bring together a group of people and homogenize their life spheres constitute a common repertoire of beliefs and behaviors that can be used to define ends. Rituals, including repetitive actions, articulations, and movements, provide a realm of behavior that connects the members and keeps selective parts of the religious doctrine alive. They form a basis for political mobilization. The frequent use of Friday sermons to explain political events indicates how rituals can easily be transformed into political activities.

The fourth aspect of religion that grants it a distinctive symbolic sphere pertains to the common knowledge of religious allegories or myths. Allegories integrate competing ideas into coherent, shorthand, symbolic accounts. Looking at religious ideologies and religious elite discourses through the prism of order, commitment, and allegory illustrates their competing readings of religious doctrines.[61] Common metaphors of redemption or *cihad,* divinely guided struggle, enable religious elites to simplify complicated political messages and convey their political positions to the masses directly without much effort. As a result, common knowledge of the religious symbolic sphere facilitates political communication in a manner that is unavailable to nonreligious parties. The fifth aspect highlights how religions include a certain understanding of history marked by a list of turning points, for example, the exodus and the reestablishment of the Jewish state, as well as projections about the future, such as the common vision of the return of the Messiah and Judgment Day. This sense of a definitive trajectory of history allows the religion to draw quick, compelling conclusions regarding events and their implications.

When taken all together, the ways in which religion is shaped by and molds its social milieu warn us that one cannot study the increasing support for religious parties as a development occurring in a vacuum. Even though some religious groups define themselves as antisystemic (i.e., they reject the legitimacy of existing institutions) or adopt policies of acculturation, it is impossible to identify a specific insular group that is completely detached from the rest of the political social community. Any political choice, by definition, is affected by its context and also directed at it. Nevertheless, the institutional context, as suggested by the proponents of crisis explanations, cannot be considered the sole cause of the appearance of religious parties and the decision of religious partisans to support them. The critical question becomes how we can develop a more systematic approach for analyzing the ways in which the context shapes both the goal and decisions of the political actors and the distribution of power between them. As we describe the politics of religion as consisting of several and sometimes contradictory beliefs and practices, we refrain from a priori labeling the religious parties as extremist, ultra-Orthodox, or moderate, and instead ask how and to what extent they allow individual autonomy and a plurality of views in their practices.

THE NEXUS OF RELIGION AND POLITICS

The analytical framework guiding this work and our attempt to define the nexus of decision making draws attention to the three areas of interaction that affect religious politics: (1) the political position and capacity of religion (religion in state), (2) the rules of power sharing and political contestation, and (3) the symbolic capital of religious ideologies. Understanding the complexity of each component alone and in relation to others shows that the locus of religious politics lies in between the systems of ideas and social structures. One-dimensional causal inferences can be misleading when, in actuality, the causal arrows are reciprocal and need to be seen as going in both directions to capture the political consequences of mutually transformative interactions.

Religion in State

This study looks at religion not as a force *against* the state, but *in* the state system. We contend that a thorough portrayal of the role of religion in the state cannot be derived only from the formal institutional arrangements. Instead, such a view urges us to reexamine some reified political conflicts that laid the foundation of the formal power-sharing arrangements. Given that theses on religion and politics created their own self-affirming historical discourses, such reviews are especially important to illustrate that the formal political position and capacity of religion are not equivalent.[62] A map of the historical debates on the public role of religion, especially during the state formative years, affords us an understanding of how the state-creating nationalist ideologies viewed religion while highlighting the contested nature of the final, current institutions.[63] Looking beyond the face value of formal configurations enables us to see how, instead of purely embodying strict separation or mutual dependence, many countries fall in a gray area, where state and religion simultaneously form different levels of dependency and autonomy.

It is important to note that identifying the multiple roles religion plays in a polity's official ideology (e.g., its constitution and the hegemonic ideas guiding existing institutions) does not amount to a thorough understanding of the entire political capacity of religion. More often than not, a gap exists between the official role assigned to religion and the enforced and experienced role of religion. More importantly, religion's political position might change within the same polity. It is not rare to see a ban on religious associations followed promptly by the adoption of state-sponsored policies to promote these very same groups. Therefore, the public policies being acted upon, and not the ones being preached, give us a better understanding of the institutional positioning of religion, particularly if we focus on both continuities and ruptures. The reciprocal relationships between the state and religion require us to think in more exhaustive terms such as *dependent autonomy* or *controlled dependency*. These terms help us to differentiate ideational and institutional aspects of the relationship between religion, secular groups, and institutions and pay attention to their different interactions. For instance, under a controlled dependency model, the state claims control over religion (institutional separation) at the same time that it remains dependent on religion for its legitimacy (ideational dependence). In this situation, religion possesses a significant potential to challenge the state's power due to its critical role as a legitimizing force.

Terms such as *controlled dependency* also alert us to the fact that the state's institutional control of religion (e.g., control of religious clergy and education through a directorate of religious affairs) does not necessarily amount to an ideological autonomy from religion (e.g., it does not grant the state the capacity to justify its policies without referring to religious). Likewise, a religion's ideological independence and, in some cases, its institutional independence can be offset by its dependency on the state for its own needs. Depending on its structure and specific practices, a religion may fail to sustain financially autonomous communities and thus rely on the state to support its activities, rituals, and education. Furthermore, the plurality of religious beliefs and practices, combined with conflicts within the religious bloc itself, might also make religion trust in the state's capacity and unifying authority to coordinate diverse groups. For instance, in Israel, the long hours of study required to master the Halakhic traditions prevent students from accepting full-time employment. Ironically, the more ultra-Orthodox the group, the more they depend on the state's largesse for the support of their religious practices. In Turkey, the diversity of Islamic groups makes them turn to the state for the coordination of some of their religious practices.[64] Despite the religious groups' opposition to state secularism, they continue to endorse the state's directorate of religious affairs. Thus, regardless of the rationale, religion's own internal structure might foil its search for and realization of full autonomy.

Power Sharing and Political Contestation

In any polity, power sharing and political contestation are subject to various constraints. The religious parties' engagement in politics is not an exception. The main rules of the contestation shape the final appearance, the number, and the strategies of the religious parties, but not the ideas embedded in their ideologies. Rules of competition are not simply limited to the distribution of the seats in the parliament. Rather, they cover both formal and informal rules, ranging from those that define acceptable party platforms or the national threshold for parliamentary representation to the allocation of the state funds to parties. Thus, in our analysis we need to ask how the electoral competition is designed and what advantages or disadvantages it poses for religious parties. Existing political practices might diverge from the institutional map of the country. Therefore, we also need to take into account practiced rules of politics, which might nullify some formal state policies. For instance, we can identify the tolerance extended to the settlement movement in Israel or the lenient application of policies for some religious associations in Turkey, despite strict, official rules against them.

Electoral rules are especially important in defining the number of religious parties. An easy entrance policy (i.e., fewer requirements for forming a party and vying for political power) results in a more pluralistic system. In contrast, in countries where the rules of electoral competition are restrictive, religious movements recede into the background or form coalitions for political survival. Nevertheless, more often than not, the rules do not limit the diversity of religious movements but restrict to what extent they are expressed in the public sphere as coherent political movements. The following chapters illustrate that rules do matter in the immediate appearance and number of the religious parties. But they also show how one of the most puzzling qualities of religious movements has been their ability to prevail despite restrictive rules and adverse power-sharing arrangements. Without exception, all religious parties embed themselves in local communities before entering the national game of democracy, thereby maintaining a remarkable level of resilient political capital—religion's political capacity, is not innate but activated and enhanced by, inter alia, the role of religion in the system and the party-affiliated network of groups, services, and associations. Therefore, it is religion's political and potent symbolic capital rather than its innate spiritual capital (i.e., self-enforcing values and beliefs) that ensure its survival even under unfavorable conditions and rules.

The Symbolic Capital of Religious Ideologies

The content of religious parties' ideologies has received limited attention, in part due to the prevailing notion that ideologies derived from the same religion generate more or less the same ideas. Nevertheless, analyses of religion's resilient social power and expanding political capital constantly remind us of the intrinsic value and significance of religious ideas. Although religious values never generate political practices ipso facto, Weber contended that no matter "how incisive the economically and politically determined social influences" may have been on a religious group, their religious ideas are derived from religious sources and "from the content of religion's promise."[65] While other spheres of interest are likely to be significant, they alone will not have a decisive influence by themselves without first working through the symbolic world of religion. Given the increasing marginalization of the specific ideas that formed religious ideologies, it is especially important to emphasize the significance of religious symbols and their uses. As noted earlier, the ways in which religious ideas are imbued with meanings and employed is not monolithic. The comparison of religious parties within Israel and Turkey shows that they differ substantially in the way they tap into religion's symbolic capital. Religious ideologies do not necessarily differ because they are rooted in different sections of their respective religious doctrines but often because they take contradictory stances on the same part. Religious party elites play a key role in infusing religious symbols with new meanings or reintroducing new issues under a religious color. Like other ideologies, the ideologies of religious parties seek to offer an internally consistent depiction of the political structure, the areas that need to be changed, and the road to an ideal society. The ways in which religious ideologies use religious symbols can be better defined if we ask how they view (1) the state; (2) the nation, nationalism, the official state ideology; (3) the community; and (4) the individuals. Understanding religious parties' symbolic constructs enables us to place their ideology against the landscape of their polity. In the process of mapping out the way to enforce their symbolic capital, we better explore how the party engages with secular and religious worlds. When its relation to the context and actors is questioned, the symbolic capital allows us to develop a typology of religious parties and to question their overall impact on their democracies without simplifying their complexities to the binaries of democratic or antidemocratic.

CONCLUSION

As Granovetter has noted, "A fruitful analysis of human action requires us to avoid the atomization implicit in the theoretical extremes of under- and over-socialized conceptions. Actors do not behave or decide as atoms outside the social context, nor do they adhere slavishly to a script written for them by the particular intersection of social categories they happen to occupy."[66] Their attempts at purposive action are instead embedded in ongoing systems of social relations and social context. Analyses that over-value one component of religious politics oftentimes create highly misleading results. After all, religious partisans are rarely simple religious zealots who follow a certain doctrine blindly; instead, they are individuals who live in complex political environments and are capable of making decisions based not only upon their beliefs but also upon the conditions of the historical institutional juncture they face.[67] The political components defined here are in constant interaction, and their overall positions can change gradually due either to the confluence of social processes or to the deliberate efforts of actors. Therefore, the critical role of *interaction* between individuals, religion, and structures urges us to place our inquiries at the nexus of key constituents of religious politics. Identifying the components of this nexus (e.g., the historical political location, symbolic capital of religion, the perceptions of individuals, and the positioning of other actors) enables us to assess the patterns of their interaction, how entrenched the modalities are, and how likely they are to change.[68]

The overall approach adopted in this study constantly reminds us that the decisions of religious partisans and parties rest on and nest in multilayered structures, and that it is not only structural but also ideational space. Both are not external factors but rather part and parcel of the politics of religion. Individuals' decisions and religious groups' articulations occur not only within their political historical context but also in relation to it and as an important constituent of it. Consequently, neither part can be studied if detached from its multilayered milieu. Nor can the potential of religious parties and the impact on their respective democracies be understood without identifying the political capacity and symbolic capital of religion. How the multilayered context, capacity, and religious capital affect the manifestations of religious politics and religious partisans' decisions is not a predetermined or perfunctory process. The promise of our comparative design lies in its ability to attend to the variant positions and contents of each component of religious politics and tease out the reciprocal transformative interactions among them. Instead of reifying religious ideologies and decisions of religious partisans, we start by asking what constitutes the web of relationships and symbols that define the political world of religious politics and how they affect and imprint the world around them. The subsequent chapters take us to the common and unique characteristics of the politics of Judaism and Islam, introduce the political movements rooted in them, and, by comparing their images in the mirror thereby explore new comparative ground of each other, to recalibrate our conceptual lenses. In this comparative inquiry, we look for an answer to the questions of what makes religious movements a common force in world politics, how their local reflections differ and converge, and how religious forces and agents shape the new holy site of world politics, liberal democracy. In order to identify the political positioning of religion in Israeli and Turkish politics, the next chapter briefly revisits some of the historical debates, the contestations, and the compromises. This review prepares the ground for the analysis of how elites of the parties central to our analysis reproduce religious symbols and why an increasing number of voters finds these messages relevant.

CHAPTER TWO

Religion in the Making of the Israeli and Turkish Nation-States

Incomplete Debates and Continuing Institutional Reformations

The greatest advantage of religion is to inspire diametrically contrary principles. There is no religion that does not place the object of man's desires above and beyond the treasures of earth. . . . Nor is there any which does not impose on man some duties towards his kind and thus draw him at times from the contemplation of himself.[1]

The politics of religion cannot be discussed without identifying the assigned and claimed role of religion within a polity. One of the challenges of what seems to be a simple task is the very language we use in locating religion in modern democracies. The assumed clear divisions between the social realms assigned to the state and to religion, one way or another, actually juxtapose religion against the state. The terms that describe this split constitute perhaps the primary hurdle for any analysis dealing with this topic. For instance, to expel the myth that the state is a single, uniform set of institutions or an ideological homogeneous collection of actors, we need to approach the state not as a static institution, but in terms of stateness (i.e., the state as a set of institutions, power sharing arrangements, and a complex web of relationships). Talking about stateness serves three purposes. First, it reminds us that the state's role and power in society does not take a single form once its institutions emerge—the entire political system may undergo significant changes that modify the environments of social actors and alter their leverages to such an extent that once marginalized groups may decisively influence the outcomes of states' actions.[2] Second, the state's ability to coerce and execute authority is not a constant, but rather a variant. Third, the state's authority and ability to wield power constantly require legitimacy and acceptance from a significant segment of the society in which religious publics often play critical roles. As a result, the state's search to make itself acceptable and the way in which it asserts its authority are not fixed but include continuous negotiations and ongoing conflicts.

In any debate on religion in politics, while the state inevitably constitutes a key concept, perhaps even more important are the terms through which we define the state's relation to religion—the terms that elucidate the ways in which we recognize or fail to recognize the assigned and achieved roles of religion. At this juncture, the ubiquitous "wall of separation" metaphor captures best, both figuratively and conceptually, the dualisms that thwart our efforts to understand religion as a political force. A quick look at the genealogy of the term attests to how once expedient metaphors or terms can limit and curtail our social imagination with significant consequences. Ironically, the wall of separation made its way into the symbolism of the political world in response to a plea from a group that feared that democratic legislators "could make laws to govern the Kingdom of Christ" and treat religious freedoms as legislative favors.[3] In 1802, Thomas Jefferson reassured the Danbury Baptist Association of Connecticut that a wall of separation would be respected and that the state would not make dictates to the church.[4] The foundation upon which the wall of strict separation was built, however, immediately proved to be unstable. During Jefferson's presidency, federal funds were allocated to build churches and to support Christian missionaries working among indigenous people.[5]

Despite its limitations, the wall metaphor did not disappear. Quite the opposite: its focus has changed from protecting religion to protecting the free public sphere, and it has gradually acquired not only a descriptive but an ascriptive (normative) status. The building of the wall came to represent one of the premises for the flourishing of liberal democracy, which was assumed to develop deeper roots in polities with a clear demarcation between religious and state domains. Many observers argued that, especially in new democracies, only the existence of a high wall would ensure that freedom and the pluralization of ideas in the public sphere would not be affected by religion's authoritative claims. Descriptive analyses that have taken the presence and status of a high and impregnable wall of separation as a reference point have often designated the interactions between state and religion as one of three ideal types. At one end of the spectrum are countries with *strict separation* of state and religion, a system where the state does not support any religious denominations and considers religious activities to be an autonomous part of civil society.

Under a second type, the *accommodationist model*, the state accepts an official religion and controls religious activities of that belief system, while nonofficial religious groups enjoy autonomy. At the other end of the spectrum reside *integrationist states*, where the state declares a certain religion as its foundation, and public policies are based on the premises of that religion.

The best textbook cases for each category draw our attention to the fact that in any polity the power-sharing arrangements rest on historical negotiations and compromises and can be understood only in relation to them. Even in cases where there seems to be a strict separation, religion's relation to the state and politics is not straightforward. Once the wall has been built, it does not necessarily remain intact and impenetrable. In fact, more and more evidence suggests that the wall of separation is more permeable than ever. To understand the prevalence and analytical consequences of the separation paradigm, it is important to remember that it rests on a powerful idea derived from modernity: religious and political spheres are deemed to be in opposition to each other. Therefore, a demarcation between them is essential for modernity and its product, liberal democracy. After all, even observers who saw the democratic capital in religion, such as Tocqueville, agreed that:

In the moral world everything is classified, coordinated, foreseen, and decided in advance. In the world of politics everything is in turmoil, contested, and uncertain. In the one case obedience is passive, though voluntary; in the other there is independence, contempt of experience, and jealousy of all authority.[6]

Although Tocqueville also concluded that these two apparently opposed tendencies could work in harmony and would be able to lend support to each other, pervasive modernist ideas successfully contended that only by assigning a carefully delineated free sphere of influence to religion would the state be able to protect the existence of religious beliefs and values without allowing them to monopolize the marketplace of ideas. Regardless of rationale, history shows that a pure form of separation has rarely materialized in practice. In fact, the entire spectrum of this theoretically robust typology of interaction between the state and religion gets immediately blurred when applied to the real world. Perhaps one of the strictest forms of separation, the highest wall of all, is exemplified by the French case. *Laïcité*, the rule of laymen, defines the French approach to religion, which emerged as a reaction to the historical tutelage of the clergy. When English-speaking countries use this term, it is often accompanied by the caveat that the historical references and allusions that gave it its meaning are missing and that no equivalent term exists. Historically, the Roman Catholic Church owned 15 percent of the land in France, ran its own health and school systems, and collected taxes. One of the first agreements signed shortly after the Revolution in 1801 between the state and the church required the church to relinquish its political authority.

Against its historical backdrop the French laïcité came to represent the idea of the disengagement of the church from the state while using the state's policies to create an open public sphere for the citizenry—a public sphere that stands beyond the reach of the conventional distinctions and competitions of layman and clergy. Nevertheless, this goal amounted to an internally paradoxical position that does not resolve but questions the precise place and, in some cases, presence of a wall of separation. For example, the state's efforts to ensure a public sphere free of religion's intrusion ultimately results in its own engagement and sometimes direct intrusion with religion's public expressions. Rather than becoming a detailed social model, the term *laïcité* developed into more of a precept or apophthegm which appealed to different groups who feared the return of "the dogma of pontifical infallibility reaffirmed by Vatican I (1870)."[7] Supporters of laïcité focused especially on education as they fought for "taking the soul of the French youth away from the [church]."[8] A law adopted in 1905 forbade the government from recognizing or subsidizing any religion and employing any clergy. Therefore, the French case commits the state to maintaining an areligious public sphere and protects its institutions from being affected by religious ideas. This active neutralization of the public sphere has often led to the question of whether the state is suppressing religious freedom for the sake of the liberating qualities of an areligious and free public sphere. The continuing debates culminated in a 2004 law (i.e., Law 2004-228 of March 15, 2004) that strengthened the state's policy of maintaining a secular public sphere by prohibiting the wearing of all conspicuous religious signs in public schools, including large crosses, kippas, and headscarves.[9] Although its first modern mosque was built with state support, the law targets French minorities, not an established and overpowering church, attesting to the situational nature of the state's laïcité and its search to reconfigure the limits of the walls of separation.[10]

In countries that adhere to an accommodationist model, for example in England, the state-affiliated church provides a certain form of religion compatible with the state's policies, along with basic religious services.[11] The system of religion and state is intertwined in such a way that twenty-six bishops sit in the House of Lords, while archbishops are appointed by the sovereign upon the advice of the prime minister. The church has its own hierarchy, essentially a replication of the institutional structure of the state. Perhaps due to the harmonious relationship between church and state or the declining religious practices within the demos, the church has not challenged the state's authority and has been able to keep its traditional values intact. For instance, the church finally allowed greater participation by the laity in the early 1970s, and women achieved priestly status only in 1994, even though the state's representative structure, which the church emulated, had become inclusive much earlier. Paradoxically, in recent times the state has helped reassert the role of religion in the public schools. According to the Education Reform Act of 1988, English state schools provide religious instruction and have regular religious ceremonies, but parents may withdraw their children from either.[12] The choice of religion to be taught is left up to the schools. Although it is an established, state-affiliated church, financially the Church of England relies heavily on the income from donations and various historic endowments. As a result, the Anglican Church is an institution that remains financially autonomous, yet legally dependent on Parliament.

At the other end of the spectrum lie regimes where religious ideas define the fundamentals of the state policies. These types of regimes are rare, but the specter of their expansion raises fears among liberal democracies. Iran is probably the most striking example in this category. Shia Islam serves as the foundation of the state's policies, and the Islamic clergy also acts as the ruling elite. At first glance, the regime seems to have resolved the tension that arises from the separation of religion and the state by granting full control to religion. In fact, Article 4 of the Iranian constitution stipulates that all civil, penal, financial, economic, administrative, cultural, military, political, and other laws and regulations must be based on Islamic criteria. A closer look at the regime, however, reveals that even in the absence of a wall, the tension between the state elite and religious groups does not vanish. Rather, given the diversity of religious groups and ideas, new questions arise. Political debates have erupted over which interpretation of a given religion (which religious tradition) should prevail and how the diversity of religious beliefs can organize the day-to-day policies under a unified state. Regardless of its effort to craft a genuine regime based on religious sources, the Iranian system relies to a significant extent on a 290-member national representative parliament and an Assembly of Experts elected by popular vote, yet the country prohibits political parties. The Iranian experience suggests that an integrationist state can obliterate the wall of separation, but it cannot claim legitimacy without an elected, representative body.[13]

Notwithstanding the dominance of religion, it is important to note that the regime had to create an Expediency Discernment Council in 1988 to resolve differences between various elected and appointed institutions and negotiate their policies to ensure their accordance with religious rules.

Iran's power-sharing arrangements illustrate that even in the case of a strict fusion of religion and the state, the process of creating a dominant religious interpretation and preventing religious ideas from challenging the unity of the state requires a careful balancing act. Ironically, elections have emerged as one of the most significant sources of power in Iran, not at the expense of the role of religion, but by creating various areas of negotiations and contestations where the interplay of social forces and religious symbols create a vibrant political competition under the guise of dormant politics. This situation has created ongoing tensions between elected and appointed elites. Paradoxically, the state gains religious authority by enforcing religious norms in the public and private domains, but its very reliance on the clergy to interpret the doctrines necessitates further state mediation. Perhaps more importantly, the increasing pluralization of religious beliefs and the varying, sometimes opposing, views on how to enforce them indicate that integrationist models do not amount to stable ones. To the contrary, the tension between religion and the state remains very high.

All in all, the review of prototypical cases warns us against an ahistorical treatment of the interactions between the state and religion and the reification of a secular state sphere as an area that can be easily separated from the religious sphere. Even in the textbook cases, it is hard to locate the wall and the presumed boundaries between the state and religion. Even if we do, we often find that the "wall" is porous and permeable. An official "separation" or integration does not necessarily amount to a creation of two autonomous or congruous domains. Nor does accommodation or integration mean an end to negotiations between actors and ideologies nested in state and religion. Ironically, separating religion from the state oftentimes requires an active involvement of the state to control religion and to build and maintain the wall. As the state seeks to curb religion as an independent political power base using a wide range of strategies, various arrangements emerge. Seen from the other side of the wall, the religious perspective, religions continue to exert their influence in the secular arena in many ways, both subtle and overt.

Rather than being a simple conceptual construct, the separation myth has significant ramifications on our analytical and empirical inquiries. The separation places religion on one side of the wall and the state on the other side, thereby precluding questions about possible forms of the state-religion relationship if the two cannot be easily separated, and about the political implications of different forms of permeability. As in many polities, religion has the potential of being a self-regulating and independent political power in Turkey and Israel. However, like any other political power, religion maintains its presence via the state, but not always at the expense of the state. Given these intricacies, the interactions between religion and the state can be better assessed by taking into account its two distinctive components: institutional (i.e., the formal rules) and ideational (i.e., the exchange and impact of ideas). Although the way in which religion and the state are institutionally and ideologically positioned in a particular society can tell us the state's institutional arrangements and declared official position on religion, it is unable to indicate its exact ideational positions. Questioning the formal rules permits us to evaluate whether and to what extent the state regulates the religious domain (e.g., training of clergy, maintaining of ritual places, religious education). On the other hand, the ideological and ideational interactions determine the degree to which the state's legitimacy and policies are independent of or remain dependent upon religious justification. Turning the lens around, we can gauge the institutional position of religion by asking to what extent the religious elites and publics maintain their presence without the support of the state. Likewise, we can determine religion's ideological independence from the state by how central the state's role is to the realization of religious ideals and the existence of religious communities.

Even a cursory look at the role of the Israeli and Turkish states beyond the separation paradigm suggests that describing the Israeli state as integrationist and the Turkish state as strictly separatist excessively oversimplifies the continuing tensions and dependency between and within various secular and religious groups. In each case, a unique set of power-sharing arrangements defines the role of religion in the state and in politics, while the boundaries separating the state from religion remain contested. In the following discussion, we identify the main conflicts and compromises that lie beneath Israel's and Turkey's political and historical settings. The countries' ideational negotiations and compromises suggest that we need to describe the various ways in which religion and state can interact in different terms. For instance, the perspective of the *state-dependent autonomy* (i.e., formal autonomy results in not independence but ideational and structural independence) or *controlled dependency* (i.e., formal separation controlled by the state fosters not ideational autonomy but dependence) might be more appropriate. As the state-constituting periods in Israel and Turkey have made clear, any attempt to understand the current manifestation of religion in these countries cannot be successful unless we review their ideational struggles and institutional arrangements unfettered by a priori assumptions. The state-constitutive periods and the negotiations that followed are especially remarkable for the revelation that conflicts often occur within the same person and that some of the most significant, enduring compromises have been reached on the premise that they were temporary.

RELIGIOUS IDEAS AND INSTITUTIONS IN ISRAELI
AND TURKISH POLITICS

The ideational environment of the Israeli and Turkish nation-state formations was shaped by the disintegration of the Ottoman Empire, the establishment of the nation-state system in Europe, and the strong appeal of
socialism that resulted in the Bolshevik Revolution in Russia. The associated nationalist ideas eventually became state-constitutive political movements under the leadership of Theodor Herzl (who later adopted the name
Binyamin Ze'ev) in Israel and Mustafa Kemal Atatürk in Turkey.[14] Both
nationalisms exhibited significant similarities due, in part, to the ideological environment in which they were born and the common political hurdles they faced. In both countries, the political leaderships faced difficult
quandaries in their efforts to build a wall between religion and the state
and to limit the role of religion in the public sphere. Israel and Turkey
were part of the second wave of nationalism following the establishment
of nation-states in Europe. The idea of nation and the various ways to
achieve one had already become part and parcel of the political debate.
Yet each country's nationalism confronted unique challenges: Jewish nationalism did not have clearly defined geographical limits, while Turkish
nationalism faced the institutional and ideational legacy of the Ottoman
Empire. Both Herzl and Atatürk envisioned a limited role for religion in
their idealized polity, yet this imagined role became one of their state's
main conundrums. As the following discussion details, the state-founding
ideologies of Israel and Turkey, namely Zionism and Kemalism, relied on
Judaism and Islam, respectively, to define a common denominator for
their national identities. At the same time, the secular state-founding elites
sought to contain the political role of religion. As a result, the role of
religion has been one of the most controversial aspects of the nation-
building processes of these two countries and remains an important area
for political competition.

The Challenge of Jewishness in the Modern Israeli State

Ideas   Understanding the current issues of Israeli politics requires an
understanding of the debates that occurred prior to and during Israel's
formative years. Perhaps the most unifying yet divisive issue was how to
define Jewishness as a national identity and, likewise, the nature of its
relationship to Judaism. On the one hand, religion served as a unifying
force for bringing broadly scattered Jewish communities together as a
nation. On the other hand, it also became a source of conflict over the
definition of the common institutions and ideals of the nation-state.

The so-called Jewish problem became a pressing political predicament, especially after the emerging European nation-states failed to grant equal rights to Jewish populations as part of universal citizenship. Despite their promises to generate stable and inclusive regimes, neither European nationalism nor emerging socialist regimes seemed to prevent the exclusion of Jewish groups. In fact, exclusion often became part of the official practice and in some cases escalated to pogroms and enforced ghettos. The Israeli nation-state building process occurred in the midst of various radical political shifts marked by the disintegration of the Ottoman Empire, the struggle of the emerging nation-state system with the legacy of multiethnic polities, and the challenge of creating national industries and markets. In this ideational setting, two parallel political struggles marked the emergence of Zionism and its formation of the Israeli state. The first struggle occurred *within* the Jewish community over the question of how to define a common Jewish identity and determine the final form of the nation-state. The second struggle involved the reactions of non-Jewish groups that opposed the establishment of a Jewish nation-state. Ironically, this opposition proved to be instrumental in uniting the feuding Jewish groups. Like other nation-state building processes, Zionism was formed amid centrifugal and centripetal forces.

The conundrums of the emerging Jewish identity and the configuration of the state institutions manifested themselves best in Herzl's own writing. The title of one of his early pamphlets, "The Jewish State: An Attempt at a Modern Solution of the Jewish Question," captured the disillusionment of Jewish intellectuals with the ideas of the Enlightenment. The Jewish question was, Herzl argued, neither social nor religious, but a national question. Many other intellectuals believed, with Herzl, that Jews could maintain their presence and acceptance in the world only by ceasing to be a national anomaly.[15] Otherwise, Herzl insisted, Jews would remain a perpetual minority in the countries they lived in. Their continuing exclusion, even in cases of full assimilation, affirmed that Jewish groups constituted not merely a religious minority with different levels of observance, but a nationality, a people, a *Volk*. Only a Jewish nation-state would offer the world a welcome "final solution of the Jewish question."[16] Only cultural, secular nationalism would transform Jewish minorities into a distinct nation-state and normalize them as a member of the family of modern nation-states.

The basic line of thought is defined by the two parallel visions that characterized Zionism as a political project. One saw Zionism as a nationalist movement, and the other approached it as a religious revivalist or religious messianic movement. Attesting to the forceful push-and-pull effect of these ideas, some intellectuals moved from one stream of thought to another, embracing each with similar fervor. Such ideational transitions were not without tension and often generated rather unique syntheses. For instance, according to Hess, the Jewish tradition in its secular aspect would form the foundation for egalitarianism and socialism, rather than universalistic values or Judaism. [17] Hess was not alone. Disenchanted by socialism and cultural nationalism, a growing number of intellectuals turned to Judaism as a source of emancipatory social models. A closer look at Hess's writings helps us understand the intellectual roots of this trend. "Internationalism" for Hess, as it manifested itself in Europe, rested on not only a contradictory, but a politically self-defeating approach: internationalism did not recognize the principle of nationality in order to move beyond it. This lack of recognition became the main hurdle on the road to its political success. Internationalism became an "empty, artificial component of cosmopolitanism" by avoiding both the critical issue of nationalism and the consequences should its ideal fail and the world divide along national lines.[18] Therefore, true internationalism first and foremost necessitated the recognition of ethnic, cultural groups. Acknowledging and addressing the existence of nationalities was not a weakness but the sine qua non of internationalism. Jewish nationalism was thus a political necessity for achieving internationalism and Zionism's universal ideals.

The symbolic language developed by the Jewish elite during the state-constitutive years allows us to get a sense of the countervailing thrusts, clashes, and creative reconciliations in the emerging national Jewish identity. Perhaps one of the most revealing terms embedded in this emerging symbolism was *Zion*. The name of the movement, *Zionism*, was introduced by Nathan Birnbaum, who drastically changed his intellectual positions by moving from the nationalist end of the spectrum to the antinationalist one. Zion, the biblical symbol of the city of David and a part of Jerusalem, came to articulate the yearning for an original state of both the traditional and the modern Jewry. Although Zion signified the critical historical role that nationhood and the nation-state played for the Jewish people, it also came to justify the emerging secular national movement as a return to Zion. The word *Zionism*, which was already a part of Jewish culture before the first Zionist Congress, became a powerful unifying sign of the collective effort of the Diaspora Jewry to end the segregation of Jewish populations. Along with Zion, a long list of Halakhic terms and symbols served as important signifiers in the movement. The modernist elite quickly learned that religious symbols offered religious and secular Jews a common ground by accentuating the religious aspects of the Jewish culture and allowed the Zionist leaders to compromise with the religious elite.

Perhaps Herzl's book titles represent the best manifestation of the coupling of the religious and secular imaginary. In his *Altneuland*, Old New

Land (1902) the conversation of an estranged Jew with different characters introduces us to the underpinnings of how the old and new came together in the Zionist movement. In order to explain his ideals, Herzl relied heavily on anecdotes from the old community, from the history of the Jewish people, to describe the new one, the modern nation-state. For instance, he articulated the concerns of the secular Jewry through the conversations of a disheartened Jew who often found himself saying: ". . . We have really died. There's nothing left of the Jewish kingdom but this fragment of the Temple wall. And though I fathom my soul to its depths, I find nothing in common with these traffickers in the national misfortune." Herzl then would turn to a stranger, representing those who understand the constructive power of religion and the old, and speak through his responses:

I see what you are—a stranger to your people. More remains of the Jews than the stones of this ancient bit of masonry and these poor wretches here. . . . If you ever come to us in Russia, you will realize that a Jewish nation still exists. We have a living tradition, a love of the past, and faith in the future. The best and most cultured men among us have remained.[19]

Overall, Herzl's explanations did not reflect a strategic prima facie use of the terms, but at a deep level, he reinforced the idea that today's questions have been asked before and that tradition empowers people to tackle them. The Hebrew adaptation of Herzl's writing, which altered the title of his work to *Tel Aviv* (literally "the Hill of Spring"), captured how the distance among isolated and parallel symbolic worlds of Jewish communities were being abridged. While the hill signified the layers of an old land in which ancient cities are buried, the spring symbolized hope for a new land with a better future. Within the essence of the new symbols and titles lay the revival of a fecund symbolic world where, like Tel Aviv, religious terms and places served to describe the promise of the nation-state. Yet while using the religio-national symbols extensively, Herzl was quick to point out that the Jewish state would be secular, liberal, and free of clericalism: religion and state would be strictly separate. The climax of Zionism's achievement would be the inauguration of the new temple, a religious sign of promised redemption. "The Jewish state," Herzl wrote, "would be known for its tolerance and interdenominational harmony."[20]

The use of religious symbols by secular nationalist Zionism did not mean that a deep level of unification of the religious and secular Jewry was in the making. On the contrary, such compromises often created controversy among both religious and secular circles. Mirroring the arguments raised by religious critiques of emerging Zionism, Birnbaum, the inventor of the term *Zionism*, eventually gave up on cultural nationalism and turned to religious nationalism. He later became the secretary general of the anti-nationalist Agudat Israel. In his writings, we can find some of the most explicit accounts of how Zionism's secular national and religious meanings clashed:

There was a time, at first, when I used to believe that all those who recognized the Jews as a people were full, *national* Jews—no matter in which soil they had their spiritual roots. At that time, I did not think at all about religion. . . . Somewhat later I came to realize that it was not good enough merely to acknowledge allegiance to one nation or another, as one pleased; to belong to it, one had to enter into its life and spirit. Of course this view did not let me treat religion with my former indifference: it was in religion that the Jewish spirit had expressed itself through the ages. *For the Jewish nationalists, the Jewish land is not the land given by God to our people so that it may there live for Him, but merely a historic domicile in which we can live "like all the nations."* They do not demand national rights and autonomy in the diaspora as an opportunity to live as a community dedicated to God, with its own religious culture, but only in order to imitate the newest European fashions. (emphases added)[21]

Religious rejectionists like Birnbaum saw Zionists as pragmatists devoid of any religious understanding of the regathering of exiles in Zion. The struggles over the Jewish identity and the incorporation of secular values into religious ideas and vice versa introduced a broad ideational spectrum. Some Orthodox rejectionist groups denounced Zionism altogether as a further assimilation and deviation from the authentic Jewish identity and as a desecration of the divine promise of redemption. Others, whom we call accommodationists, came from both religious and secular sides. For religious accommodationists, Zionism per se represented the unfolding of divine redemption and messianic ideas (gathering from exile and the beginning of redemption).[22] The Zionist call for a nation-state, for *Hamizrahi*, which later became the National Religious Party, was a call for the return to the historical land and religious origins in order to achieve religious redemption.[23] For secular accommodationists, the acknowledging of and referring to religious symbols was an inevitable step toward forming a new Hebrew national culture. If Jews were a Volk, the religious traditions of Judaism constituted an indispensable component of the modern Jewish nation. The ideas of accommodationists carved out a new discursive sphere but did not resolve the paradox of emerging nationalism: that is, how to build a nation-state by acknowledging its common image in its religious history without turning religion into the dominant political force in Israel's emerging society.

Despite the convergence of the social imagery of different secular and religious groups, the contesting views on the ultimate form of Jewish unification ignited intense debates in the Zionist congresses and during prestate *Yishuv* period. According to Don Yehiya, because of the symbolic dependency of Zionism on Judaism and its desire to unify all Diaspora Jews in one nation, Zionism never defined itself as a secular movement. However, there were always intense arguments about the extent to which secular nationalism would co-opt the religious elite. For instance, prior to the first congress, Max Nordau, its vice president, declared, "Zionism has nothing to do with theology; and if a desire has been kindled in Jewish hearts to establish a new commonwealth in Zion, it is not the Torah or the *Mishnah* that inspire them, but hard times."[24] Herzl's efforts to form the broadest coalition possible led him to denounce such statements, often on rather pragmatic grounds: "We must not," Herzl argued, "drive the Zionist rabbis away. Let us not discourage them, even if we have no intention of handing them the leadership."[25] Such arguments were justified by the idea that one could be strongly attached to Jewish religious traditions without being an Orthodox Jew, and Orthodox Jews were an important part of the political coalition formed to realize the Jewish nation-state.[26]

A closer look at the early years of Zionism reveals that the movement hosted a gamut of competing social projects with distinctive and different visions of the Jewish nation. There are several explanations as to why there was such a great divide in the imagining of the Jewish nation.[27] One of the most pertinent explanations traces the divide to the disparate transformations of the state-religion interactions in the political communities in which Jewish groups were embedded. When defined in the broadest terms, these groups included (1) Western European, (2) Eastern European, and (3) North African and Middle Eastern Jewry. The first group, Western European Jewry, witnessed the gradual separation of the role of state and religion in conjunction with the emergence of the Western European nation-state system. This group mirrored Europe's nationalist ideals and did not rely on religious beliefs for the construction of a national collective identity. Birnbaum considered these trends alien to Jewish tradition and called them "pagan rebellions in a Jewish garb." The Jewry of Eastern Europe, with their experience of systematic segregation and the resultant reactionary strengthening of religious leadership, supported conservative religious movements such as Hasidim[28] and Mitnaggedim.[29] Overall, in both groups, the very experience of the strong state and secularism created Jewish groups that embraced these ideas but also reacted to them by creating inward-looking communities (see table 2.1 later in this chapter for a timeline of this movement). In Birnbaum's writings, we can see how the politics of their respective geographies divided these groups:

What goes for the modern Jewish nationalists of Western Europe, also applies to their Eastern European fellows-in-arms. I must give them even more credit than to the others. I respect the great Hebrew and Yiddish writers, who draw their power from the eternal font of Jewish life, even though they do not share in its profound and fervent faith and great religious self-discipline. I also acknowledge that particularly the younger generation among them seeks the spiritual soul of the Jewish people; they have not fallen prey to the fallacy of those nationalists who are proud of the sacred Jewish past, but in effect, deny this past by excluding our spiritual traditions from their own picture of national life. But, on the other hand, the nationalists of the Eastern European brand are even more dangerous than their more assimilated Western friends, because of their closer contact and greater influence upon the Yiddish-speaking religious masses.[30]

The third group consisted of the Jewry of the North African and Middle Eastern countries, whose political experiences had been imprinted primarily by Ottoman rule where a millet system granted religious communities cultural autonomy. The culturally decentralized polities in this region did not force the Jewry to choose between assimilation or conservatism in order to maintain their communal identity.[31] Therefore, this third group differed drastically from the others. While the Jews maintained their religious and cultural identity and autonomy, which effectively made these groups—popularly described as Sephardi—more community-centered and less isolationist, their traditions were affected by the dominant Muslim practices.

Given the broad audience of Zionism and the distinctive experiences that participant groups brought with them, religion appeared as the only common, unifying denominator. In Vital's words, "Zionism itself (in its secular-cultural form) could never claim more than a large minority of its people as true supporters. The traditionalists of religious Orthodoxy, the socialists, and the autonomists substantially outnumbered them."[32] The Jews' cultural diversity and different positions on religion further complicated the question of religion in the emerging polity.

Institutions　　The founders of the emerging Israeli nation battled over critical questions such as how to mold the national Jewish identity, the final form of institutions, and the state's role in redistributive policies (both symbolic and financial). The content and form of education was most intensely fought over because of education's decisive role in shaping and maintaining hegemonic ideas and the future of the polity. The multifaceted groups supporting Zionism differed from religious leaders in their vision of the core values and policies that would guide the future of the state. The phrase "The Cultural Controversy" emerged, in essence, to capture the contested understanding of the ideal citizen and polity, as well as the debates that exerted a special bearing on the structure and content of education. Fundamental questions dominating the agenda ranged from who is a Jew to what is the main purpose of the emerging state. For some, the Jewish religion was and still is contradictory to the needs of modernity and the modern nation-state. According to this group, a "new Hebrew Culture" was necessary to replace the fragmented and conservative Diaspora culture and achieve national unity. The debates on what form this new Hebrew culture should take opened up additional contested spaces.

One of the rather popular visions advocated a largely aesthetic synthesis of Judaism and Europeanism and/or a European culture in Hebrew form. Others believed that the new Hebrew culture would grow naturally from within a modern Israeli society. Still others thought that education needed to be religious in nature to reconnect with the Jewish essence and community from which the Jewish masses were estranged. From this broad array of positions emerged yet another set of political groups hosting some somewhat contradictory names, such as Secular-Zionism, Cultural Zionism, Religious-Zionism, and anti-Zionist Orthodoxy. To maintain the broadest possible coalition for the establishment of a Jewish nation-state, the political leadership under Herzl accepted the demands for religious education. Although this concession engendered strong opposition among secular nationalists, it also helped to reach what was perceived as a temporary agreement between competing groups. (See figure 2.1.)

In a paradoxical way, Herzlian Zionism, which set out to transform religious groups under the new identity of a modern nation-state, in the end relied on religion as the unifying force in the creation of the Jewish nation. One of the unintended consequences of the Cultural Controversy was the strengthening of the position of Israel's ultra-Orthodox movement, Agudat Israel. Historically, when placed along the conventional secular-religious spectrum of groups that joined Zionism, the Agudat movement (later the party) was placed at the religious end of the spectrum. From the perspective of world Orthodoxy, however, Agudat appeared to be relatively more integrative than other groups, as its supporters did not opt for isolationism or engage in debates with non-Orthodox Jews while seeking to define Israel as a Halakhic state. Some religious groups perceived and continue to treat any Zionist thought as blasphemous, and therefore refuse any interaction, regardless of the purpose. According to the Agudat movement, a Jewish state bereft of its religious identity would be illegitimate, regardless of its form; ironically, this danger compelled the Agudat movement to contribute to the emergence of the state and its Jewish identity, despite the movement's generally isolationist policies. What can be called the religious dilemma or paradox of Orthodoxy faced by Agudat followers was clearly described by Rabbi Itzhak M. Levin in his speech to the Agudat Israel Executive Committee on January 20, 1946:

To declare whole-heartedly that we are in favor of the state is difficult for us so long as there is no guarantee regarding religious affairs. A Jewish State in Palestine

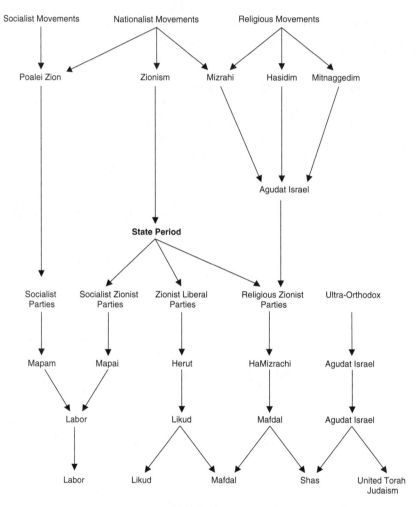

FIGURE 2.1

An ideological map of the prestate movements and the genealogy parties in Israel

that does not conform with the Torah is a profanation of God in Israel and among the nations and a danger to the Jewish religion. However, just as it is impossible to favor the state in good faith, so too is it impossible to oppose it. Otherwise, the name of God would be profaned as all blame is attributed to us, Orthodox Jewry, for hampering and thwarting [the establishment of a Jewish state].[33]

In fact, Agudat proved to be very successful, first as a movement and later as a political party (see figure 2.1 for a general review of these ideological movements and parties).[34] The movement's articulation of religious demands led to important agreements in education and religious services, culminating in the formation of an autonomous religious educational system for ultra-Orthodox groups and the establishment of the office of the Chief Rabbinate. These compromises later became part of the constitutional framework of the Israeli state in what is commonly called the Status Quo Agreement.

The formation of Israel's pillarized education system reflected the provisional compromises reached regarding how to reflect and build the Jewish national identity in Israel. In spite of, or perhaps due to, the lack of consensus on the definition of modern Hebrew culture, the 1911 Zionist Congress agreed to support religious schools in the national educational system. The 1920 Zionist Congress in London recognized the existence of two streams of Jewish education in Palestine—one general (secular) and the other Hamizrahi (national religious movement).[35] Finally, the 1925 Zionist Organization accepted Hamizrahi's schools as an autonomous stream in the educational system of the Yishuv. In 1953, after official statehood had been achieved, ultra-Orthodox schools formed another section of Israel's national education system. Eventually, Israel consolidated its three-pillar educational system in which state-secular, state-religious, and self-governing religious schools perpetuated different ideological blocs.[36]

The intricacies of the conflicts and compromises of the country's formative years resulted in a rather unique state system consisting of a set of semi-independent blocs or semi-self-governing spheres.[37] The emerging institutional arrangements combined tenets of both full control and full autonomy. Educational institutions exemplify how political power was distributed and "layers of authority" were formed to balance the demands of religions and secular groups. The public rules were designed in such a way that religious groups acquired authority over a significant part of Israeli society, religious and secular alike, while also becoming subject to secular scrutiny and dependent on financial support.

The institution of the Chief Rabbinate draws our attention to the historical continuities and renewed agreements that characterize Israel's political landscape. The state established the office of the Chief Rabbinate in

TABLE 2.1

Turning points in the incorporation of religion into the state structure

Israel		Turkey	
1892	Zionism first used as the name of Jewish nationalism	1920	Declaration of Misak-1 Milli (National Pact); definition of citizens as Ottoman Muslims
1897	First Zionist Congress	1921	Establishment of the Second Group (including the proponents of decentralization) in the First National Assembly
1902	Emergence of Hamizrahi movement	1923	Declaration of independence
1911	Zionist Congress agreed to support Hebrew culture	1924	Abolition of caliphate
1920	Zionist Congress at London accepted Hamizrahi's schools as autonomous	1925	Closure of religious schools, lodges, foundations, and shrines
1921	Separate establishment of Ashkenazi and Sephardi Chief Rabbinates	1926	Abolition of religious law and adoption of new civil code
1947	Status Quo Agreement	1928	Elimination of the statement that the state religion is Islam
1948	Declaration of state	1931	Declaration of secularism as one of the main pillars of Kemalism
1948	Establishment of the portfolio of religious affairs	1937	Declaration of the state as secular
1953	Official acceptance of two-tier religious-secular school system	1946	Establishment of Democrat Party including first opposition
1956	Establishment of Mafdal, the first nationalist religious party	1951	Establishment of the state religious schools

1921. The office was meant to accommodate different Jewish traditions but also to connect religious authorities directly to the state structure (see table 2.1). The institution failed, however, to provide religious groups with full autonomous power in a pillarized social structure. Instead, a rather complex "wall" emerged, bringing together the tenets of separation, control, and dependency. Ironically, the generalized principles that govern the rabbinate and the public order were originally developed during the Ottoman Empire.[38] From the perspective of the separation of church and state, the presence of the Chief Rabbinate might appear to extend state control over religion. In fact, during the state-formative years, the chief rabbi was a member of almost all the Zionist Executives. Thus, the position of chief rabbi not only provided a recognized conduit for religious views, especially those of Hamizrahim, to be heard in the political system, it also wielded great influence on the emerging institutional structure.[39] It is important to note that the office also engendered quite the opposite power-sharing practice. Ironically, some Orthodox groups asked then and continue to ask now for a "wall of separation," not as a disestablishment of the rabbinate but to gain autonomy and independence from the state. The government officially accepted the Chief Rabbinate as the supreme and autonomous religious authority of the first Yishuv, the prestate community, after the establishment of the state, thereby reserving an official space for religion to exert its influence on both state and society.

Even a cursory look at the gradual establishment, ongoing regulatory changes, and internal structure of the rabbinate helps us to gain insight into the negotiations of the Yishuv period. In 1928, religious and secular authorities accepted a set of regulations that redefined the powers of the Chief Rabbinate, with the first election for the rabbinate held nearly forty years later, in 1964. In order to accommodate conflicting traditions within the religious community, the powers of the Chief Rabbinate were divided into two blocs: an Ashkenazi chief rabbi (roughly representing the Jewry of European descent) and a Sephardi chief rabbi (Jewry of Middle Eastern descent). Both bore the title of *Rishon Letzion*. Although this compartmentalization reinforced and reconciled the differences within the religious bloc, it had even broader implication for Israel's ethnic politics.

A later decree ruled that the chief rabbi was to be elected by a 150-member electoral body that included 75 Ashkenazi and 75 Sephardi, of whom 80 were rabbis and 70 were representatives of the public.[40] Some Orthodox groups perceived the election of the chief rabbi as a delegitimization of the traditional institution of the rabbinate, which had previously rested on community approval and personal merit. Making the chief rabbi subject to an election polluted the meaning and the structure of the institution. Taken together, these changes meant that the Chief Rabbinate and the Chief Rabbinical Council were ultimately considered public bodies because they were publicly financed and subject to the judicial control of the secular High Court of Justice, even in some matters of religion. Religion was given an ultimate layer of authority, along with becoming subject to a layer of control. The compromise did not satisfy the parties at either end of secular–ultra-Orthodox spectrum. To further complicate the picture, the state created the Ministry of Religious Affairs to coordinate religious state schools, rabbinates, and the court system. Although the ministry was dismantled in March of 2004, its responsibilities were dispersed among different ministries and its heritage has continued.[41] Paradoxically, the ministry did not attempt to create a common area in which to address the differences between religious groups. Instead, the intense competition to control religious institutions forged alliances and sharpened the differences between groups. Any religious group that gained a political position, in effect, had gained access to state support at the expense of the others. With the dissolution of the Ministry of Religious Affairs, its responsibilities and its authority were transferred to the Ministries of Education and Infrastructure. More importantly, the ambiguous position of "Minister Without Portfolio" was given to a member of a religious party. Such a political position continued to attract the religious parties to the government by allowing them access to funds for their communities.

The complex institutional framework and web of autonomous positions established religion as an important political factor in the polity, but did not end the ongoing conflict regarding the boundaries of religious and secular authority. The formation of a secular and a religious pillar did not translate into the presence of two homogeneous blocs either.[42] For instance, the divisions in the religious community were so deep and striking that a significant portion of the ultra-Orthodox community objected to the institution of a Chief Rabbinate, which, they felt, explicitly flaunted Orthodoxy's collaboration with, and acceptance of, the secular state. Nevertheless, the vibrant political debates that marked the constitutive years of the Israeli state did not result in institutions that could resolve the main political issues and questions of the time. Instead, perhaps due to the emergence of numerous parties and factions, the process created institutions that continued to contest the nature of the emerging nation-state.

Two parties, Mapai, which represented secular brands of Zionism, and Hamizrahi, the national religious Zionist movement, joined in what later came to be known as the "historical coalition." In the Zionist Congress of 1935, the coalition "agreed that no public desecration of the Sabbath was to occur and dietary laws were to be maintained in the public institution." The foundation of the current religious system was complete when an agreement (Status Quo) was reached between non-Zionist Agudat Israel and the then-chairman of the Jewish Agency, Ben-Gurion.[43] To prevent what could have been divisive debates after the declaration of statehood, Ben-Gurion, in 1947, sent a letter to the executive committee of Agudat Israel, allowing the group control over certain religious matters.

The political environment that formed the background of the agreement shows, however, that the term "Status Quo" was something of a misnomer (or, perhaps, a strategic labeling) as the agreement in no way constituted a final contract or reflected the existing compromise. It only provided a modus vivendi, an interim solution to controversial issues. The specific agreements of the original Status Quo established a religious stratum in the Israeli civil society, which included (1) the recognition of the Sabbath as the day of rest for the entire Jewish population, (2) keeping of the dietary laws in government-run or state-subsidized bodies and services, (3) the enforcement of Halakhic rules for marital and burial ceremonies under the auspices of the rabbinate and rabbinical courts, (4) the establishment of a religious stream in the national school system and of an independent ultrareligious school system which is not supervised by the state; and (5) public financing for religious services for various communities and for religious institutions. (For a chronological review of the incorporation of religion into the state, see table 2.1.)

The political power of the Status Quo agreement lies in its role of creating autonomous areas for the religious bloc and a strong religious layer of control over the civil society in general. Yet at the same time, the agreement neither separated the religious and secular worlds completely nor allowed one to dominate the other. In the Israeli case, the seemingly high and impervious wall of separation turns out to be a fence with multiple gates of access to various forms of religious and secular ideas.

According to some scholars, the Status Quo agreement anticipated such a permeable structure. Aviezer Ravitzky, for instance, contends that rather than being a contract, the Status Quo is an institution that recognizes the necessity for vagueness and ambiguity in place of decisiveness in the political discourse. Such an approach has been adopted in other political documents and agreements. The classic example is the expression, *Tzur Yisrael*, Rock of Israel, in Israel's Declaration of Independence, an expression that each person can interpret according to his own understanding and belief. The rock refers to God or to the land, depending on the reader's perspective.[44] Using Ravitzky's terms, the ideological foundations of Zionism include an inherent "imperative duality," and due to this duality, religion remains at the heart of today's political controversies. These dialectical tensions are contained in the founding principles in order to prevent the potential for conflict. They intentionally allow for multiple answers to questions such as, "To what did the Jewish nation return? To its original language? To its national homeland? Or to the Holy Land, the holy language, and holy scripture?"[45]

This ability to avoid giving just one answer and to accommodate different responses proved to be an effective compromise that highlights both the power and the vulnerability of the Israeli system.[46] Many polities, not only

Israel, underpin secular national symbols with religious meanings, creating a reciprocal relationship that is in part enhanced by the sacred aspect of nationalism. If there is a crisis of legitimacy or a social crisis, this very dependency between religion and the secular becomes the source of greater conflict. In the Israeli case, many state policies were given and continue to carry dual meanings, as best exemplified in the case of religious holidays imbued with national meaning. Among other holy days, Hanukkah and Passover (or Pesach) were reinterpreted to encompass some liberation themes.[47] Passover became the symbol of national independence, while Hanukkah exemplified rededication.

Although Zionist nationalist and Halakhic ideas proved permeable at the ideological level, at the level of individual practice, the seemingly propitious symbolic agreement between religious and secular blocs evoked strong feelings and continues to generate critical questions. Defining the shifting boundaries between state and religion has always been one of most crucial areas to which various groups have attended. Intense political conflicts often seek to modify the Status Quo in favor of one or the other group. The Status Quo was challenged, for example, by disagreements over the type of education that would have to be provided in development towns, new social units (in 1950), and over the law exempting girls from military service based on religion (in 1952). The conflicts reached their zenith over the definition of who is a Jew, which directly affected the scope of the law of return.[48] As will be explained in the following chapters, religious parties have various positions on the Status Quo debates, ranging from restructuring to protecting it.

The Challenge of Islam in the Kemalist State

Ideas   Like Zionism, Turkish nationalism emerged as a political force during the disintegration of the Ottoman Empire. The unraveling of the Ottoman state system generated three distinct streams of thought: *Islamism, Ottomanism, and Pan Turkism*. These were not necessarily mutually exclusive social projects. On the contrary, they marked the ideological territory in which a multiplicity of groups offered distinctive prescriptions to prevent the empire's disintegration or to salvage the most meaningful political units out of it. While Islamism aimed at uniting Muslim subjects under the empire, Ottomanism sought to create a sense of imperial citizenship or transnational Ottoman identity. Pan Turkism's objective involved the creation of an ethnic state comprising all Turkish-speaking people (see figure 2.2).

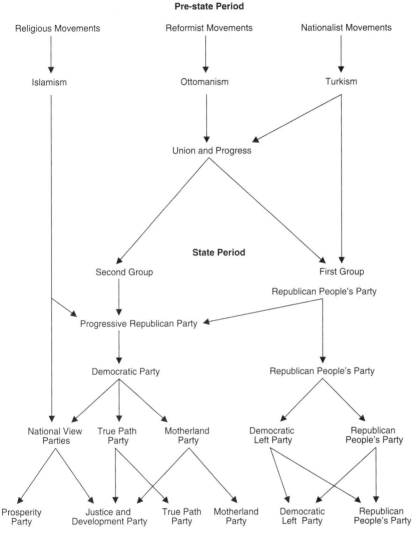

FIGURE 2.2

An ideological map of the selected major movements and the parties in Turkey

NOTE: In order to emphasize the plurality of ideas and institutions only a selected group of movements and institutions are included here; for more details see Zafer Tarık Tunaya, Turkiye'de Siyasi Partiler (İstanbul: İş Bankası, 1952).

Before discussing the role of Islam in the formation of Turkish nationalism and its specific form, Kemalist nationalism, it is important to note that
there were two components to Islam under the Ottoman system: Islam as a
source of state power and bureaucracy (political) and Islam as an important
aspect of communal life (social). At the beginning of the nineteenth century,
religion and religious institutions were still part of the Ottoman governmental machine. During that time, the Ottoman state leadership and bureaucracy actively sought to prevent the empire's decline by restructuring
the imperial system. A prime example of such efforts was the *Tanzimat*
(Reorganization) reforms (1836–1876) that constituted a political resusci-
tation operation intended to respond to the changing demands on the Ottoman monarchy and to forestall its disintegration. The sweeping reforms
focused on institutions and the state apparatus rather than society. They
targeted primarily the military, administrative, educational, and judicial
systems. The seeds of Kemalist nationalism and its challengers were sown
in the Tanzimat process and the political environment it created.

The Tanzimat reforms had several unintended consequences: the intended de-traditionalization of the relationship between the Ottoman
state and its citizens at the social level set in motion a process that ultimately threatened the conventional role of the traditional and bureaucratic elite by making them increasingly subordinate to the new emerging
religious elite.[49] The *ulema*, the religious elite, responded to the reforms
by looking for new venues to maintain social and political influence.
Among other impacts, the religious elite exerted a crucial influence on the
newly emerging Muslim Ottoman public opinion.[50] Ironically, the failure
of the reform period resulted in a reemphasis of the religious symbols and
Islamic identity of the empire. Caliph—which symbolized the "leader of
the Muslim world" and was the least emphasized part of the title of the
sultan, the Ottoman monarch—was revived and used more assertively
than ever.[51]

This period of political crisis highlighted the role of religion in general
and Islam in particular because a political rhetoric emerged that sought to
justify the role of religion in society. Until then, the Ottoman public had
perceived religion as a foundation of disparate social communities, but religion did not have a separate political discursive sphere of its own. The
confluence of these changes manifested itself in the increasing visibility of
the clergy in the Young Ottomans movement. The Young Ottomans were
members of the Ottoman elite who were openly critical of the Ottoman
bureaucracy.

At this point it is important to note that the analysis of the Ottoman
Empire and its millet system continues to imprint our understanding of
Islam in Turkish Politics. Conventional accounts view the central role of

the state under the Ottoman system as a source of the Kemalist state's authoritarianism and perceive the Muslim millet as the key reason for the invented nature of Turkishness (an identity adopted not because it emerged organically from the ashes of the Ottoman Empire, but because of its dominance in the Western model). Furthermore, despite its aggressive reforms, Islamist circles often idealize the Ottoman system due to its ability to contain religious identities. Such conclusions, according to Ortaylı, use the perspective of the nation-state to explain the Ottoman system, thereby dichotomizing identities and amplifying some of the differences between the state elite (center) and the masses (periphery). Nevertheless, especially during the Tanzimat period in the nineteenth century, the Ottoman identity reinforced a multidimensional sense of belonging by blending the cosmopolitanism of the Ottoman elite, often expressed in the linguistic unity of the Turkish language, with the significance of religious identity. In this context, a sense of Turkishness prevailed, albeit in some cases for instrumental reasons, both at the elite and mass levels. When we focus on the broad undercurrents, they indicate that both the cosmopolitan elite and the Muslim groups who had been content with their Muslimness increasingly embraced their Turkishness because of the social impacts of, inter alia, the Balkan wars, the First World War, and the increasing exposure to different groups. Thus Turkishness and Muslimness did not necessarily compete but actually, in some cases, reinforced one another in the ongoing identity formations.[52]

Against this ideational background, in the early years of the state formation, Kemalist nationalism, like Herzl's Zionism, operated in a political environment where different ideas based on religious, ethnic, and multiethnic citizenship were battling over the identity of the emerging polity. Kemalist nationalism surfaced as a political struggle at three interrelated levels: (1) against the ancient regime (i.e., against the Ottoman state, its claim of sole legitimacy, and its institutionalized form in education and court system), (2) against religion as a source of legitimacy, especially in areas where traditional and religious beliefs were seen as inconsistent with the citizenship requirements of a modern nation-state, and (3) against the colonial powers. Kemalism as a national project emerged out of these various levels of conflicts. It was formed through a process of negotiations and compromises, with concessions to various political movements, rather than springing up as a complete political project.

Kemal argued in his public statements that it was not possible to base a political project on the renewal of the Ottoman system: The nationalist movements based on religious ethnic distinctiveness, in Kemal's view, were destroying the empire's multiethnic foundation by violently clashing with each other. For Kemal, only a nation-state could create the political sovereignty and independence necessary for all peoples who would be part of it.[53] In his various writings, Kemal asserted that perhaps one of the most challenging aspects for founding such a nation-state would be the disestablishment of the Ottoman institutions. Creating a new polity out of the fallen one required a political unlearning of the practices and the spirit of legitimacy created by the millet system, in which the citizens' relationship to the state was defined through their religious-communal and local identities.

Unlike Tanzimat, which focused on the institutional structure of the state, Kemal's policies focused on contravening the influence of Islamism and Ottomanism (i.e., the social role of religion) among the masses and on altering their perception of Islam. With the introduction of the reforms, an institutional reconfiguration mode surfaced: new institutions were formed and served parallel to the old ones; the official introduction of the new institutions occurred only after the established institutions proved incongruous with the new practices and their dissolution was justified to the public. For instance, the establishment of the Grand National Assembly under the leadership of Kemal in Ankara on April 23, 1920, was justified only after the sultan-caliph had officially closed down the last Ottoman Parliament on April 11, 1920.[54] In his analysis of the challenges facing the emerging nation-state, Kemal singled out as the most pressing issue the pervasiveness of religion and tradition in people's perception of the government. Notwithstanding the obvious failure of the Ottoman system, most people could not conceive of a state legitimized through means other than religious and traditional ideas: "the idea that the country could possibly be saved without a Caliph and without a Padishah (sultan) was impossible for the masses to comprehend."[55] Given the intertwined nature of political identity and religious identity, Kemal claimed that those who sought a political solution without referring to the traditional institutions "have been looked down upon as men without faith and without patriotism."[56]

This well-entrenched religious legitimacy of public institutions and the continuing relevance of symbols in the public sphere made the use of a dual language similar to the one adopted by the Zionist movement necessary, especially in the early years of the republic. Reflecting the influence of the dominant political discourse of the time, Atatürk used religious symbols extensively and carefully, differentiating the war against the ancient regime from the war against foreign invaders. He announced the opening of the Grand National Assembly in the following way:

On Friday, 23rd April, after prayer, the Grand National Assembly, God be willing, will be opened. As the duties of the National Assembly will be of a vital influence and of the utmost importance—such as, securing the independence of our country and the deliverance of the seat of the Caliphate and Sultanate from the hands of our enemies—and as it will be opened on a Friday, the solemn character of this day will be acknowledged by offering a solemn prayer, before the opening, in the Hacıbayram Mosque. . . . We pray God to grant that we may be successful.[57]

Kemal Atatürk also used Islamic terms to emphasize the religious unity of the emerging nation, calling for a redefinition of some traditional practices at the same time. The bivalence of Kemalism, that is, its effort to inhabit both the Islamic and the secular nationalist world and its attempt to transform Islam, revealed itself best during one of Kemal's public addresses in the mosque in Balıkesir. "Friends, the great prophet possessed two dwellings, two abodes for his endeavors. One was his own house; the other was abode of God." Instead of using this dichotomy to denounce the role of religion in the public sphere, Kemal continued:

Mosques are not built in order for us to prostrate ourselves and then stand up again without looking at each other. Mosques were built for discussion, that is for consultation of what had to be done in religious and worldly affairs as well as for the obedience to god and prayer. Let us divulge what we have thought about with respect to the sacred and profane, about the future and our independence, and especially about our sovereignty.[58]

On the one hand, Kemal called for a new approach to religion and the adoption of a more individualized and proactive Islam. On the other hand, several other early documents attest to how he emphasized the unifying role of Islam for the emerging polity. In one of the first agreements of the nationalist movement, the National Pact *(Misak-ı Milli)*, signed January 1920, the nation was defined as a religious, cultural, and geographical unit. Interestingly enough, the language of the National Pact clearly avoided the term *Turk* and described the people as Ottoman Muslim.

The totality of the parts within the lines of the armistice which are inhabited by an Ottoman Muslim majority, which is united in religion, race and origin and imbued with feelings of the fullest mutual respect and sacrifice and with full consideration for each other's racial and social rights and circumstances, forms a whole whose partition cannot be accepted in reality or in law for any reason whatsoever.[59]

The variety of names used for the newly established nation-state and its citizens during the early years of the republic reflected the political shifts and contending sources of legitimacy of the new state and Turkish nationalism. Abdulaziz Mecdi (Karesi) Efendi's speech at the first meeting of parliament epitomizes the general confusion over the description of the nation: "What we mean by Turks are different Islamic groups, such as Turks, Kurds, Cherkessians, [and] Laz. Is that right? (Yes, applause). If that is not the meaning, please use the term 'members of the Islamic community,' instead of Turks."[60] Competing answers to the question of "what do we mean by Turks?" resulted in the formation of two groups in the first parliament. The first group advocated Kemal's idea of national sovereignty and the republic and accepted the nation as ethnic Turk instead of an Islamic community. The second group, however, saw the assembly as an interim organization whose task was to reestablish traditional institutions with the goal of reinstating religious citizenship.[61] Kemal himself observed the confusion resulting from the shifting role of Islam in the emerging state in *Speech*, his historic public address that lasted thirty-six-and-a-half hours. "The role of Islam in the public sphere—and the construction of the national identity—was a conundrum in the minds of the people and the intellectuals."[62] Given the symbolic importance of religion, the massive resistance to secularism, and the formation of opposition groups, he concluded that "it was hard to disguise the terms and concepts concerning the state and government under religion, but it was necessary to avoid direct statements regarding the changing role of Islam."[63]

Many political movements that shape Turkish politics today had their roots in the constitutive years of the republic. Unlike hegemonic Zionism, Kemalism was formed by, and engaged in, a debate with diverse political movements that supported distinctly different conceptions of the nation: One of the most prolific articulators of Turkish nationalism, Ziya Gökalp, offered substantial, critical arguments both for and against Kemalism. Gökalp questioned not only all political projects that reduced the emerging collective identity to either a Turkish or a Muslim one, but he also doubted the efforts that expected their convergences to occur by chance. For Gökalp, states were not changing randomly through expansion or disintegration. They were all affected by nationalization and were moving in the same direction: the formation of a nation-state. In the future, the boundaries of states would overlap with the boundaries of nations.[64] Religious unity by itself, for example via Islam, was not enough to form a political community. Nationhood required more than a shared religion; it required shared values and ethics. In a statement considered radical in his time, he argued that religions do not constitute civilizations. Civilizations comprise more than religious values, such as shared aesthetics and scientific endeavors. For Gökalp, the emerging Turkish nation needed to become unified on three levels of identity, so that everyone could say "I am Muslim, from the Turkish nation and the Western civilization."[65] Instead of contradicting each other, religious, national, and civilizational identities complemented and strengthened each other.[66]

According to Gökalp, the biggest misconception of the Tanzimat proponents was their belief that a cultural mélange could be created, a kind of synthesis of Eastern and Western civilizations. "They did not think that two civilizations based on different principles could not be fused. The political dichotomies we have right now are the result of this mistake: Binary court system, education, tax system, budget, and laws." The task ahead for Turkish nationalism was to eliminate these dichotomies. "There are three layers in our society, folk (traditional masses), the graduates of religious schools, [and] graduates of Western schools who are dissimilar in their edification. . . . Is it normal for a nation-state to have a triple faceted life?"[67]

Gökalp's ideas were influential, but his approach to ethnic and Islamic foundations as *one* of the constitutive elements of the Turkish nation did not appeal to those who advocated a restoration of Islam or who sought to make ethnic Turkishness the core of Turkey's emerging political identity. The increasing exclusion of Islam as a political force ignited strong opposition from leaders such as Said Nursi, who later founded one of the most influential Islamist movements in Turkey. The political persona and changing views of Said represented the newly emerging religious elite, who looked at the growth of nationalism from an Islamist paradigm and remained critical of both the ancient and emerging regimes. For instance, Said Nursi opposed the traditional religious clergy, *şeyhs,* because they supported a regressive role for Islam in the communities and used their religious charisma for personal gains. Accordingly, he opposed the *fatva* (religious decree) of the *Şeyhülislam* (the leading clergy), and the leading ulema, Durrizade Abdullah, that denounced Mustafa Kemal and his role in the ongoing liberation war.[68] Nevertheless, Said also found the policies of the new parliament, the emerging trend to relegate Islam to the private sphere, as not true to the essence of the Turkish nation. In 1923, disillusioned with the new regime, Nursi warned the Grand National Assembly:

The instrument of your victory and the body which recognizes your services are one, they are the community of believers and, in particular, the lower classes who are solid Muslims . . . and it is therefore incumbent upon you to act in accordance with Qur'anic injunctions. To prefer the pitiable, rootless, Europe-worshipping imitators of Frankish customs who are detaching themselves from Islam to the masses of the Muslim people is (avam) against Islamic custom and will lead the world of Islam to direct its gaze in another direction and request assistance from others.[69]

In the midst of mounting opposition, especially from Islamist circles, Kemalist nationalism increasingly sought to *ethnify* Islam and imbue Islamic terms with secular meanings. The use and transformation of Islamic symbols was crucial in political communication as "it was only from Islam that the Muslim Ottomans could draw the emotional resonance that would mobilize both upper and lower classes. It was Islam that would provide a repertoire of symbols which could compete with the national symbols of the

Greeks or the Serbs."[70] An ethnic definition of citizenship and secularization of the state institutions became more explicit in official policies when
Kemal described the Turkish nation as "constituted by citizens who share a
common language, culture, and ideals." In short, the term *Turkish* was defined as "a name for the people who established the Turkish Republic." In
an attempt to distinguish the Turkish nation from the Ottoman millet, the
term used to describe the religious groups and main units of the Ottoman
society, the new term *Ulus* was invented. Attempts to "Turkify" Islam at
the popular level led to the official encouragement of the use of Turkish,
rather than Arabic, at all religious devotions.[71] Perhaps the most significant
of these changes was the ban on the Arabic call for prayers and its substitu-
tion with the less popular Turkish version in 1932. The first opposition
party, the Democratic Party, based its political platform on the promise to
end restrictions on religious practices and restore the Arabic call for
prayers. Thus, the official ideology of Turkish nationalism emerged out of
the conflict over the configuration of a new national identity among the
multiplicity of the identities inherited by the Ottoman Empire. Kemalism's
ethnification project seemed to marginalize non-Islamic groups, indicating
that its concept of ethnicity still relied on the unifying power of the religion.

Institutions   By any account, the institutional reforms introduced by
Kemalist nationalism have been radical and have sought to redefine the role
of religion in Turkish society. Many observers of Turkish politics have referred to Kemalism's approach to religion as one of the radical examples of
the elite-led separation of church and state. Others agree that Kemalism
single-handedly tried to disestablish religion and place it under state control,
but they view the effort not as one of separation but of extending state control over religion. Neither account, however, addresses the state's dependency on religion for its political existence; therefore, they both have the tendency to underestimate the intricacies of the process that molded and guided
the course of Turkey's transformation from an Islamic to a secular state.
      One of the most intriguing and revealing early decisions was to separate
the caliphate, the religious leadership, and the sultanate, the state leadership. Finally, in 1922 the office and title of the sultanate was abolished, but
the caliphate was protected. As the last sultan left the country with the help
of the British military, the issue of abolition of the sultanate was unprob-
lematic. Ironically, the Grand National Assembly *elected* Abdulmecid II as
a new caliph, asking him to acknowledge the sovereignty of the nation and
the national assembly. The negotiation changing the caliph's official title
from "Caliph of Resullah" ("the successor to god's messenger") to "the
Caliph of Muslims" was not merely symbolic, but sought to end the traditional religious legitimacy of the office. The first title claimed divine

authority, and the assembly advised against its use. Kemal described the caliphate as a political, not a religious, institution that had always sought to control the Muslim world and was now kept intact for historical and cultural reasons. Efforts to abolish the caliphate surfaced on the national assembly's agenda only after the caliphate appeared to be gaining political power and reasserting its appeal as "the leader of believers." When the caliph officially complained about the inadequacies of the caliphal treasury to fulfill its role, it was taken as a sign that the office would act as more than a symbolic leadership. A weeklong discussion of the caliph's request in parliament produced the bill abolishing the caliphate on March 3, 1924.[72]

Ambiguities inherent in the national identity, especially with regard to the role of Islam, continued to manifest themselves in the various policy areas where Turkishness took the central role. For instance, the population exchanges from 1915 to 1925 were characterized by a substantial emigration of minority groups and an influx of refugees and immigrants. All Muslims, regardless of their ethnic backgrounds, were considered Turkish. For example, more than 90 percent of immigrants from the Balkan countries of Bulgaria, Romania, and Yugoslavia were Muslim. Immigration policies' reliance on religion rather than language or other ethnic origins revealed how, in practice, Islam was an indispensable identifier of national identity, especially when the new identity needed to be defined in relation to Western countries.[73] Shortly after the republic was established, 98 percent of Turkish citizens were Muslim, as opposed to 80 percent in 1912, indicating that Muslimness was regarded as the main homogenizing force and encouraged by the republic.[74]

This definition of an exogenous Turkish identity matches the parallel construction of the Israeli identity. In Israel, new immigrants receive citizenship if they meet certain qualifications derived from the Halakhic definition of Jewishness. In this context, it is important to note that until 1928 the Turkish state was defined as an Islamic state. While religion maintained its frame of reference, especially in the definition of Turkishness, the reforms adopted from 1923 to 1945 amounted to a cultural transformation project with little concern for its popular political implications. Among other changes, the newly adopted policies gradually eliminated the preeminence of the Arabic script and measurement system, both religiously important traditional symbolic systems. A new institution, the Directorate of Religious Affairs, was established by the Law of 1924 to educate the religious clergy and to coordinate the activities of the mosque, thus regulating all religious services under the auspices of the state.[75] Taken together and considered from the institutional perspective, the reforms embodied an accelerated process of state-initiated laicization, where religion was relegated to the sphere of personal morals and practices. Many institutions transformed themselves radically, and some new ones were adopted directly from Western countries, such as the Swiss Civil Code in 1926. Although the private observance of religious rituals could continue, the public expression of religion and political activities by religious organizations were banned. Like socialist Zionists, some among the Kemalist elites regarded some of the existing political-religious practices as anachronisms. In its effort to strengthen the new institutions, de-Islamization of Turkish identity marked the emerging definition of Turkishness, describing the Turkish nation as a people of common ideals and ethnic unity.[76]

The laicization of political institutions and national identity was not popular with everyone. Instead the centralization of the state and the recalibration of the political position of religion created intense opposition, especially among those who lost their social status under the emerging regime and felt alienated by new social and political codes. Opposition centered on the weakening symbolic references to religion, ultimately resulting in the decline of the common symbolic system and a widening of the social and political distances, both among different social groups and between the ruling elite and the masses.[77] Islamic rhetoric had been a crucial aspect of political communication and legitimization. Given that some abstract political notions such as *nation* and *sovereignty* came into political discourse as Islamic terms, the role of Islam in the society was not limited to the social aspects of life. Therefore, problems associated with the changing role of religion had several sources. First, religion constituted the foundation of legitimacy and any claim on political life. Second, Islam was a "discourse" which enabled persons of both high and low standing to have recourse to the same store of concepts in organizing their life strategies. Third, aggressive laicization also weakened the role of the religious elites as opinion leaders who filtered various political ideas through a standard imagery of high and folk culture.[78] Thus, the de-emphasis of the traditional role of religion as part of the political identity challenged the interconnectedness of the political and the religious symbols in the political imagery of the Ottoman public. Discontent with the state's secularization policies was reflected in a widening distance between citizens and the state.

The reactions to the Kemalist laicization process varied. It is important to note that the laicization process also transformed its religious opposition. One of the most articulate critics of Kemalist policies was Said Nursi. He challenged the Kemalist state's policies as anti-Islamic, and his forced withdrawal from the public sphere resulted in his ideas being mostly disseminated through his writing. Ironically, the restriction on the public expressions of Islam within the boundaries of a new nation further contributed to the transformation of traditional Islam and the creation of a national Islamic community. His interpretations tried to reconcile scientific thought with the teaching of Islam, highlighting its compatibility with the requirements of modern times.[79] One can argue that the references to Islam by Kemalist nationalism and the incorporation of nationalist ideas by its Islamic opposition exemplified an unavoidable osmotic process, which proved that Kemalist secularism and Islamic beliefs challenge but also depend on each other: The Kemalist nation could justify itself only through religion, while the Islamic opposition could maintain its popular appeal only by accepting the boundaries and terms of the modern nation-state while simultaneously appropriating novel means of discovering scientific Islamic insights, relying on print capitalism (i.e., production and consumptions of pamphlets), or increasing engagements in public discussions and private household meetings.

Ironically, while the Kemalist nation sought to "bring modernity" in the form of a nation-state, it perpetuated the Ottoman tradition of an authoritarian state by forcing the modernization and secularization on an unwilling population. Kemalism's relationship to Islam became neither monolithic nor devoid of controversy. The institutional disestablishment of ancient religious institutions and the public role of Islam proceeded in tandem with the establishment of new institutions. The founding of the Directorate of Religious Affairs was the last installment of a process that had started in 1939 with the reduction of *Şeyhülislam*'s influence. Until that time, Şeyhülislam had retained significant power, especially in the areas of education and the judiciary. In a historical context, the establishment of the Directorate of Religious Affairs meant, therefore, not only a step toward reducing but also institutionalizing the authority of religion in the state system. The mere existence of the directorate allowed the state to control religion at the institutional and, to a certain extent, at the individual level. The directorate assumed the role of writing the main part of the Friday *hutbas*, to be read in all mosques while *Hodjas* (prayer leaders), who often enjoyed the legitimacy of being the state's representative, had the latitude to present their ideas and religious interpretation in the remainder of the hutbas. On the other hand, the state-sponsored mosques created a state-dependent clergy integrated into society and backed by a state legitimacy that they could use on behalf of religion. More importantly, in Yasin Aktay's terms, the new setting created "the Muslim Paradox" for Islamists who felt caught "between modernism and superstition defendership,"[80] neither of which they supported.

When westernization began in Turkey because the westernist heads couldn't direct their attacks directly against Islam, they tended to the superstitions living among people. For the criticism was coming from the franc admirer snobs, the religious men refrained from supporting the criticism, although they too had potentially been burdened with such a criticism. So, the religious men fell unwittingly in a position of "superstition defendership."[81]

Likewise, even those who tried to promote more rights for religious expression and were critical of Kemalist nationalist policies adopted them to some extent. Ali Fuad Başgil, in *Din ve Laiklik, Religion and Laicism*, on the one hand rejected the idea of serving as a state-employed intellectual and faculty member at the state-sponsored divinity school, arguing "in a faculty under the frame of secular university a pious, religious man cannot emerge, just as the rice cannot grow on the stones." On the other hand, the real problem for Başgil was that the state's investment in theology schools did not meet the expectations for the number of clergy needed to serve in district mosques. The state misallocated its resources by investing in those who studied philosophy of religion instead of supporting those who prepared to serve the immediate religious needs of communities. Only through a more extensive role for the Higher Islamic Institutes, Başgil argued, would these institutions educate true men of the Islamic religion. Overall, his critique, like that of many others, was directed more at the misapplication of the state's policies than the state role and the policy's premises.

The permeability of Islamic and Kemalist ideas and the paradoxes it creates show us once again that the wall of separation is frequently rather porous. Not only do ideas move back and forth across the supposed wall, but along the way they transform each other. Based on how people perceive and study secularism (*laicite, laiklik,* or *layiklik* in Turkish) in Turkey, Andrew Davison concludes that "no separation between state and religion ever occurred under Atatürk—only partial areas of separation developed within the structure of the state and society's control, in some dimensions, enhanced state control. Disestablishment does not capture the mechanisms of reestablishment. Indeed every label needs *a qualifier . . .*" (emphases added).[82] It is this qualifier that often points to where the tension over the public role of religion is occurring.

CONCLUSION

The separation myth and its derivatives, the control- and conflict-centered explanations, do not allow us to capture how the state and religion often engage in mutually transformative and dependent relationships. The dependency of the state on religion and vice versa and not the state's control of religion seem to make religion one of the most contentious areas of Israel's and Turkey's politics. Power-sharing arrangements rarely result in the complete autonomy of religion from the state and vice versa. In Israel, the questions posed by Zionism drastically changed the symbolic capital of religious traditions. As the Turkish case shows, even in cases of the state's attempts to control religion institutionally, the symbolic capacity of religion can remain an indispensable element of the state's legitimacy. Thus, we need to see religion in the state and the state in religion to understand the political capacity and position of religion in a society. This framework also releases us from dichotomous perceptions of religious parties as antisystemic (i.e., seeking to alter the power-sharing structure of their respective systems) or status quo (i.e., legitimizing the system). For instance, in countries where the state relies on religious values and beliefs implicitly or explicitly, religion might take an oppositional role without much cost. Likewise, in countries where the state allows institutional autonomy, the lack of opposition to the state does not amount to an ideological consensus among religious and other political views.

Moving beyond the separation paradigm and its variations lets us focus on a more detailed description of the institutional and ideological latitudes and constraints that affect the forms and political positions of religious parties. As the following chapters illustrate, Israel and Turkey have opted for different sets of specific rules to govern both their power sharing practices and the contestations of their respective political spheres. For instance, the Israeli political system rests on an easy entrance policy, assigning a parliamentary seat to all parties that pass the low 1.5 percent national threshold. Even very small parties can successfully compete for parliamentary representation. In contrast, Turkey's public sphere has remained very restrictive. The law on parties limits the content of party platform at the outset, and the high 10 percent threshold to gain parliamentary representation disfavors small and regional parties. Strikingly, despite different electoral rules, the overall transformation of the party system in both countries has been remarkably similar. In both countries, a one-party system was succeeded by a two-party system. The main oppositional parties to the dominant secularist parties, Likud in Israel and the Democratic Party in Turkey, have based their platforms on a critique of secularism and the state-centered economy. The countries' two-party systems were eventually replaced by multiparty competition. During the multiparty era, the religious parties consolidated their power. The parallel transformation of political competition in both countries, notwithstanding their different electoral rules, suggests that we need to look at the overall power distribution in the political system as well as the specific rules of electoral competition to capture the underlying political currents.

In short, understanding religious parties requires examining the role of religion in the state and in the broader framework of the political system. Religious parties are nested in their respective power-sharing arrangements, and their questions and quests are rooted in their polity's historical debates on the role of religion. In Israel, the successors to the Hamizrahi movement and Agudat Israel, along with the newly emerged Shas, have established themselves as pivotal religious parties. In Turkey, the main center-right parties represented the religious opposition until the establishment of the National Order Party in 1969. Later, pro-Islamic parties took on three different forms under the Prosperity Party, the National Action Party, and the Justice and Development Party. These parties' current electoral fortunes and ideological platforms are not a drastic rupture in the contested political realm marked by religion; on the contrary, they are new manifestations of religion's continued ability to make itself relevant in respective politics regardless of assumed barriers.

PART TWO

Ideologues or Pragmatists? The Ideas
and Ideologies of Religious Politics

Representing the Sacred
in Mundane Politics

The Ideologies and Leaders of Mafdal and Shas

Orthodoxy is in fact not an unchanged and unchanging remnant of
pre-modern traditional Jewish society, but as much a child of modernity and change as any of its "modern" rivals.[1]

The common conundrums faced by the politics of Judaism and Islam in
the constitutive years of Israel and Turkey show that (1) no institutional
arrangement can deprive religion of its political capability and (2) the capacity to define new policy positions makes religion a resilient force. Even
when they are suppressed institutionally or faced with opposing ideologies, religious beliefs and symbols transform themselves and their environment by both adopting and adapting to new ideas. Recognizing religion's relevance in politics as a resilient discursive and practical area that
embodies critical social ideational changes allows us to pose some basic
questions and look for their answers not in external, structural factors
but within religious ideologies' own ideas. In what ways do religious convictions continue to make themselves politically relevant in the face of
new issues and developments? How do these parties use their respective
religious symbolic capital? What are the distinct ways in which religious
beliefs interact with institutions and ideas put forward by their secular
opponents? Why do the new interpretations that form the foundation of
religious ideologies diverge?

At the conceptual level, these questions enable us to explore how and
with what consequences religious parties embedded in the same religion
diverge from each other. Are the differences among religious parties merely

rhetorical, or do they have a real impact? If they do matter, what implications do they have on their respective democracies? At the heart of these questions lies a basic puzzle: whether these parties, (1) under the guise of their strictly religious appearance, constitute new hybrid entities that are the product of the dissemination of the values of modernity among its challengers or (2) carve a new space in modern politics that is ultimately antithetical to the premises of liberal democracy while using its norms and tools (e.g., its commitment to the diversity of ideas and party competition).

Any discussion of religion in politics in the form of political parties requires some caveats. The striking electoral fortunes of religious parties often direct attention to the process of electoral competition and lead many to treat these parties as one cogent body and as a master of the electoral game with untamed powers. The electoral bias in the study of parties stems from their perceived role as pivotal and precarious actors in the formulation of policies and in defining the course of democracy. Such views often, however, obscure these parties' ideational components. The institutional rules of a polity define what specific institutional forms religious parties take, how they present their political rhetoric, and their ability to participate in parliament. However, it is in the ideational realm that religious parties face more complex constraints and ample opportunities. These parties often make their most permanent mark on their respective political systems through their ability to bring novel positions to the marketplace of ideas rather than through their immediate electoral success.

Conventionally, we describe political parties as institutions that only *represent* political ideas and interests. The power of political parties in general and religious political parties in particular, however, lies in their ability not to simply articulate or mirror, but to *define* and *shape* religious interpretations and "collective interests." In other words, religious parties do not always express already well-defined views or represent clearly delineated communities. Instead, they often are constitutive agents—they bring different constituencies together and define their common ideals while imbuing religious symbols and beliefs with new meaning. The very resiliency of religious parties lies in the combination of their expressive and constitutive practices. Therefore, the most important asset of religious parties is their capacity to bring otherwise contradictory interests together and give meaning to and link what could otherwise be disconnected political developments and views via an ideological framework rooted in religious symbols.

The prevalent opinion among observers that religious parties are reactionary agents, offering only ideas antithetical to those offered by others, is quickly disproved when the composition of their political ideas is dissected. While nesting their ideas in their respective religious doctrines, the parties not only grapple with abstract questions pertinent to the legitimacy of the state, they also deal with more tangible ones elicited from daily political issues. As a result, on the one hand, they try to position themselves on diverse issues consistently in line with their respective doctrine. On the other hand, they seek to maintain their bivalence, their presence and relevance in both the secular and religious worlds, to enhance their popular appeal. Every religious party is, therefore, pulled in two different directions as it strives to make its interpretation believable and coherent in the eyes of religious supporters while also forging political positions appealing to a wider public. Rather than simply drawing on tradition, religious parties are challenged to reconcile conflicting positions and effectively use them to build broader political capital.

Any quest to assess religious parties' symbolic capital and role in a democracy requires us to review their approaches from the inside out by asking how they view (1) the state's main ideology, (2) the diversity within its envisioned political community, and (3) the limits of political unity. In fact, these areas surface as the main battle zones of competing ideologies in many polities. Rather than reverting back to traditional ideas or reacting to the secular ones, religious parties offer their most unconventional positions in these areas that define critical components of a polity. In order to understand how religious parties position themselves vis-à-vis competing groups and how they substantiate their position via religious symbols, the following two chapters draw on a three-level analysis. Guiding the discussion at each level are the questions of (1) how religious parties in Israel and Turkey view their hegemonic secular nationalism and the role of the state, (2) how they balance individual differences against the cohesion of community, and (3) to what extent and how they recognize and include nonreligious groups and other communities in their policies. The way we approach the words *state* and *community* draws on how religious groups use the terms. For instance, we do not ask whether the envisioned communities in fact meet the analytical characteristics of the terms—that they indeed form entities whose members share a certain place, set of commitments, obligations, and the like—but how the party conceptualizes them.

It is important to note that, as indicated in Chapter One, our detailed account of the internal debates and use of symbolic capital in this and following chapters serves three purposes. First, it unpacks discursive practices through which religious symbols are contested and reinterpreted. Second, it shows how simple analogies and symbols can be used to encapsulate and communicate significant political views. Third, it demonstrates how these debates across and within religious and secular groups do not consist of a dialogue among the voices of a unified chorus, but rather an argument between multivocal and at times disharmonious groups. These dimensions altogether indicate that symbolic capital does not come at the expense of other components of religious politics but rather that it illustrates their mutually dependent positions and relations by underlining the significance of (1) the traditional role of symbols and ideas as originator of ideas, (2) their religious authority as interpreters, (3) the social networks by which new meanings are communicated, and (4) the political capital accrued via these ideas. At the broader level, all these components together depict a spiritual-political cycle that evolves in the politics of religion.

An inquiry into the symbolic capital of religious parties through this type of inside-out reading reveals how sacralization (i.e., imbuing secular ideas with religious meaning and elevating them to the level of an unquestioned position) or internal secularization (i.e., redefining religious ideas and symbols to allow them to accommodate secular practices and constructs) can help us to describe these parties' engagements with the so-called secular world. Viewing the ideational world of religious parties from these lenses helps us identify the mutually transformative ideas and probe into what lies beneath the parties' ostensibly odd coupling of ideas and incongruous positions. Comparable configurations in religious parties in Israel and Turkey illustrate how viewing religious parties from one narrow angle within a country or across countries compromises our ability to describe and analyze them accurately. Only a systematic multifaceted analysis can illustrate that the contribution of religious parties to their particular democratic systems is not a question of whether their respective doctrines are democratic or antidemocratic. Given that the majority of religious parties incorporate aspects of both extremes into their praxis the question is *to what degree* these parties engage in democratic and anti-democratic ideas and how we can incorporate their contradictory elements into our answers.

MAFDAL: MODERATE RELIGIOUS-ZIONIST PARTY?

Religious nationalist parties initially appear to be products of a politically expedient and easy synthesis between two competing ideologies and venues to depict ideal societies: nationalism and religion. However, the intricate relationship between nationalism and religion, which includes both tenets of rejection and dependency, makes this combination anything but an easy ideological coupling. In fact, a review of Mafdal's ideational history shows that the party's resiliency stems from its positioning in an area where crosscurrents of secular-nationalist Orthodox ideologies exist only in a parallel way. This ideological map begs the question of how the party makes itself relevant to not only contesting but what also appear to be mutually exclusive views and how they adequately interconnect them.

Mafdal (*Miflaga Datit Le'umit*, which literally means the religious national party), one of Israel's oldest parties, dates back to *Yishuv*. Although it took its current name and form in 1956, its ideas are rooted in the writing and teaching of various religious scholars from the state's constitutive years. Mafdal was born out of the alliance of three movements: *HaMizrachi* (an acronym for Merkaz Ruchani or "spiritual centre"), *Hapoel Hamizrachi* (Worker's League Spiritual Center), and *Hakibbutz Hadati* (often translated as the religious kibbutz movement). The coalition was further strengthened by the incorporation of the *Bnei Akiva* youth movement.[2] These movements differed in their reasoning on how to reconcile the nationalist and religious ideas. Nevertheless, they all shared the view that Zionism was in essence a religious project and maintaining it as such was crucial. The shared spiritual component of their names stems from their convictions that materialist aspects of political ideologies need to be complemented by bringing to the fore their spiritual foundations. Yet each movement separately and together faced the question of how materialist and, in some cases, overtly antireligious movements could have spiritual underpinnings.

Mafdal's overall ideological position is best understood by exploring the broader context of its initial appearance, which was marked by two questions that continue to stir up heated debates within both secular and ultra-Orthodox circles. Since the constitutive years of Zionism, various groups disagreed on whether and to what extent the state should incorporate religion into its structure and policies. Equally important but less recognized is the parallel controversy within religious circles over the theological status of the state and its nationalist project. From the Halakhic perspective, the main question Zionism posed was whether and under what conditions the formation of the state was a theologically acceptable process. It is this second and somewhat muted debate that reveals the fault lines that still divide Israel's religious blocs and distinguish Mafdal from other parties. Paradoxically, in both debates the religious ideas of "ingathering of exiles" and "redemption" emerged as critical symbols and proved their capacity to bridge and polarize secular and religious groups while they created more divisions among religious publics.[3] After all, the religious notion of the ingathering of exiles included a very political idea of uniting separate Jewish communities, forming a unity that could be seen as a creation of a nation-state in secular terms. The

meaning of the emerging state and its founding ideology, Zionism, formulated two religious answers. One, for the Orthodox accommodationists,
in the end the creation of the Israeli state meant an embodiment of redemption; thus Zionism needed to be embraced as a critical step toward
promised divine salvation. Two, Orthodox rejectionists, on the other
hand, viewed Zionism as not only a religiously unacceptable project but
also as a hollowing of the religious meanings of the key religious terms,
thereby putting a major obstacle in the path to redemption.

Ironically, the religious circles turned against Zionism and questioned
the legitimacy of the state not because of Zionism's position on the role
of religion but because of its appropriation of religious ideas to accomplish the secular nationalist goals. Although the idea of the Messiah and
its relation to the redemption were not clear in the religious texts, some
arguments put forward (such as those of Birnbaum) indicated how religious groups challenged not the concept of nationalism per se but its
claim of being redemptive. In effect, the debates *incorporated* the idea of
nationalism with religious discourse as an increasing number of critics
agreed that the Halakhic idea of the ingathering of exiles could be analogous to nation-building. In the writings of those such as Birnbaum, we
can trace back the complex ideas that challenge the concept of nationalism per se and its justification by adopting the symbols of redemption:

I was not surprised to note that the pagan Jews [Zionists], if they did not reject,
had crippled this glorious messianic conception of [redemption]. . . . There has
been put in its place the fiction that the Jewish people as a whole is the messiah.
Instead of the longed-for act of redemption and era of the messiah, the liberal-
ethical ideal of cultural progress has been set up—to be realized by assimilation
and apostasy, stock exchange and journalism—summed up in the phrase of "the
special Jewish mission." . . . The sages erected "fences" around every one of its
provisions, to preserve the pious from unwittingly transgressing them and drifting
away from the Jewish ideal and losing its powers of self sanctification. Let them
[Zionists] to go out and "seek" Him in the jungle of their stock-phrases. Let them
crowd the theatres, lecture halls, and newspaper columns, befuddling their own
minds . . . instigate their petty rebellions, and try to *govern the course of history* . . .
worry about the *Jewish question*. I know they cannot succeed.[4]

Birnbaum's arguments contain the seeds of two objections to the religious justification of the state as the embodiment of redemption. First,
Zionism elevates nationalists and nationalism to the level of divine instrument, Messiah. This is not only an un-Halakhic, but also a dangerous
thought. Redemption in the Halakhic sense is a divine process that does
not require human intervention. In other words, the very idea of divine
promise of peace and stability does not rest on human activism and intervention for its fulfillment. Second, from the perspective of groups like

Agudat Israel, Zionism not only emptied a divine concept but did so for the wrong reason. After all, ultra-Orthodox critics argued that Zionism's ultimate goal, namely the "normalization of the Jewish nation, by creating a Jewish state," contradicted the uniqueness of the Jewish people and also delayed its promised redemption. Only the divine has the power to initiate redemption on behalf of its chosen people. "Religious Zionism," assisting in the commencement of the divine project, was therefore "a contradiction in terms."

It transpires that the ideology of Religious Zionism cannot really be implemented simply because Zionism and religion are mutually exclusive. We are obligated to Zionism for the very existence of the State, but we have to understand that Zionism set as its aim the establishment of a new nation in a new state. The fundamental problem that Zionism was intended to solve was that of the difference between Jews and gentiles that found expression in anti-Semitism. The basic Zionist idea is to be accepted in the family of nations, to be a normal nation, a nation that has a state like all the other nations. When this was achieved, Zionism assumed, the Jewish problem would be solved. A nice idea, but there is only one small problem—it conflicts with Judaism. Judaism maintains that the Jewish people are different from all other nations, and this is both the Halachic and the desirable situation. As we have said, Religious Zionism is a contradiction in terms.[5]

The conclusion that religious Zionism cannot be a justifiable position in the Halakhic tradition continues to separate ultra-Orthodox from religious Zionists. Mafdal's political ideas therefore need to be assessed against Orthodox ideas that reject the legitimacy of the state and all shades of Zionism as a deviation from the predetermined course of redemption.

The State and Zionism: Sacred State and Redemptive Zionism

Mafdal's leadership distinguishes itself from other religious party leaderships by claiming to be the only modern Orthodox Zionist party fully committed to the Halakhic tradition. Nevertheless, what sets religious parties apart from others is not their declared commitment to what seem to be politically expedient syntheses but the elaborate reasoning in religious doctrine and value rationality behind their objective. As explained before, such political syntheses do not mean much to their audiences unless they are coherently grounded in their respective religious traditions and perceived as credible by religious publics. In other words, it is not the position per se but the theological justification and the ultimate intended religious promise of political positions that matters most to religious audiences. Thus Mafdal's ostensibly simple claim of being a national religious party begs the question of how nationalism, a secular movement that emerged in Europe, could be given a cogent Halakhic meaning. More significantly, what does modern Orthodoxy mean to Mafdal and to what extent does it translate it into an inclusive political project? Furthermore, what does modern Orthodoxy mean to Israel's democracy?

The writings and teachings of Rabbi Avraham HaCohen Kook, the first Ashkenazi chief rabbi, introduce us to the foundations of religious Zionism and the blueprint for the ideas behind Mafdal's both accommodating and confrontational views.[6] While many religious groups reduced politics to a perpetual conflict between secular Zionists and religious anti-Zionists, Kook brought to the fore a discursive space beyond these dichotomies by using the long static concepts of the *holy* (religious) and the *unholy* (not religious). This distinction helped him reintroduce the driving forces behind Zionism and its actors, modern nation-states and citizens, from a Halakhic perspective. Holiness, Kook argued, was not a question of either/or as many contended, but consisted of different dimensions. The divine was like the lightlike essence revealing itself at two levels: "latent" holiness (religiousness), the innate presence and concealed in the inner soul, and "overt" holiness, which could be acquired through actions and deeds by choice. While the former constitutes an intrinsic and immutable part of the Jewish soul, the latter is based on free will and acquired through one's deliberate choices, actions, and Torah study.[7] Thus, what is apparent and reasoned is not always what is divine and intended.

This seemingly simple approach to the individual's relationship to the divine led to a halakhically grounded ambivalence toward the meaning of apparent and hidden religiousness. Such a stance not only undermined conventional binary terms based on absence and presence of religious devotion and holiness but opened the door for many drastically different political conclusions. For instance, one important aspect of intrinsic holiness was its deceptive nature and evasion of strict classifications—even for those who carried it. Remarkably, Kook believed that a certain level of holiness existed within an individual notwithstanding his or her free will. Most important, latent holiness, which is given to each member in an unknown quantity, was described as infinitely greater in importance than acquired holiness, which is received by deliberate religious commitments and learning. Such distribution of religiousness compelled the religious public to think that the façade of religiousness can be highly misleading.[8] Thus, Kook's definition of religious essence created delicate strategic ambiguity in regard to individuals' *real* religious standings and level of religiosity, thereby dismissing any classification along the religious-secular divide. Being secular, according to this definition, did not amount to an adverse relationship to the divine. On the contrary, Halakhic history showed that in some cases secular individuals would serve religion more than others, regardless of their immediate or self-claimed intentions.

Many of the adherents of the present national revival maintain that they are secularists. If a secular Jewish nationalism was really imaginable, then we would indeed be in danger of falling so low as to be beyond redemption. But what Jewish *secular nationalists* want they *do not themselves know*: The spirit of Israel is so closely linked to the Spirit of God, that a Jewish nationalist no matter how secularist his intention may be, is despite himself *imbued with the divine spirit even against his own will*. An individual can sever the tie that binds him to the source of life but the house of Israel as a whole cannot. All of its most cherished possessions—its land, its language, history and customs—are vessels of the Spirit of the Lord. (emphasis added)[9]

In Kook's view and later in Mafdal's ideology, secular Zionism and the commitment of its advocates are nothing more than the collective appearance of latent holiness. The secularists' desires and actions to achieve the unity of the Jewish people and the founding of the state of Israel were instigated by their religiously predetermined roles. "In all paths of life, it is the secular which awakens first, then the holy is compelled to awaken, to complete the renewal of the secular, to beatify and redeem it from dirtiness" just like the tree grows before the fruit.[10] Secularists were part of the process of the reestablishment of the promised Jewish state, regardless of their perceived wills, and the fact that they awakened first and fulfilled their pioneer role was not unforeseen but consistent with the Halakhic process of social transformation. The holy land, in contrast to other spaces, would make the release of intrinsic holiness easier. The completion of Zionism in the sanctity of the holy land would eventually bring the veiled light and intrinsic holiness in the Jewish people as a nation to the fore and manifest itself in unprecedented ways.

Against the backdrop of these ideas, Mafdal's religious Zionism explained how Zionism and the Israeli state carried a deep religious meaning and had critical religious functions despite their ostensibly antireligious outlook and seemingly theological fallacies. Rather than simply appropriating Zionism as a foreign entity or changing it altogether, this explanation redefines its ideological premises and adopts its praxis as it is. For religious Zionists the establishment of the state reflected not "normalization" but the uniqueness of the Jewish nation.[11] The revelation of Zionism's religious value turned secular Zionism, not religious Zionism, into an oxymoron. By placing redemption and intrinsic holiness at the center of its ideas, religious Zionism cultivated a model of social change where immediate political agents and processes play a role in the broader process of redemption. Not surprisingly, this sacralization of Zionism and the secular state made Mafdal a perfect political partner for Mapai, the secularist Zionist bloc, since Mafdal saw its role as merely a spiritual partner and compass to ensure the state's religious character.[12] The diverse political movements Mafdal came to represent shared the common approach of placing Zionist ideals in a religious framework, despite their different positions on social and economic issues. Perhaps due to the spiritual division of labor or a lack of consensus on other topics, the party often avoided divisive issues derived from social and economic policies; instead it focused on policies in areas such as education, public services, and the definition of citizenship to ensure that the state would not lose its Jewish character.

Mafdal's approach to the idea of religious activism, another contradiction in terms in the ultra-Orthodox world, distinguished it further from other religious groups. Ultra-Orthodoxy rejected taking an active role in the political community and instead emphasized counter-acculturation, the creation of pure religious communities, not to force but to get ready to receive the redemptive process. Religious Zionists challenged the ultra-Orthodox practice of disengagement in insular communities and asserted that taking part in the nationalist project did not constitute a desecrating action but rather, due to their immediate religious essence and ultimate goals, a hallowed observance of religious commandments. The religious core of some political activities rendered them not only acceptable but desirable. Thus, what seemed to be an antiredemptionist move for the ultra-Orthodox, in essence served as "a spur to the ultimate Messianic Redemption."[13] Religious Zionists needed to embrace *Halutziut*, a term often used by secular Zionists that means "pioneering spirit," as at heart such endeavors were religious acts.

Religious activism found a more pronounced expression in other religious Zionists' writings, especially during the constitutive years of the state. Some, such as Zvi Hirsch Kalischer, confronted the ultra-Orthodox critics, calling their refusal to participate in Zionism and their justification for refusal, namely, waiting for redemption, a misconception: "The redemption of Israel, for which we long, is not to be imagined as a sudden miracle. Cast aside the conventional view that the Messiah will suddenly sound a blast on the great trumpet and cause all the inhabitants of the earth to tremble."[14] Redemption would only progress by diplomacy and by awakening support for it among different groups.[15] Religious activism, engaging in mundane politics with sacred ideas, became part and parcel of the unfolding redemption and a guiding principle of Mafdal's activities.

Mafdal's placement of Zionism under a sacred canopy did not mean the settlement of all theological questions regarding the legitimacy of the nation-state. On the contrary, resolving theological questions in centrally important areas only generated other theological questions. In fact, the establishment of the state posed a set of new conundrums, such as whether and how policies made by government officials who lacked willed holiness would be accepted by the religious public. The opinions given by the former chief rabbis of Israel illuminate how religious legitimacy is neither static nor unequivocal given the presence of competing positions.[16] Laws have two sources of authority in the Jewish tradition: *dina d'malchuta dina* (the laws of the land where one resides are binding) and *takanot* (regulations) established by the community. The first rule, a product of the Diaspora, requires for reasons of political survival and coexistence the recognition of the law of *any* state, yet it does not consider them Halakhic. The second source of legitimacy, however, carries more weight than the first one, as the laws take their strength from the community. For religious communities, this traditional distinction begs the question of whether and on what grounds the laws of the Israeli state would be legitimate.

The reasoning of Rabbi Mordechai Eliahu, the former Sephardi chief rabbi, suggests that regulations of a community must be ratified by a "highly reputable contemporary Torah scholar."[17] In the absence of such consent, "the laws of the Knesset do not possess the validity of takanot."[18] On the other hand, Rabbi Avraham Shapira, the former Ashkenazi chief rabbi and one of the spiritual leaders of Mafdal, gives a conditional answer that portrays the common rationale of Mafdal's approach: Among other conditions, Shapira argues, a law that has been passed with the approval of the religious opposition in the Knesset is considered legitimate. If religious Knesset members opposed the law, it is contrary to the Halakha and not binding.[19] Although it is relatively easy to justify the state's laws under "the law of the land is the law," as it is done by Agudat Israel, Shapira offers a more nuanced approach that captures the essence of Mafdal's policies and its assumed function in Israeli politics. Due to their overall redemptive role and connection to the Jewish community, the state's policies are legitimate, but this legitimacy is not reflexive and absolute. It is only the presence of a religious party in parliament that ensures their legitimacy. In a way, the legitimacy of the state is subject to a daily plebiscite of the religious public represented by religious parties. Thus, Mafdal's role in the government or outside of it is to ensure that the government's policies will be imbued with spiritual meaning.

Indeed, Mafdal's assumed role of spiritual guardianship reveals itself in different ways in the party's policy statements. Using a rhetoric that weaves the main terms and claims of Zionism and Judaism together, the party program declares that "The National Religious Party sees in the very existence of the state of Israel a revelation of faith and holiness. . . . It is vital in the growth of our redemption, strong gathering of the exiles, in the building of the land, and for the establishment of a governmental life for the light of the Torah of Israel."[20] This opening statement at first suggests that the party is a state-centered and status quo party, in full support of the state, but caveats follow immediately: "The combined belief in Torah and the State of Israel was the driving force behind the establishment of Mafdal which has led to historical achievements including the definition of the Jewish character of the Israeli Defense Forces. . . . The work, however, has not been completed."[21] To this end Mafdal seeks to influence policy from within the government to follow the basic tenets of Torah. One of the party's popular election slogans "Zionism with Soul" captured this role and the party's desire not to replace, but to guide and complement the secular bloc.

Given this religiously justified yet qualified commitment to the state, the crucial question is: what if the state fails to fulfill its religious function? What appears to be a rhetorical question became a very significant political issue in the post-1967 era in which the status of the land seized during the war was discussed. Religious Zionists were faced with a new puzzle: the state's relationship to the land. Mafdal's position in this era can be elicited from the speeches of Rav Zvi Yehudea Kook, the son of Avraham Kook. Yehudea Kook's ideas were shaped by a different political context than his father's and brought to the fore different religious precepts. A comparison of the ideas of father and son captures the transformation of Mafdal's ideas. While father Kook incorporated the two pillars of a modern nation-state, its ideology (Zionism) and leadership (Zionists), into Halakhic thought, the son Kook focused on the third pillar: the boundaries and territories of the nation. The son Kook's thoughts revealed themselves most forcefully in his historic speech, which was later regarded as prophetic. It epitomized the belief that the establishment of the state came at the price of accepting the partition of the Holy Land, leaving Zionism as redemptive ideology incomplete. In order to receive the full extent of the promised redemption, a new activism toward the settlement of the entire land was required:

On the night when news of the United Nations decision in favor of the Re-Establishment of the State of Israel reached us, when the People streamed into the streets to celebrate and rejoice, I could not go out and join in the celebration. I sat alone and silent; a burden lay upon me. . . . I could not accept the fact that indeed "they have . . . divided My land." (Joel 4:2)! Yes [and now after nineteen years] where is our Hebron—have we forgotten it?! Where is our Shechem, our Jericho,—where are they?!—Have we forgotten them? And all that lies beyond the Jordan—each and every clod of earth, every region, hill, valley, every plot of land, that is part of *Eretz Israel*—have we the right to give up even one grain of the Land of God! . . . the first step is [required after this]—the settlement of Israel on their Land! [22]

What makes this statement powerful is that the 1967 War, in fact, ended with the capture of Jerusalem, Hebron, and other holy cities. For the religious public in general and Mafdal supporters in particular, the miraculous outcome of the war meant a new stage of the process of redemption had begun. The ideological fulcrum of the party started to gradually shift from protecting the sanctity of the state to protecting that of the land. Facing theologically complementary yet politically contradictory goals, Mafdal confronted the new puzzle of how to balance the sacralization of the state, the unity of the nation, and the sacralization of land toward the fulfillment of redemption.

Community and Individual: Cohesive Nation, Divided Individuals?

Mafdal's common description as a modern Orthodox party initially suggests that it would emphasize individuals over community. After all, one of the trademarks of any modern ideology is its appeal to individuals as autonomous, free-willed constituents of societies, not closely tied communities. In fact, many ideas in religious Zionism confirm this expectation. Individuals and their differences are the main element of Israeli society and, according to religious Zionism, it is important to understand the root cause of these differences. For instance, individuals seem to have a different relationship to the land of Israel. Some seem attached to it due to its elevated, spiritual properties, while others are driven to it due to the material gains it offers in various areas, ranging from academic and cultural to economic. These differences are based on different forms of devotion to the Land of Israel. Those whose devotion focuses on self-interest come from those who are not cognizant of their intrinsic holiness. Therefore, the challenge for those with a deeper religious consciousness is to advocate and promote the unity of all Jews, because only they understand the theological sources and reasons for the confounding diversity among groups. A lack of understanding and animosity toward those who are not religious defies the role of religious people and has a detrimental effect on the community in general:

The Midrash tells us, God held Mount Sinai over Israel like a bucket, forcing them to accept the Torah. This act demonstrated . . . that we acknowledged our subservience to God. Similarly, in the future end of days, *God will not wait until the people of Israel have perfected themselves*. Accordingly, as the Temple had been destroyed, according to the Talmud, because of *sinat hinnam* (undeserved hatred) among Jews, it will be rebuilt only because of *ahavat hinnam*, i.e., love for Jews even if it is undeserved. Because in his theological system, that the youthful, secular and even anti-religious Labor Zionist pioneers *halutzim* were actually part of a grand divine scheme. The Sages wrote that Omri merited to be king as reward for establishing a city in the Land of Israel, even though his intentions were certainly pragmatic [not holy].[23]

The political implication of this view is that although their immediate actions seem antireligious, it was important to accept nonreligious Jews and keep the community unified. The undeserved hatred among Jews has brought the most destructive changes upon Israel. The undeserved love extended to all community members would serve as a panacea to the ills of what might be a divided society. After all, "it is *the unity* which paved the way for receiving the Torah. The Torah cannot be given to individuals or diverse groups, no matter how exalted (pure) they are, but to the entire nation of Israel, and only when they are together, 'as one man, with a single heart.' "[24] Likewise, not individuals, but the community altogether would receive the awaited redemption. Therefore, it is not the individual commitments but the overall characteristics of the community that matter the most for the theological status of the nation:

Even though regional differences might delay the group's unification, this condition will not be forever. These differences have limited and local value, only as long as the nation has not reorganized itself and set up its external and internal institutions and their connections. But once the national structure has been completed, then the tradition itself demands that we establish for the whole people an over-all high court, in the eternal, holy center that God will choose for the people in the Temple. From there will come forth one Torah for all Israel. Then we shall abide by a living tradition which wells up in the soul of the nation and is bound up with God's Torah.[25]

In part due to the political conflict that marked the constitutive years of Israel, Kook's writing continuously addressed questions derived from the unavoidable differences in the community, a theme that manifests itself in the views of Mafdal's leadership: what happens if there are unbridgeable disagreements among Jewish people? Kook describes two venues that may settle divisive issues. One is based on the search for the truth. If the questions are about the truth, then a consensus based on the majority opinion creates the solution.[26] What if there is no clear consensus? Kook then introduced his notion of self-reliance, "which does not mean not trusting the holy," but promotes the idea that through the enlightenment of Torah, it is possible to reach sound collective decisions.[27] Thus, the consensus that emerges through the enlightenment of Torah serves as the ultimate means to sustain the community.

The controversy on the status of the territories and settlements tests some of these notions and exemplifies how sacralization of secular ideas and institutions does not necessarily result in full harmony. Problems arise when popular perceptions and Halakhic rules conflict in the absence of a broad Torah community. For instance, amid the growing support for territorial compromises (which amounts to the growing opposition to a decision justified by Halakha), the party-affiliated weekly argued that right political decisions were not always centrist. There are times when "[t]he leader who doesn't stick to the center can inspire the nation with stages of an uplifting spirit and not 'stages' of withdrawal." The real duty of the leader, beyond the pragmatic concerns of politics, is described as follows: "He was leading the sheep not to be led by the flock." An ideal leader of the nation does not seek middle-of-the-road popularity. A true leader is infused with a vision of the redemption of Israel, even if the nation is not worthy of it or does not want to be redeemed.[28] The vision of redemption informs the leader in matters of politics and guides him toward pursuing what to some might appear to be costly short-term policies.

Notwithstanding the challenges posed by how to handle religious and ideological differences in Israel, Mafdal's program indicates that the national community and the call for keeping it intact are not limited to the people who reside in Israel but include the community of Jewish people in the broadest sense:

Where is Am Yisrael? Where are the Jewish people for whom the State of Israel was established? Today, Jews are scattered throughout the four corners of the earth; in North America, Russia, Morocco, South Africa . . . Every year we lose more than 100,000 Jews through assimilation and even here, in Israel, there are times when we feel as though we have lost the feeling of being "one nation." The achievement of National Unity—between Jews in Israel and the Diaspora, and between Jews at opposite ends of the Israeli political spectrum—can only be achieved through *Aliyah* and a return to the original Zionist ideologies that created the State. We must re-establish the concept of brotherhood and we must reach out and bridge the political, social and philosophical gaps that separate the nation. We must do this now, because National Unity is more than a political concept—it is a "mitzvah."[29]

Essential for Mafdal is the forging of a national unity, a goal considered a religious commandment and not a political choice. Treating unity as a mitzvah offers another example of how Mafdal raises political positions to the level of sacred, thereby removing them as a subject of political debate. The party believes that the boundaries of the ultimate community stretch beyond the Jews living in Israel and that any policy that prevents the assimilation of Diaspora Jews becomes highly detrimental to the party's efforts toward achieving its idealized community. In fact, a review of the educational programs endorsed by the party shows that many of them oriented towards strengthening the ties among Israel's different communities and between the Israeli and Diaspora Jewry. A significant number of the party organizations, such as Bnei Akiva, are transnational, among others, they gather the leaders of youth movements to address issues that can and do cause social rifts.[30] Other party-affiliated institutions, such as Emunah, one of the largest religious women's organizations, maintain branches in countries ranging from Uruguay to Belgium and focus on providing social welfare services for women and children to build strong communities from the bottom up. A common outlook emerges from the wide spectrum of party-affiliated groups: instead of relying on the existing communal relations or establishing themselves as a part of the community, party-affiliated institutions organize around a number of different issues or training programs with the goal of uniting different communities within and beyond Israel.

Paradoxically, Mafdal does not take the divinely ordained unity of the Jewish community for granted in its programs. Rather, it focuses on the dissonance between the divinely ordained and existing conditions and makes closing the gap between the two central to its political agenda. Indicating the new discursive areas that tie individuals to communities in distinctive ways, the key role of the Jewish community for the overall transformation of the Jewish people compels the party to focus on the individual. Continuing the Judaization of the public sphere and bridging communities through religiously grounded education is of prime political and religious importance—only such a type of continuous education would succeed in bringing out Halakhic enlightenment and in forging the unity that the party seeks to attain at a higher level of holiness. Achieving national coherence, a characteristic of any nation-state, becomes a religious obligation for Mafdal. Consequently, secular constructs and ideas that serve this end are seen as part and parcel of religious doctrine.

A review of the basic tenets and overall transformation of the party's ideology shows that a constant tension exists between the party's view of the differences between individuals and the desired unity of the Jewish nation. Although individuals are the main units of society, their role is defined only within the narrow and restrictive framework of national unity and the community. In fact, Effi Eitam (one of the former chairmen of the party) did not hesitate to state that the party's efforts to balance individual and collective interests impaired its policies. As Zionism moves along in the redemptive process, a new political restructuring is necessary. The third stage of religious Zionism, the new "post-Zionist redemptive" era arrived after the normalization of the nation (i.e., building of the nation-state) and the normalization of the state (i.e., building of the strong state).

While the current era is expected to present the nation with the rebuilding of the second temple, this final stage meets with both internal and external opposition and requires an increasing emphasis on unity: "Every person has a momentary flash of transcendence. But what is new here, is to take this flash from the individual core to the community. Because we are not only *individuals* who possess the image of God—we are *a nation* that possesses the image of God. That is the great innovation. What is new is that there is a nation that has this. There is a nation with a soul."[31] These collective responsibilities will define the course of the new era of religious Zionism. What makes Mafdal's ideological map hard to read is the fact that, while its core ideas accommodate individual difference as given and acceptable, they ultimately espouse a homogeneous society rather than a plural diverse one. The centrality of redemption conceives of the nation as a unit and history as not open-ended but as moving in a certain direction toward the fulfillment of redemption. Ironically, however, the more collective responsibilities are emphasized, such as the rebuilding of the temple, the more individual differences are likely to be perceived as a polarizing threat. As captured by a Bnei Akiva's motto "Al Tifrosh Min Hatzibur," it is forbidden for any individual to separate himself from the community. This perpetual internal tension in the party's ideas brings to the fore a certain crucial question: to what extent can the individual foundations of the party resist the ideological reconstruction that would likely make individuals subservient to the community?

Inclusiveness Versus Exclusiveness of Mafdal's Zionism:
Redemptive Pluralism

Perhaps warned by the polarizing currents of his time, Rabbi Kook wrote that the multitalented diversity of the Jewish people has its downside. As a society, the Jewish people are more prone to internal frictions and conflicts: there can be times that "each talent and faculty strives to express itself fully, even at the expense of others."[32] The dire consequences of the lack of cohesion are explained by many Halakhic metaphors: a society divided is like *a palace built on top of many boats*. As long as *the boats are tied together, the palace stands*. Not guided by a shared vision, however, "each boat normally tries to make its own, separate way in the sea" (emphases added). It is only the unifying existence of the palace that directs the boats to sail together along the same path. Given the internal divisions, there needs to be a force, a strong palace that protects against internal strife and unifies the Jewish people. This force emanates from the Torah itself.[33] Therefore, the more people are enlightened by Torah, the more they recognize "God's hand within the natural universe. The holy land eases one's emancipation, strengthens the palace and thus also the unity of the Jewish nation."[34] Ultimately, the unifying force of Torah would eliminate the ostensible differences in the Jewish nation.

As a reflection of the nation's inherent unity, Mafdal's leadership claims inclusiveness as the main pillar of the party's ideology. In the words of Zevulun Orlev, a member of the upper echelon of the party, Mafdal's average supporter comes from among those "who have contact with all sectors of society unlike the supporters of other parties: He can pray in the morning with *Haredim,* go to work in the afternoon where his boss votes Shinui (a secularist party), and go to a nighttime Israel Defense Force drill, where he will be in a tank with someone from Meretz (another secularist party)."[35] Contact among different sectors and consensus on the existing social institutions, such as the necessity of the state and military, stand not only a politically expedient position, but also a religious necessity. Mafdal's role is especially important because ultra-Orthodox groups in general reject both Zionism and service in the military, continue to divide religious and secular groups, and are the main source of social fragmentation: "The *Haredi* community, which by and large never shared in the brotherhood of blood, cannot feel the same inseparable partnership of statehood, and so it drifts time and again into a *Milhemet Tarbut* [culture war]."[36] Quoting Kook, the party leadership argues, ". . . those who are truly righteous do not complain about the darkness. Instead they add light. They do not complain about wickedness. Instead they add righteousness. They do not complain about impurity. Instead they add purity."[37] Thus, social contact with nonreligious segments of society is also a religious obligation.

What happens if the divisions persist and tensions emerge because of ethnic and socioeconomic disparities? One of the intriguing answers to this question can be found in the party's weekly, which starts with the Halakhic question of why a bird was declared impure although its name, *chasida,* derived from the root "kindness," suggests otherwise. "If the bird is so kind, why is it impure?"[38] The answer, says the weekly, rests on a well-known but neglected moral theme: "It is kind to its [own type of] comrades, but not to anybody else." Repeated proper religious acts are not enough to move one from the category of the impure "if [one's] good deeds are directed only toward friends and colleagues."[39] This discussion comes as a surprise because the main question in this weekly column is whether Ashkenazi hegemony exists and what implications it has on the society. The article concludes, ". . . without a doubt, the problem (Ashkenazi supremacy) exists. [It is the] secular brand of political Zionism that considered (and still considers!) a religious way of life as a somewhat primitive, dark custom which is the opposite of the light of modern living."[40] Yet what seems to be the only conclusion drawn from Ashkenazi hegemony, the exclusion of Sephardim, overlooks the fact that it is the absence of a shared commitment to tradition that turned the Ashkenazi secular elite into a problem and provided fertile ground for growth of "weeds." Commonalities between Ashkenazi and Sephardim exceed their differences. More fundamentally Torah says, "Do not make separations" [Devarim 14:1], regardless of the reasons.[41] Accordingly, bringing sectarian or other narrowly defined interests to the fore is inconsistent with the party's ideology. This is why Mafdal leaders consider religious parties like Shas, which focuses on Sephardi interests, as organizations that are kind only to their own people and are thus impure.

The discussion shows that even though the party acknowledges the presence of ethnically and economically based problems, its unity-centered paradigm does not allow it to attend to the distinctive needs of these communities on their own terms (as ethnic and/or socioeconomic disparities). The party follows the belief that "the living contact with our heritage and the daily life of tradition [eventually] lead to similar outlooks and approaches."[42] On the other hand, when the issue is the land, the party moves to the opposite direction and presents contacts and negotiations with Palestinians as not only futile, but dangerous. "This danger, of losing the land, is the worst of all, since it can be put into effect by a single word. That is why the Almighty warned Lavan in a dream: 'Take care not to talk to Yaacov, neither good nor evil' [Bereishit 31:24]. Lavan was forbidden even to talk, to make any effort to convince Yaacov to return to Aram Naharayim."[43] This sentiment turns into an even more contradictory position in the party program by stating, on the one hand, that "there will only be one state between the Jordan River and the Mediterranean Sea—the State of Israel, no independent national Arab entity will exist within the limits of the Land of Israel; no part of Israel will be given over to a foreign government of authority." On the other hand, the program concludes that "the State of Israel will strive for peace and make every effort to attain it."[44]

As a result of its clashing stances, the party finds itself supporting the ideal of peace, while objecting to any negotiations that might lead to territorial concessions. The Shas party's argument that the Halakhic tradition justifies territorial concessions only if the concessions save Jewish life does not resonate with the Mafdal leadership. According to Shlomo Goren, the former Ashkenazi chief rabbi of Israel, who is considered to be one of the most influential rabbis from the Orthodox Zionist camp in Mafdal's recent history:

We are in a state of war with the Arabs, thus our fight is a defensive one and a commanded one and *pikuach nefesh* (protection of life) does not apply. Our duty is to continue to fight towards a military victory and the liberation of all of *Eretz Yisrael* [Land of Israel]. We have only the word of God from the mouth of the father of the prophets, "But if you will not drive out the inhabitants of the land from before you, then shall those be as thorns in your eyes, and as pricks in your sides, and they shall harass you in the land wherein you dwell" (Numbers 33:35). Onkelos [the authoritative Aramaic translation of the bible] translated this to Aramaic as reading "they shall take up arms against you." This warning of the Torah according to the Onkelos translation is being fulfilled today by the *intifada*, which is organizing against us armed terrorist groups, threatening our lives and disrupting our ways. Against them we must accept upon ourselves the command "Let us go up and possess it for we are well able to overcome it" (Numbers 13:30).[45]

Ironically, it is the party's unity and land-centered platform that do not allow it to develop policies that acknowledge sectarian interests and exploit venues through which agreements on the status of the settlements and territories can be reached. Overall, the sacralization of the nation and the land gives the party a rich ground to be accommodating, yet at the same time, it narrows the domain of issues that can be subject to political negotiation and compromises. The party's strength, its ability to reconcile religious and secular ideas, also becomes its main political hurdle when it takes issues such as ethnic differences off the agenda. Therefore, it is not surprising that Sephardi moderates among Mafdal members formed *Tami*, Movement for Tradition, while the National Zionists, who accept some forms of concession of land for peace, formed *Meimad* (a Hebrew acronym for "Jewish State, Democratic State"). According to Sephardi leaders such as Avner Shaki, Mafdal "consistently failed in understanding the needs of the Sephardi population and in fully integrating Sephardi leaders into the upper echelon of the party." Attesting to some implicit strong ethnocentric stances not addressed directly in its views, it is not rare to hear comments in certain party circles that the party cannot divorce itself from its European Jewry, Ashkenazi elite-centered roots, which inform its ideas on national unity. Socioeconomic issues plague different populations and require the party to step out of its paradigm and look at Zionism not as a redemptive but as a social and economic project. While these topics never found a place in the party's deliberations, the question of the land gradually moved to the center of the party's agenda and became an issue beyond debate and thus beyond politics.[46]

Placing Mafdal's position on a spectrum from inclusive to exclusive highlights its contradictory visions. The root of the party's teleological view and the puzzling impact of it on the party's vision of an inclusive community can be best seen in Kook's statements that "Just as all wine contains sediment so the sinful form part of society; and just as the sediment sustains the wine, so the gross passion of the wicked enhances the vibrancy of life. Ultimately, however, the sediment will sink to the bottom of the barrel . . . and cease to be objectionable . . . whereupon our minds may, unencumbered, contemplate the wondrous unfolding of the Divinely preordained ideal fruition."[47] The party's trust in the redemptive process results in some policies that put its electoral coalition and ideological consistency at risk; for example, the party's description of settling the land as mitzvoth effectively alienates its moderate supporters. However, from the perspective of the party's ideology, its position on settlements allows the party to take a critical step toward eliminating desecrations for the unity of the polity. Unless prevented, such unholy actions become the root cause of real social tension and disunity. As a result, in the view of the leadership, some of the party's short-run "radical policies" are unavoidable in order to ensure the political unity in the long run.

Thus, Mafdal's novel sacro-secular position has been a mixed blessing. One can argue that the party's unequivocal emphasis on unity let it address the deep-seated fear of the disintegration of the Jewish people and potentially even Milhemet Tarbut, a culture war. Its assumption of intrinsic sameness makes it more inclusive but prevents it from looking at social tensions that cannot be reduced to different levels of holiness. The centrality of redemption in the party's ideology defines the current differences as inconsequential, which may keep it from looking inward at the Israeli nation. This is why Yehuda Ben Meir, a Mafdal defector who founded Meimad, attributed the raison d'etre of their split to the hollowing inconsistencies in Mafdal's principles: its practice did not exhibit a genuine commitment to pluralism, despite or perhaps because of its ideology. Mafdal's belief that divine redemption requires human effort makes it a progressive agent in the ultra-Orthodox world but turns into an obstacle when the party has to deal with issues of diversity and open negotiations. Mafdal's unique coupling of Judaism and Zionism enables the party to embody two competing approaches and positions at the same time: while it is dovish and willing to compromise on the domestic level, when it comes to international issues, it becomes a hawkish, uncompromising party.[48] Yet both positions are rooted in the same conviction, namely that the unity of the nation and the land is both a reflection of and a prerequisite for redemption.

The Mafdal Leadership

The life and career of Mafdal's early spiritual leader, Avraham Kook, shows that his reading of Zionism as a Halakhic project was not merely an isolated theological exercise, but the result of efforts to make the Halakhic tradition relevant to the political context marked by a formation of a nation-state. Kook was born in Latvia and moved to Israel when he was in his late twenties. He first served in Jaffa, Israel, surrounded by secular pioneers and agricultural development areas. His early years show how his approach was developed and how his views both responded to and reinforced the plurality of ideas forming within the nascent Israeli society. For instance, upon the requests of the religious public, he would write warning letters encouraging the secular pioneers not to defile Shabbath while also using these pioneers as example in his religious teaching. His religious leadership therefore was more one of passive guidance than active mobilization. When he left Israel to attend a meeting of Agudat Israel in London, he was marooned there by the outbreak of World War I. His forced exile turned out to be very important for the formation of his ideas. Kook experienced the different communities and political negotiations that accompanied the formation of Zionist nationalism. In his writings he recognized the modern idea of the nation-state and religious tradition as two separate entities but a reflection of the same essence. In contrast to his emphasis on unity, his argument for the necessity of having both a spiritual and a secular leader symbolized his view of the political and religious communities' dual yet interdependent roles. For Kook, as long as the Jewish people's level of holiness is such that conflict continues to exist between the physical and spiritual realms, it will be necessary to have two distinct leaders.[49] When the Jewish people merit the revelation of God's unity in all realms, then one leader will govern them: holiness.

Mafdal's leadership structure reflects the disparate pillars of its ideology. For example, Mafdal not only incorporated religious movements that had joined Zionism in Israel's early years; it also included groups that focused on labor relations as the main source of tension in Jewish society. Israel was to establish not only a Jewish state, but a state with principles of egalitarianism, collective property, and responsibilities. The broad range of ideas supported within Mafdal led to a series of intense conflicts, such as (1) whether to enter the secular socialist Histadrut labor organization, or to join an alliance with other religious elements, including the non-Zionist Agudat Yisrael (socialists versus religionists); and (2) whether to balance the sanctity of the state versus the sanctity of the land. The party leadership managed to contain the party's internal competition as long as it remained politically moderate and kept the main party faction focused on the common goal of promoting state and national unity as a religious construct. The party's strength also became one of its weaknesses: The party had always maintained strong institutional ties with a wide range of interest groups and civil movements (e.g., labor, agricultural, women's, and rabbinic/educational groups). Mafdal's failure to balance the interests of its disparate supporters and the increasing power of the radical groups with which the party became affiliated gradually led to a narrowing of its ideological spectrum. Still, the party serves a platform to represent all non antisystemic religious groups willing to recognize the government and negotiate with it.

Yet the party's messianic ideas and openness to groups with radical views make it exceedingly reactive against and susceptible to political developments that either confirm to or deviate from the trajectory of the historical transformation it advocates. Paradoxically, the more the party's redemptive ideology is corroborated politically, the more religious, teleological ideas dominate the party platform. Events that made Israel's national boundaries nearly identical to Biblical boundaries reinforced the view that they were signs that redemption was unfolding. Such views encouraged Mafdal leaders to treat many political questions, including the territorial ones, as theological questions. The transformation of Mafdal's ideology was most visible in the aftermath of the 1967 War and during the debates on territorial concessions in 1992 and 2005. Together they illustrate how political context can alter the opportunity structure for religious movements, or how once-marginalized ideas and groups can take on central roles.

Perhaps due to the constant internal struggles between competing blocs, Mafdal rejected the idea of a popular selection of its leadership and its slate of candidates, while other Israeli parties, especially Likud and Labor, the two major parties, adopted internal democracy. In order to limit the power of the radical factions within the party, Mafdal opted for a mixed system: the party's central committee elects the party leadership, and the candidate list is decided upon by a unique process. Each of the approximately thousand-member central committee chooses seven out of seventeen candidates, and those with the highest vote totals are slated. As an overall policy, Mafdal seeks to maintain a moderate political leadership in order to provide balance among its internal factions. The leadership of Zevulun Hammer was followed by another moderate, Shapira. However, the party's ideological alignment with the extremist groups *Tze'irim* and *Gush Emunim*, which advocate the establishment of settlements in the occupied territories as a way of maintaining Biblical boundaries, changed not only the party's overall ideological outlook but also challenged the conventional moderate leadership.[50] The decline of the party's electoral fortunes and the intensifying competition within the party was reflected in the continuing changes in its leadership. First, replacing Hammer with the moderate ethnic Sephardi Yitzhak Levy was meant to expand Mafdal's popularity among Sephardim. Later, the radical party member Efraim (Effi) Eitam's rise to a leadership position sought to galvanize territorial nationalists to the party. These leadership changes show that the party is in search of a common ideological ground within its organization and a leader who can prevail over the centrifugal forces tearing at the party's ideologies. The resignation of both Effi Eitam and Yitzhak Levy to form the Renewed National Religious Zionist party in protest of Mafdal's moderates showed that its leadership consistently finds itself at a crossroads and that the way it resolves (or fails to resolve) its questions affected Israel's ideological landscape in a substantial way.

In contrast to other religious parties such as Agudat Israel, Mafdal's religious and political leaderships do not overlap. However, the party's control of the office of the Ashkenazi chief rabbi and its distinctive religious-Zionist school system forged institutional ties between Mafdal and certain segments of the Ashkenazi religious elite. Mafdal's first leader, Moshe Shapira, who represented the moderate bloc and mediated the party's internal dissensions until 1977, geared the party's policies toward ensuring religious content in the secularist nationalist policies of the Zionist elite. Mafdal's legislative focus and opposition to government policies such as the marriage law led Ben-Gurion to declare that the party itself was "more dangerous than those of anti-Zionist Agudat Israel," despite its politically moderate leadership.[51] The political cost of this era has been the party's exclusive focus on promoting the role of religion as a central factor in education and political culture (e.g., marriage law, the debate on citizenship) at the expense of other core issues, such as economics, defense, and foreign policy. The question of the territories, which lies at the intersection of domestic and foreign issues, became the focus of the party's interest only after 1967. This repositioning was not because of a random policy change. Rather, exemplifying a general pattern of transformation in religious parties it rested on a finely tuned ideological response to these shifts in the context.[52]

The religious leaders, despite opposition from within the party, continue to play an important role in shaping Mafdal's policies by presenting their views to the political leadership directly or indirectly. The lack of explicit religious party leadership similar to that maintained by Shas and Agudat Israel indicates the party's reluctance to undermine its modern party structure. The religious leadership announces its opinion in the form of a Halakhic ruling but does not directly act as part of the party organization.[53] For instance, Eliahu became the final authority for several significant decisions, such as whether to participate in the government coalition. Other spiritual leaders, such as former Ashkenazi Chief Rabbi Avraham Shapira, Rabbi Dov Lior, Rabbi Eliezer Waldman, and Rabbi

Zefanya Drori have had their voices heard in the party's decisions and in some cases have become actual party members. The dividing line between Mafdal's moderate and extremist supporters can be defined by the contrasting views of how central these advisory opinions are to the party's policies. Moderates assign a less critical role to the "advisory" opinions of the religious leadership.[54] In contrast, the party's right wing opts for a more comprehensive inclusion of religious leadership in the decision-making process, even if that means promoting religious values at the expense of opposing the state's main policies.[55]

Notwithstanding the fragmented ideological structure of the party elite and the constantly negotiated role of spiritual leadership, a closer review of the party indicates that most of Mafdal's top posts are reserved for people of a certain ethnic origin and educational background. Most of the leaders were educated in Bnei Akiva schools, which emphasize both Jewish tradition and Zionist ideas, and a high percentage of them get their college education at Bar Ilan University.[56] Only a few of the top party elite, including Yitzhak Levy, Hanan Polat, and Haim Druckman, had solely religious educations. The average age of the party's top leadership is fifty-six.[57] Although the party does not diverge from the general profile of the Israeli political elite, its average leadership age is higher than that of its main competitor, Shas.

Women provide a striking contradiction within the party's leadership. Despite the presence of a very strong women's movement, Emunah, a high rate of female attendance at Bar Ilan University, a large volunteer system, and *Sheirut Leumi* for religious girls in the military, the party has failed to incorporate women into its upper echelon. In 2003 Mafdal slated its second female Knesset representative, Gila Finkelstein, after Sarah Stern-Katan's successful bid in the 1977 election. Finkelstein's own account shows how several of her earlier attempts to become a candidate failed. Only after getting an endorsement from one of the spiritual leaders of the party was she given a winning position on the party's ticket.[58] Finkelstein's efforts to bring issues salient to Orthodox women, which are buried under Mafdal's national agenda, to the forefront exemplified the critical contribution of women. For example, Finkelstein brought *agunot*—"chained women" whose husbands refuse them a religious divorce and force them into long legal-religious processes—to the public's attention. Although Mafdal is the only religious party that has allocated seats to women, this low level of representation clashes with the party's claimed critical role for social integration and the reconciliation of modern and traditional values. According to the party-affiliated weekly, these results must be seen against the background of ongoing theological discussions on the status of women's representation. Although written in favor of women representation, one weekly states that:

There is one issue which has cropped up more than once as a reason for not establishing a joint religious party. This is the question of nominating women as candidates for municipal office, a practice which the Mafdal has refused to abandon in several municipalities. . . . It is common to quote the above Midrash, which suggests how ignorant Manoach must have been to be under his wife's influence. For some reason, the second part of the Midrash is quoted less often: Elkana and Elisha followed women, meaning that they followed their advice. Women have something to say even to the greatest prophets. . . . [However] it must be kept in mind that there are limits which should not be crossed. This is the reason that the sages emphasized in the above Midrash that Rivka and her maids went after Elazar, and did not precede him. There is a red line of personal modesty which must be maintained in all relationships.[59]

While Mafdal's tenuous ties to the Sephardi community cannot be explained by the rather significant number of Sephardim included in its upper ranks, it can be attributed to the party's inattentiveness to the socioeconomic problems that plague Sephardim. Although Mafdal continues to recruit more Sephardi to its core leadership group, in part to counter the increasing recent popularity of Shas, the electoral impact of this incorporation has been marginal. One of the party's recent leaders, Yitzhak Levy, epitomized the limited impact of such attempts.[60] In contrast to the dominant profile of the party elite as Ashkenazim with Western and Eastern European background, Levy was born in Morocco and educated in Talmudic schools. Ironically, his education and overall profile did not differ from other Mafdal leaders as drastically as that of other Sephardi members. The party's well-entrenched educational institutions do not allow it to incorporate leaders from different backgrounds that could strengthen the party's ties to communities not mobilized by the party.

In part due to the delicate ideological balance that it seeks to strike, Mafdal is a party with active internal debates. The conflicting ideas brought together in the party's ideology make it vulnerable to defection and ideological reformation. The main fault lines of the party's policy can be deduced from the desertion of two of the party's own elected leaders and their efforts to establish a new political party on the grounds that it would renew the party's ties to ultra-Orthodox communities and consolidate its policy of no territorial concessions. Still, despite the fluctuations, Mafdal remains an important agent of Israeli democracy, not because of its electoral power, but because of its capacity to coin novel sacro-secular positions on pressing and emerging issues while carefully placing itself among competing ideological groups and playing critical roles in defining religious meanings of secular policies.

SHAS: AN ENIGMA OR A NOVEL SYNTHESIS
IN ISRAELI POLITICS?

Unlike Mafdal, which had its roots in diverse movements of the prestate period, Shas appeared on Israel's political scene in 1983 as a local initiative in the Jerusalem municipal and Bnai Braq elections—the main political battlegrounds for religious groups. Shas's emergence appears to be a fairy tale of modern politics with a trajectory of success that many new religious parties appear to follow. A small group of Sephardi, led by Nissim Zeev, defected from the dominant, ultra-Orthodox Agudat Israel and ran as a separate candidate list, designated as SHAS. The acronym and the party's name no longer match, attesting to the exponential growth that moved it beyond the limits of its initial appearance. Nevertheless, the acronym SHAS stands for *shisha sedarim*, sixth order or section of the Talmud. Therefore, even though it is not an accurate short form for the party's current name (*Hit'akhdut ha-Sephardim ha-Olamit Shomrey Torah*, International Organization of Torah-Observant Sephardic Jews), it communicates its religious persona. The Shas list gained three seats on the Jerusalem city council in its very first bid.[61] From this local success sprang one of the most popular religious parties in Israeli politics, the Sephardi Haredi, or Sephardi ultra-Orthodox movement, which won four seats in the Knesset in its first national election.

A closer look at the timing of Shas's emergence shows that its formation and sudden rise were no random occurrence but the culmination of various factors. The context into which Shas was launched was marked by at least five political processes. First was the fragmentation of Israel's conventional electoral blocs since 1977: Shas emerged shortly after the Israeli party system moved from a one-party-dominated (Labor) to a two-party-dominated system (Labor vs. Likud) in 1997. The Sephardi alignment with Likud played a crucial role and established the Sephardim as an effective voting bloc. Second was the crisis in the representation of Sephardim: The son of a traditional Sephardi religious leader founded the Traditional Movement of Israel, TAMI, a sign of Mafdal's inability to deal with the question of ethnicity in its own ranks. Third was the increasing questioning of Sephardi identity in Israel, especially in relation to the new wave of immigration: In 1984 the rescue of around ten thousand Ethiopian Jews raised the question of whether they were really Jewish, echoing some doubts on the authenticity of the Jewishness of groups located in Asia and Africa, and thereby making the Sephardi identity once again a central issue of political discussions in Israel. Fourth was the fragmentation within the ultra-Orthodox and religious bloc: The political rivalry within the ultra-Orthodox bloc divided religious parties along two ethnic-religious blocs, Hassidic and Lithuanian, and further marginalized the Sephardim. Fifth was the decline of the state-centered economic policies: The state's disengagement from the social welfare system precipitated a crisis, especially in economic and social sectors dependent upon government funding.

More interestingly, Shas was born shortly after the tenure of the charismatic Sephardi religious leader Ovadia Yosef as chief Sephardi rabbi ended. Notwithstanding Ovadia's enormous popularity within the Sephardi community, the Knesset adopted a law that limited the tenure of all chief rabbis. The Sephardi community saw this law not only as an attempt to undermine Ovadia's growing popularity and his capacity to challenge the domination of Ashkenazi rabbis but also as a challenge to Mafdal in the religious bloc and the Hassidim in the ultra-Orthodox bloc. Ironically, the chief rabbinate position served as the springboard for Ovadia's engagement in politics, even though the position was originally created to limit or depoliticize religion. The current law specifies that chief rabbis be elected by what would be considered an electoral college representing different religious factions. Being elected as a chief rabbi requires survival among warring factions, making it more of a political position than a bureaucratic one. Instead of curbing the power of the position, the introduction of term limits made the office more susceptible to political influence. It is possible that depriving Ovadia of his public position through the introduction of term limits encouraged him into the sphere of party politics so that he could continue to wield his influence.

What makes Shas an electoral miracle and democratic puzzle is not its emergence but its ability to survive in Israel's very competitive electoral system with its narrowly defined political platforms: Sephardi and ultra-Orthodox. Instead of disappearing from the national scene after a few elections, as many small parties do, Shas has expanded its appeal, receiving 13 percent of the votes, the highest number of votes ever cast for an "ultra-Orthodox" party in Israel's history. In 1999, it became the third largest bloc in Israeli politics after the center-right secular Likud party (see figure 5.1). Although the party's support declined in the 2003 elections, Shas has established itself as one of the pivotal agents in Israeli politics through its ideas and its political network.

The State and Zionism: An Ethnic Orthodox Zionist Party?

From its first appearance in the Israeli political arena as an offshoot of Agudat Israel, the political positioning of Shas has been readily designated as ultra-Orthodox, extremist, Haredi, and therefore anti-Zionist.

All parties once affiliated with Agudat Israel evolved from one of the most isolationist and stable political blocs in Israeli politics and exhibit a similar political profile.[62] Using Birnbaum's analogy, Israel's conventional ultra-Orthodox parties adopted a policy of counter-acculturation or "sitting inside the fences" (i.e., seeking refuge in religious communities from the influences of the secular world).[63] According to Agudat Israel, the state of Israel is not a genuine Jewish state given its current structure. As a result, the Jewish people remain in spiritual exile. The premises and self-description of religious Zionism misled its followers. Redemption will occur only through the revelation of the divine will, not through human intervention.[64] As a corollary to these perceptions, the ultra-Orthodox bloc has adopted a mixed political strategy of "reserved participation"; this strategy permits the ultra-Orthodox bloc to take part in elections and "represent" its constituency, but prevents it from accepting government positions, since that could be seen as a legitimization of the state. Other groups within the ultra-Orthodox bloc advocate complete isolation from politics and perceive even participation in elections as moving beyond the protection of the "fences." An election poster distributed before the 1988 election by Neturei Karta, an ultra-Orthodox group, captures such isolationist ideals:

Jew! Did you know that a state, even if [run] according to the Torah, contradicts the passage: "Then ye shall be Mine own treasure among all peoples . . ."? [Exodus 19:5] [And] . . . denies the coming of the Messiah; . . . that the state is a means of uprooting the entire Torah; . . . that by participating in the elections you are maintaining this state and consenting to all the above? Participation in the elections is a denial of the Holy Torah.[65]

Overall, the Agudat Israel bloc continues to host all shades of anti-Zionism and non-Zionism (which sees Zionism as irrelevant to the Jewish people) that recognize the state for instrumental reasons. Given the intractable positions in the Haredi world, it was a drastic step in the ultra-Orthodox world when Yitzhak Peretz, Shas's first political leader, presented Shas to the Knesset on September 13, 1984, as a Zionist party. However, Peretz's introduction came with a caveat and set the tone of the party's public appeal. Shas was a "Zionist Party in the *real*, deep, wide, and true meaning of Zionism."[66] Still, many considered a Haredi ultra-Orthodox party an oxymoron. Peretz's introduction only raised more questions about Shas's identity and labeled it an ultrapragmatic party that sought to expand its political bargaining power in Israel's coalition governments.

An ultra-Orthodox party's claim to be Zionist begs the question of how the party justifies such an unconventional position in an ideological

world in which consistency is not only an asset but an absolute requirement, and views without rigorous religious justifications do not have any
political appeal. The genealogy of Shas's views on Zionism documents
that the party's claim of Zionism is not simply a rhetorical position.
Shas's overall ideology appropriates the meaning of secular terms by engaging in a debate over their meaning while incorporating them into its
own ideological framework—an example of what this study defines as
internal secularization.

Although it is still a relatively new party, the core of Shas's political
and religious positions is rather settled, and its underpinnings can be
found in the ideas of Shas religious and political leaders, Ovadia Yosef
and Aryeh Deri, respectively. Ovadia Yosef's ideas on the state and other
issues are available from three main sources: his *responsa*, rulings mostly
initiated by questions, his books, and his weekly sermons. There are striking differences between these sources in terms of style. Detailed, highly
nuanced complicated responsa contrast with very colloquial, simple sermons that are often embellished by sarcastic remarks and political humor.
While the audience for the first type is the religious public, the second
audience is mixed, ranging from those on the brink of becoming religious
to curious observers to Torah scholars. Although Yosef does not address
political questions directly, important political views are embedded in
many of his decisions. Often what appears to be a meticulous discussion
of a simple question brims with important revelations about current issues. Loaded with religious terminology and metaphors, these decisions
are often not easily accessible.

Although Yosef's views were shaped in the Haredi ultra-Orthodox
world, his views differ substantially from Agudat Israel. For instance,
regarding the religious status of the state, it is important to note that in
his various rulings, such as the one in the journal *Torah She-be-Al Peh*,
Yosef wrote: "I wish to emphasize first that the state of Israel and the independent Jewish reign in our holy land is of the highest historical and
religious significance."[67] Such simple acknowledgement separates Yosef
and the Shas party from others in the ultra-Orthodox world who treat
the state as external to the religious world, having no religious significance. The ruling is perhaps one of the most revealing , and it permits us
to elicit the theological underpinnings of the party's views on the state.
In one responsa, Yosef addressed the question of whether one can recite
Hallel and *she-heheyanu* on Israel's Independence Day. Although the
question seems like another ritualistic query that has no significance beyond religious circles, it asks, in essence, whether the establishment of
the Israeli state is worthy of religious recognition and celebration. Hallel carries great significance in the Jewish tradition, as they are cited

only on days on which the Jewish people witnessed redemptive miracles, such as Passover (freedom from slavery) and Hanukah (liberation of the temple). Thus, Hallel citations serve to mark events as unquestionably significant enough to demand collective remembrance and gratitude. Accordingly, the subtext of the question, or its reflection in secular terms, is whether the state is legitimate or not. In his *Yabia Omer*, Ovadia Yosef answered:

> While despite all this, there are many and great *Gedolei Yisrael* who see in the establishment of the state the beginning of the Redemption. . . . However, since we still have before us a long path before we reach peace, both in political and military aspects and in ethical and spiritual aspects, we should not obligate the completion of *Hallel* [on Israel Independence Day]. . . . I will not fear [to state] that despite all of these areas of shade [i.e., the lack of religiosity among many in Israel], there are still great lights from which we should not hide. The state of Israel today is a center of Torah in the world and thousands of wonderful boys from among the best of our delightful children are studying Torah day and night in holy *yeshivot*. The Torah is returning to its host, for there is no Torah like the Torah of Israel. . . . However, since now we have only a good beginning, therefore there is no obligation to recite *Hallel* with a blessing.[68]

Beneath his discussion lies Shas's overall approach, which can be described as a cautious, somewhat elusive, but nevertheless radical interpretation of critical issues, especially those pertaining to the legitimacy of the state and other institutions. Yosef's decisions are often radical by the standards of Haredi principles, yet cautious by the criteria of religious Zionists and elusive by the norms of secular Zionism. For instance, from the perspective of the Haredi world, Yosef's extension of Hallel to Independence Day opened a dangerous door, not only for legitimizing the state, but also for changing the Halakhic tradition by bringing the Zionist state under the sacred canopy. Many in the Agudat Israel bloc readily dismissed Yosef's decision on the grounds that one does not have "the authority to add or expand days of celebration. The expansion of celebration was placed into the hands of members of the great assembly 3000 years ago."[69]

Yet a closer reading of Yosef's response from the religious Zionist perspective shows that his treatment of the status of the state was rather cautious. When Hallel is cited for a miracle of lesser caliber than those of the Exodus or Hanukah, it is said at prayer's end. Therefore, it is not only the citation of Hallel, but also the place of Hallel that defines an event's religious significance. Yosef wrote that if the congregation prefers to say Hallel on Israel's Independence Day in the usual place, they should not be stopped, but his preference was to recite it at prayer's end. As a result, while Yosef elevates Independence Day to a significant day, he carefully distinguishes it from others by assigning it a lesser status. In contrast to Mafdal's sacralization of the role of the state as the main tool of redemption, according to Yosef, the state is an institution with a mixed character. On the one hand, the presence of the ever-expanding Torah community legitimizes the state's presence; on the other hand, due to its mixed character, it does not deserve to be elevated to the level of sacred with full religious recognition.

When viewed from the perspective of Agudat Israel, Shas's ideology does not treat the current polity as a state of spiritual exile, but rather considers it a polity in the process of spiritual emancipation. While the repeated statement of the ultra-Orthodox worlds (i.e., in the Land of Israel "we are not yet at home") has made inroads into Shas's ideas, Yosef's explanations reject the belief that Jews in Israel remain in spiritual exile. Yosef does not consider the emergence of the state an obstacle to divine redemption; thus, Independence Day cannot be treated as a day of mourning. Unlike Mafdal, Yosef also refrains from declaring it a day of decisive divine intervention. For Yosef, spiritual homelessness takes a special meaning in modern Israel: that is, the weakness of the Torah community. It is the status of the Torah community, not the state's structure, that is the most salient issue. Yosef's legitimization for settling the land, the main goal of Zionism, does not rise to an unqualified acceptance of Zionism.

One of the key ideas in both Ovadia and Deri's appeals is that while Zionism itself is one of several mitzvoth, its political expression made it a destructive practice. With Zionism the Ashkenazi tradition became dominant in both the secular and the religious blocs, leading to the estrangement of non-Ashkenazi people from the state and from the world of ultra-Orthodoxy. Thus, Shas's opposition to Zionism is not simply a strictly ethnic or antisecular claim, but a claim against the destructive effects of political and religious domination by various Ashkenazi groups. This domination via the political power of Zionism caused the decline of the original religious traditions of the land of Israel, which were Sephardi. However, Sephardi communities object to the domination by Ashkenazi values not only for political reasons but also on Halakhic grounds. The European Jews who immigrated to Israel in the prestate years were not coming to a religious and cultural tabula rasa, but to a land whose customs and religious traditions were Sephardi. This observation is not just a simple factual statement, but provides grounds to challenge the Ashkenazi hegemony of both the religious and secular blocs from a religious perspective. Jewish tradition requires that the people accept the rule of the community in which they locate; thus, Sephardi traditions must be regarded as Israel's "rule of the locale."[70] Acting in opposition to this tradition leads to the deterioration and fragmentation of the religious community, not to its elevation.

The concept of estrangement and deterioration of the religious community is especially important for Shas's ideas. Unlike Mafdal's conviction that redemption is a predetermined process that requires the presence of the Jewish state, for Shas the unfolding of redemption is not a linear, self-governing process. The community needs to be ready to receive the redemption. Repairing the destructive effect of the Ashkenazi domination of the land is only one step in the process toward this goal. In this regard, Yosef's objection to the Ashkenazi domination seems to be not a problem of ethnic domination but of religious decline; ultimately, in his view, however, the ethnic and religious aspects of Ashkenazi hegemony are inseparable. The Ashkenazi tradition became dominant through its political and economic power, not through its Halakhic practices and conventions. When the first chief Sephardi rabbi, Rabbi Uziel, agreed to accept the Ashkenazi chief rabbinate as a partner, his idea was to create a unified religious custom, *minhag*. However, the establishment of the state led to the Ashkenazi's hegemony in both the religious and secular blocs, which eventually undermined the unity of the Torah community. Deprived of its original (Sephardi) religious traditions, the Torah community lost its roots in Israel. The religious decline was followed by social decay that plagued the general Sephardi community. While the Shas leadership accepts the basic principle of Zionism's willingness to settle the land as a religious commandment, it refuses to accept Zionism's political expression, especially those policies that entitled Ashkenazim to power and authority over other religious communities.

By adopting a dual position that couples the acceptance of core Zionist beliefs with the rejection of Ashkenazi domination as against the mitzvah, Shas possesses a unique rhetoric that can be likened to a form of compliant protest. On the one hand, Shas's rhetoric questions the legitimacy of all institutions; on the other hand, it does not ask for radical institutional change. Yet the transformation of the existing Sephardi community is a prerequisite for restoring Sephardim to their original position. For instance, Deri describes the internal dilemma of Zionism and Sephardi objections as follows:

The real intention [of Ashkenazi Zionism] was not only to mold people into Israelis, but to westernize the Sephardim. Either way, one thing is certain: it didn't work. So our path is now the only way. *The people of Israel are destined to live as tribes.* But to live together peacefully, we must make the tribes feel equal to each other. Having one segment of the people feeling inferior will not lead to a healthy situation. Shas has returned a measure of pride and self-confidence to an entire segment of the population that has, for whatever reason, lost it since they came to Israel. The key was avoiding the anti-establishment rhetoric and negative message that previous ethnic parties like Tami employed. Our message is positive. We talk about tradition, about education, about recreating what was lost. This gives people something to identify with and a feeling of pride.[71]

Shas's position vis-à-vis Zionism continues to be a source of controversy, in large part because of its dual strategy of questioning the main state institutions without being an antisystemic party. After all, a Haredi Zionist party is an oxymoron in Israeli politics and unacceptable in the Haredi world. Yosef often explains that all those who express the love of land and embrace its symbols need to be regarded as Zionist. Despite Shas's criticism of Zionism, since the party accepts its underlying premises, the party should be identified as Zionist. "We pray for Zion, Jerusalem and its residents. For [the people of] Israel, for the [religious] teachers and their students. . . . According to our definition a Zionist is a person who loves Zion and turns the commandment to settle Zion into reality. When I am in foreign countries, I use my sermons to encourage immigration. In what way are they more Zionists than we are?"[72] These answers do not end the debate, but show how Shas opens a new discursive sphere in Israeli politics, where its identity not only defies existing rules, but its rhetoric increasingly adapts itself to a symbolic world that ultra-Orthodox parties avoid.

Community and Individual: Restoring Old Communities with New Individuals?

Shas's ethnic religious appeal obscures an important key for analyzing its current policies, namely the religious leadership's description of the relationship between the individual and the divine. Unlike Kook, who sees different degrees of holiness in each member of the Jewish community regardless of their expressed will, Ovadia rejects the idea of unintentional will. The party leadership's discussions of the differences within the Jewish community reveal an interesting symbolism that is not obvious to those unfamiliar with Judaism. For example, the symbols used on priestly garments, such as pomegranates and bells, "contain deep meanings" and are important icons for the religious essence and the obligations of the people. These symbols are not mere images, but epitomize "the souls of Israel that were hewn from under the Heavenly Throne and are divided into two categories."[73] Because it has a dual message, the image of the pomegranate is especially important: it seems empty, yet when ripe, it is full—a symbol of the transformation of a nonreligious soul. Despite their perceived hollowness, these souls are attached to sanctity too, hewn from the Heavenly Throne and yearning for correction. "These pomegranates on the cloak were multicolored, for these souls come in various forms."[74] Bells, on the other hand, represent souls that are pure. They represent those who observe all mithzvot and focus on their perfection.[75] However, this symbolic and dichotomous view of the Jewish people does not translate into an expectation of inevitable conflict. On the contrary, while the party leadership sees clear distinctions within the Jewish community, all souls are redeemable due to each individual's attachment to the holy roots.

These images represent a social transformation and echo Mafdal's views of social evolution, but not in deterministic redemptive terms. Religious leaders point out how the three different ways in which the symbols can be ordered correspond to distinct forms of community and signify divergent levels of responsibility of the pure: there are symbols that include lines consisting of only bells, while others place one bell next to pomegranates, and finally one where bells are placed in pomegranates. This is not an arbitrary order but provides guidelines for the religious community: In isolated communities of Torah, only bells exist and easily fulfill their missions. In the present, Torah communities face a new mission of having to break away from their isolation to form mixed communities and transform all individuals into the golden bells; this transformation can only happen, however, when the pious is situated next to the unreligious, symbolized through the order of one bell and one pomegranate. Therefore, for Shas, religious communities are at the stage of reaching out to others and cannot isolate themselves. According to Deri, "detachment, separation, and erecting a wall [of separation]" is an easy solution. Yet "this is not our approach. . . . Rav Ovadia Yossef does not separate himself or erect any barriers. [He] feels their pain, teaches and guides, and offers counsel and instruction . . . works toward returning the nation to its heritage, and restoring the glory of Torah to its rightful place."[76]

The party-affiliated weekly repeatedly contrasts two different approaches regarding the secular bloc: "The first one is that of our leader, Yosef, who stands and works endlessly on behalf of the general good. The second approach centers on internal development, retreating to Torah study and solidifying our own fortresses."[77] The religious publics are called to this duty according to the recurring themes in the leaders' public speeches: Because "the nation's sins can work their way to the *kohen gadol* [the leading Torah priest], and lead even him to sin. Am Yisrael exists as a single body: an infection in the foot brings discomfort to every other part of the body. Then even the inadvertent sinner harms himself and the world. One who places his hand through fire suffers a burn whether he meant to or not, and one who falls is wounded, even if he slipped by accident. How fortunate we are, and how great is our lot, that the Creator guided us along the path of goodness and warned us of the stumbling blocks that bring about tragedy. And, if we do slip and fall—He has shown us the path of *teshuvah* [return to religion]!"[78] Similar statements promote the idea that Israel is about to reach the third stage of the ideal community, which requires the establishment of a Torah center within the city, "like a bell to fill the vacuum inside the hollow pomegranate." Therefore, Shas calls for the opening of "more and more Torah classes in all neighborhoods, more and more active rabbis of Batei Kenesset, flourishing communities—full Torah lives in every city and town!!"[79] As individuals turn to Torah, social problems will fade away, and the divine redemption will be received.

The emphasis on teshuvah might be an expected approach from a religious party. In the Israeli political context, however, such an approach is rather novel. For example, the leadership of Agudat Israel and the religious communities focus on their own perfection and social and intellectual isolation with strict commitment to Halakha.[80] The Mafdal leadership, on the other hand, believes that individual differences will be ultimately eliminated during the course of divine redemption, thereby delegitimizing the large-scale active recruitment of nonreligious Jews to Orthodox communities as a political priority. Shas's unique approach begs the question of why the party makes the "rapid massive expansion of Orthodoxy" its priority. Even if it is politically expedient, how can the party justify such an unconventional perspective, given its roots in the quiescent ultra-Orthodox world?

The answer can be gleaned from the party's interpretation of how the divine is related to the individual and in its understanding of redemption. As explained earlier in the case of Mafdal, redemption involves a social political change that follows a clearly laid-out Halakhic historical map to reach an eternally stable state. Redemption takes on a different meaning, however, in Shas's outlook. The divine is eager to reveal its redemption, but, according to Ovadia, the individuals simply fail to receive it: "The skies want to produce rain and the ground wants to give forth its produce. Blessing and prosperity want very much to burst forth in abundance."[81] This poses the crucial question of "if this is true, then why do so many crises and terrible disasters occur" and why is redemption still not complete? For Ovadia, the inability of individuals to discern the divine and to accept it is "draining its [blessings] to the very dregs, all the wicked of the earth drink. As a result of our sins, people absorb from this fancy wine only the harmful sediment. If only we perform *teshuvah* and increase our observance of mitzvot, then we can *remove the blockade and earn* the bounty of the goodness of blessing" (emphases added).[82] The failure to follow mitzvoth is at the heart of the nation's social problems and the cause for the failure in unfolding of the divine redemption. Thus, teshuvah is a movement toward creating a permanent stable political community. In Deri's words, "If we desire life, if we are interested in bringing the redemption closer, then we have no choice: we must work with all our might against those who destroy us. We must form an opposing weight, closing the breached areas and building additional layers. We must dig the wells anew, so that they give forth fresh water to provide spiritual life, bring an end to our troubles. We ourselves have no concept of how critical a role we play in the elimination of our troubles and speeding the redemption—even the empty ones among us are filled with *mitzvot!*"[83]

In order to expand the religious community, the party familiarizes those who are foreign to the religious world with the rules of ultra-Orthodoxy. For example, rather than focusing exclusively on theological debates, Ovadia Yosef's weekly sermons are loaded with stories, analogies, and cynical remarks, which often outrage the secular public. Shas's approach is geared first and foremost to making the traditional and secular Jews religiously observant, rather than converting them to ultra-Orthodoxy directly. In an ironic way, Shas's desire to create a community of Torah allowed it to focus on individuals and open its religious tradition to the needs of newcomers. Since collective redemption cannot happen without individual redemption, the teshuvah movement tries to accommodate individual differences. The expansion of the Torah community does not need to be a radical transformation of the community or of a person's life. In fact, Shas circles refrain from using the term *teshuvah*, or penitence, which implies a rupture and drastic upheaval in one's beliefs and practices. Instead, offering an example of its internal secularization the party uses *hit'hazkut*, spiritual strengthening.[84]

The lenient policies Shas adopts to expand hit'hazkut pose the question of whether the party has launched a Sephardization drive under the guise of neo-ultra-Orthodoxy and whether or how the teshuvah movement will create a homogeneous community. Two visions of community compete in the religious and political imaginary of Shas leadership: creating a community of Torah or placing the Sephardi minhag at the center of Israel's religious traditions. However, many of Yosef's and Deri's statements adopt the recurring theme that one needs to follow one's tradition. The Shas leadership appears to regard "tribes," or cultural religious groups, as their political reference point instead of the nation-state. For some observers of Sephardi tradition such as Zvi Zohar, Shas's leadership approach is rooted in the distinctive Sephardim historical experience: "the Sephardim have the notion that community should pre-empt ideology; you should not, because of your ideology and belief, break apart the unity of the community; and *it is better to have a community which is internally diverse than it is to have several communities which are internally consistent."* (emphases added)[85]

Shas's depiction of community further differs from Mafdal's with respect to its relationship to the lands. For Yosef, according to pikuach nefesh, the Halakhic principle of the protection of Jewish life, the positive commandment to settle the land is preceded by the commandment to avoid unnecessary loss of life. "If the heads of the army with the members of the government declare that lives will be endangered unless territories in the Land of Israel are relinquished, and there is the danger of an immediate declaration of war by the neighboring Arab [states], . . . and, if territories are relinquished the danger of war will be removed, and that there are realistic chances of lasting peace, then it appears, according to all opinions, that it is permissible to relinquish territories of the Land of Israel."[86] In the remainder of the ruling, however, Rabbi Yosef also notes that military officers, government officials, and security experts are divided on this issue. Some have concluded that withdrawal from the territories could increase the dangers, and he suggests that these opposing views should also be considered.[87] Beside its unique position that challenges the sanctity of the land, the idea of basing the applicability of a religious rule on the expert's view is quite a novel step in the religious world.

The way Yosef referred to the pikuach nefesh principle contradicts the central role assigned to the land by religious Zionism and further shifts Shas away from the conventional Haredi world. For some observers of Israeli politics, the party elite strategically adopted this position just to better position itself as a potential coalition partner. Such interpretation has a massive effect in the symbolic world of religion, regardless of its political rationale and implications. Once symbols become sacred and are believed to be inherently accurate and beyond the reach of politics, challenging their meanings requires a significant shift in the overall network of religious interpretation. It is not Ovadia's decision per se, but the discursive sphere it opened in the Haredi world that carries significant weight.

Despite the reactions, Yosef's statements did not remain alone. The party's political leadership expanded this discursive sphere with further arguments. For instance, Deri also argued that the Jewish nation had not reached a state of permanence as long as it was surrounded by enemies. "The only true feeling of permanence is when we are in the *bet hamidrash*, in the study hall. Establishing additional settlements in the Shomron will not guarantee our existence, and will not add to our security. The opposite is true; it will only increase the hatred of our enemies."[88] Given the priority of creating a Torah community, Shas sees maintaining unity within the Jewish community and saving it from conflicts as more important than establishing settlements. Overall, Shas's ideas create a community-centered

Orthodoxy as opposed to the land-centered Orthodoxy of religious Zionism. The debate surrounding pikuach nefesh exemplifies how the same religious term lends itself to polarized policy positions. Even if its justification of territorial compromise is only a rhetorical appeal, Shas has managed to question from within the religious bloc some well-entrenched thoughts that have dominated the religious Zionist and ultra-Orthodox worlds.

Inclusiveness Versus Exclusiveness of the Shas Social Program: Unity in a Communal Pluralism?

Shas's origin as an ethnic movement and the focal point of the Sephardi identity suggests that it is an ethnically exclusive party. Before drawing any conclusions, however, we need to address some crucial questions that are often buried under the party's ethnically colored language: What is the Sephardim's common interest that the party earnestly strives to enhance? More importantly, what groups actually constitute the so-called Sephardi community? On what grounds does Shas claim to represent them? Tackling these questions requires us to revisit the use of the term *ethnicity* in general and *Sephardi* in particular. Because of the strong emphasis on the unity of the Jewish people, the plurality of ethnicities is a contested area in which religious ethnic claims do not translate into appreciated political currency in either religious or secular circles. Therefore, the rise of a Sephardi ethnic identity movement is a critical question in its own right. Nevertheless, any attempt to understand the ideas of the Shas leadership necessitates a disentanglement of the highly loaded term *Sephardi*.

Ethnic identity in general signifies a group of people who identify with one another (i.e., claimed) or are identified by others (i.e., ascribed) on the basis of a boundary drawn by their common racial, cultural, linguistic, or religious traits. When we apply this simplified definition to the Sephardi identity, its complex nature comes to the fore immediately. In contrast to a conventional ethnic identity that emphasizes a common language or a shared geographical and/or ancestral origin, the Sephardi identity is defined by none of these. Sephardi have their origins in areas ranging from Argentina and Yemen to Iran and Bukhara and speak languages that include Ladino, Arabic, Persian, and Bukharian. Although many groups subsumed under the name Sephardi have upheld the teaching of the same Torah sages, the sage Yosef Karo in particular, this unity was only created after the groups moved to Israel. Karo, who was expelled from Spain in 1488, lived in places such as Greece, Turkey, and Egypt before settling in Safed, Israel. Besides the common guidance of *Shulkan Aruch*, Karo's major work, Sephardim share the cultural marks left by the predominantly Muslim countries in which they lived. What distinguishes Sephardi from other groups in Israel is their distance from the dominant views of both the religious and secular blocs.

The breadth of cultural and lingual diversity represented by Sephardim raises questions of how Shas brings these very different groups together, how it forges a sense of unity out of diverse experiences, and how it explains its ethnic platform and policies in religious terms. In the views of Shas's leadership, the Sephardim relinquished their dominant position in Israel on the expectation that it would promote the unity of the Jewish people. The concessions were made for the purpose of expanding the Jewish community around its local culture; this actually resulted in their removal to the periphery of Israel's political, cultural, and religious life.

Ovadia Yosef's mentor, Ezra Attiah, the head of Yeshivat Porat Yosef between 1925 and 1970, provides a striking account of how Ashkenazi and Sephardi communities were gradually detached from one another as the Ashkenazim started to play a dominant role. According to his students, during Attiah's meetings with Agudat Israel's Council of Torah Sages, he could not understand the participants because they spoke in Yiddish. Despite the language barrier, he continued to attend and was uplifted by observing their gatherings.[89] Such meetings eventually led to the establishment of Yiddish as the main language of the ultra-Orthodox community. Yet instead of creating unity, the consolidation of Ashkenazi traditions occurred at the expense of the peripheralization of others. This gradually increasing and pervasive Ashkenazi hegemony amounted to the destruction of the religious core of those who shared the characteristics of neither the Ashkenazi ultra-Orthodox nor the secular elite. The economic and political weakening of the Sephardim exacerbated this exclusion, creating a vicious cycle in which Sephardim felt culturally and politically trapped. This background explains why the locus of Shas's appeal lies in the idea that all cultural-religious groups and tribes prosper in their original religious tradition. Breaking the vicious cycle requires first and foremost that the Sephardim reclaim their lost traditions.

Shas's view of the Sephardi identity demonstrates the confluence of ethnic, religious, and political positions. The name *Sephardi* does not describe an already existing community; instead it gathers the claims of various groups who seek to change their socioeconomic and political status vis-à-vis the dominant segment of society. The Sephardi identity is introduced as a positive and uniform character, in some cases constituting a stricter religious identity than that of the Ashkenazi tradition. It is defined by the group's differences from others, not by its commonalities. The party's motto of "restoring the throne to its rightful place" refers to the era before the Ashkenazi domination, *pax Sephardi.*

The main ideas expressed in Yosef's decisions and sermons carefully distinguish Sephardi practices from those of Ashkenazim, and he raises them to a central position when addressing current political questions. His approach combines a reevaluation and revaluation of Sephardi and Ashkenazi customs in various forms: "A Sephardi who generally attends a Bet Kenesset of Ashkenazim should make a point of listening to this reading from one who reads with the Sephardic pronunciation," says Yosef.[90] Based on its Halakhic premise that one should follow his or her tradition, many of Yosef's explanations normalize Sephardim cultural practices that have been marginalized under the Ashkenazi hegemony. In some cases, Yosef goes to the other extreme to make the distinctiveness a norm: "[A] Sephardi is not permitted to change his accent or pronunciation. This is true even if he is the *shaliah sibur* among Ashkenazim (and vice versa)."[91] Yosef's decision not only justifies already existing differences, it also challenges the notion that Sephardi pronunciation is neither up to the standard of high Hebrew nor the effective language of ultra-Orthodoxy. Perhaps more importantly, he repeats the main premise of the Shas movement: that Sephardi tradition is the authentic tradition of the land and thus has primacy. For instance, "Sephardi pronunciation is more proper and authentic than that of Ashkenazim, and many Ashkenazi rabbis went out of their way to learn Sephardic pronunciation."[92] This view reverses the overall approach that languages used by Ashkenazim, such as Yiddish, are the more authentic venues to study Torah and suggests that Sephardi practices, currently relegated to the margins of secular and ultra-Orthodox society, need to be reclaimed. Rather than being simple or deformed, "Proper pronunciation (Sephardi pronunciation) is difficult, and it behooves each person to learn pronunciation properly."[93] Thus, many of these religious norms promote a shared sense of identity among Sephardim and reinforce their religious traits.

An overall look at the ideas informing the Shas movement shows that instead of expressing an already well-defined Sephardi identity, the movement is trying to create one out of a multiplicity of traditions. Yosef's codification of the Sephardi religious rules and his discussions of political leadership play a central role in defining this identity. The emphasis on distinctive Sephardi religious traditions justifies the unique conditions and traits of Sephardim in other fields. "Diligent" explanations of religious rules carefully construct alternative practices for the hegemonic ones. One of the recurring statements clarifies the approach: "According to the authorities among the Ashkenazim, the practice is this, but *We*, however, follow the ruling of the Shulhan Aruch and differ."[94] Such statements end with a simple comparison that shows the differences. After all, to strengthen religious communities, Halakha allows each person to follow his or her own tradition.[95] Thus, Yosef's meticulous codification of the Sephardi rules is more than reviving a tradition; it is forging a new frame of religious reference for his followers. Therefore, labeling Shas an ethnic ultra-Orthodox sectarian party masks how the party developed a religiously grounded ethnic language not only to express but also to shape the Sephardi identity.

The political success of Shas's religious-ethnic appeal requires a discussion of the overall political position of religion in Israel and its manifestation in Israel's political context. It is not the ultra-Orthodox opposition to the secular world but the implications of internal tensions in the ultra-Orthodox world that define Shas's successful ideology. More significant still is Israel's multilayered power structure and the hegemonic role of religion in legitimizing political demands. In many areas, religion mediates the individual's relationship to the state and offers a unique venue to engage in political negotiations. Immigration policies and the immigration status of a community turn into questions about the religious origins of communities and the authenticity of their Jewishness. The recent immigration of members of the Ethiopian Jewish community has stirred the greatest controversy. The Shas leadership regards the treatment of Ethiopians as a prime example of the marginalization of the non-European Jewry. Given that religious decisions are the most decisive element of the immigration discourse, Yosef's statements carry great weight, not only in religious circles, but also for government decisions. When the Ethiopians' religious identity was questioned, Yosef's input was influential, primarily because Israel's power-sharing structure places the religious leadership in the position of one of the key authorities on this issue. Using stark language, Yosef concluded, "I will not fear [to comment on] what I saw from R. Yitzhak Isaav Halevy Herzog . . . who wrote to question the Jewishness of the Falashas. . . . I was very surprised to see that he disputed the words of great scholars who determined with certainty, without question, that they [Ethiopians] are from the tribe of Dan."[96] This simple statement was crucial for authenticating the Ethiopians' identity. In Israel, ethnic discussions are basically discussions of religious roots. Yosef's ideas and Shas's policies on ethnic issues are affirmed by the existing political structure.

The latitude Shas's leadership has in articulating and justifying political demands raises the question of whether they opt for confrontational ethnic policies to capitalize on the politically expedient issue areas that were, in part, created by the systemic role assigned to religion and the changing ethnic power structure. In his response to questions from Shas supporters, Deri uses the conflict between Abel, the shepherd, and Cane, the farmer, to explain the overall political approach of the party:

What was Abel doing in the field, in Cane's domain? . . . At first Cane started an argument with his brother: "Cane spoke to Abel . . ." What should Abel have done? He should have ignored his brother, but, instead, he decided to try to persuade Cane of his own stance. He was therefore drawn to Cane's field to continue the argument, unaware that arguments are ineffective. To the contrary, they reinforce the feelings of animosity, they push the participants into corners, arouse violence and force. As we know, tragically, the end was bitter indeed.[97]

Deri's conclusion is pertinent to modern politics: one should not leave one's domain and try to confront others to change practices. Abel's futile attempts to confront Cane only increased the animosity between them. Likewise, confrontational politics to alter the status of Sephardim or Haredim would be only counterproductive. Instead of polarization, there are many people in Israel who fall into transitional domains: "The majority of Jews in Israel are believers. They attend synagogue services, they are connected to our heritage, some more and some less." Given the presence of the overall religiously lenient public, the solution is not to confront the small minority but sow the seeds for a new domain. "If the networks decide to schedule programs for the minority, who insist on desecrating that which is sacred, then so be it. We have no business listening to their programs. Let them listen to their own venom, they can have their friends, whose opinions correspond to their own, listen to their shows. We have our own radio hosts, and plenty of listeners waiting to hear what they have to say."[98] The party's strategy appears not to be focused on the secular or Ashkenazi opponents, but on attracting an acceptable religious following for building a broad political domain and for creating alternative options that attract others to the party.

Consistent with the party's rhetorical argument and in contrast to Mafdal's desire to engage in dialogue, Shas sends its messages mostly through its own communication channels. Besides the extensive broadcasting, the leadership led the establishment of one of the most extensive educational, social, and school network systems in Israel, called *El Ha'maayan* (to the wellspring), which embodies various aspects of the party's ideology and its conundrums. In its founding statement El Ha'maayan lists as its goal to (1) promote the traditional and Jewish values of religious Jewry in Israel, (2) advance religious Jewish education in the educational system in Israel, (3) advocate the improvement of religious services, (4) bolster the quality of religious life, and (5) supply the religious needs of haredi religious Jewry.[99] These broad goals, which seek to integrate religion into the lives of many, contradict some specific terms of the contract the Shas schools sign with their teachers. For instance, teachers in Shas schools are not allowed to take labor disputes to the secular courts. The institutions also enforce strict gender segregation.[100] Despite their strict rules, the schools still provide unique employment opportunities and tuition rates for ultra-Orthodox groups. The party-sponsored, wide-ranging, low-cost services turned into an instrument for reaching a previously nonaccessible part of the public. Activities in El Ha'maayan address every community need, including fertility clinics, cheap produce markets, occupational training, religious lessons for adults, support for the absorption of immigrants, and funds for yeshivot, religious higher education.[101]

Furthermore, Shas's network also claims to provide a stable environment, especially for those who are caught between different lifestyles. In the words of Deri, the party-sponsored meeting places and schools are invaluable shelters because

the lives of youngsters are stormy. So many different forces influence them. Considering the destructive forces that yield so much power, they need an educational system that can combine general studies—language, mathematics, and computers—with the treasures of the *siddur* and the spiritual wealth of our heritage—*Tanach*, *Midrashim*, *Mishnah* and *Gemara*. They need this not only to become Torah scholars—though why not?—but in order that they grow rooted in faith, attached to their ancestral heritage, devoted to their parents, and emerge as adults with fine qualities and character.[102]

Although Shas's school system appears to consist of loosely tied, community-based schools that cater to the party's supporters, perhaps the Shas leadership's most important accomplishment was to add its school system as a new pillar to Israel's official educational system. This recognition by the state legitimizes Shas as an established bloc and provides the party with a share of the state budget without being subject to strict state control.[103] According to Shas reports released in early 1999, state funds and volunteer donations together enabled the party to expand its educational network to 682 kindergartens, 86 day-care centers, 146 elementary schools, and 50 junior high schools. The numbers translate into a total of 40,000 students, 2,400 teachers, principals, and supervisors, and 2,200 kindergarten teachers and teacher aides, in a country where the national threshold for a seat in the Knesset representation is 25,936 votes.[104] Instead of viewing education as a means to establish a more homogeneous community, statements of leaders such as Rabbi Reuven Elbaz present the party's training as an effort toward summoning redemption from its dormant state.[105]

The party leadership's ability to establish a nationwide network has had mixed results. Placing the party's social service institutions at the center of their respective communities has resulted in an increase in school hours, a lower student-teacher ratio, and an increasing number of teachers. The *Ma'ayan Hahinuch Hatorani* network has 7 children per teacher, while the secular school system nationwide reports one teacher per 10.5 students.[106] Yet with this success, the leadership faces a dilemma inherent in its policies overall. Given that the party funds this system mostly through the state budget, the more the Shas community expands and becomes autonomous, the more its dependence on the state increases and requires it to open its system to state scrutiny. Although a parallel expansion of its electoral support strengthens the party, its harsher tone in budget negotiations alienates moderate supporters. Reflecting the incongruous position of the state in Shas rhetoric, it appears to be an institution that is needed to improve the condition of the community but that also needs to be avoided when possible. In addition, the more the party has to rely on the state to continue and expand its services, the more it needs to prove its Haredi identity. Despite, or perhaps due to, its dependency on state funding, Shas focuses on a bottom-to-top solution to restore the status of religion. When faced with specific issues that can be achieved by private initiative, Deri turns to the public and nonstate elite: "This matter is not in the hands of the politicians. It is completely in the hands of the administrators of intellectual institutions, and doctors at all levels. They are the experts in the rights of the minority and public welfare, individual freedoms and all those beautiful words. . . . Yet the answer given is that the hatred and estrangement have reached such a level, have poisoned to such an extent, have brought about such thoughtlessness in the general public."[107]

Shas's emphasis on community, as opposed to the state and land, manifests itself best in its policies toward Arab populations. Pikuach nefesh, protection of Jewish life, once again surfaces as a guiding principle. The leadership accommodates coexistence with other communities to avoid animosity and to "save Jewish lives." "I was asked by God-fearing physicians," says Ovadia, "who work in public hospitals, even on Sabbath, whether they are allowed to treat gentile patients even if it would mean violating Torah prohibitions." The answer shows the underlying logic of similar decisions. "In our times, when there is fear of greater animosity in the world, if Jewish doctors forbore from treating non-Jews . . . if non-Jewish doctors heard this they would stop treating Jewish patients."[108] These explanations, although rooted in the idea of protecting Jewish community, enhance the sense of coexistence. Yet in areas where protection of life is not a primary concern, we see a different level of acceptance. Attesting to the cultural proximity between different Sephardi communities in predominantly Muslim countries, Ovadia permits the use of melodies "from non-holy sources for the singing of holy lyrics during prayers."[109] This decision applies mostly to Arab music that Rabbi Yosef himself favors and that is used by many Sephardi rabbis.[110] Perhaps more important is Yosef's consistent referral to Arabs and Moslems as non-idolaters. In the religious symbolic world, granting Muslims and Arabs such status allows their inclusion into certain practices and gives them the right to dwell in the land of Israel. Referring to the rule that excludes idolaters from the land of Israel, he states that "this applies only to idolaters—Moslems are

not considered idolaters by the majority of early Rabbinic authorities."
By taking this stance, Shas does not reduce the current Jewish-Arab tension to a religious dispute. Instead, Muslims are integrated into Yosef's
teaching as an adjacent tribe. In a myriad of his rulings one can find statements such as this: "If a non-Jew [like a Muslim] who does not worship
idolatry, makes one of the blessings instituted by our sages, one may answer amen to it. However, if an idolatrous non-Jew makes such a blessing,
we suspect that he may have had idolatrous intentions, and thus we are
forbidden to answer amen to his blessing."[111]

Underlying Shas's approach to other groups is the party's perception of
"tribes" as the main unit of political unity and the belief that the people
of Israel are destined to live in distinctive communities. As a result of the
party's emphasis on tribes living next to each other, the leadership accepts
the extension of the social network that benefits Arab constituencies. Mohammed Barakei, the leader of Hadash, a secular Arab-led party, publicly
announced his support for Shas. Although this coalition was in part
rooted in Shas's antisystemic rhetoric, an endorsement of an ultra-
Orthodox party by an Arab party is a political miracle in itself. Barakei
stated, "an alliance of *Mizrahim* (Sephardim) and Arabs, those who have
been discriminated against [is natural politically]," as both groups seek to
carve out a place in Israeli politics.[112] In Deri's opinion, the party received
electoral support from many Arab precincts because of Shas's "genuine
effort to correct what was done by positive discrimination."[113] Although
the extent and the stability of such a coalition is very questionable, the acceptance of a religious party by the Palestinian population is very indica-
tive of Shas's sweeping power of mobilization and its ability to reach segments of the society beyond the immediate scope of religious politics.
However, Shas's political aspirations to transcend the boundaries of ultra-
Orthodoxy do not free it from its desire to appeal to the Haredi world altogether. In the ultra-Orthodox world, the party tries to show that it remains true to its original haredi identity. Through both its positions and
efforts to make itself relevant as a viable political option for different
communities, Shas has transformed many of the conventional Halakhic
views from within and spread them via its social network, thereby creating political positions that are out of the reach of other parties.

The Shas Leadership

Shas's leadership structure reflects the complexity of its policies and
ideology. For instance, despite the prevalent notion among observers of
Israeli politics that the party was established under the leadership of the
ex-Sephardi Chief Rabbi Ovadia Yosef, the party's political elite has

stated that Ovadia endorsed Shas only after the movement had begun independently in Jerusalem.[114] Paradoxically, after Yosef supported the movement, the Lithuanian Ashkenazi Rabbi Eliezer Menahem Schach assumed the spiritual leadership of the party. Schach's leadership of the Sephardi movement seems contradictory at first, but it allows us to understand the structure of the ultra-Orthodox bloc and the internal constraints on forming a separate political movement. Having a Lithuanian rabbi lead the Shas party was neither paradoxical nor a coincidence. One reason is that Lithuanian schools have always been more open to Sephardi students than other Ashkenazi schools due to their emphasis on the transformative power of religious education. In fact, the party's leader, Aryeh Deri, himself was recruited by a Lithuanian school. Second, after the end of the one-party dominant system, the political competition within the Right bloc intensified. The diversification of politics challenged the hegemony of the Agudat in the religious bloc and brought to the fore the ethnic-religious fault lines within the ultra-Orthodox world. Finally, Sephardim, lacking an independent religious or secular political bloc, became both the main target of political competition for other parties as well as a potent force for forming a new political movement. Schach's Lithuanian religious leadership of a Sephardi party reflected this transitional phase in Israeli politics and captured the changing map of the ultra-Orthodox bloc. The current spiritual leadership established itself only after the party leadership dethroned Schach and cut its ties with Agudat Israel. Perhaps the most revolutionary aspect of the Shas movement was its effectiveness within the religious bloc rather than the secular world.

Since the beginning of the movement, Shas's leadership has rested on two intertwined pillars: religious and political leadership. The period from 1983 to 1992 constituted the party's formative years, while the years from 1992 to 2003 amounted to a consolidation of its power. Unlike Mafdal, which was formed in the Diaspora addressing the question of the nature of the emerging state, the Shas movement responded to local concerns and reactions regarding the complexities of the Israeli system. According to Nissim Zeev, the movement was formed as a result of Agudat Israel's decision to have two different branches of education for girls: one with an academic emphasis and one with a vocational emphasis. Confirming well-entrenched exclusionary patterns, all Sephardi girls were chosen for the vocational branch in spite of the intense opposition from Sephardi circles. When a group of Sephardim ran on an independent candidate list during the Jerusalem municipal elections of 1982, they revolutionized the ultra-Orthodox world. The rise of Shas needs to be seen against the background of the ultra-Orthodox bloc with its own diversity and highly hierarchical pillarized structure. The rigid structure, as well as the overall position of Sephardim within the religious bloc, left Shas's leaders no choice but to accept the mentoring of the Lithuanian Rabbi Schach. The selection of Shas's first leader, Yitzhak Peretz, who was closer to Schach than Yosef, attests to the extent of this influence.

The 1992 election campaign marked an important turning point for the party's leadership. Ironically, perhaps due to the unexpected growth of the movement, Schach stated his opposition to a completely independent Sephardi party by declaring publicly, "the time has not yet come for Sephardim to take positions of leadership" and as a result "Sephardim should not be allowed to take control of the whole Yishuv."[115] Schach's overt opposition to Shas's defection from the Agudat bloc led to its consolidation as an independent Sephardi ultra-Orthodox movement.[116] Shas's emergence is intriguing, not because of the party's opposition to the secular world, but because of the reaction of the Haredim to an ethnic Sephardi party.

Yosef's personal history captures the social developments that affected the formation of the religious elite active in today's Israeli politics. Unlike many Sephardim who moved to Israel after the establishment of the state, Yosef moved to Jerusalem in 1920, when he was three or four years old. Although coming from Baghdad, a city with many Jewish scholars, Yosef did not belong to any established religious family.[117] Despite his Sephardi background, he had to attend an Ashkenazi yeshiva first (a Sephardi one was not available), thereby immersing himself both in Ashkenazi and Sephardi religious traditions. Yosef's establishment of himself as a religious scholar was prompted by the decline of Sephardi hegemony in Jerusalem. His service in Egypt consolidated his tie to the non-Ashkenazi culture and helped him forge a unique style that allowed him to combine the tenets of different symbolic spheres. As captured in Yosef's habitual practice of commenting on Ashkenazi traditions while listening to Arab music, Shas has distinguished itself with its ability to inhabit several worlds simultaneously.[118]

Ovadia contradicts the images of religious leaders as local and insular. He is neotraditional in the sense that he redefines religious traditions, making them relevant to urgent, contemporary questions. He himself is a self-accomplished Torah scholar and thus represents not a traditional lineage, but the importance of achieving religious status. His unconventional ideas draw on his expertise and intricate positions vis-à-vis tradition. More specifically, his legitimacy results from (1) his expertise in both the Ashkenazi and Sephardi traditions, (2) his understanding of other Sephardi communities gained during his tenure as chief rabbi in Egypt, and (3) the recognition he achieved from 1973 to 1982 as the chief Sephardi rabbi, the highest religious state office in Israel. In general, scholars assess Shas's political appeal by its impact on the secular world; however, what makes Yosef and Shas revolutionary agents is their ability to challenge the settled power relations and dominant traditions of the ultra-Orthodox world dominated by Agudat Israel. By creating an alternative Council of Sages, Ovadia Yosef not only became the spiritual leader of the party, he also forged an additional religious authority. The Shas council includes seven rabbis from countries as diverse as Bukhara, Yemen, Tunisia, and Morocco. Ironically, although the Council of Sages plays a central role in the formation of the party's policies, the council's decisions often carry an advisory tone. Announcements stress that decisions are reached through a series of consultations that include the political leadership. The political leadership statements claim that the council's decisions are not binding. Aryeh Deri, for example, has explained the relationship between the political and religious leadership as the relationship between advisory and executive bodies:

I took it upon myself to accept his [Ovadia Yosef's] decisions, and I have never been disappointed. Conversations with Ovadia are a cleansing of the mind. It's not like a dictate. It's a discussion. And although sometimes I have disagreed with decisions made, in retrospect I also saw the wisdom in them. I know this is difficult for you to understand. But believe me, I wish every politician had an authority like this to turn to. It's good to have a division between men of thought and men of action.[119]

Nevertheless, the line separating the decisions of the political leadership from those of the religious leadership is rather blurred, as the decision prior to the 1996 election of the prime minister shows. The resolutions are phrased in a way that suggests that the religious leadership consults with other branches in the party before formulating a decision. Given the secrecy of the council's meetings, it is hard to gauge whether the Sages rubber stamp the spiritual or political leadership's decisions.

Despite its short history, Shas has had two spiritual and three political leaders or party chairmen so far: Rabbi Schach, Rabbi Ovaida Yosef, Rabbi Yitzhak Peretz, Aryeh Deri, and Eli Yishau. The changes in the leadership correspond to the public scrutiny it receives as well as the rapid transformation of the party.[120] The first leader was chosen due to Schach's influence on the party. Aryeh Deri's leadership announced Shas's political independence from Schach. After all, Deri is one of the members of Yosef's inner circle. Yosef trusted him as a tutor to his children and later as leader of the party. It is noteworthy that Ovadia's sons, even after Deri lost office, did not claim the political leadership, possibly reserving their bid for the spiritual leadership of the party. Regardless, the dominant role of Ovadia raises the question of how the party will reinvent itself after Ovadia's spiritual leadership ends.

By some accounts, Yitzak Peretz, the first leader of the movement, was a rather random choice except for his closeness to Rabbi Schach.[121] Searching for a moderate who would also appeal to the Ashkenazi Lithuanian public, Peretz's name was found on a list of rabbis. Peretz was serving as the chief Sephardic rabbi of Raananna and was not active in the formation of the movement before he became the leader of the Shas party. Indeed, Peretz sought to appeal to the party's main opponents, and he defined the party's raison d'etre *not* as a challenge to Zionist secularism.[122] His closeness to Schach and his exclusive rhetoric in his position as minister of absorption of new immigrants eventually led to his resignation. Aryeh Deri's intraparty coup, the decision to join the Labor government, which qualified Shas as the first ultra-Orthodox party to collaborate politically with the secular bloc, helped secure Peretz's departure.

It would not be an exaggeration to argue that it is under Deri's leadership that Shas has found its niche in Israeli politics. Deri, a Moroccan Jew, came to Israel at the age of nine. When he was recruited by a Lithuanian religious school, his decision to attend was motivated mostly by the financial support offered. His family maintained its traditional Moroccan identity, while Deri became more religious than they were. Deri's emphasis on how the Shas school system transforms parents reflects his own experience. More importantly, Deri's ability to function in both the secular and religious worlds reflects his social background rather than an adopted ideology. Although seen as a rising star and becoming the youngest minister ever in Israel's history, Deri's political career ended upon his conviction for bribery. Binjamin Netanyahu was also one of the accused, but Deri was the only one convicted. Deri's resignation led to the emergence of another leader, Eli Yishau, whose career started in the shadow of Deri's legacy.

The leadership changes were initiated under unique circumstances, yet as a whole they show a rather active and resilient political leadership. Despite the lack of clearly identified factions within the party, there is some evidence that Deri represented a more moderate and pragmatic side of the party than Eli Yishau, who comes from a more conservative part of the movement. Peretz's brief leadership and his de facto ousting reflect some of the party's emerging modus operandi, in that a conflict with the religious leadership is highly likely to be resolved by excluding the member from the party. Deri's political views epitomized the reasons for the party's defection from the Agudat bloc and its integration into the Israeli political system as an independent agent with hybrid characteristics. Under Deri, Shas has publicly stated and shown its willingness and ability to cooperate with the Zionist secular Labor Movement. Similarly, Shas's clear objection to counter acculturation and isolation allowed the party to consolidate its bivalence (i.e., its ability to inhabit and appeal to the secular and religious worlds at the same time). For instance, the rhetoric used by Shas's leadership allows it to challenge immigration policies not only as anti-Halakhic, but also as ethnically discriminating. However, the leadership must constantly prove its ultra-Orthodox identity. The leadership's remark that "we are Zionist" is often accompanied by the statement that Shas is no "less Haredi than other parties."

Deri's conviction for bribery actually strengthened the party's overall political arguments since the Sephardi Deri was convicted, while similar charges against non-Sephardi Benjamin Netanyahu, Likud's leader (or "the leader of Likud"), were dropped. According to the leadership, the court proceedings proved that Shas skeptics treat the party and its leadership unfairly. They believed Deri was convicted because of Shas's ability to challenge the Ashkenazi-dominated secular elite. The party also referred to the infamous Dreyfus affair by turning it into a popular campaign slogan, "J'accuse," and by distributing more than two hundred thousand copies of a 72-minute videocassette, which portrayed Deri's trial as an unfair prosecution. After being convicted, the charismatic Deri was followed by Eli Yishau, showing that the religious leadership preferred to continue existing policies with a leader who was very familiar with the party's network. Yishau had been active in the party at different levels, as head of Shas's educational system, El Ha'maayan, and as Minister of Labor. Yishau's leadership lacks Deri's charismatic appeal but demonstrates that the party has a consistent ideology and that leadership changes do not result in radical policy shifts.

The background of Shas's political leadership and the party's Knesset members reveals that, despite some variations, the leaders have a common profile that differs from that of other party elites. A majority of the Shas elite received their education in Talmudic colleges, and they are first- or second-generation immigrants, mostly from predominantly Muslim countries. A significant proportion of them had community work experience in the Shas-affiliated educational and welfare system. In 1999, seven of the seventeen Knesset members were immigrants from Morocco, Russia, and Georgia, or were children of immigrants. Only two had bachelor's degrees in education. The party's members of parliament are quite young, on average only thirty-nine years old, making them the youngest members of parliament. With their predominantly non-Ashkenazi backgrounds and youthful ages, the Shas elite can be described as a "counter-elite." In 2003, the party maintained its profile, with the youngest average age and representatives fluent in both Hebrew and Arabic.

One of the party elite, Sholomo Benizri, shows that the party leadership is not a pure product of the ultra-Orthodox world, but also accommodates newcomers. Benizri turned to religion only during his military service in Hermon in 1980 at the age of nineteen. He attended the Or Hahaim Yeshivah in Jerusalem, a leading venue for the newly religious

Sephardim. In 1992 he was placed on the list to represent Reuben Elbaz, the head of Or haim. Benizri operates in two worlds: attesting to the complexity of his background, he plays basketball (an unconventional position in an ultra-Orthodox world), but he refuses to play in the Knesset team because it includes females. [123] Like Deri, his parents are not as religious as he is, and they remain merely traditional. In such profiles of the leadership one can find the intricacies of Shas's political stance, where the ultra-Orthodoxy of Sephardim does not express itself in a strict structure but contributes to a new version of ultra-Orthodoxy.

CONCLUSION

While the ultra-Orthodox Haredi world chooses to only live next to the secular world, religious parties such as Mafdal and Shas, like other religious parties that establish themselves as pivotal actors, actually deal with the secular world and face the question of how to incorporate the problems and issues posed by different groups into their ideologies. Although Mafdal and Shas are perceived as part of the religious bloc, they use religious doctrines and approach politics in radically different ways. The popular election slogans of Mafdal and Shas capture the contrasting positions of these parties in the Israeli political space. While Mafdal describes itself as a proponent of "Zionism with soul," arguing that its mission is to complement Zionism, Shas promotes itself as a new political movement by asserting that it is "neither Right nor Left"; "Shas is an Identity." While Mafdal seeks to complement Zionism, Shas seeks to support a new religio-political identity that promotes Judaism for the soul among the Sephardim and in Israel. Religious groups differ in the ways in which they approach Zionism, incorporate religious ethnic differences, and view the role of individual or community in their idealized polity. Therefore, diversity within a given religious doctrine and across religious parties is not an exception but needs to be seen as unavoidable and perhaps as the norm. This is why Mafdal's and Shas's ideologies often draw opposing political conclusions from similar religious reference points (see table 3.1). The parties' distinctive approaches to Halakha bring to the fore the importance of the leadership for their endorsement of one interpretation at the expense of others and as one of the main driving forces of diversification in the religious bloc. Nevertheless, the leadership alone cannot explain the differences. The role of the leadership needs to be placed within the context of the broader political conditions. Contrasting interpretations of the two central terms in the Jewish tradition, redemption and pikuach nefesh, provide excellent examples of

TABLE 3.1

A comparison of the ideological premises of Mafdal and Shas

	Mafdal	Shas
Hegemonic nationalism	Supportive (Regardless of its façade, Zionism is inherently a religious project.)	Critical but also supportive (Zionism must be pluralized including ethnic Zionism, e.g., Sephardi Zionism)
Nation	Combines global ethnic unity and territorial sanctity	Pluralistic communal; nation consists of communities
State	Supportive; treat it as sacred as it supports redemption	Indifferent to the state as long as it supports Jewishness of the community
Authority of religious leadership	Loose authority of religious leadership	Strict authority of religious leadership
Individual vs. community	Individuals are ultimate unit	Community is ultimate unit
Inclusive vs. exclusive	In ideology: inclusive, considering the differences in the Jewish community. In practice: exclusive, considering non-Ashkenazi groups and Palestinians	In ideology: critical of groups that challenge the purity of communities. In practice: inclusive, considering Jewish community and to a certain degree Palestinians
Dominant process	Sacralization	Internal secularization

how the Jewish symbolic sphere can sustain multiple and often opposing political positions. While Mafdal integrates secular terms and makes them a part of its vision of the unilinear history projected in Halakha, Shas's encounter with the history of Israel and the pressing questions that inflict the party-affiliated communities constantly transforms its religious stances to address them.

The parties' understandings of redemption offer them different paradigms for their assessment of the main trends in politics. Mafdal believes that the future is not open-ended and that today's politics are merely an opportunity to secure the unfolding divine journey. Ovadia Yosef's responsa indicates that Shas is, in a sense, ultrarealist and that it clearly opposes constructing policies around "teleological" views; for example, Ovadia states, "In reality, we have no expertise in predicting the future, and often that which was imagined to be salvation turned out to be injurious. We do not take the distant future into account." Rabbi Elbaz's argument that Shas's activities are geared toward "summoning the dormant

(not self-governing) redemption" illustrates a fundamentally different understanding than that of Mafdal's. Ironically, ultra-Orthodox Shas differs
from modern-Orthodox Mafdal in that it sees the future as uncertain and
recognizes the independent power of today's decisions in defining tomorrow.[124] In Mafdal's view, current politics are an unfolding process with
futuristic explanations of the Halakhic tradition. Thus the predetermined
future defines today's politics. Mafdal's policies are difficult to understand because the redemptive process appears to be somewhat tautologi-
cal: it not only explains today's policies via a predetermined future, but
ascribes today's policies to the efforts to ensure tomorrow.

The idea of community plays a central role in both parties' ideologies,
further illustrating that it is not the positions but the underlying ideas that
define religious parties' democratic capital. The different conceptions of
Jewish community lead to different political projects. The centrality of
messianic views, which rests on the presence of a unified nation in Mafdal's ideology, allows the party to be tolerant of differences in the Jewish
nation. The party's endeavors to create national unity coincide with the
goals of modern nations and encourage it to be active in higher education
through creating its own educational pillar and thereby undermining the
isolationist perspective of Haredi communities. The party, in this sense,
accepts the idea of individualism and individual success for the better-
ment of the nation with respect to its assigned religious value. Yet since
Mafdal's tolerance is based on a teleological view, the party has difficulty
in expanding its tolerance to different ethnic, cultural, and religious
groups. Mafdal's sacralization of the people of Israel and the state of Israel comes with a mixed balance sheet. It enables the party to be an inclusive political stabilizer but does not allow it to address issues of diversity
beyond the secular-religious conflict.

Due to the marginal role assigned to auto-redemption in its ideology, it
is not possible to find in Shas a parallel of Mafdal's emphasis on the unity
of the nation. Although the party treats the Israeli nation as a religious community, it tacitly accepts its pluralist structure. The state plays a peripheral
role, as the party views the Jewish community, not the Jewish nation-state,
as the ultimate political unit. Differences and diversity in the community are
not an issue as long as the overall Jewishness of the community is protected
and different religious traditions are not suppressed. As the idea of redemption and the importance of Biblical lands lose their significance in its
religious symbolic world, Shas is less critical of territorial compromises.

In Shas's ideology, Zionism failed to create an egalitarian Jewish community because it did not include Sephardi on equal terms, and it imposed its foreign ideas on them in the name of being a nation. The alienation from the nation-state community resulted not only in the social but

also the spiritual marginalization of Sephardim. For Sephardim to be part of a Jewish community, they need to return to their Sephardi roots and reestablish themselves in the modern Israeli nation on their own terms. Thus, Shas's ethnic rhetoric allows it to approach the ethnic elements in Zionism from a critical perspective. In this regard, Shas's critique of Zionist nationalism carved out a significant place in Israeli democracy by highlighting its ethnically exclusive practices in different sectors.

The leadership structure of both parties shows that they are hierarchical organizations with limited internal democracy. Similar to other Israeli parties, a small elite dominates the party structure. Even in cases where the religious leadership is not visibly dominant, their opinions and interpretations of the Torah, as well as their party structure, provide the backbone of party ideology. Still, they cannot be easily labeled as charismatic parties. Mafdal's long history proves that the party's ideology and political appeal survived its originator, Avraham Kook, and reached the level of routinization despite incessant internal crises. Likewise, although Ovadia Yosef and Aryeh Deri exhibit some characteristics of charismatic leaders with their remarkable popularity among supporters, the removal of Deri, for example, did not damage the party's electoral success. Similarly, Yosef's immense popularity did not protect many of his decisions from internal opposition.

In short, Mafdal and Shas represent two different responses to the changing political landscape of Israeli democracy through two distinctive applications of Judaism. The ideology of Mafdal is rooted in a process of sacralization, whereby the party justifies every aspect of nationalism as internal to Judaism. What lies beneath the party's modern outward look is a deeper process of traditionalization and inward perspective. The party assimilates the new issues, questions, and political constructs within the old. The political power of such an approach is that it normalizes changes by encompassing the new within the tradition while also presenting them as a continuation rather than a rupture. A less-recognized aspect of this approach is that, as these changes are internalized into religious traditions, the broader spectrum of ideas that exist in the outside world is negated. This negation differs from other ultra-Orthodox groups whose negation of the outside world equals their recognition of it. Religious Zionism negates the independent presence of the "external," because in essence, what seem to be external developments, such as Zionism or the 1967 war, are all "internal" to the Halakhic tradition.[125] It is this process that makes Mafdal one of the most fascinating interfaces of modernity and religion, and thus of religion and politics. The underlying processes point to a contradiction. An embrace of modernity by Mafdal defeats its struggle to revisit the core ideas that challenge modernity. Tradition is modernized to justify a modern look without abandoning its core ideas.

Shas's ideology reflects an internal secularization of Judaism, where the leadership redefines conventional religious positions by assigning them new meaning and making them germane to current pressing issues. In contrast to Mafdal's sacralization of politics, Shas confronts the ideas of modernity, ethnic differences, and the centralized state by adopting them and thereby internally secularizing its version of Judaism. Shas's innovations are thus especially important in their effect on the Haredi world, where certain symbolic innovations can have revolutionary effects, such as the acceptance of the expertise and the decisions of secular authorities when religious principles require a detailed assessment of the existing situation. Again, although it seems to be miniscule and insignificant progress when viewed from the perspective of pure equality, some of Yosef's public decisions—such as when he proclaimed "in truth, the prevention of *bat-mitsvah* celebrations enables criminals to denounce the sages of Israel, as if they deprive the daughters of Israel and discriminate between sons and daughters"—open the door for gender equality in religious terms, one of the most deficient areas of democratic capital in religious communities.[126] Yet the limited role of women in the party shows that despite the fact that the party is innovative in promoting the position of women, these changes remain within the parameters of traditional roles. For instance, new educational opportunities are provided to women, but only to train them as teachers and nurses, thereby "emancipating" them to fulfill their traditional roles more effectively. Although these opportunities are limited, given the absence of such efforts in Haredi communities, they amount to important changes in the Haredi world, forcing it to reconsider some roles from within.

To conclude, the diversity of religious parties has significant consequences for Israeli politics. The dissonance among the religious parties is more than a question of nuances and throws doubt on the very title of "religious bloc." Capturing the political agenda of religious parties and locating them in their respective system first requires a recognition of the parties' ideological prisms through which they define politics. Their ideologies reflect different modes of mutually transformative processes between the religious and secular. Describing these parties by imposing upon them the binary term of secular/ultra-Orthodox, Zionist/anti-Zionist, democratic/undemocratic, or traditionalist/progressive only fortifies their existing images and falls short of providing an understanding of their role in Israeli politics. The successful political appeal of these parties lies in the very fact that they have found their niches in an ideological space that cannot simply be captured by these terms.

CHAPTER FOUR

Representing Islam in Secular Politics

The Ideologies and Leaders of the Nationalist Action, the National View, and the Justice and Development Parties

Synthesis is not simply the downright new quality leaping forth from definite negation; it is the return of what has been negated. . . . Progress is always a recourse as well, to that which fell victim to the progressing concept.[1]

An Islamic party is a contradiction in terms in Turkey, where the secular political system prohibits the use of Islam for political ends. Nonetheless, through the adaptive power of religious ideas, pro-Islamic parties have been part and parcel of Turkish politics since the first Parliament. The first opposition party, the Progressive Republican Party, defined itself as an organization "respectful of liberties and religious beliefs and convictions." This ostensibly neutral expression later became a marker for parties that sought more room for Islamic ideas in the public sphere. Although a party that adopted an overtly Islamic or antisecular rhetoric risked closure, pro-Islamic parties persisted by inventing a new rhetoric and new venues for political action, representing "prayer rugs" in Turkey's secular politics.[2] The ideologies of pro-Islamic political parties take a highly complicated form as a result of the constraints imposed on religion's public role in Turkey's intricate political environment, but at the same time they serve as an essential part of the national identity and a potentially (de)legitimizing political force. In fact, the rapid changes and the increasing adoption of secular rhetoric in their public appeal led the secular public to call religious parties practitioners of *takiyye* (i.e., intentional deception to promote a certain cause). Takiyye has become not only a part of Turkey's political lexicon but a constant reminder of the pervasive secular skepticism. Religious parties are assumed to tactfully suppress their real agenda in order to maintain their political presence in the secular public sphere.[3] Between its institutional constraints and its vibrant Islamic politics, the Turkish case offers a unique venue to ask how Islamic ideas not only prevail but also how they make themselves increasingly relevant to individuals.

Given their institutional constraints, self-preservation strategies, and rapid transformations, any attempt to understand Turkey's religious parties requires a careful reading from the inside out. Only through such an analysis can we pass beyond accounts that reduce Turkey's pro-Islamic religious parties to *expressive* movements poised to confront others, especially secularist groups. This approach gives a vantage point from which we can delve into the constitutive aspects of parties' ideologies via their core religio-political ideas. These ideas ultimately define the ideal community of these parties and what it means to be its (Muslim) citizens. With an eye on this broad objective, the following discussion focuses on how Islam and secular ideas engage in mutually transformative interactions. Guiding each section are three questions. The first question is how the three sets of parties, (1) the Nationalist Action Party (NAP) and its splinter Büyük Birlik Partisi (the Grand Union Party, GUP), (2) the Milli Görüş, National View (NV) parties and (3) the Justice and Development Party (JDP), approach the hegemonic secular nationalism.[4] A second question is how they balance the importance of individual differences and the cohesion of community. The third question is how and to what extent they accommodate nonreligious, heterodox, or ethnic groups in their appeal. Our analysis treats the NV and the JDP as two separate ideological blocs. Such division is not meant to argue that the JDP is a new, separate movement. Instead, treating them as separate blocs highlights the striking continuities and differences between the two, and more importantly, allows us to tackle the question of whether and how the politics of Islam has taken a new form under the banner of the JDP.

This chapter analyzes the Turkish case using the heuristic approach and goals explained in the previous chapter. Viewing religious parties in Turkey through the same lenses applied to Israel's religious parties illustrates that a parallel path of diversification has emerged in both countries. However, unlike in Israel, one cannot find easily discernible, separate religious party leaderships in Turkey. Instead, political leaders often assume this role and develop complex ties to religious groups, orders, and intellectuals. The distinctive ways in which religious parties appropriate Islamic ideas into their ideological outlook become critical to understanding the foundations of their elusive positions. Again, we look for the state within religious ideologies, instead of placing religious ideologies at opposite ends from the state and secular nationalism. Developing a fine-tuned description of each party's position vis-à-vis ethnic and religious differences enables us to discern conflicts between the parties' ideals and practice. Important to note is that each party's strong platform is challenged when the party is compelled to attend to political demands of ethnically or religiously heterodox groups. Our broadened and deepened scope brings to the fore the areas in which the parties remain silent, which can be as revealing as their vocal positions. Our efforts to examine how these parties' ideologies sacralize Turkish politics and internally secularize Islam reveal a clustering of political positions reminiscent of the positions of Mafdal and Shas.

This nuanced picture draws our attention to the critical role of the area glossed over by conventional categorizations. In fact, it shows that the very ubiquitous and pressing question of whether religious parties are secular or antisecular, democratic or antidemocratic reinforces categorical answers when, in fact, these parties often both enhance and thwart their respective democracies in multifaceted ways. When viewed without ascriptive labels, their overall democratic records confound our expectations and cannot be defined unidirectionally by mirroring the complexity of the process of democracy. An inventory of their ideas from within affirms that we can only avoid unidimensional and simplistic accounts of these parties' democratic capital (or lack thereof) when we fully understand and incorporate the content and implications of their ideologies into our assessments.

THE NATIONALIST ACTION PARTY: A NATIONALIST OR A RELIGIOUS PARTY?

According to Esat Öz, the NAP is "the least understood party" in Turkish politics.[5] The NAP's once-popular image as a dogmatic and ultra-nationalist party has been reinforced by limited analyses of the party's ideology that habitually have focused only on explaining the radicalism of party-affiliated groups. A distinctive image of the party emerges when we look at the NAP without assigning it to the radical nationalist camp of Turkish politics or trying to disprove its extremism. This new perspective reveals the party's unique ideological position and its Islamist-Turkish idealism, which locates it in the crosscurrents of Kemalist ethnic nationalism and Islamic ideals. The party's history can be divided into three periods: from its foundation to 1973, from 1973 to 1980, and from 1980 to today. Across these three periods, the party has gradually adjusted its ideology.

The predecessors of the NAP entered Turkish politics in 1948 under the leadership of field marshal Fevzi Çakmak of the Nation Party (NP). It is important to note that the NP did not associate itself with the main body of opposition that had formed against the strict enforcement of secularism and authoritarianism of the Republican People's Party (RPP). Despite its relative independence from the main opposition and its search to find a third way, the party was closed down in 1954 on the grounds that it hid its real policies and based itself on religion. Çakmak was often described as the "believer general" (as opposed to the common image of a secularist soldier), who constituted the image that personified the NAP ideology of the state, that is, a soldier serving the state for higher religious ideals. Ironically, his party's closure was endorsed by the Democratic Party, then the ruling party, as much as by the secularist RPP. Under the name of Republican Work Nation Party, the Nation party preserved its presence and eventually evolved into what we know today as the NAP. Alparslan Türkeş was elected as chairman of the NAP after resigning his military position in 1965. Following his election, the party adopted not only its current name, but also the core of its current ideology, *Dokuz Işık* (*Nine Lights*).

The party's lasting image was formed during the 1970s, when Turkish politics appeared to be a form of polarized pluralism. The 1961 constitution had created multiple access points to state power that allowed groups to easily organize. In the absence of a consensus on the fundamentals of the regime, various groups advocating different shades of Marxist, nationalist, and Islamist ideologies clashed violently. In this context, the NAP stood out by interpreting the political divisions from a nationalist religious perspective. For instance, the leadership asserted that communism was nothing but a camouflage for Russian nationalism and anti-Islamism. If the Turkish nation as a whole was set to move along a trajectory of growth, the elite needed to protect the state from destructive ideologies. Given this sense of history, the NAP leadership described its followers as *Ülkücü*, idealists, and set as its objective the protection of the state and the Muslim nation against foreign, antireligious and nationalist intrusions. This polarized political arena provided the backdrop for the party's internal changes, which culminated in Türkeş's declaration on June 9, 1973: "Today Turkish nationalism ceased to be a main theme of our association and group, but became our party's fundamental programmatic philosophy."[6]

The political and economic crises of the 1970s resulted in the 1980 coup d'etat. As the party had centered its ideology on allegiance to the state (i.e., sacralized it), it assumed that it would survive the coup intact. More importantly, according to the party's followers, the military's ideology embodied the pillars of NAP's own arguments. This perceived affinity between the NAP and the regime, however, did not protect the party from the fallout of the 1980 military coup: its organization was closed down and the party leadership was banned.[7] The 1980 crackdown by agents of the state shook the NAP's ideological foundations. The party's slogan, "our ideas are in power, we are in prison," voiced the sense of persecution and "mistreatment" at the hands of the state, despite the NAP's own selfless "altruistic sacrifice" for the state and the nation. Paradoxically, the 1980 coup's efforts to purge the Turkish political sphere of all divisions not only introduced NAP supporters to an increasing degree of skepticism about the state's policies, but they also highlighted its previously weak political alliances and brought to the fore its Islamic ideas. Many leaders who were imprisoned in this era referred to their experience as attending *Yusufiyye medrasha,* referring to the prophet Janus's years in prison. In fact, as the NAP activists often shared their cells with other Islamists, their imprisonment, according to some party leaders, had a significant impact on the party's overall ideological repositioning.[8] The party's closure and the absence of a clear enemy such as communism initiated a process of ideological reformulation and generated intense leadership rifts that ultimately resulted in an official split. Against this background, it can be argued that the post-1980 environment initiated a process whereby a third NAP incarnation came into being. In this (so far) final incarnation, Islam became a more decisive force and served as a focus of its political vision.

Following the overall pattern of Turkish politics after party closures, the NAP reentered the political scene in 1983 under the name of the Conservative Party. By 1992 the party retrieved its pre-1980 name, *Nationalist Action Party,* and Türkeş again became the leader of the movement, yet this time in a context devoid of the threat of communism. In this setting, where the Turkic republics were independent and the Kurdish problem was on the rise, the party transformed itself from an ethnic-religious party to a religious-ethnic party, establishing itself as one of the pivotal actors in Turkish politics with fluctuating, yet steadily significant support (see figure 6.1). One of the most important steps in passing the 10 percent national threshold and in inaugurating its ideological reconstruction was the formation of a pre-election coalition with the overtly religious Welfare and Reformist Democratic parties. The introduction of the coalition to the public as a "coalition of believers" or "holy alliance" illustrated the newly pivotal role of Islam in the party's ideology.

The "holy alliance" received 16.1 percent of the vote. Though the NAP's exact share is difficult to determine, the amount of total support clearly indicated the growing popular appeal of the party in its Islamic incarnation. The party's failure to pass the national threshold in the 1995 election without the blessing of the coalition of believers further strengthened the process that placed the Turkish-Islamic ideal at the heart of the NAP's appeal. Interestingly, some party members defected from the NAP not because of its Islamization, but because of insufficient Islamization. The Islamists who left the party on the grounds that it had not fully completed its Islamic conversion later established their own independent party, the GUP. Despite the defections, the NAP alone finally received 18 percent of the votes in 1999.[9] In this election the NAP established itself as the second-largest voting bloc in the Turkish National Assembly with 128 members of Parliament, but failed to maintain its electoral success at the same level in the next election, when the JDP emerged as the new popular political actor.

The Nationalist Action Party and Kemalist Nationalism: A Turkish-Islamic Ideal?

At first glance, the NAP's emphasis on a strong state and ethnic Turkishness suggests that the party would be in harmony with Kemalist nationalism. Party history, however, shows that the NAP from its inception both challenged and was challenged by the Kemalist state. One of the most revealing incidences of this oppositional relationship revolves around the conviction of the party's leader, Türkeş, in the *Turancılık,* or the *Pan Turkism* trial of 1944. The trial was instigated by the protest of a group of nationalists against the state elite and its cultural policies. Following President İsmet İnönü's talk denouncing the rising wave of nationalism, a group of protesters, including Türkeş, was arrested. In their reading materials, the party's youth organization explained this incident to new recruits in the following way:

During the 25 years that followed the establishment of the Republic, Turkish people accepted nationalism along with religion. Materialistic nationalism was limited to a small group. These two conflicted at times, but created some useful results forging national solidarity. Starting in the 1940's, Turkish nationalism lost its ideological stronghold in the state. For instance, among the 496 classics the education ministry picked for the school curricula, 63 were Russian and none were Turkish. The state ignored the Russian control of the Turkic republic. Facing the mounting opposition from nationalists in his public speech on May 19, 1944, then president İnönü described Pan-turkists as a real danger. Pan-turkists who were dragging Turkey to Turkism and racism were indeed serving foreign interests. His talk promised that the government would take all necessary measures to prevent these *sinisters* from succeeding. This overt repression of the Turkish nationalists was also a political gesture towards Russia who seemed to be gaining against Germany.[10]

The intraparty discussion of the *Turancılık* case introduces us to the roots of the NAP leadership's paradoxical relationship to the state. On the one hand, the party viewed the state as the sine qua non of the Turkish polity. On the other hand, the party became the state's harshest critic when its policies seemed to be undermining the state's historical role of leading and protecting Turkish communities worldwide.

The NAP's intricate relationship with Kemalist nationalism manifests itself best in Türkeş's *Nine Lights*, which outlines the founding principles of the NAP ideology. At first glance, *Nine Lights* basically replicates Kemalist ideals that seek to promote nationalism, idealism, moralism, science, populism, peasants, freedom, development, and industrialism. A closer review indicates, however, that despite its commitment to the Kemalist state, *Nine Lights* does not include its devotion to the pillar laicism. Instead, moralism defines the goal of protecting the spirit and traditions of the Turkish nation. Missing also is a notion of "social development" depicted in Kemalism as a race toward Westernization. Rather, *Nine Lights* defines social change as both moral and material progress without any reference to Westernization or modernization. Kemalism's idealization of the West as the highest form of civilization is replaced by a reference to "Turkish tradition."

Nine Lights shows that the NAP's quest to couple Turkish secularism and Muslimness in one unified core of Turkish nationalism both aligns it with and pits it against Kemalism. While many view its ideology as a Turkish-Islamic synthesis, the party rejects this type of characterization on several grounds. The coupling of the secular state and the Islamic nation, for the party, cannot be reduced to an ideological synthesis, that is, a deliberate effort to reconcile the two opposing views. To the contrary, from the party's perspective Turkish Islam emerged out of an organic historical transformation marked by inherent affinities and historical necessities.[11]

State means order. In the Ottoman Empire religion was important, but the major sources of Islam, namely *Qur'an* and *Sunnah*, did not provide a state regime. The Ottoman regime was not a theocracy. Tradition and customs define the regime. A nation that establishes a state defines the regime in its own terms.[12]

For the NAP leadership, religion, that is Islam, cannot create a strong state; religious communities cannot be self-sustaining and must be sheltered by a strong state. It is no coincidence that the dominant streams of thought during the collapse of the Ottoman Empire—Turkism, Ottomanism, and Islamism—asked how to save the state. Due to this common question, they all eventually merged under *Misak-ı Milli* and Kemalist nationalism. Kemalism prevailed over the others as it mobilized the diverse groups and built the necessary alliances and institutions to contain the divisions in the polity, thereby reinventing the state.[13]

The NAP's justification of Turkish-Islamic ideals formed two theses. In each thesis we can find how the party engages with the Islamist critique of Kemalism and the nationalist critique of religion. The first argument contends that even pre-Islamic Turkish traditions exhibit Islamic attributes. *Kut*, the god of the pre-Islamic Turks, embodied the ninety-nine adjectives used to describe the image of Allah, God, in Islam.[14] The traditional religions of the Turkish peoples, in essence, were always monotheistic and maintained moral standards comparable to those of Islam. Therefore, when the Turks adopted Islam, they merely completed their ethical and spiritual growth. By embracing Islam, Turks not only integrated Islamic principles into their national characteristics more explicitly and systematically, they also contributed to Islamic civilization by introducing the tools to build a strong state with a sphere of governance beyond religious affairs. For the NAP, laicism is derived from the reading of pre-Islamic and Islamic history and represents an organic historical compromise created from the merger of Islamic ideas and progressive Turkish state culture.[15]

Approaching the conflict between secular nationalists and Islamists from an Islamic point of view, the second thesis focuses on the Islamist objection that nation and nationalism undermine the universal unity of Muslims under *ummah*, the overarching Islamic community. In the views of the NAP, such an approach expediently ignores *Surah Al-Hujurat* (the section called the Chambers) in the Qur'an. The verse "O Mankind, We created you as males and females and rendered you distinct nations and tribes, so that you may know one another better" refers to nations, not ummah, as the main unit of society and demonstrates how nations are not artificial constructs, but divinely ordained units.[16] Therefore, for the NAP's leadership, the Qur'an not only recognizes nations as distinct cultural groups, but sees them as the main instrument of universal solidarity. This is why the verse ends with "so you can understand each other better."[17] National loyalties do not induce fragmentations within the Islamic world. To the contrary, national identities are compatible with human nature and facilitate progress toward forming the global Islamic community of ummah.

Regardless of their different interpretations of Islamic traditions, both theses claim that Islamic values are inherent in Turkish tradition and that Turkey's strong state structure protects its Muslim community—a state structure that rests on a unique institutional tradition protected by laicite—forming not contesting, but mutually dependent relations. In contrast to the RPP's statement that Turkish nationalism is limited solely to Turkey, the NAP argues that the Turkish nation is a historical polity beyond its present-day borders with roots in Central Asia. The symbols that anchor the movement's ideas capture this transnational historical perspective. For instance, a gray wolf, *bozkurt*, which according to a widely shared mythology guided the Turkish peoples during their first migration from Central Asia, was commonly used to identify the NAP's followers. Just as they did with the image of bozkurt, the party successfully revived many symbols based on national myths and made them the common currency of its daily discussions of religion and politics.

In this practice of fusing ethnic and religious symbolic worlds, the NAP not only creates a popular language to be shared with sympathizers but also blurs the boundaries that separate popular Islamic and national history.[18] Thus, instead of being the source of mutually exclusive values and political forces, the state and the nation actually work to reinforce each other. The overlapping concentric layers of Turkish identity are represented in the banner of the *Ülkü Ocakları*, which depicts a gray wolf engulfed by a crescent and symbolizes the mythological unity of the nation rooted in its Islamic foundation.[19] In its ideological articulations, the NAP—like its Israeli counterpart, Mafdal—elevates the state's status to religious significance by declaring it to be the only institution capable of maintaining the national religious community. The argument that laicism (the disassociation of Islam from the state ideology) did not start with Kemalist nationalism, but evolved throughout Turkish history, places pressing political issues posed by Kemalist laicization into a broader historical framework with roots and relevance beyond Kemalism. Some party members believe that it was Ismet İnönü who succeeded Atatürk as leader of the RPP state founding party and president of the Republic, and that it was İnönüism and not Kemalism that conflated laicism and Westernization in an authoritarian way.[20]

Likewise, the NAP's emphasis on the historicity of laicism and the significance of nationalism in Islam allows it to question views that depict Kemalist secular nationalism as ex nihilo, due to Western influence, and to redefine the role of secularism as the foundation of the state and thus the foundation of a Muslim society. By doing so, the NAP emerges as a party that questions both the blind Westernization of the so-called Kemalist parties and the denial of Turkishness of the Islamist parties.[21] For the NAP, the question of Islam is not one of a clash between Muslimness and Turkishness, but of reinventing and restoring the *real* characteristics of Turks. In the NAP's Turkish-Islamic ideal, Islam appears as neither an independent nor a synthetic value system, but more of a culturally imbued *Islamic* value system. "Islam does not have a nationality, but each nation adopted Islam in a unique way according to its national characteristics." Thus, the Turkish Islamic ideal is not a strategic invention, but the evidence of how the blend of culture and Islam is inevitable.[22] For example, in Turkey one can speak of Anatolian Islam, that is, Islam formed through the historical consensus of groups living in Turkey's territory.

The NAP's commitment to the state's secularism as well as to a strong Islamic community might first appear to be a politically expedient position. In fact, the party assumes that unity between Islam and Turkishness is as effortless to achieve as proclaimed in its motto "Islam is our soul and Turkishness is our body" and "one without the other cannot be alive." In its praxis, however, due to its effort to be a Kemalist Islamist party, the NAP often finds itself at a crossroads and is forced to reconcile the conflicting demands of Islamic and secular groups—the groups that the party perceives as intrinsically harmonious. The dilemmas of the party and the way the party addresses them can be traced through its two popular and parallel campaign slogans. In the 1999 election campaign, which took the party to the apex of its power, the NAP declared that it was not only a party "respectful of the faith" but "the only party to solve the *türban*, headscarf, problem." After all, the NAP "was the only valiant, not timid party," in comparison to other Islamic parties, when the state needed to be confronted. Ironically, the party's success in the 1999 election put its ideas to a test in an unexpected way: one of the two women with headscarves whose parliamentary election bids succeeded was a NAP candidate.

The election of a woman with a headscarf on its ticket not only embodied the dilemma faced by the party but also its unique solutions. Turkey's strictly secular structure requires the removal of the türban, which is considered to be a religious symbol, when attending parliamentary meetings. Confronted with this rule, the NAP member followed the parliamentary dress code (i.e., took her scarf off when she needed to be present at parliamentary meetings). To further avoid "unnecessary" and potentially destabilizing conflict, she pursued her parliamentary activities mostly from her local office. This "solution through compartmentalization," which de facto sanctioned the removal of a woman's headscarf in the state's secular public domain but not in other areas, reflected the NAP's complex policies, which treat the state domain and its rules as sacrosanct. The NAP's compromise contrasted with the reaction of Kavakcı, the Virtue Party's Istanbul Member of Parliament, who did not take her turban off, an action that lit a firestorm of protest because it violated the secularity of the state domain.[23]

The party's strategy in the case of the woman representative, Ünal, was neither a unique nor an ad hoc solution. Instead, it captures the principle of compartmentalization, that is, the acceptance of some compromises in the state domain when they serve a higher public or religious good. The party also tries not to confuse objections to the authority of the state with a critique of its policies from the religious perspective. For example, following the same logic, the NAP questions many of the milestone events that exemplify the secular state's oppression of pro-Islamic groups. In this revised history, Sheyh Said, a leader who has been widely used in Islamist circles to exemplify the state's oppression of Islamic groups, was severely suppressed by the NAP, not due to his religious demands, but because the rebellions were undermining state control in the region, challenging not the state's secularity but its stateness (i.e., the state's ability to control and protect its polity). The rebels were suppressed not because they were Muslims, but because they were insurgents.[24] Thus statist, national, and religious principles clash only when they put the state at risk.

Similar views conveyed by the leadership indicate that instead of being a static, ahistorical institutional arrangement with sharp boundaries, laicism generates an area of debate and reorganization to secure the state's continuity and political order. Thus, one needs to not only focus on the policy outcomes of such debates but also on the processes to achieve them and their broader implications. As a result, the party both objects to limitations regarding the public expression of Islam and also warns that not all antisecular policies translate into the strengthening of the Muslim community. Any solution to the question of Islam in the public sphere needs to avoid a crisis in stateness. Accordingly, Bahçeli, the party leader, often states that "the issue of the türban cannot be resolved on the campuses [referring to the campus protests], but should be addressed by the state." This approach mirrors the idea promoted by Kemalism but via a different rationale: religion is a matter of individual conscience and not a public issue. Thus, issues pertaining to religion cannot be resolved through civil negotiations in the public sphere without state involvement. It is the state that must reorganize the role of Islam in society.[25]

In its current program, the NAP reflects its unconventional position by defining laicism as a public order rooted in positive law, which is neither affected by religious publics nor allows them unique power and immunities. Yet the same section argues that "a state order is secular only to the extent that it protects the freedom of religion and conscience."[26] It is unacceptable that these freedoms will be limited by *unlawful* venues. As a corollary to this argument, the party declares the Islamist critiques that question the state's practices as the suppression of believers, thereby undermining political order and stateness, as antireligious. After all, the short-term implications of the state's policies are irrelevant, unless they are in grave violation of religious principles. Although the NAP's Turkish-Islamic synthesis enables the party to appeal to secular and religious worlds at the same time, again similar to Mafdal, the NAP achieves this conciliatory position by elevating the state to the level of sacred, limiting the scope of politics and rendering some political questions *nonnegotiable.*

Individualism Versus Collectivism: A Search for a Lost Community and Order?

When different aspects of its ideology are viewed together, individuals have a Janus-faced role in the NAP's ideology: they are seen not only as natural members of and subservient to their ethno-religious community but also as the main agents in forging communal ties and in fulfilling the nation's ideals. As a result, the NAP's ideology frequently refers to individuals not as members of insular communities or actors in domestic politics but as critical agents against the foil of global transformations. As such, the NAP's ideology, mapped out in *Nine Lights,* contends that with their ideas, faith, and idealism, individuals are the foundation of the nation. After all, Türkeş argues, "a man without religion is an empty shell, a ship without compass, rudder and anchor. Religion is also a social institution. None of the societies can survive without religion."[27] This is why even countries that view religion as opium for the people eventually abandon this view. The weaknesses of these ideologies rest on their approaches to sacred values, individuals, and community. Despite their different façades, all ideologies originate from *hırs* (uncontrolled interest or ambition) and *hased* (distrust and competition), and thus they are reactive and seek to create regimes that control interest and distrust. The West spread its social model by creating an almost new religion [out of Western values].[28] Accordingly, liberalism and capitalism are not universal values, but reflections of the West's global domination. The NAP supports an alternative and local view of a polity rooted in Islam, one that seeks to restore the role of individuals as moral agents and the role of community as the source of moral values.

Accordingly, at each level of its activities, the party teaches the consciousness and pride of Turkishness, the ethics and virtues of Islam, the sense of justice and brotherhood, and the duty to fight against poverty, as all of these together enhance one's service, *hizmet,* on the path of Allah, God.[29] In the party's discourse, serving the nation and the religious community have become synonymous. Leadership statements often serve as a reminder of the party's and its members' idealized, altruistic positions. Statements such as the one made by the party's current moderate leader, Bahçeli, that "we, the Turkish nationalists and *Ülkücü* youth, are ready to pay any price to protect the state and the future of this nation if an urgent need emerges" define politics as a choice between the collective good versus personal interest. The recurring message intends to distinguish the NAP and its followers from other political parties, as people capable of fully transcending individual, short-term considerations and benefits.[30] Politics, in this view, appears as an area not for negotiations of interests, but as almost a site of religious, ritualistic expression that requires the pursuit of collective good as opposed to personal interest.

The party's local organizations, the neighborhood-centered *Ülkü Ocakları*, Hearths of Idealists, serve as microcosms of its idealized, communitarian political sphere. The nationwide connection through *ocaks* amounts to one of the most comprehensive party-affiliated associational networks in Turkey. Ocaks provides members with a sense of overarching ideology, identity, belonging, and protection, regardless of the size and leadership of each local group. It is not uncommon to see a visiting Ülkücü from one town using another ocak as a hostel, a testimony to the party's power to connect otherwise isolated communities through neotraditional ties.[31] The ocaks' character as party-affiliated institutions in the public domain is frequently obscured, because many look like typical family homes, even though they are used as schools and meeting places. Like the meeting places of other pro-Islamic groups, they successfully blur the boundaries between public and private domains, providing a strong link between the two. Approximately 1,090 ocaks carry out a centralized training program in all provinces of Turkey. In Istanbul, 63 ocaks attract a wide range of youngsters, mostly from high school and college.[32]

Just like the NV parties and the JDP, *Ülkü* Ocaks aim at establishing a branch in every neighborhood in order to compete against other parties and to organize and educate young NAP supporters. Once they are established, ocaks serve as both community and party centers. As defined in their statute, activities at ocaks are geared toward creating a strong group identity and cultivating a sense of solidarity through continuous interactions and discussions. The party's national motto "leader, organization, and doctrine" is meticulously applied at the ocak level. The structure at the local level translates into a clear division of labor in the Ülkücü movement at large. Ocak leaders assume the role of elder mentors and regularly meet with members to answer questions, explain the party's ideology, and give their take on current events. Leaders act as intermediaries between the central party organization and local groups. The party's internal hierarchical ladder is well defined and promises to carry new recruits to the national leadership of the party. Stemming from the popular belief that they have already proven their merits in Ocaks and at various levels of the movement, the merits and ideological commitments of the members who climb the ladders of internal hierarchy are not questioned when they achieve a leadership position.

Through ocaks, Ülkücüs learn a rather simplified version of Turkish history from the pre-Islamic past to today's Turkic republics. The leadership offers a political map to the attendees that explains the historical foundations of current global changes. This historical trajectory also emphasizes that, since the 1990s, Turkish history has reached another critical juncture. A window of opportunity exists for materializing the ideal of *Nizam'i Alem*, the world order, but there is also the danger of becoming a perpetually peripheral country. In the GUP-affiliated *Alperen* Ocaks, where Islam plays a more overt role than in Ülkü Ocaks, achieving the ideal of Nizam'i Alem is presented as a five-step transformation: "The disciplining of the self (*Nizam-ı nefs*), the family, the neighbors, and the re-creation of a nation, and a world order."[33] This multilayered process replicates the Islamic sufi understanding of disciplining the self to achieve moral excellence. In fact, Ülkücüs perceive themselves as the almost nationalist-religious equivalents of selfless religious servants. Many Islamists uphold the image of *mücahid*, a self-sacrificing laborer for an Islamic cause, as the heroic figure in *Ummah*. In its more Islamized version, the GUP leadership defines its archetypical public persona as Alperen, which combines the characteristics of saint-like believers and soldiers. With these images, the NAP carves a new space in the public mind by blurring the lines between the national and religious spheres. The NAP does not hesitate to claim historical figures as the guiding spirits of the party, whose legacy is used by various religious and nationalist groups, but rarely by both.

Ülkücüs often refer to each other as the people of *dava* (common goal) and are committed to the mission of a just order at all levels of community, neighborhood to national. This sense of mission makes them cognizant of their broader responsibility to their immediate milieu and active in creating a new order, first in the nation and later in the Turkish world.[34] In fact, GUP party-affiliated groups warn the idealists about the challenges of rekindling dava in communities already alienated from communal values, especially Islam. "In many places Muslimness is confined to the mosques and Ramadan. . . . Therefore, many of your families will not have sympathy for the values you are fighting for. They need to be convinced. While doing this, do not fall into the trap of disrespecting, disobeying, offending, or blaming your family and other authorities."[35] In similar messages, idealists find themselves called upon to raise the awareness of Turkishness and Islam in their community without undermining traditional structures. Both in Alperen and Ülkü Ocaks, teachings emphasize that "even though people resist some ideas, a good honest person's ideology earns respect in his community over time. Movements that have initially been endorsed by a few in their local community later became mass movements." Thus, the challenge that Nizam'i Alem advocates and which includes both the NAP and GUP supporters is to change society starting with its basic unit, the neighborhood, while maintaining its traditions and keeping the communal structure intact. The NAP's Ülkücüs' oath, which is taken on the Qur'an before their meetings, not only epitomizes the centrality of Islamic references in the party's post-1980 self but also the party's new sacro-secular expressions. Expressed in the vow is a sense of the perpetual threat and untapped potential of the dormant Turkish-Muslim transnational community, offering a fusion of both religious and nationalist goals: "In the name of God, Qur'an, Flag, Nation . . . our struggle will last until [we achieve] the nationalist Turkey and Turan [unity of Turkic nations] and prevail against any form of fascism, communism, Socialism, capitalism and imperialism."[36]

The embodiment of the NAP ideology in Ülkü Ocaks as well as its more Islamic variant Alperen Ocak together show us that the NAP's vision of the individual focuses not on the principle of autonomy but on the person's role as an idealistic member of a national ethnic community. According to the NAP program, it is not only the local currents but the process of globalization that represent a major challenge to the individual and the community. At one point it states that globalization "undermines the collective sentiments and responses and social ties, especially due to the decline of face to face communication. None of this should change the fact that we live in a distinctive social order."[37] Paradoxically, instead of forming new communities, the party attracts supporters more effectively in settings where a sense of collective identity is already present. Devlet Bahçeli, the current party leader, attributes the NAP's limited success in urban centers where communal ties are weak to the Ülkücü Ocaks' failure to establish political ties other than face-to-face communication. In fact, election results show that the NAP was most successful in villages and in middle-range cities with a population between twenty thousand and seventy thousand. Despite the initial hurdles, Bahçeli contends that NAP voters are primarily looking for an alternative form of organization, and that the sense of trust developed in their communities empowers them in the face of major changes. Although party members are slow to build communities, once established, these communities form lasting party ties.[38]

Perhaps due to its emphasis on the Turkish-Islamic roots and its ability to serve as a bridge between the cultural expression of Islam and the state, an important aspect of the NAP's ideology is dedicated to discussions of Turkey's role in relation to other countries. This interest has been intriguing, given that other parties, especially center parties, have failed to provide an explicit discourse for understanding Turkey's politics in a global context. For the NAP, the end of the cold war created a new context that allowed countries to reposition themselves. Although communism's threat is over, the forces of globalization do not automatically create a just international order. On the contrary, the new order is more prone to injustices than ever. Nationalism and the state are the only shields against globalization's negative effects. Only by resisting the homogenizing forces of globalization through bringing to the fore its unique national characteristics can a country find its proper niche in the global order. This approach requires both a strong hold on tradition and the permanence of the state to effectively guide social transformation. To this end, securing continuity, "change without alienation," is essential. In this global context, the Islamist ideal of ummah cannot serve as the only goal and, more importantly, it cannot be realized without national ummah.[39] Turkish communities span a vast area across the world, giving Turkey additional political leverage in global politics. Thus, by reclaiming the strengthening of their national and religious ties, Turks will not be isolated in the process of globalization, but will complete their own globalization and eventually change its course.

Inclusiveness Versus Exclusiveness: National Unity Within Religious-Ethnic Community?

Any ideology that anchors its ideas in an ethno-religious unity has the potential for serving both pluralistic civil and exclusive political projects. Locating a party on a spectrum ranging from inclusive democratic to exclusive authoritarian requires an understanding of what constitutes membership in the party's idealized political community. The answer at first seems straightforward. In the NAP's ideology, the attraction between the national characteristics of Turkishness and Islamic values is rooted in their ipso facto congruence. It is the acceptance of the now-lost unified sense of Turkishness that serves as the foundation of NAP membership. However, the NAP's *Report on Cultural Issues* captures the strenuous relations in this pluralistic yet homogenizing lost community.

Recently some intellectuals and politicians have referred to a cultural mosaic which is a very threatening term for Turkey. Because a cultural mosaic assumes that there is no dominant culture; to the contrary, it indicates the presence of various cultures and their external reflections as civilizations. It presumes that none of the cultures throughout the history could shape the geography. . . . In a society which displays the characteristics of a mosaic, nationalization cannot be realized. From Turkey's point of view, where the whole population is Turkish, it is a misperception and betrayal to argue that Turkey is a mosaic.[40]

For the NAP, Turkey's geography includes distinct cultural groups. Nevertheless, it is congruity, not difference, that has come to define the foundation of the country's social fabric. Thus, Turkishness came into being not as an exclusive ethnicized religion but rather as a historical infusion of differences. According to Alparslan Türkeş, "history witnessed over and over that the same group of people, without religious unity, could not form a nation." Thus, the incorporation of Islam cemented the ethnic and racial roots of Turks as the foundation of the Turkish nation. Given this historical and inherent Turkish unity, any claims to distinctive group identities are unacceptable. The NAP's party program states that "As the Turkish identity has been shaped by Islam from the beginning and has included various Turkish groups, under the rubric of Turkish nationalism the term 'others, excluded groups' by no means includes Islamic elements and Kurdish citizens."[41]

Accordingly, although its Turkish-Islamic ideal allows the NAP to reach out to all cultural, religious, and ethnic groups with success, some distinctive groups, for instance the Alevis and Kurds, are incorporated into this unity only to the extent that they accept the deeply rooted organic unity. Their identities, therefore, become a contingent, yet integral, part of Turkish identity. According to Ali Baykan, Kurds are essentially another Turkish clan. They were organized in closed, inward-looking groups; they developed their culture in this closed community and thus distanced themselves from other Turkish groups. Despite this distance, however, the Kurds could not develop a common, coherent language completely different from Turkish. One cannot talk about the existence of a nation without, at minimum, a common language. Without addressing other contradictions in the Kurds' distinctive national identity, the language barrier itself raises questions about the Kurds' claim to cultural and ethnic distinctiveness.[42]

Important to note is that while the party questions the claim to ethnic or religious uniqueness, it also expands its own vision of ethnic-religious Turkishness to better accommodate various groups. For example, the party most eagerly seeks to incorporate the Alevis, a group the NAP found itself in conflict with in the 1970s. The Alevis are regarded as ethnically Turkish and religiously heterodox. According to some authors, such as Bora and Can, it is not a coincidence that the NAP's stronghold throughout the 1970s was the triangle of Çorum, Erzurum, and Gaziantep in Anatolia, where Alevis are concentrated. The relative deprivation of the dominant Sunni, who are the traditional merchants and artisans in that region, led them to direct their frustrations to Alevi groups. Alevis were considered a destabilizing segment of society with their unconventional religious beliefs and affinity to leftist ideas and communism.[43] The party's doctrine was especially effective in Eastern and Central Anatolia, where the ideological rivalry between the pro-leftist Marxists and nationalist groups transformed into intercommunity conflict between Alevi-leftist and Sunni-rightist groups. Although this political history alienated many Alevis from the party, an open letter by Bülent Yahnici, one of the leading ideologues of the NAP, exemplifies the party's ongoing transformation and new inclusive approach. Referring to one of the most popular expressions attributed to Alevi tradition, "do not hurt even if you are hurt," he wrote:

Dear Alevi citizens, please also follow the above mentioned motto yourself. Let's assume that we indeed hurt you in the past; please do not hurt in return. We love all our citizens and embrace them without discrimination. We are trying to amend all our mistakes and shortcomings.[44]

In fact, beyond its rhetorical appeal, the party's increasing emphasis on Anatolian Islam, a cultural, geographically defined version of Islam, enables the NAP to moderate its strict association with dominant Sunni Islam.[45] By emphasizing Anatolian Islam, an amalgam of traditions, culture, and religion, the party leadership contends that all practices of Islam found in Anatolia, not just the Sunni orthodox version, are constitutive elements of Turkish-Islam. This strategic construction of Anatolian Islam forms a basis for claiming the unity of distinct ethnic and religious groups. As the party takes Anatolian Islam into its core ideology, it easily justifies its acceptance of Alevi practices as an ethnic-religious construction, thereby cutting its ideological distance from Alevi groups. This inclusion is further enhanced by the party's strong repulsion of the distinctive Kurdish identity. Religious bonds alone do not seem to stem the Kurdish groups' demands for political recognition. The insistence of Alevi groups that their identities are integral to Turkishness creates a strong ideological affinity. The party's commonly repeated slogan repeats the Alevi proverb calling for unity, "Let's be united and let's ease the load," and reveals the confluence of these forces.

The NAP's vision of history appears to guide the party to embrace all groups that do not contradict their assigned historical roles with respect to national unity. Nevertheless, at a deeper level, the NAP's rhetorical commitment to diversity seems to rest on the assumption that these differences will be eliminated through a gradual and holistic evolution and widespread acceptance of Islamic and Turkish values. In a more nuanced definition of Turkishness, Enis Öksüz describes the Turkish nation as "consisting of groups not only from the race of Turan, but also those who acquired kinship with the Turkish nation, and all those who sought refuge in this nation's sense of Justice."[46] Nevertheless, the centrality of being a part of and accepting this evolving historical, ethnic Turkishness in the party's rhetoric marks the limits of its inclusiveness. Questioning the terms of membership is not allowed, oftentimes creating a highly conditional language that even pervades into the area of the fundamental rights. Under the heading of "human rights" the party program declares, "our party believes that each individual is entitled to inalienable rights and the party is committed to enact them and protect them from any abuse. In that framework we respect all fundamental human rights, especially those rights that have bearing on the protection of freedom of belief and expression, and the ability to pursue all beliefs *unless they oppose the indivisible unity of state and nation*" (emphases added).[47]

For basic rights to have any meaning in a polity, there first needs to be political order. The failure of the state to shelter the individual and radical pluralism of religious-ethnic communities creates a Hobbesian world. More importantly, the commonly accepted logic of globalism rejects group-centered rights: "globalization is based on individual rights; emerging ethnic identity is not seen as a fundamental right." Thus, the Kurds' demands should not be considered as demands for a separate identity as "the presence of separate religious and ethnic groups in the public sphere without any common values can only lead to chaos."[48] All differences can be harmonized as long as common national-religious values are accepted, and political order is secured. This conclusion captures the underlying assumption that informs the party's policies across a wide spectrum of issues.

In essence, the NAP's national community is not a voluntary political union based on individuals' wills but an evolving ethnic-religious community that each Turkish citizen is inherently a member of. As a result, the party considers citizenship not as a contractual relationship between state and individual. Membership in the ethnic community is historical, perpetual, and a given, unless its terms are rejected or negotiated. The party gains ideological leverage from this ultimately community-centric approach and sees the individual only in relation to the political community and the state, that is, from the perspective of their common goals and transformative role. Individuals' claims to differences are acceptable as long as they do not collectively coalesce to challenge the state. Thus, the party's recruitment focuses on awakening individuals to their inherent membership and emphasizes unity as opposed to diversity. The state and the unity of the nation lie beyond any political scrutiny and negotiations. However, the ambiguity and lack of consensus in Turkish politics, especially on basic ethnic and religious rights, constantly challenges the party's sacralization of the unity of Turkish-Islamic nations, and in return, leads it to turn issues based on genuine differences into nonissues.

The Nationalist Action Party's Leadership

The NAP's ideology was forged by its long-term charismatic leader, Alparslan Türkeş. A brief review of Türkeş's personal history reveals the main determinants of his and the NAP's ideas. Türkeş was born on Cyprus in 1917 before the establishment of the Turkish Republic. His political socialization was defined by the British occupation of the island and the clash between Turkish and Greek identities. Türkeş's political persona and his political ideology reflect the imprint of having lived on a politically contested island. In 1932, after the establishment of the republic, Türkeş moved to Istanbul to attend a military high school, and later, college. When he became politically active in the early 1940s, his ideology centered on the vulnerability of frontier Turkic groups and the centrality of the state in protecting them. His vocal involvements in the protests against the government's lack of interest in Turkish communities around the world, and especially the lack of reaction to Russia's invasion of Turkic republics in central Asia, led to his conviction in the *Turancılık* case of 1944 on the grounds of spreading nationalist extremist views.[49] Since his imprisonment lasted less than a year, he managed to finish his military education, but his ideological perception of the state had altered drastically. Türkeş played an active role in the 1961 military coup, which declared to end the authoritarian populism of the Democratic Party as its goal. He then joined the ruling military elite, the National Union Committee. However, the military ruling body marginalized him and thirteen other officers for fear of a countercoup. Ironically, Türkeş and his fellow officers were forced to resign and leave Turkey.

Upon his 1965 return from exile in India, Türkeş turned to the civilian political world. He first joined the Work and Peasant Republican Party and was elected chairman. In part due to his military background, Türkeş developed a highly hierarchical party institution with special emphasis on youth groups. His followers created a myth surrounding his deep religious devotion, and Türkeş is believed to have received regular advice from Mustafa Aziz Çınar and Mehmet Faik Erbil from Arusi, a branch of the Nakshibendi religious sect.[50] Many observers of Turkish politics attributed the political appeal of the NAP to Alparslan Türkeş's charisma and authoritarian leadership and predicted the party's disintegration without his leadership. However, once his reign was over, the NAP weathered its leadership crisis and managed not only to maintain its presence but to increase its electoral support and emerge as a stronger political contender.

A review of the party's leadership structure shows that the NAP created a centralized role for the leadership at the same time that it established a closely linked, nationwide grassroots organization. Despite its rigid structure, this framework gave the NAP a remarkable institutional capacity to adapt to changing political conditions and prevented the party's collapse, despite electoral fluctuations. The teaching and ideas of Alparslan Türkeş still serve as the ideological anchor of the NAP, and he continues to be referred to as *Basbuğ* (commander-ruler) in the party's traditional military-like organization. The party members pledge "allegiance to the leader, the doctrine and the organization" at each meeting. The emphasis on loyalty to the leadership, however, has not prevented internal opposition. On the contrary, even the charismatic Türkeş faced serious leadership challenges. The defection of Muhsin Yazıcıoğlu evidences the intensification of internal strife, especially when the party's ideology undergoes internal changes.[51] Although the GUP itself formed around the strong appeal of Yazıcıoğlu, the leadership contended that "it rejects any organization that centers on the idea of infallible leaders, idolizing of leadership, and the domination by leaders." The GUP leadership thus implores the Islamist nationalists to avoid compartmentalization and defines its mission as removing "any restrictions on the individuals' ability to pursue their beliefs in *private and public.*"[52] Absent in the GUP emblem and ideology is the NAP's nationalistic symbols, such as the gray wolf, and its ideas, such as Türkeş's assumed leadership of Turkey, which for GUP is tantamount to idol worship, a deviant anti-Islamic practice condemned in the Qur'an. The GUP considers any form of nationalism centered on such symbols as un-Islamic. As opposed to their ability to form the state, the GUP highlights Turks' ability to organize and form civil society institutions for their political resiliency. Challenging the myths around Turkey, the GUP emphasizes the teaching of Seyyid Ahmet Arvasi who first used the term "Turkish Islamic ideal." Since Islam cannot be embraced selectively, only a full incorporation of the thirty-two *farz*, basic principles of Islam, into the party's nine guiding principles would save the NAP from being an incoherent religious nationalist party.[53]

In the same vein, the political background of Yazıcıoğlu epitomized the strong currents that shook and molded the NAP in the 1980s. Yazıcıoğlu served as the head of Ülkü Ocaks and, like many other Ülkücüs in the aftermath of the 1980 coup, was imprisoned for almost eight years without a conclusive conviction, a period that had a decisive Islamic influence on his ideology. Epitomizing the strenuous relationship between the state and Ülkücüs, he became the leader of the foundation that tried to protect the rights of the Ülkücüs who were imprisoned during the 1980s. As the wave of Islamization swept the NAP in the 1991 elections, Yazıcıoğlu's personal motto became "He will carry your beliefs to the parliament."[54] The defection of the GUP founders resolved neither the internal leadership nor the ideological conflict within the party. In fact, After Türkeş's death in 1997, the NAP skirted the edge of disintegration when competing groups such as the ones led by Devlet Bahçeli and Tuğrul Türkeş, son of the charismatic leader, disagreed on how to change the party's ideology. Devlet Bahçeli, a moderate academic lacking the appeal of Türkeş, emerged as the new leader, suggesting that the party had become more of an ideological party than a leader-centric party.[55] Bahçeli is a member of a Turkmen clan in the region known as the Fettahogullari, and he climbed the internal ladder of Ocaks while pursuing an academic career. This background increases his legitimacy in the party.

Even though many thought that Bahçeli lacked charismatic leadership qualities, he proved to be highly effective, confirming the *ülkücüs'* resiliency. Instead of reversing the party's Islamization, Bahçeli's statements such as "the *indecision* has come to an end, the transformation period is over, and the Turkish-Islamic Ideal has become the principal reference point for the party" marked another intriguing turning point in the party's history.[56] By adopting Islam as the main characteristic of "Turkishness," Bahçeli's leadership claimed religious issues as the party's natural political domain while maintaining its ethnic-nationalist party position. With its newly adopted Turkish Islamic rhetoric, the NAP reached the apex of its electoral success and surfaced as the second-largest party in the 1999 election.

Ironically, this electoral victory initiated a new wave of dissent within the party's leadership. On the one hand and in response to the party's growing popular appeal, Bahçeli maintained the idea of traditional leadership by incorporating Türkeş's entourage into the upper echelon of the party leadership. On the other hand, the party's search to strike a balance between Islam and nationalism while using their confluence as the driving force behind Turkey's role in a global world attracted a new group of experts and activists from different fields, who traditionally had not been affiliated with the party's Ocaks. People who do not move up through the party's grassroots organizations and still achieve high positions in the party's leadership are often distinguished as "not from ocak." The conflict between the party's internally developed and imported leaders defines the rivalry within the current party elite.[57]

Perhaps due to the recent transformation of the party's upper echelon and its previous ties to the student movement, the NAP's elite profile differs significantly from that of other parties. In 1999 the NAP's 127 members of Parliament had the highest level of education of any party in Parliament.[58] Since the party leadership came largely from *Ülkü Ocakları*, the party continues to rely on its traditional political mobilization tools. Compared with other parties, the NAP also has one of the lowest average ages (forty-five) among its elite. Furthermore, 82 percent of the NAP representatives are age fifty or younger.[59] In terms of women representatives, the NAP has the second-lowest number after the NV parties. This result is partially due to its dilemma regarding the turban issue, which forces the NAP to take a position between the state and Islam. In contrast to the Prosperity Party, the NAP also does not have well-organized women's groups, and the recent revival of its symbolic women's organizations has had limited success.[60]

In sum, the NAP's hierarchical leadership structure and institutional resilience has not prevented internal conflict or equipped the party with a highly adaptive capacity to accommodate diverse views. Although the party's efforts to incorporate Islamists and nationalists generate continuous clashes, the party has proven to be effective in sailing through crises and keeping its organizational structure intact. The party's embeddedness in local associations, the central role of the party network, and its relationship to the leadership allowed the NAP movement to go through a significant ideological transformation without disintegration. Its ideal of being a Kemalist Islamist Nationalist Party, which many in Turkish politics consider a contradiction in terms, represents both the most vulnerable point and the greatest asset of the party.

THE PROSPERITY PARTY: AN ANTISECULAR ISLAMIST OR A POPULIST MASS PARTY?

According to its leadership, the Prosperity Party represents "one of the youngest parties, but the oldest political movement in Turkey."[61] Ironically, all of the now-defunct parties affiliated with NV parties applied the same statement to themselves. In fact, the NV was one of the first overtly political Islamic movements that emerged when Turkey moved to a multiparty system. As explained earlier, the term *Islamic party* is an oxymoron when viewed in the official parameters of Turkish politics. According to the Turkish constitution and the Law on Political Parties "no one can use religion, religious feelings or things considered sacred in religion to change the state's social, economic, legal foundations for personal or political benefit."[62] In fact, although the movement in general remained intact, different incarnations of the NV parties were outlawed five times on the grounds that they encouraged divisions in society by using religion for political ends. It is important to note that the parties were closed down not because of their declared programs, but because of the praxis and statements the leadership made after making inroads into Turkish politics. After each closure, a new party was immediately established. The wholesale termination of all parties after military coups (see figure 4.1 for the reason for the closures) complicates the picture of the NV parties further. As explained earlier, the following discussion uses the term National View (NV) parties and the party's most recent name, Prosperity Party, interchangeably, so as not to confuse the reader with the multiplicity of names adopted after each closure. The NV movement, a broad grassroots network, avoided official legal scrutiny by organizing itself around civic associations and a *vakf* (foundation). The use of *National View* as the common name emphasizes both the popular foundation and the ideological and institutional tenacity of the movement that generated five successive parties.

The NV's main political positions are reflected in the views and the political biography of its leader, Erbakan. Prior to his NV leadership, Erbakan's efforts to be elected on the ticket of the Justice Party (JP), the main opponent of the Kemalist and secularist RPP, failed twice. While his bids to serve in Parliament were not successful, Erbakan managed to get elected as president of the Union of Turkey's Chambers of Commerce and Stock Exchange, an important political and economic position, by receiving the support of the emerging Anatolian bourgeoisie (as opposed to the established one). However, the dominant party, the JP, canceled the election of the chamber of commerce to prevent him from taking office. Thus, Erbakan's political career started out in opposition to both the secular RPP and its main opposition, the JP. He ran as an independent candidate only after exhausting the existing political venues, and in part, in order to leverage the endorsement of the emerging Anatolian bourgeoisie for political power. Yet his candidacy came in response to the encouragement of his spiritual leader Zait Kotku, a *Nakshibendi* leader.[63] Once his bid as an independent candidate succeeded, his national visibility was established, allowing him to take a leading role in the nascent NV movement.

Erbakan introduced the new National Order Party (NOP) to the public on January 26, 1970, with a statement that epitomized the party's emerging discourse: "After seeing diverted from its right path, today is the day we launched the rockets to reinstall our nation, to the orbit of its holy and glorious historical path, our dear nation who believes in *Hak* (which literally means both God and Justice), walked along the highest spiritual path who enjoins what is right and opposes what is wrong."[64] This perplexing but adeptly crafted hybrid rhetoric blended scientific modern terms and traditional Islamic expressions, thereby declaring the party's political success as a step forward in establishing a genuine religious community not in conflict with but in charge of scientific progress. When viewed from the Islamic perspective, this very statement included an allegory of

Quranic verse Al Imran 3.110, which says, "You are the best of the nations raised up for [the benefit of] men; you enjoin what is right and forbid the wrong and believe in Allah." With its first public appearance and
unique discourse, the party clearly indicated that it would be instrumental
in creating an Islamic world in Turkey's secular politics while also creating a secular world in its supporters' Islamic visions.

When religious and economic components of the similar statements
are accounted for, we can identify the two major objectives of the NV
parties: (1) to reestablish an Islamic community in the Turkish public
sphere and (2) to promote the interests of the emerging bourgeoisie that
existed on the periphery of Turkey's economic sphere. These two goals
reinforced each other, since the emerging bourgeoisie was not part of the
secularist elite and continued to adhere to Islamic symbols. At a deeper
level, the shared religious beliefs often lent themselves to the formation
of alternative economic relations, thereby reinforcing the ties among the
peripheral elite. By coupling the question of moral and material development, the NV promoted the idea that only moral development can initiate material progress. Therefore, the religious values of the nation, which
were suppressed by the Kemalist laicization process, should be liberated
to initiate genuine, locally grounded growth in the public sphere. Paradoxically, although the NV objected to the venues of the Kemalist project, it adopted its preoccupation with state-centered massive growth and
social transformation.

The Constitutional Court banned the NOP, the first party to represent the NV movement, one year after its first public appearance on the
grounds that the party's ideology was "divisive" and tacitly endorsed a
"theocratic state."[65] The court's decision initiated a reiterative process
in which parties were closed down and reopened immediately under a
different name. The NOP's successor, the National Salvation Party (NSP),
was founded on October 12, 1972. In its first parliamentary election,
the NSP won 11 percent of the total votes, positioning itself as a potentially pivotal coalition partner. The party's political abilities and the
competition between the center, Right, and Left became evident when
the NSP managed to form coalitions with two competing ideological
blocs: First, the coalition with the secularist RPP, the party the NSP
challenged the most, was formed in 1974. Although the coalition lasted
only a year, its decision to intervene militarily in Cyprus defined it as one
of the most significant governments in Turkish history. In relative terms,
the Cyprus events brought the NSP closer to the military, the traditional
protector of Turkish laicism. Then in 1975, the party joined in a right-
wing coalition government, the National Front. As a result of this alliance, the ideological lines that had strictly separated the participant

parties were reshuffled and became somewhat clouded in the eyes of their constituencies.

It is important to note that the NV parties' decisive electoral successes came only after the 1980 military coup, an event that marked a critical turning point in Turkish politics. The coup was launched in reaction to the ideological polarization and violent confrontations of the 1970s, which brought Turkey to the brink of civil war. According to some estimates, the fighting between different ideological groups claimed 1,606 lives in the eight months prior to the 1980 coup.[66] In reaction to the "ideological polarization and clashes" among nationalist Islamist and socialist-leaning groups, the military regime sought to purge Turkish politics of all divisive trends and associations. In the aftermath of the coup, all political parties, including the NSP and other civil society organizations, were banned.[67] Attesting to Islam's deeply ingrained power to justify policies during a crisis of stateness, the military government referred extensively to a Turkified and modernized Islam.

Kenan Evren, the leader of the military coup, introduced the new constitution as a novel contract not adopted from the West. More importantly, added Evren, it differed from other constitutions as it placed "compulsory religious education under its protection."[68] In the opinion of the military elite, the use of Islam was necessary to counterbalance "anti-systemic" leftist, antinationalist and secular ultranationalist ideologies. Given the global rise of Islam, only a reformed Islam and individuals well equipped with Islamic ideas could shield the country from the threat posed by the "Islamic Revolution" in Iran and its overt efforts to export the revolution. In the ideological vacuum following the 1980 coup, the military regime introduced a moderate Islam as one of the main pillars of the country's resuscitated politics to ensure its "continuing stability." The newly established Motherland Party, a morally conservative, Islamic and pro-free-market coalition, emerged as the largest party into the political sphere opened by the coup. In fact, the leader of the party, Turgut Özal, was a member of the NV parties in the 1970s and was at one time a candidate on its national ticket. Thus, the emerging political elite in the 1980s already possessed or had begun to forge close ties to Islamic circles and had successfully mobilized religious votes in a bid facilitated by the political environment of the post-1980 regime.

In 1983, the Welfare Party (WP) was established in the ideologically sterile environment of the postcoup era. Erbakan resumed his leadership role only after the restrictions on the political leaders of the pre-1980 parties were abolished in 1987. The party, however, failed to enter Parliament by missing the 10 percent national threshold—an unusually high limit that was set to eliminate small factions.[69] As described earlier, the Welfare Party overcame the restrictive electoral rules by forming the pre-election alliance, the "Holy Union."[70] The union, not the WP by itself, received 16.2 percent of the votes, documenting a sharp increase in the so-called votes of believers.[71] The coalition collapsed when the NAP members of Parliament resigned, but the sharp lines separating these three parties had already blurred. Despite the negative reactions from each bloc's hard-core constituency, what appeared to be a strategic partnership unintentionally promoted the ideological affinity between the parties and their supporters around the role of Islam.

In an electoral growth pattern similar to that of Shas, the NV parties consolidated their power at the local level first, establishing new political communities in peripheral urban areas as well as in towns and villages. In the 1994 local election, the WP won municipal control in six major cities, including Istanbul, Ankara, Konya, Kayseri, Erzurum, and Diyarbakır; twenty-eight provinces; and approximately four hundred smaller towns and districts, including almost all of the predominantly Kurdish municipalities in the southeast. The results were especially striking in that the party established itself not only in Ankara and Istanbul, the symbolic secular centers of Turkish modernization, but in Diyarbakir as well, the symbolic center of the Kurdish ethnic movement. The Welfare Party received 21.8 percent of total votes in the December 1995 parliamentary election, hitherto the highest number of votes received by a religious party in Turkey's history. Erbakan became the first Islamist prime minister of the "Welfare Path" government he formed with the True Path Party in July 1996.

A closer look at the electoral success suggests that the NV's electoral ascendancy rested on and was later challenged by several powerful crosscurrents:

1. The party's political leadership severed its ties with the religious order, *İskenderpaşa*, and its new leader Esad Çosan. This separation eventually forced the political leadership to use a more radical Islamic language to justify his Islamic credentials.

2. The party's success reflected the effective expansion of a new generation of economic and political elite at the local level that sought government power not only to represent their moral views but also to enact more supportive market policies.

3. A growing grassroots movement that also included a strong women's movement demanded policies not only to represent Islam in the public sphere, but to promote an internal reform of Islam.

4. The rapid expansion of the party created a need for leadership experts in different fields, which led to initiatives to recruit new members outside of local organizations. Some of these new recruits, such as Abdullah

Gül, aligned themselves with the emerging leadership within the party and eventually challenged the traditional party leadership.

5. The party changed its position on some core issues, such as European Union (EU) membership. Initially opposed to joining the EU, the leadership eventually toned down its criticism and finally endorsed membership. The strategic use of the European Court of Human Rights to overturn domestic decisions and the exposure to a free public sphere experienced by Turkish immigrants in European countries were instrumental in effecting this turnaround. Yet some party followers saw turning to the West to save Islam in Turkey as inconsistent with the party's policies.

6. The party's increasing political power raised public awareness of radical leaders and groups, heightening the secular public's anxiety about an Islamic takeover.

These countervailing trends placed the party at a crossroads and pulled it in opposite directions. A broad spectrum of ideological positions emerged, ranging from support for forging a more liberal platform through reform within the Islamic bloc to a movement toward becoming a more conservative Islamic party. The broader spectrum did not prevent the National Security Council (NSC) from centering its meetings on the growing radical and antisystemic Islamic activities. At the historical meeting on February 28, 1997, the NSC issued a set of "advisory decisions," a de facto ultimatum to limit the power of Islamic groups. The declaration, later described as a "soft military coup" or "post modern coup," showed how the secularity of the state continues to be seen as a security issue by the military.[72] Acting in violation of its own program, the NV government passed a set of laws embodying the military's decisions. Among other decisions, it introduced massive reforms that made eight years of state-controlled education compulsory and closed unregulated Quranic schools, undermining the main activities of the neighborhood religious communities. The weekly *Selam* published one of the best assessments of these policies from the pro-Islamist perspective:

On February 28, 1997, while the "Islamist" Necmettin Erbakan was prime minister, Turkey's generals declared war on the country's Islamic movement. This included curbs on Islamic education and social activities, the exclusion of "Islamists" from government jobs, sanctions against "pro-Islamic" businesses, and crackdowns on Islamic newspapers, organizations and student groups. Above all, it led to the persecution of Muslimahs [female Muslims] wearing hijab, headscarf. The crackdown and the popular resistance to it are continuing.[73]

Overall, the culmination of Islam's political power under the WP and the party's acceptance of policies that adversely affected the power bases of Islamic groups represented a sea change for Turkey's Islamist movement. The failure of the NV to deliver on its policy promises (1) reinforced the emerging fault lines over the appropriate strategy that would restore Islam's role in Turkish politics (e.g., confronting or co-opting existing institutions); (2) caused the alliance of various Islamic groups behind the NV to disintegrate; (3) showed that, although the military was under increasing pressure not to interfere with politics, a perceived challenge against the pillars of the regime still prompted it to take up its role as protector of the public sphere against religious intrusions, but in a way where it only exerted its power through the existing institutional venues; and (4) ushered in the decline of the NV's traditional leadership and of Turkey's first wave of state-oriented and confrontational political Islam.

In January of 1998, the Constitutional Court decided to dismantle the Welfare Party on the grounds that it promoted civil unrest by promoting religious hatred and sought to launch a theocratic state.[74] Unlike previous decisions, this time the party was not only depicted as antisecular but also antidemocratic. Public statements of NV leaders were used to prove that the party intended to undermine secular and democratic practices. Erbakan's statement, which has been repeated by the JDP leader Erdoğan, that "democracy is not an end, but a means for us" and Oğuzhan Asiltürk's assertion that "the order we shall bring has a big difference, as big as mountains, from the secularist and democratic order. Ours is on the mountain top, and democracy is in the abyss" were seen as evidence of the party's lack of commitment to democratic principles.

Following the closure of the Welfare Party, yet another NV party, the Virtue Party (VP), was born in 1998. The transfer of all but 5 of the 147 elected Welfare Party members of Parliament to the VP allowed the new party to be represented in Parliament.[75] It is important to note that the closure of NV parties led to forced leadership changes. However, the changes did not amount to real alteration in power in the movement. The term "trustee leader" emerged to describe newly chosen party leaders who took on the leadership positions, as Erbakan and his close entourage could no longer hold the official title due to the legal restrictions. Although Recai Kutan assumed party control in 1998, Erkaban's leadership remained intact. Proving its massive popularity and resiliency notwithstanding the high possibility of yet another closure, the VP still won 15.39 percent of the votes and 111 seats (out of 550) in the April 1999 election. When the VP was finally closed down in 2001, the closure prompted the bifurcation of the pro-Islamist movement into two separate parties, the Prosperity Party and the Justice and Development Party. The latter were established only one month after the VP's disappearance from the political sphere. Both parties competed in the 2002 national election. The Prosperity Party's astounding loss (i.e., it garnered only 2 percent of the total votes)

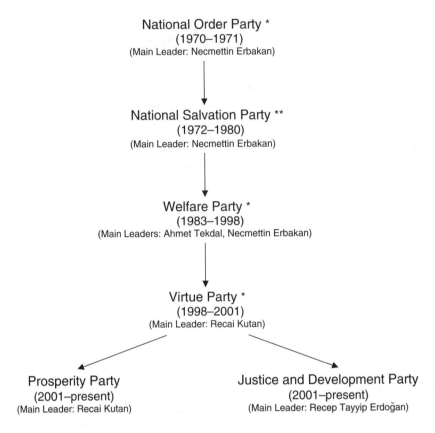

National Order Party *
(1970–1971)
(Main Leader: Necmettin Erbakan)

National Salvation Party **
(1972–1980)
(Main Leader: Necmettin Erbakan)

Welfare Party *
(1983–1998)
(Main Leaders: Ahmet Tekdal, Necmettin Erbakan)

Virtue Party *
(1998–2001)
(Main Leader: Recai Kutan)

Prosperity Party
(2001–present)
(Main Leader: Recai Kutan)

Justice and Development Party
(2001–present)
(Main Leader: Recep Tayyip Erdoğan)

FIGURE 4.1
Genealogy of National View parties

* Closed by the Constitutional Court.
** Closed by the military coup.

and the surprising emergence of the JDP (i.e., it received a remarkable 34 percent of the total votes) manifested another critical juncture in the NV's overall transformation and continuation.

The National View Parties and Kemalist Nationalism

A review of the National View parties vis-à-vis Kemalism first requires an understanding of how the establishment of the republic affected religious communities beyond the suppression/reaction paradigm. While Kemalist policies banned religious orders, the *tarikat,* the policy did not amount to a wholesale dismantling of these orders. More often than not, the orders responded to their closure by adjusting their overall organization and searching for a venue in the Islamic imagery to maintain their position.[76] As a result, many different religious institutions and interpretations came into being. One of the most successful organizations was the *Nakşibendi* (Nakshibendi) order. The order remains one of the oldest and most successful tarikats; it has followers in countries ranging from Australia to Pakistan.[77] The order's transformation following the state-constitutive years gives an indication of how the Turkish version of laïcité molded the Islamic groups. Under the leadership of Zait Kotku, the order promoted a new religious view, *Halvet der encumen*, the possibility of religious solitude amid people in society. Kotku understood the necessity of creating solitude for pursuing a pious life outside of the isolated, exclusively religious community where tarikats had traditionally dwelled. This new religious view of spiritual growth and learning opened a space for a life similar to that lived in a religious tarikat, but in an urban setting. *Sefer der vatan,* which originally meant traveling to be exposed to different ideas and moral enlightenment, became a voyage to one's inner world, thus endorsing not only a greater engagement in daily life, but also a more intense form of politics.[78]

The order's centers are located between major universities in the historical Istanbul neighborhood of Fatih, an area surrounded by universities. The center attracted a broad audience including the residents of the neighborhood (who are traditionally conservative in their religious views), college students, and the rising economic and intellectual elite. In this emerging community, the sect established one of the strongest ties between Islam and politics. The NV leaders were among those who were exposed to the new approach of the post-Kemalist revolution—an inward-looking, yet socially engaged religious community without seclusion. This reinterpretation of the order's basic moral principles explains the resilience of the tarikats but also shows the increasing need for the leadership to appropriately adapt tradition to new conditions. One of the unintended consequences of secular republican policies was to move tarikats closer to society while proclaiming any overt autonomous public expression of Islam to be a threat to the republic.

The NV parties' critique of Kemalism was articulated by Erbakan in his project *Adil Düzen,* Just Order. To understand Erbakan's political views, we need to refer to two sources: (1) the ideas shaped by his exposure to Zait Kotku and the Nakshibendi sect and (2) his education as an engineer and his experience of different political rules and cultures in

Europe, first as a graduate student, then as a professional. Reflecting the core of NV doctrine as well as his own personal encounters in Germany and France, Erbakan's book, *Milli Görüş*, calls Kemalism into as question as an unauthentic paradigm inspired by Western social models. Erbakan argued that, despite their regimes' "pseudo" successes, Western countries all contradict human nature and create deprived and alienated social communities. Most revealing for Erbakan were the monetary interactions that were absolutely mechanic, that only attended to the value exchanged and that failed to evaluate the state of the individuals involved in the transactions. "If you owe them 1 lira and gave them a 1000 bill they will make you wait for hours on Sunday until they find the right amount of change."[79]

Similar observations proved to Erbakan that excessive materialism had undermined the nature of human interactions. In the search of wealth, the worth of human interactions became secondary to the pursuit of monetary gain. Despite the Eastern bloc countries' criticisms of Western materialism, they failed to create a viable alternative. Lacking the competitive nature of Western countries, they substituted state control for competition in the regulation of the market. The result was an inefficient bureaucracy created just to "control the control."[80] This extreme concern with materialism contrasts with the deep attachment of Muslim communities to the spiritual benefits of Islam. No doubt, Erbakan surmises, Westerners would be puzzled if they saw how some shop owners in Muslim countries would ask them to shop at their neighbor's store to make certain both were earning enough income daily.

According to Erbakan, Kemalism looked for solutions to Turkey's problems in social models generated in the West due to its reflexive revulsion to tradition. These models, however, formed out of extraneous (non-Islamic) social conflicts and values and thus failed to address local issues or, more importantly, tap into Islam's innate progressive ideas.[81] In his Just Order, Erbakan concludes that to ameliorate the chronic ills of its system, Turkey must make a sharp turn and reclaim its roots in Islam. The Qur'an offers a model for balanced political and economic development, guiding people toward becoming morally responsible agents. For instance, good tradesmen, the driving force of growth, are part and parcel of Islamic culture, so much so that Islamic tradition promises that tradesmen will be summoned together with martyrs and prophets on the Day of Judgment. The Islamic system already incorporated the seeds of genuine economic development, yet Kemalism borrowed an approach that centered on interest and spending, perpetuated an unequal distribution of income, and fostered an understanding of the nature of the individual devoid of collective moral values. What Turkey needed, according to Erbakan, was a homegrown "Just Order," a moral, liberal economy where the establishment of local values, like trust among the participants, takes priority over the overall efficiency of the system. Moral individuals, not broad centralized economic programs, lead economic growth. According to the NOP program, the first openly Islamic party in Turkish politics,

When there are moral individuals, the nature of the political regimes becomes secondary and the economic performance reaches its highest. Regardless of whether the individual works in the public or private sector, they do not diverge from justice and do not squander each other's or the public's potential. We oppose the orders that deny this basic fact and the regimes that undermine the foundations of the social orders and then use the instability and disorder created to further deprive individuals of their economic and social rights thereby turning the country into a big prison. We also oppose regimes that leave the capital flow uncontrolled. The only solution to these economic regimes is first and foremost an installation of moral order. Thus, we support a morally ordered, mixed economy.[82]

The cardinal sin of Kemalism was to impose its inauthentic collective identity on Turkey through top-to-bottom social engineering that estranged people from their own values. The six principles of Kemalism, namely statism, reformism, populism, nationalism, secularism, and republicanism, were a poor adaptation of Western modernism and rationalism and an *ex post* rationalization of loosely related policies. Statism (i.e., the state's role as a pioneering and active agent of modernization) came at the expense of populism, which argues that the political sovereignty is vested in the people as a whole. Nationalism was defined in a minimalist sense as the indivisibility of the nation and the state. After the upheaval of the Nakshibendi Sheik Said, the Law for the Maintenance of the Public Order in 1925 and the Independence Tribunals led to the emergence of a political system that did not allow for the sharing of political power.[83] Thus, under the guise of modernizing the state, the Kemalist state reinvented Ottoman authoritarianism, denying any role for Islam.

The deep roots of Kemalism's suspicion toward Islam lie in the Kemalists' adoption of positivism, which accepted the Western idea that the Islamic way of thinking was not conducive to social progress.[84] In an effort to correct this fallacy, Erbakan dedicated an important part of his *Milli Görüş* to detail the scientific contribution of Muslims to the global culture. Instead of being antithetical to science, Islamic contributors helped to form the roots of positivism. Kemalism's fear of religion resulted in its misidentification of both Islamic and Western history. The very word *laicism*, which cannot be translated to Turkish, captured the Kemalist paradox. The phrase "such a critical word cannot stay as a foreign word" became one of the NV's main slogans.[85] The vague meaning attached to the term became a tool for implementers to marginalize believers. As a result, Turkish secularism distanced itself from its Muslim community, as well as from its European counterparts upon which it was modeled, by making it a tautology. Its practice is justified by its own elusive meaning: "When one says that every country has a *sui generis* democracy, that indicates that the person is off track in his thinking. Likewise, it is not possible to talk about a *sui generis* laicism."[86] The contradiction revealed itself in the contesting legal provisions. Penal Code item 632, which prohibits "abuse of religious beliefs," contrasted with the constitutional provisions that oblige the state to promote the moral development of individuals.

Recurring debates in the NV-affiliated *Milli Gazete* show in less abstract terms how the leadership's critique of secularism was presented. Mehmed Şevket Eygi, the former chairman of NSP, for instance, under the title "why Turkey is not a secular country," lists ten different policies that demonstrate how the state violates its own principle of laicization. Eygi contends that the state (1) through the Directorate of Religious Affairs employs and controls more than 100,000 *imams, müezzins, müftü,* and *vaiz,* namely those who provide religious services in mosques, conduct religious ceremonies, and offer religious consulting in the provinces; (2) has the right to confiscate any of the properties belonging to the *evkaf-i-islamiyye,* Islamic foundations, and may decide single-handedly to sell or rent this property; (3) regulates over a thousand religious vocational *İmam Hatip* schools and controls their curriculum and teaching directly, without delegating this authority to the Directorate of Religious Affairs; (4) intervenes in the daily practices of the believers, for example, in the matter of Islamic clothing, especially the veiling of Muslim students and civil servants; (5) not only organizes pilgrimages to Mecca, but also prevents pilgrimages through any other means, despite constitutional guarantees for freedom of travel; (6) adopts an official policy that opposes Muslim Iran, and instead, collaborates with "Zionist" Israel; (7) gives permission to protesters in the streets who often shout "damn Shariah and Islamic rule"; (8) continues to monopolize the collection of the skins of sacrificed animals (for religious rituals); (9) interferes in the matter of Muslims' clothing, such as *cüppe* and *teseddür*; and (10) while allowing non-Muslim minorities, Armenians, Greeks, Jews, and Assyrians to choose their chief priest and rabbis, prevents Muslims from electing their religious leaders.[87]

These objections to the "secularity of the Turkish state" are based on the NV elite's argument that Kemalism not only institutionalized its mistrust of religion in the public sphere, but that it also set in motion a self-fulfilling prophecy by weakening the existing political community and, thus, (inadvertently) the state. Regimes, especially democracies, easily degenerate into oppressive regimes in the absence of just individuals or in situations when political institutions are not open to its citizens' moral scrutiny. Thus, for the NV parties the restoration of the public role of individuals compels a wide range of reforms, from reducing the size of Parliament, to introducing the direct election of the president of the republic, to providing people with direct access to the Constitutional Court if their petition contains at least one hundred thousand signatures. It is important to note that all of the NV's novel projects remain, in one way or another, within the blueprint of the Kemalist paradigm. The invention of a parallel terminology and the depiction of a communal unity in the discussion of these models illustrated both appropriation of and opposition to Kemalism as a mutually reinforcing process. For example, *milli* is a dual term—both religious and national community—that is used in place of Kemalism's *ulus, nation.* The term "national consciousness (*şuur*)" replaced "general will (*irade*)." Any yearning for "economic growth" is always tied to the condition of "spiritual development." Only a common "deep consciousness of Islamic identity" and not laicism could eliminate differences in the national community and ensure *in pluribus unum.* Erbakan declares the conquest of Istanbul the national day of celebration instead of the opening day of the Grand National Assembly.

Despite the NV parties' broad, multilevel criticisms of Kemalism, the leadership adamantly opposed and continues to oppose being identified as an antisystemic or antilaicist party.[88] First of all, the party leadership believes that identifying the NV parties as antisecular only seeks to delegitimize the religious parties' political platform.[89] Given that Turkey's *laiklik* has not been true to its essence, calling the NV antilaicist is a misnomer. Second, and more importantly, an antisystemic and antisecular labeling in the Turkish context implies the rejection of nationalism altogether. *Milli Gazete*, the NV newspaper, which publishes the opinions of the movement's elite and ideologues, reiterates frequently that nationalism and religion must not be considered binaries.[90] "Some people want to set the flag against the mosque. But, the flag represents our independence and mosques are the guarantor of our ownership of this land."[91] The NV challenges not nationalism per se, but the nationalism invented and imposed by the secularist Kemalist regime, which claims to be the only form of patriotism.[92] According to Asım Yenihaber, a writer for *Akit,* one of the NV-affiliated newspapers:

A member of the nation does not necessarily need to be a nationalist. Patriotism is not a novel phenomenon that started with nationalism, and there is not an inevitable link between the two. Nationalism is not a historical and sociological concept, instead it is an invented theory sustained by sociological myths. Nationalists invent nations. It is unquestionable that a nation has been in the making in Turkey in the last 80 years. The name, shape and content of the nation were delineated clearly in the official documents. Inclusion of Atatürk Nationalism into the 1980 Constitution resulted from the efforts to suppress alternative conceptions of the nation, such as the one proposed by the National View Parties.[93]

A genuine nationalism should be expressive of the desires of the nation rather than forcefully imposed. Kemalism was invented as a tool for the continuation of the Western colonization of Muslim land following the decline of the Ottoman Empire. It was no coincidence that Kemalist policies strove to deprive religion of its independent financial and political sources. Nevertheless, reflecting the idea that noninterference lies at the heart of laicism, secularism in its Western form entails not only the protection of the state from different religious groups but also the protection of religious groups from the state and the religious groups from each other. When the state moves beyond its role as an apparatus to serve the political community and becomes a means to achieve political order and moral community, a Leviathan emerges from the process that ultimately destroys all citizens. This is why, according to Kutan, "the state should not be considered as a sacred institution owed incontestable allegiance."[94] Views regarding the state as sacred can only lead to authoritarian or totalitarian regimes like those prevalent in the European countries before the Second World War.

Community and Individual: Muslim Individuals Versus a Community of Believers?

The NV parties' rejection of the state's leading role and the "invented" nature of Kemalist nationalism is often taken as a sign of their communitarian commitment. In fact, the NV does differ from state-centric parties that define the state as a primary agent of change and the basic avenue for implementing social justice policies.[95] When we view the NV's understanding of community from the bottom up, a more detailed picture emerges that highlights two main components: a vertical understanding of community that stresses its relationship to the state and a horizontal view that centers on the relationships within and across the communities. The first dimension is a by-product of the movement's belief that limiting the state's power ipso facto expands the freedom of individuals and creates a system where communities coexist harmoniously in the public sphere.[96] When we analyze the specific beliefs that underpin the horizontal interaction, however, the NV parties' community-centered, emancipating ideas take on a rather different character. At this level, individuals are described in reference to their assumed shared identities such as "believers," "Muslims" or "folk," making the line between individuals and community vague.

One of the NV's most popular projects, establishing "a pluralistic judicial system," enables us to explore both how the party addresses the differences within and across communities and how secular ideas operate in Islamic practices. In essence, the NV contends that political arrangements need to protect individuals against the state's hegemonic and suppressive practices. For many Islamic intellectuals, *Medina Vesikası*, the Medina Contract, a social agreement that was introduced by the prophet, offers a blueprint for an ideal pluralistic community. Historically, the contract effectively coordinated the relationships between Muslims, Jews, and polytheists. One of the significant debates contributed by wider circles of Islamist intellectuals and the NV elite promoted the idea that new social models elicited from the contract would balance the rights and freedoms of members without relying on the heavy hand of the state to regulate differences. When facing their critics, however, the proponents of the contract had to represent the terms of the agreement to fit the paradigm of the nation-state. After all, skeptics contended, the contract treated different groups as ummahs and assigned them to distinctive territorial communal zones—practices incongruous with the idea of a nation-state. Even more importantly, the prophet's unrivaled appeal as a trustee who crossed communal lines was critical for the contract's success. In the eyes of the NV parties, the secularist elite was unable to recognize the contract's social and historical relevance and capacity to address social issues; they dismissed such models as anachronistic Islamic projects developed solely to promote Islamic ideals. For instance, comparable practices under the Ottoman Empire that shored up its multiethnic structure provided evidence that the contract could serve as a model for coexistence beyond the prophet in a society with diverse groups. Islamic communities had always been heterogeneous, and Islam had addressed plurality since its inception. Inspired by similar practices, the NV also proposed a set of new participatory institutions, such as an elected court system to empower individuals. Under such pluralistic legal systems, the configuration of the main courts would be decided by their constituencies. The courts would consist of members chosen by a majority of the elected officials in a given province. However, given the importance of the human-rights court, the members on that court would be elected directly by the citizens. Underneath this model lies the NV-affiliated elite idea that, regardless of their susceptibility to different levels of popular pressure, the discretion of elected judges promises to be more effective than the court decisions of the Kemalist state.

What makes the NV's Medina model and elected court system signifi-cant are not the details of the model itself, but its heuristic potential for explaining how the leadership applies idealized Islamic institutions to the anomalies of Kemalism and its tendency to turn to society to fix the social problems that the party attributes to the state.[97] The NV discourse regarding a pluralistic legal system suggests that an idealized society based on *millet*, autonomous communities and participatory institutions, addresses conflicts rooted in individual differences. The common notion of *ummah*, a unity formed by shared beliefs, makes individual communal differences irrelevant to the common identity. The conspicuous absence of any debate on individual rights beyond the rights from the state's inter-vention suggests that in the NV ideology, individuals are reduced to homogeneous units that are invested with collective ideas. According to Erbakan, for instance, "if a saint becomes a candidate for a colorless party (a party other than the NV parties), his sainthood would *not make any difference*, he cannot serve in the path of God. Nevertheless, even if a mentally ill person joins the ranks of our party, he can serve in the path of God" (emphases added).[98] What matters at the end is not the individual himself, but the community of individuals and their collective presence and actions. Similar statements reinforce the idea that the community of believers serves as the foundation of society, not the individual. The NV electoral slogan argues that the endeavors of just one group that spreads truth and justice can save the entire community.[99] Although the individu-als and the community are interdependent, the community's welfare takes precedence over that of the individual.

A nation is a union of communities under the protective gaze of the state. The state acts only as moderator. The NV parties' exclusive em-phasis on the public against the state allows it to promote the idea that the demos, the people, and not the state are essential for democracy. Ac-cording to the party elite, while the state does not have any nationality, the nation owns the state. The power of the state must be the same for all members and equally accessible to all.[100] The political community should have autonomy from the state. The assumption that a community con-sisting of Muslims inherently includes order allows the party to ignore the critical question of how internal conflicts will be resolved. However, the existence of multiple interpretations of Islam and numerous distinc-tive identities in Islamic communities challenge the NV's view of the Is-lamic community as a political unit that is intrinsically coherent (free of conflicts) and inclusive. The NV takes a risk when it embraces the indi-vidual in relation or in opposition to the state because the individual per se becomes an empty rhetorical image.

Inclusiveness Versus Exclusiveness of the NV Parties'
Turkish-Muslim Nation: Boundaries of Just Order?

When Aksal argued in his column in *Milli Gazete* that "the only forces that can undermine the peace and stability in the Middle Eastern Islamic territory are racist, nationalist tendencies," he captured one of the NV's key beliefs.[101] In the NV's view, nationalism is a tribal, exclusive ideology that undermines unity and order in society. Nationalism becomes especially problematic in regions such as the Middle East, where there are diverse cultural groups that are not represented by the existing nation-states. Ummah, on the other hand, allows for the existence of cultural, ethnic, and language differences and their expressions in the public sphere. The inherent incompatibility between ummah, the community of believers, and the modern concept of nation is the root cause of many social and political problems. The Kurdish problem, for instance, is a dilemma created by the Kemalist national character as it pushes the existing shared beliefs to the background of collective identity while failing to create new ones. In his speech on February 25, 1994, in Bingol, Erbakan made this argument:

They said to the children of this nation, leave your prayers and follow the world [materialism]. As a result neither the world nor prayers were left. The children of this nation started their school days with prayers for centuries. What did you do? You replaced it with the pledge of allegiance to the nation "I am Turkish, just, hardworking. . . ." When you make this statement to others, you give others, like the Kurdish Muslims, opportunity to say "I am Kurdish, I am more just, and more hardworking . . ." Parliament will be captured by believers one day. All rights were given back to [religious publics] without shedding blood.[102]

In countries like Turkey, problems pertaining to collective identity derive from coercive ethnic nationalism. In a striking contrast to the NAP's views, NV leadership's discussion in *Milli Gazete* and party programs reinforce the idea that "Turks are not a nation, neither are Arabs, Bosnians, Cherkessians, Kurds, or Albanians. They are communities."[103] They existed in history, lived together, and expressed their identity in their established institutions. According to the NV, nation-states, at best, are human artifacts and are bound to disintegrate unless maintained by people.

Bringing Islam back into the definition of national identity thus is an antidote to an exclusive national discourse. Vehbi Hatipoğlu, the Welfare Party's Kurdish Member of Parliament, echoes this argument and contends that addressing the Kurdish question requires recognizing that shared Islamic identity transcends the demands based on ethnic identities. Kurdish support for the Welfare Party needs to be seen not as a quest for separation, but as a quest for an integrative political community. "Not only Kurds, there are more than one million families with mixed ethnic backgrounds that cannot be forced to choose. We need to reject both the Turkish Islamist and the Kurdish Islamist syntheses which tries to divide *ummah.*"[104] Turkey's ethnic problems result from the policies of the state, not from the approaches of individuals and communities toward each other. In Eygi's open letter to Kurdish groups, the party's position was expressed more directly:

> Dear Kurdish citizens, just like you I have also complaints against the state. I am an Islamist who spent an important period of my life in exile and in prison. I am Turkish but not a Turkish-nationalist. I plead that you also keep away from Kurdish nationalism. Like our Muslim brethren, you are not a minority but a real owner of this state. Our flag also symbolizes our religion. Language is just a means . . . and the Kurdish language will be free soon. You should not undermine the entire unity because of the problems in the existing rule.[105]

The NV parties' idealized ummah draws on the idea of a Just Order grounded in shared values and Islamic brotherhood. Unity and consensus are both a premise and a promise of the Just Order. According to Erbakan's discussion in *Milli Görüş*, National View and Just Order include a transformative process. The ruling elite, a core group of believers, acts as the central agent for change, guiding other social groups toward moral perfection and economic progress. Gradually, new groups imbued with National View ideas are expected to replace all nonnative beliefs, strengthen unity, and liberate the local forces of economic progress. The dual promise of moral restoration and economic welfare enables the party to define itself as "the party of all those who are oppressed and excluded" under the Kemalist ideology and its current embodiments. These anti-status-quo and developmentalist ideas wrapped in an Islamic rhetoric allow the party to tie the problems of cultural and socioeconomic exclusion together and appeal to the masses who consider themselves culturally and economically marginalized.

Overall, the NV appears to replace the function of the state in the Kemalist project with religious community. The recurring lack of attention to the community's internal structure and opposition to any ideology that divides them, however, begs the question of what will happen when there are conflicts within the ummah or when individual differences cannot be associated with religious identities. When we turn to areas where the NV remains relatively silent, its views on "oppressed groups" take an intricate form. Especially intriguing is the NV's position on groups whose membership in *ummah* is controversial. The Alevis, one of the most significant heterodox Islamic groups in Turkey, are a prime example. Despite efforts by the party leadership to include Alevis in both the NV community and its leadership, only a small number of Alevi leaders currently participate at any level of the NV organization.[106] To make up for this deficit, *Bektaşis*, relatively more orthodox and more urban Alevis, are often brought to the fore and described as a group whose practices are commonly accepted by Islamic scholars and who are thus a part of *Ummedi Muhammediye, ummah.*[107]

Even among the NV's progressive wing and the current leadership of the JDP, one can find statements such as the ones offered by Erdoğan, "*if Alevism is following Caliph Ali, I am an Alevi,*" which carefully differentiates the current practice of Alevism from its origin and founding principles, that is, embracing Caliph Ali's leadership. Implicit in many similar statements is the idea that "we are all committed to the essence of Alevism, but Alevism diverged from its essence."[108] A full recognition requires that the Alevis return to their roots and prove their genuine membership in ummah through strengthening their ties to orthodox Islam. This conditional acceptance manifests itself in many opinions in *Milli Gazete*, which "urges a summit of the leaders of the Sunnis and *theirs* [Alevis]," and in essence, treats these groups as separate (emphasis added). In addition, sporadic remarks by NV leaders such as Kutan, who called Syrian Alevism "a deviant belief system," keep Alevi distrust alive.[109] According to party activists, the party's strategy of appealing to Alevis at the grassroots level is further handicapped by the NV's unfamiliarity with cultural religious symbols used to reach out to marginalized groups.[110]

In short, the NV's inclusive ideology is challenged by ummah's unity and its reduction of Islam to mostly hegemonic orthodox Islamic practices. The limitations of such reductionism manifest themselves best in the conditional acceptance of heterodox communities. The public practice of Islam becomes decisive in defining Muslim identity, notwithstanding the promise of inclusive membership in a Just Order and its national and transnational community. Arabic remains the language of religion, which with its shared, yet reified, Islamic symbols rooted in a common global community of ummah, prevails over different cultural practices and identities. Thus, in a paradoxical way, the initial acceptance of ethnic and cultural differences in ummah is homogenized at a deeper level.[111] The party's rhetoric does not address the status of groups who do not share the NV's symbolic religious system or those who interpret them in unconventional ways, such as the Alevis. As a result, the party's silence on how to deal with differences that result from divergent interpretations and historical constructions of Islam poses significant questions regarding the boundaries of its inclusive rhetoric.

The National View Party's Leadership

Until 2001 the National View movement and its political parties were led by Necmettin Erbakan alone. Even when Erbakan was barred from political activities, his leadership continued through surrogates. A closer look at Erbakan's personal history helps us to tease out some critical ideas inherent within NV parties. Erbakan's father was a lawyer who belonged to the relatively privileged class during the final years of the Ottoman Empire. In a striking contrast to the religious authority he exudes in his explanations, Erbakan had neither an extensive religious education nor an understanding of Arabic, skills that would have allowed him to read religious texts in the original language and offer novel interpretations. As a young man, he established close ties to the Nakshibendi Order's Gümüşhaneevi lodge in Istanbul and its leader Mehmed Zait Kotku. An argument can be made that some of Erbakan's core political ideas were formed under the spiritual mentorship of Kotku. These ideas crystallized during his graduate studies in Germany, his failed attempts to start a local motor factory, and his efforts to lead a massive industrial revolution in Turkey. It is important to note that Erkaban ran for public office only after Zait Kotku endorsed his involvement in politics "to stand closer to the rule[rs] to protect the believers from its oppression," a motto of Nakshibendi tradition.[112]

To understand the core ideas that guided Erbakan and later that of JDP founder Recep Tayyip Erdoğan, it is important to note that Seyh Ahmed Ziyauddin, the founder of the Gümüşhaneevi Dergah—who was tutored by, among others, Abdurrahman el-Harput—was known as a Kurdish Hodja. The core of Ziyauddin's teaching was shaped by the events that marked the early 1800s—the period when the Ottoman-British agreement opened the market to foreign capital. Ziyauddin, who himself came from a merchant family, started a movement to protect the local capital against Western penetration. Gümüşhaneevi came to be known as the house of *milli-Islam*, national Islam. Thus, Erbakan's ideas must be viewed within the framework of this tradition, where religious networks lend themselves to economic solidarity, where milli meant strengthening the local market, and where ethnic differences became secondary to common religious bonds. It is in the same tradition that Erdoğan's core ideas were molded.

It is also important to note that Zait Kotku remained close to the movement but remained invisible to the secular public and never became an overt leader of the NV. His weekly sermons resembled those of Ovadia. Like Ovadia, Kotku constantly translated religious arguments and rules from the Arabic texts into Turkish and gave specific advice on how to follow Islam in daily life. Perhaps as a reaction to the closure of his order in the early years of the republic, politics for Kotku has constituted a venue to protect the order and ensure its self-sufficiency. The Erbakan-led parties moved beyond a mere representation of this group of believers and defined their goals as becoming mass parties capturing the parliamentary majority. Interestingly, Erbakan's Islamic rhetoric became more radical after he distanced himself from the Nakshibendi order in the 1990s. One can argue that organic ties to religious groups allowed the leadership to use an areligious rhetoric more effectively. During this period, Erbakan likened his political efforts to *cihad*, the holy struggle, and embraced the title of *mücahid*, those who engage in cihad. Erbakan's relationship to the Naksi sect was weakened by the party's increasing political success. Esad Coşan, who succeeded Kotku, eventually began to openly question Erbakan's legitimacy and religious credentials. For instance, Coşan dismissed Erbakan's claim of mücahid as not only misleading but unsubstantiated by Islamic principles. "There is no war or conflict, but teaching the right way and spreading good news. Erbakan says he is *mücahid*. What is the basis of this claim? Those who are not well trained [in Islam and make such claims] do not help but ultimately hurt the Islamic movement."[113]

Interestingly, the NV's electoral power increased after the movement distanced itself from Coşan. Or one might argue that the party distanced itself from the Naksibendis when it attained a certain level of political influence. Lacking the support of a religious tarikat led directly to the transformation of the NV into a sect-like organization that closely resembled that of the Nakshi's religious order. The transformation increased Erbakan's role as a religio-political leader, which in turn became one of the reasons for the closure of NV parties in the 1990s and the eventual split of the party. Notwithstanding their tumultuous history, Erbakan, as well as the other members of the political elite, dominated the NV parties' leadership and managed to have the second-lowest rate of candidate change across all Turkish parties (30.63 percent), runner-up only to the Motherland Party.[114] Despite its populist image, the party leadership is highly educated, with an average age of fifty. A significant segment of the top leadership comes from among engineers, lawyers, and technological experts.

The NV's network (now inherited by the JDP) rests on a heterogeneously composed group of supporters who back a relatively homogeneous party elite. Although the network differs from those of other parties in Turkey, it has remarkable similarities with those of religious parties elsewhere in the world. Local activities center on *mahalle*, a main social unit consisting of a few streets where residents share shops and schools, elect their *muhtar*, the head of the neighborhood, and share the same voting booth. The party organization builds on the existing ties but also deepens them by adding new dimensions. Like Shas representatives, the NV's neighborhood representatives visit households and invite the families to join the party, identify their needs, or discuss ideas. These visits enable the party to collect demographic, social, and political information about each household, creating perhaps the most comprehensive database in Turkey about the electorate. Party activities, like those of Shas, focus on programs at the intersection of charity, community development, and individual empowerment and blend traditional activities with new ones. For instance, women's groups attend training programs that teach them how to sharpen their communication and political mobilization skills and visit orphanages, all on the same day.[115]

In fact, the party's ability to mobilize citizens and its responsiveness to diverse popular demands has made it the most effective civil and political organization in Turkey. One of the keys to the NV organization's success is the party's successful expansion of the political sphere into the private domain. Private household visits offer "natural domains" for political activities, where new ideas are expressed and exchanged in an informal setting. Such distinction is especially important for women. The party activists provide information about current political events or programs and further identify the household's expectations in order to coordinate the distribution of financial aid, reinforcing solidarity. In addition, the party provides public buildings and highly organized meetings, where men and women are allocated different spaces. The extension of the political to the private facilitates women's participation, and its activities are often explained as not intended for immediate political benefit, but for serving the collective good, hizmet, which also means serving a higher cause and Allah. This sacro-secular approach and the use of private-public hybrid domains changes the nature of politics in the eyes of the activists and strengthens the position of the leadership.

It is important to note that although women play a significant role in the party's local organization, female party activists are not represented in the upper echelon of the party. Only a very few female elite members who do not wear Islamic clothing or use Islamic rhetoric have joined the NV leadership by invitation. Along with the NAP, the NV parties have the lowest number of women candidates as a percentage of all candidates, 3.27 percent and 3.09 percent, respectively. The NV parties also have the lowest percentage of candidates with only elementary (2.18 percent) and secondary school education (16 percent). A majority of NV candidates have obtained higher education and, in spite of their religious rhetoric, only a limited number of them were actually educated in theology, although many of them received informal religious training, or learned Islam in a tarikat. The party's claim to be the true representative of the people raises a number of questions considering its rather homogeneous elite profile.

Despite their relatively similar background, it is misleading to describe the NV party leaders, including the JDP, as ideologically uniform: The leadership consists of two camps corresponding to *transformationalists,* those who focus on the rapid transformation of the political system, and *accommodationists*, those who promote pursuing incremental adaptive policies to allow Islam a greater role in public life. The original founders of the party come primarily from the transformationalists. For instance, Eygi, who can be called a purist and who expresses the former group's ideas most radically, denounces any attempts to reform Islam and condemns any efforts at interfaith dialogues as a conspiracy against Islam. Instead he advocates a bottom-to-top reformation of the political system, hoping to end the spiritual exile of Muslims in their own country.[116] The average age of the transformationalist group members is around sixty-nine, and their policies were shaped in reaction to the aggressive secularist policies of the 1940s, as well as the political environment created by the 1960 Constitution, which encouraged the expansion of civil organizations. Most members of the accommodationist group, who later formed the core of the JDP leadership, climbed to the upper levels of the party through their successful roles in local government. This group also includes those who were activists in the party's local organizations and graduates of *İmam Hatip*, religious vocational schools.[117] In contrast to the transformationalists, not only do the accommodationists have a significantly lower average age (forty), their views have been molded by their local governing experiences, therefore inhibiting a state-centric perspective within their ideology. A small cadre of accommodationists bypassed the party's training because Erbakan invited them personally to become members. Among those is one of JDP's current leaders, Abdullah Gül, or Merve Kavakçı.

Even though their opposition to and perceived exclusion by the secular regime forged a sense of unity under the leadership of Erbakan, the NV parties experienced a growing rift in their leadership cadre, which culminated in the birth of the JDP. The fragmentation surfaced visibly during the 2000 party congress, when Erbakan's leadership was formally challenged for the first time. Forty-five percent of the party delegates voted for Abdullah Gül as party chairman, virtually splitting the party in two and ushering in the brand-new JDP.[118] The internal party debates revolving around the Gül candidacy help us to better assess the importance and limits of the NV's internal democracy that has been inherited by the JDP. Although the party elects its Central Decision Making and Executive Board, opposition to Gül's leadership bid demonstrated that the core leadership favored *istiare*, consultation and deliberation, over elections with respect to internal party matters. According to Lütfü Esengün, "Until 2000 the party [the NV parties] did not have any internal tension, not due to the party's control of the groups, but because of the principle of letting everyone express their wishes. *Democracy is not just voting.* Those parties that equated democracy with elections have faced significant

problems, such as the RPP, which supported elections but omitted consultation. The RPP [therefore] teetered on the brink of disintegration."[119]
As a result, the RPP's intraparty voting processes have seemed to be destructive, despite their central role in the party's efforts to gain political
power beyond the party. For critics within the party, Erbakan's charismatic appeal makes internal deliberation processes defunct and leaves
voting as the only venue to secure internal democracy.

Against this background, the JDP leadership cannot be seen as an emergence of a novel alternative Islamist elite but rather as a political alliance
that was formed to strengthen the political bid of accommodationists as
opposed to transformationalists. The differences between these two
groups help us to understand not only the way in which the political fulcrum of the NV movements changed with the emergence of the JDP but
also how the JDP shares the political and intellectual accumulation of the
NV parties. Despite the Prosperity Party's and the JDP's different
emphases on the state and the individual respectively, both the NV parties,
under the leadership of Erbakan and Erdoğan, oppose counter-acculturation
(isolation from the secular world). On the contrary, they reconcile secular
and religious practices by endorsing state-level and individual-level policies
in distinctive ways. Both parties play a leading role in the transformation
of Turkey's Islamic and secular spheres, and they constantly reinvent
themselves in response to the changes in them. As a result of its harsh critique of the laicization policies of the state, the NV core leadership's rhetoric continues to hold a unique place in Turkey's politics. The divergence
of the NV parties and the JDP, and the establishment of the JDP as an independent and pivotal party, indicates two different levels of internal secularization processes and multiple uses of Islam.

THE JUSTICE AND DEVELOPMENT PARTY: A NEW
BRAND OF ISLAMIST PARTY?

Notwithstanding the JDP founders' strong ties to the NV leadership and
their reliance on the same grassroots organizations, the JDP described and
continues to identify itself as a brand-new party, the first conservative
democratic party in Turkish politics. This distancing is in part a forced
strategy required by the law that prohibits the continuation of a closed-
down party. Given the presence of a deep organic connection, the transformation of the NV begs the question not of whether, but of how and to
what extent the JDP's leadership and ideology differ from those of the NV
parties. In the following section, we place the JDP amid the crosscurrents
of changing approaches and continued ideas.

The JDP: An Islamic-Democratic Party?

The JDP's approach to the state and Kemalist nationalism cannot be understood without taking into account the legacy of the NV parties and the new social forces that imprinted the party's formation. A review of the JDP's rhetoric quickly illustrates that the JDP forgoes the NV's anti-Kemalist rhetoric, which questions the legitimacy of the existing system. In fact, Cemil Cicek's statement that "one can not engage in politics while waging a war against the tank [i.e., the military], we need to be realistic," summarizes the party's decision not to swim against currents and clash with the main institutions such as the Constitutional Court, the military, the NSC, and the Institute of Higher Education.[120] Reflecting this shift, the word *realistic* and its derivatives are used more than thirty times in the JDP's succinct political program, begging the question of what realism entails.

One of the most striking manifestations of this new "realistic" approach is seen not in the JDP's avoidance of a confrontation with Kemalism, but rather in its pursuit of an adaptive incremental transformative process. Instead of treating Kemalism as an external project to the Turkish Islamist, the party's rhetoric and policies adapt Kemalism's own goals and question them on their own terms. Driving this approach is the idea that confrontation at the expense of exclusion from politics is not a sound political strategy. The simplest and most popular expression of this stance can be found in Erdoğan's use of sports analogies to explain the avoidance of an antisystemic approach. Comparing the constraints imposed by state institutions to decisions made by referees in a soccer game, Erdoğan argues, "*Even if your objection is right,* there is no example where a referee reverses his decision. So it is futile to argue with referees and no one gains if you are expelled from the game"(emphases added).[121] As result, instead of pursuing radical changes, the JDP applies its political power to launch institutional reforms and assumes that the trickle-down effect of the implemented restructuring will eventually alter the political democratic practice and political culture.

The JDP's approach compels it to revisit the politics of Islam using references that were externalized by Islamic groups. For instance, missing in the JDP's program is the NV's main thesis that laicism is not a local term; thus in its foreign form, it is not a guarantee of Turkey's democracy but a main obstacle in its path. In contrast, the JDP program states, "Our party considers secularism as a pre-requisite of democracy, an assurance of freedom of religion and conscience." Indicating the party's compliant protest, the same section also concludes that the party "views religion as one of the most important institutions of humanity."

Our party rejects the interpretation and distortion of secularism as enmity against religion. . . . It considers the attitudes and practices which disturb pious people, and which discriminate against them due to their religious lives and preferences, as anti-democratic and in contradiction to human rights and freedoms. On the other hand, it is also unacceptable to make use of religion for political, economic and other interests, or to put pressure on people who think and live differently by using religion.

Perhaps most paradoxical is that in the party's continuous questioning of the misapplication of secularism, it rarely uses the word *Islam*. Instead, the broad categorical word *religion* is used sixteen times while *Islam* appears three times in reference to art and foreign relations. More importantly, the party's rhetoric does not treat the West categorically; instead, it pluralizes it and refers to certain parts as a positive model. Accordingly, the JDP's program states, Turkish laicism "tries to emulate the French model instead of the Anglo-Saxon one, but unsuccessfully. Based on its practice, we can conclude that Turkey's secularism is in fact more of an Anglo-Saxon model, where religion is put to the service of the nation state."[122] For the party, it is not laicism but an interventionist form of laicism that poses a problem in democracy as it seeks to *regulate* the marketplace of values, while politics, in essence, draws upon *free* and *competing* sources of values. Echoing the views of other pro-Islamic groups, the JDP contends that while a politics based on free expression of values can generate consensus, a merely interest-based political system is doomed to result in conflict. Therefore, stable politics cannot be free of values, especially in societies where politics increasingly relies on interest groups.[123] Likewise, in its *Temel Kavramlar, Fundamental Concepts,* the JDP defines the moral mission of politics as the deliverance of justice in the public sphere. The term *justice* does not mean a dry application of legal rules. Justice has rational meanings, such as being impartial, not erring, treating people equally, being balanced. It also has spiritual and virtuous connotations, such as being fair, moderate, equitable, tolerant, and compassionate. Thus, secularism as practiced in Turkey embodies self-defiant ideas, crippling the idea of justice.

According to the JDP's official documents, the *qualifiers* attached to the term *democracy* capture their distinct core values and identify the various ways in which the polities define social justice. Social democracy and liberal democracy each adhere to different understandings of social justice and use different tools to achieve it. In this tradition, the JDP contends that its understanding of democracy is *conservative democracy*. Conservative for the party is not blind adherence to habits or customs. Instead, conservative entails restoring wisdom, *hikmet,* tradition's divine and hidden reason, passed collectively from generation to generation. In contrast to its sweeping reform programs, the party leadership states that it objects to any social engineering and radical transformation. In a conservative democracy, commitment to deeply shared values is treated as the sine qua non of political transformation rather than an obstacle to it. All in all, the adoption of the new label of conservative democracy, a term that has no precedent in the country's history, allows the party to open a new political sphere beyond the Islamic-secular tension:

We are bringing about a new concept [conservative democracy] not in an abstract manner, but also in a concrete manner, and this is something that needs to be discussed, debated. Our objective here is to look at all sorts of different approaches and attitudes to find out what we can accumulate from them. Supporting a process of change that is evolutionary, gradual, and based on transformation in its natural course, we emphasize the importance of preserving values and achievements, rather than the preservation of present institutions and relations. The ideal is not to have a mechanical democracy that is reduced to elections and certain institutions, but an organic democracy that pervades the administrative, social, and political fields. We refer to this—we coined a new term for it, and I'd like to underline it—we refer to this as "deep democracy."[124]

Echoing the NV parties' stance, the JDP's policies rest on the premise that the discord between the state and society is the root cause of Turkey's problems. As a result, the party reduces the question of Islam to the state's approach to religion and its inability to respond to the individual's desire for religious rights. As a corollary, for the party all pressing political problems can be solved with two major efforts: reforming the state's institutional structure and limiting its coercive power and autonomy vis-à-vis the public. From the perspective of the JDP, a small state does not necessarily amount to less Kemalism. Instead, the original goals of Kemalism will be realized when the overexpanded state disengages from areas where it has impeded organic developments. As a result, unlike the NV, the JDP does not focus on the ideology of the state but on its institutional configuration and efficiency. Likewise, the question of Kemalism has been redefined as a question of restrictive democracy.

To make Kemalist secularism compatible with liberal democracy, the JDP leadership argues that laicism must be understood as having bearing on both institutions and individuals. Although institutions can be secular, individuals cannot. The state can and must distance itself from religious traditions in order to create an environment of religious freedom, allowing individuals to *naturally* express their religious views via their political choices. To achieve a real democracy, the state's role must be confined to redistributive and regulatory policies and its secularism should be understood not as active neutralization, but as a passive "non-intervention" in public expressions of Islam. At the individual level, however, the party contends that the official discussion of secularism entails offering individuals the means to

learn and practice their religion. Thus, the party's program declares that
"as a requirement of the principle of secularism all facilities shall be provided for our citizens to learn their religion. In addition to the lessons of
Religious Culture and Ethical Science, based on the wishes of the parents,
the provision of selective Religion Lessons shall be made optional."[125]
Thus, in a contradictory way, the same state that is noninterventionist at the
institutional level is also given the role not of an enabler but of a provider
(i.e., interventionist) in individuals' religious training and education.

The JDP's critique of secularism as a question of democracy also manifests itself in its justification of its efforts to join the EU. For the NV parties, the West embodied Islam's "other" and was characterized as an exclusive and oppressive entity with neocolonialist approaches. Furthermore,
the EU was often depicted as a Christian club, where religious mores defined the political goals. Surprisingly, however, taking the NV parties'
moderating approach to an unexpected level, the JDP religiously committed itself to Turkey's EU bid. This change can be mainly attributed to five
processes: (1) Turkey's acceptance of the European Court of Human
Rights' authority, which opened the way for Islamist groups to challenge
the Turkish state's authoritarian policies, especially with respect to religious freedoms; (2) the rising Islamic bourgeoisie's demand for the free
movement of capital; (3) the increasing pressure on Islamist groups after
the February 1997 soft military coup, which reinforced the sense of an in-
tractably constricted political sphere in Turkey and a need to look for
new venues; (4) the increasing mobilization and mobility of Turkish populations in Europe and their political impact on Turkey's pro-Islamic
movements; and (5) the unifying power of EU membership, which brings
diverse groups with conflicting interests together and offers significant
political capital. For some, EU membership meant achieving the Kemalist
ideal of "reaching the level of modern countries"; for others it meant liberating the public sphere to allow more public expressions of Islam.

However, a review of its raison d'etre indicates that JDP's EU policies
rest on two premises: First, the Copenhagen criteria captured the JDP's
domestic project because of its capacity to create a limited state and free
public sphere, especially for marginalized groups. The EU in this regard
serves as a means to an end and "the party would [have found] another
conduit" to achieve similar goals if the EU had not been present.[126] And
second, given the global discourse on the clash of civilizations, Turkey's
role in Europe is to act as a catalyst in reconciling differences across
divergent religious communities. Engaging with the West through EU
candidacy gives the JDP the power not to become a part of the Christian
club but to represent Islamic identity in it. The party presents its policies
and engagement with other countries as a conservative Islamic party as

the only way to prove that the clash of civilization thesis is not inevitable. This role has become especially important in the post–September 11 world, where clashes along religious lines gained remarkable salience. The party's claim of being a moderate voice of Islam in an increasingly difficult intercivilizational dialogue makes it a credible agent in world politics and in return increases its leverage in domestic politics.

Using its parliamentary power gained in the 2002 elections, the party unleashed massive institutional reforms to meet the Copenhagen criteria, which require the launch of the free public sphere, a decentralized administrative structure, and a free market. This structure-focused approach allows the party to put identity-related questions in domestic politics to the back burner. Attending to such identities in Turkey, the JDP leadership argues, brings to the fore the contradiction between the state's official policy and individuals' Muslim identities, which cannot be addressed within the framework of the existing institutions. Instead, the party addressed identities using the terms of the global debate (West vs. the rest, Muslims and others) attending to the increased emphasis on the transformative forces of transnational currents.[127] As the party aims to represent Islam in the global community, it also plays an active role in the Muslim world. Not accidentally, for the first time in its history, a Turk was elected president of the Islamic Development Institute. This politics of engagement or "rhythmic politics," in the words of the JDP leadership, adopts the values of the West to challenge Kemalism and to deprive it of its main political discourse. Thus, the JDP not only effectively appropriates the end goal of Kemalist ideals, it also uses the Kemalist yardstick, Westernization, to measure and legitimize the policies it pursues.

Community and Individual: Democratic Community and Muslim Individuals

In *Fundamental Concepts*, the JDP describes its main approach as "human-centered politics." Although this new discursive appeal maintains the NV's views regarding community, the individual appears as the new anchor. While the NV parties proceeded on the assumption that a moral community was already present but handicapped by the state, the JDP expands this view by including less visible social changes that have undermined that community. For example, the changes happening in cities today are seen as crucial developments in linking individuals and communities in Turkey's democratic society. The attention to urban centers differs from the NV's rhetoric, which focused on the needs of traditional communities that lived in peripheral urban settings and fringes of newly emerging markets. Conversely, the JDP depicts individuals as active and able residents of

the cities and able and effective players in the market. Attesting to this vision, *Fundamental Concepts* depicts the urban setting in great detail: Living in the city changes not only the lifestyle, but also the identities of those
who immigrate there. The natural ties among individuals weaken, while
new ties are created based on different foundations, such as nostalgia for
traditional communities. The change process yields varied outcomes. For
example, some individuals or groups emerge who see differences with outsiders in absolute terms; other communities rest on fragile emotional ties.
In modern societies, reason is expected to dominate other values and guide
social life. In contrast, the JDP leadership argues that a postmodern society
is unfolding where the role played by reason has been left unclaimed. The
overall postmodern identity in the cities is based on suspicion and vulner-
abilities. "Thus there are two challenges facing modern democracies: reconciling the reason and ethics that modernity separated and balancing the
claims to equality and difference."[128]

The JDP's critique of Turkey's present and changing urban settings allows it to differ from the NV parties' emphasis: the NV parties view
transformation as an extraneous exercise where individuals play more of
a reactive than a proactive role while the JDP sees transformation as a
pervasive and ubiquitous process where individuals have the capacity to
mold this change in particular directions. The party's claim to center its
models on the "human" not only highlights the party's difference from
state-centered parties like the NV but also reminds supporters of the social transformation in which individuals play a key role. The party defines
the restrictions on Islam as a question of human rights and reinforces the
necessity to separate the discussion of Islam from the question of state.
The importance of this new distinction can be seen in the party's ideological justifications. Yalçın Akdoğan, one of the leading architects of the
party's ideology of conservative democracy, identifies two radical approaches to politics: (1) political congregations create political groups
based on community and unquestionable allegiances and (2) political
firms form political "companies" or "corporations" drawing solely on
material interests.[129] Although both approaches differ drastically, each
can be equally dogmatic and deprive politics of alternative ideas. While
other parties are galvanized to these extremes, embracing conservative
democracy lets the JDP distance itself from them. As the party tries to find
a place above state-, community- or interest-centered politics, it turns to
a new foundation to substantiate its political claims.

Notwithstanding the rhetorical centrality of individuals as opposed to
the community, some homogenizing generalizations continue to permeate
the JDP's views in new forms. On the one hand, the individual as the carrier of collective reason surfaces as one of the main justifications of the

JDP's policies. Not only was "collective reason" never used in the NV's rhetoric before, but the term also opens a new discursive sphere with the potential of valuing deliberation and cooperative decision-making processes. However, despite its initial promise, collective reasoning faces several limitations. For instance, the discussion of conservative democracy reveals that the party equates collective reasoning not with an open-ended deliberative process, but with a discovery of ideas informed by the "common values" shared by society. In the process of discovering their ideals, the party rhetoric increasingly reifies common values, ultimately reducing them to resilient values derived from traditions and religion. More importantly, although the terms indicate a significant shift from the elite to civil society, instead of relying on inclusive participatory processes to unearth this reasoning, the party declares itself to be the voice of the people on the grounds of its close ties to society. As a result, while the reference to collective reason and common values seems to empower individuals, the terms' vagueness risks subduing individuals to another level of collectivity.

In fact, a closer reading of the party's program and the leaders' explanations presents common values as a critical yet increasingly ambivalent term as the party avoids defining what these values actually convey, how widely they are shared, or whether they can be changed. "What we [the JDP] understand from conservatism is not the protection of [all] existing institutions and relationships [values] but *only some of them*. Conservation does not mean being resistant to transformation and progress, but to adjust to changes without losing your *essence*"(emphases added).[130] The JDP objects to blind rejection or acceptance of tradition and modernity and emphasizes the necessity of a synthesis between the two: "It is necessary to accept modernity in its full extent, especially its progressive pillar of advanced technology, higher education, and urbanization. Nevertheless, its philosophical foundations, individualism, secularism, rationality, and materialism should be first differentiated from their misconceived practices and descriptions, [and only then] mixed with local values."[131] Similar statements suggest that while the party presumes to know what constitutes common values, the values themselves have remained highly elusive in the JDP's newly generated ideology, rendering them susceptible to authoritarian interpretations and political practices.

How the party defines common values and what its rejection of deteriorated "individualism" entails is not a rhetorical question. On the contrary, the party's justification of its failed attempt to criminalize adultery as a response to popular demands indicates that its perceived common values guide its policies. More importantly, the fact that punishing adultery is both an Islamic rule and a traditional practice often used to defend honor killings, a tradition the party's women branches are especially critical of, points out the intricate nature of these values and the complex situations that they generate. Such multifaceted practices beg the question of how the party would treat questions where values conflict and how they would address those intrasociety issues that are often observed in traditional, patriarchal, and sometimes semifeudal family structures. In fact, the JDP's Islamist women activists vehemently disparage the overtly patriarchal and traditional values espoused under religious principles—a point often overshadowed by their critique of the secularist state. In fact, in areas where the traditional role of women and the individual political identity of women conflict, the party's rhetorical commitments and praxis have also been seen to clash. For instance, although the party commits itself to promoting women in politics, its efforts to support women as independent political agents remain limited. On the one hand, the party adopts a 20 percent rule to allocate one-fifth of the seats in the local governing councils to women. On the other hand, notwithstanding the party's unprecedented legislative power and organizational control, only a limited number of its centers (five in 2005) enforce this rule. It is important to note that the national secularist constraints are not often applied rigidly at the local level; that is, conservative Muslim women are able to serve in local elected positions *and* wear headscarves.[132] Although the party declared its goal to increase the number of women candidates, its placement of only 21 (out 550) women in "potentially winnable" positions in the 2007 elections further confirms the gap between its rhetorical commitments and praxis. Although the party now has a greater number of women representatives, in part due to the wide criticism it faced from its observers, many of these women joined the party by invitation of the leadership and do not have close ties to the party's grassroots.

In essence, instead of echoing pro-Islamist groups' critiques of Kemalism as Westernist and anti-Islamic, the JDP, through its conservative democracy, turns to Western political traditions to present its ideas.[133] Allying itself with the worldwide family of conservative ideologies, its manifesto, *Conservative Democracy,* declared that the party rejects the tension between individuals, family, and society. "Society is not the coffin but the cradle of individuality." Yet conventional wisdom tells us, the manifesto argues, that individuals are bound to err; thus society's accumulated wisdom comes first and the family serves as a link between the two.[134] Interestingly, the party's ideological support for private property and free enterprise is also presented as a venue to strengthen the family structure. Thus, the concept of family represents the middle ground, where the party can merge its moral and economic stances. All in all, in the JDP's vision the individual gains strength as the agent and carrier of common values, yet he or she also becomes a member of a rather ambiguous group, neither purely traditional nor purely market oriented but rather a hybrid of both. This diffused understanding of community frees the JDP from seeing religious communities as the ultimate reference point of its policies and offers a new individual that the party seems to not only represent but to define.

Inclusiveness Versus Exclusiveness of Conservative Democracy: The JDP's Others?

According to Akif Gülle, one of the founders of the JDP, the party is best represented as the "Kızılay circle of Turkish Politics." Kızılay is one of Turkey's main cultural, educational, and financial districts in the capital. "The residents of Mamak [a working class neighborhood] and Çankaya [a region where many secular bureaucrats live] come to the circle in different vehicles (sometimes on foot) and for different reasons."[135] Unlike its predecessors, the JDP does not define its role as a party of the oppressed or a party of believers, but a party responsive to the "demands of society" and a mere reflector of the people's values and beliefs.

The JDP represents the feelings of our cherished nation in the government of Turkey. This is our mission as a party. Values, which underlie these feelings, have become and shall continue to be the fundamental values for the formation of policies. We have achieved a great convergence by opening our door to everyone who embraced the aspirations of the nation. A sulky and burdensome state shall be eliminated, and will be replaced by a smiling and capable state. The concept of *"a nation for the state"* will not be imposed any longer, and the concept of *"a state for the nation"* shall flourish instead. The state shall be prevented from becoming fetters around the legs of the nation, which prevents its progress.[136]

Following the NV tradition for the party, the Kemalist idea of "the nation for the state" made the state's acceptance of different groups contingent on their embracing Kemalism's secular, ethnic, nationalist vision. In reaction to that, the JDP program clearly spells out that "there is no obligation, in our understanding, for differences to be converted into homogeneity. This diversity is the culture of different people living together in peace, filtered through our historical experience." This idealized approach to diversity, however, begs the questions that were raised in the party's own publication: Does the party favor absolute pluralism or diversity, or is it reacting to state-controlled limited pluralism? More importantly, what will keep the diverse groups together if all groups were to claim the fullest recognition? To determine the premises that lie beneath the party's commitments requires a litmus test of the debates on Turkey's ideologies inclusiveness, the most notable of which are the Kurdish question and the status of the Alevis.

The JDP's position on the Kurdish question both diverges from and resembles that of the NV parties. On the one hand and on the ground of common Islamic elements in the Turkish identity, the JDP declares Kurdish rights to ethnic difference as indispensable to Turkey's political unity. On the other hand, the party's public rhetoric, unlike that of the NV parties, openly defines the Kurdish problem as a problem created by state policies. In the words of Erdoğan:

We don't need to name each quandary [in Turkish politics]. But if we have to name this problem let's describe it [as] "the Kurdish problem." It is not the problem of the one part of the country but it is our problem. It does not suit a powerful state to disregard the mistakes committed in the past. Even when I was in prison I sent out a message: "I am not angry at my state. This state and this flag belong to all of us. There will be a day that mistakes will be repaired." I sent this message to you from prison. It is my and my friends' dream that everyone will be a first rate citizen under this flag. The rule of law won't be a visitor, but the owners of this land, the freedoms will be realized fully.[137]

To place this statement in perspective, it is important to note that it was not until 1995 that the Turkish Parliament changed Article 8 of the antiterror law, which had been adopted to fight the Kurdish insurgency, so that a public discussion of Kurdish issues would not be a legal offense. Erdoğan's speech was one of the first public statements on the state's role in the Kurdish problem. Conventional framing of the issue cultivated the idea that the state's policies were only a reaction and not an integral part of the Kurdish question. Erdoğan, however, not only defined the issue as an ethnic Kurdish problem, but also depicted it as a vicious cycle created from the claims of difference and the state's policy of repression. According to the party program, the Kurdish problem turned to a perpetual conflict based on "terror and oppression [that] respectively feed one another. Any approach which ignores that terror is *a consequence* [not a reason] produces only oppressive solutions. Cultural diversities do not require that commonalities with the region's population be disregarded. Expression of language and other cultural traits do not challenge national unity."[138]

The JDP's assessment included an invitation to the state to acknowledge its past mistakes. Despite its reformist façade, however, at a deeper level the party's approach reiterates its ideological premises that (1) the Kurdish problem is a vertical problem, that is, a problem limited primarily to the distorted relationship between the state and Kurdish groups; and (2) the withdrawal of the state and the installation of free-market institutions will transform the region's conflicts into havens of permanent consensus. A less obvious side of the JDP's approach to the Kurdish issue, as well as the broader question of how to level the playing field for disadvantaged groups, surfaced immediately after Erdoğan's historical speech in a simple exchange between Erdoğan and a Kurdish member of the audience. In a response to a request from a person in the local audience, Erdoğan expressed another aspect of the party's overarching principle. "We want a factory," shouted a Kurdish villager, a common outburst in any meeting held by politicians in a region where the unemployment rate is much higher than the national average. "We won't build a factory here," answered Erdoğan. "We passed a law encouraging investment in this region. We want businessmen from Diyarbakır to return and invest here." Indicating how the party's approach deviated from conventional policy positions, Erdoğan carefully explained to the crowd that, "We provided them with free land, a 5 year tax break and a 50% reduction in their energy bills, as well as low social security insurance payments. What else do you want? You should not ask for a free ride."[139]

Rather than being a simple routine exchange, the leadership's comparable statements reveal the party's persistent framing of Turkey's problem in vertical terms, that is, its treatment of pressing concerns as issues between the state and the citizenry. Attributing social and political problems to the state's malfunction characterizes the party's insistence on economic liberalization programs as a panacea. This recurring recipe illustrates how the party entrusts conflict-ridden issues to the corrective and homogenizing power of the market. The transformative forces of the market have been brought to the fore not only to address the Kurdish problem but also to deal with Turkey's economic, social, and political conflicts in general. While the recognition of the problem per se is an important step forward, the party seems to couple state-centered diagnoses and market-dependent solutions. As a result, the party's policies fail to recognize the non-state aspect of the social issues, such as the hurdles facing individuals to become potent agents in the market or the cultural, social, and economic foundations of the conflicts across different communities and within society.[140] More importantly, the party's reliance on the trickle-down effect of institutional and market-based reforms seems to substitute the forces of the market for the role of the state as the main institution for resolving social problems. The latent homogeneous and moral free-market community appears as the ultimate reference to the NV's ideology, and the party assumes that loosening the state's hand in the region and unleashing free-market forces will create novel power relations that replace traditional ones. This near sacralization of the market by the JDP reminds us of Karl Polanyi's critique that there was nothing natural about laissez faire; free markets could have never come into being and functioned equitably merely by allowing things to take their course.[141] Such an approach also ignores the fact that the concept of citizenship, both horizontally and vertically, is rather weak in Turkey, and on average, individuals live at a minimal level of welfare, preventing them from being full members of a free-market community. An aggressive market economy in a country where 25.6 percent of the country's population lives under the poverty line and the official unemployment rate remains at 10.3 percent can be as oppressive as the state.[142]

Perhaps a more decisive litmus test of the JDP's inclusiveness than the still-problematic Kurdish problem is its ability to incorporate the heterodox Alevis. As in the case of the NV parties, the Alevis' controversial religious identity lends itself as a trial case to show the limits of the JDP's tolerance toward groups with distinctive religious understandings. While the party program is silent on this issue, the leadership views suggest that the JDP has yet to develop a coherent program and remains wedded to the NV's approach with respect to the Alevis. To better assess the JDP's policies toward religious groups in general requires an understanding of the policies and reform projects of the Directorate of Religious Affairs. For instance, one of the JDP's most noticeable reform projects is the establishment of a quota system that allocates a percentage of the positions of religious assistant provincial leader, *müftü,* to women. In fact, this reform exemplifies the party's own approach that views quotas as corrective tools to ensure gender equality. The party's failed attempt to fill the women's quotas in its own organization was matched by that of the directorate: the quotas for müftü were left unfilled due to the unavailability of qualified candidates. Indeed only 2,450 of the 80,000 (0.02 percent) directorate employees are women. Many of them are Quranic teachers for girls at the elementary school level.

Considering the broad reform projects launched by the Directorate of Religious Affairs, an institution that the party maintains significant control over, the Alevis' vocal claims that the directorate has not acknowledged the group's distinctive religious rituals makes the party's response especially significant in assessing its policies. Despite the growing demands, the JDP leadership has refrained from recognizing Alevis as a distinctive group with different religious needs. The JDP leadership asserts that, had the Alevis been recognized as an "other religious group, the Aczemendis (an extremist eccentric Islamist group) would have to be included as well." Similar statements identify two premises: Alevis are regarded as esoteric or marginal religious groups even though they constitute an estimated 5 million to 25 million people. More importantly, refuting religious demands by declaring that groups are marginal implies that the JDP's policies conceive of Islam as a homogeneous practice that needs to be sheltered against heterodoxy:

We have a religious approach that embraces both who come to the mosque and who don't. Alevis are our Muslim brethren. They might be regarded as an order and not a sect. It is a culture in Anatolia. We need to review the textbooks and the Directorate's approach to religion to include *them.* We need to shed light straight on. We are ready to serve whomever benefits from it . . . however, the issue of Alevi *dedes*, religious leaders, needs to be taken to the ministry of cultural affairs.[143]

This somewhat contradictory approach treats Alevism as a cultural practice that is internal yet different from the hegemonic Islam. This recognition disregards the Alevi groups's own claim that their beliefs embody a unique collection of Islamic values and practices and thus grants them with distinctive religious needs that need to be addressed in the country's religious sphere. Yet the recent popular suggestion that the issue of Alevis' needs should be addressed by the Minister of Culture, not Religious Affairs, indicates that the party also addresses Alevism as an issue residing *outside* the framework of Islam. Such approaches reify Alevism as a cultural practice, thereby divorcing it from Islam and dismissing Alevism's own claim of being an original Anatolian Turkish religious practice. Other leadership statements suggest that the JDP simply mirrors the NV's perspective on heterodox groups and only advocates a conditional inclusion that requires Alevis to adopt dominant Sunni practices in order to be fully recognized by the Directorate of Religious Affairs. These debates beg the question of what exactly constitutes Islam for the JDP and whether the party understands diversity to merely be limited to variations within the dominant version of orthodox Islam.

A review of the JDP's policies from its practice brings to the fore its cautionary notes against politics of difference that take an essentialist or absolutist tone by disregarding others. In fact, the party documents state that when claims of difference discount the importance of equality, they can create chaos and tyranny instead of diversity. According to Erdoğan, the JDP's seemingly paradoxical policies with respect to Alevis result not from the party's approach, but from the Alevis' self-perception. All Muslims, including Alevis, are represented by the directorate. Consequently, Alevis' claim to more rights is at odds with their claim that their beliefs constitute a core part of Turkish Islam. Justifying such assertions on the grounds of being a non-Muslim minority is inconsistent with the group's overall identification, thereby creating deadlock.[144] The JDP's approach, however, ignores the fact that the Directorate of Religious Affairs, since its inception, has taken the Hanefi version of Islam as its foundation, has adopted a limited understanding of diversity within Islam, and has failed to take notice of unorthodox religious practices. Regardless of its justification, the JDP's attitude toward ethnic religious communities signals a contingent commitment to pluralism while its emphasis on the freedom from state restrictions and the loosening of the state's tight grip on social actors saves the party from having to define the "pluralism" it seeks to launch. The JDP avoids addressing horizontal equality across groups or within society, thereby reinforcing the idea that its opposition to the status quo translates into an automatic acceptance of the diversity of societal actors. Neverthe-less, like the NV parties, the JDP embraces diverse groups when their im-mediate or ultimate commitment to Islamic tradition is not questionable or when they are clearly defined as un-Islamic minorities. The treatment of unorthodox or hybrid groups, such as the Alevis, shows that the party's in-clusiveness is not based on a principled commitment, but limited to those actors who do not challenge the presumed religious unity.

The JDP Leadership

The common profile of the JDP's leadership epitomizes the changing profile of the Turkish political elite in general and the pro-Islamic elite in particular. Tayyip Erdoğan differs from other leaders in Turkish politics. Unlike his colleagues, Erdoğan is a product of the state religious school sys-tem, which provides students with an education that focuses on Islam, the history of the Ottoman Empire, and Ottoman Turkish literature. He was born in one of Istanbul's peripheral neighborhoods in 1954. His struggles represent those of others from the shantytowns of Istanbul who were trying to move up the urban social ladder into the middle class. The elementary school he attended, Piyale Pasa, was located in a neighborhood dominated by one of the biggest historic mosques and in an area populated by a diverse group of people including immigrants from rural areas and Gypsy groups. In contrast to many other party leaders, he was not raised in a stable small town, but grew up in a microcosm of Turkey's changing social terrain.

Interestingly, according to Erdoğan's biographies, the decision to attend Imam Hatip religious school was made for him by one of his teachers based on his class performance. The religious schools, created as a result of Turkey's secularism, gave him comprehensive training in Islam and an un-derstanding of religious texts based on original sources. In striking con-trast to Erbakan, his training and lifestyle make it unnecessary for Erdoğan and many in the party's upper echelon to defend their Islamic credentials. Erdoğan's imprisonment, which ironically is seen as political capital by many, further confirms his reputation as a deeply devout and courageous Muslim. As a result, when Erdoğan and others in the party's elite remain silent on religious issues, it does not raise questions regarding their com-mitment to Islamic ideals. Erdoğan first encountered secular restrictions when he decided to pursue higher education. As a graduate of a religious vocational school, he had to first take an equivalency test for a regular high-school degree to be eligible to enter the university in a field other than theology. His college education was limited to two years of vocational training. Throughout his high school and college years, he was active in many school organizations and the National View youth branches. Following Erbakan's path, he adopted Mehmet Zahid Kotku of *İskenderpaşa* Seminary, a branch of the *Nakşibendi* called *Gümüşhanevi,* as his mentor.

Like many others in the party, Erdoğan is a product of the NV parties' local organizations. His first party position was as head of the WP's Beyoglu district branch, one of the most heterogeneous districts in Istanbul. Although he was elected on the WP ticket during its coalition with the NAP, his seat selection was annulled due to internal party conflicts. This loss reinforced Erdoğan's oppositional position in the NV parties and delayed his national political career until his election as mayor of Istanbul in 1994. The Istanbul mayoralty is the most visibly important and nationally recognized local governance position in Turkey. Despite the public scrutiny, he preferred to open the city assembly with a prayer, *fatiha,* instead of the national anthem. Along with his political career he also established himself as a businessman, working as a distributor at a job that made him overly invested in trade and the market.

It can be argued that the success of the NV parties at the local governance level changed the views of many of their leaders from transformationalist to accommodationist. In this transitional period, some of Erdoğan's statements as mayor evoked strong reactions and raised concerns about his radicalism. He was once reported to have described himself as the imam (i.e., a religious prayer leader) of Istanbul, and he tended to give ambivalent answers to questions that attempted to gauge the JDP's leadership stance on Islamic rules. For instance, in one of his interviews he was asked whether his tie was silk. Because the use of silk is forbidden for practicing Muslim males, this question was targeted at his level of commitment to *Sunnah,* the advised but not required Islamic practices that often reveal the degree of one's devotion to Islamic beliefs. Erdoğan's answer, like those of others in the upper stratum of the JDP, revealed the complex way in which the party leadership unified their beliefs and practices. The tie, Erdoğan answered, would likely be a mix. Nevertheless, he explained, even if it had been pure silk, it still would have not raised questions in Islamic terms: After all, "I need to have a different look. During a struggle one needs to have a look that exudes power. Our prophet had similar practices. Silk was advised during time of struggle and warfare."[145]

Although some of Erdoğan's statements suggest that he interprets Erbakan's approach to politics as a contest between *Hak* (righteous or "God") and *Batıl* (unrighteous or deviant), when asked whether he saw himself in a state of war, Erdoğan suggested that his practice was not guided by being in a state of war but by the principle "following the customs of society." Yet many explanations that include the statement that "there are some leniencies (certain areas where one can disobey the religious laws) in the face of difficulties" suggest that the party leadership is likely to view their efforts as undertaken in an environment where there is spiritual struggle and exile. Although the leaders have avoided direct questions about their Islamic beliefs, interviews conducted in their early years showed how they carefully thought about positioning themselves in the secular world without violating Islamic rules. The JDP's bivalence is not a mere necessity but draws on a set of Islamically justified practices.

Perhaps due to the drastic shifts in the JDP leadership's positions after occupying local elected offices for the NV, many question whether the party's public rhetoric is increasingly more strategic (i.e., takiyye). In fact, Erdoğan's overtly Islamic discourses ended with his conviction for a speech he delivered on December 6, 1977, in Siirt, one of Turkey's peripheral cities. Although the two lines of the poem Erdoğan cited, "the mosques are our barracks, the minarets our bayonets, the domes our helmets, and the believers are our soldiers," have often been referred to as the reason for his conviction, the remaining part of his speech directly questioned the legitimacy of the hegemonic policies that existed prior to the establishment of the JDP.

We will continue our fight against those who entrusted this country to the wrong views. How beautifully our ancestors said "don't lean on a tree, it gets rotten and you won't have support" don't lean on humans, they die and you will be left without guidance. Rely on God, so you can stand up. Based on this rationale, I tell you without hesitation: my reference is Islam. If I can't say this in this land of martyrs, why should I live in this country? Our national anthem says that "these prayers called pillars of religion should echo in this land forever," they cannot silence these prayers . . . "it is the right of my people who believe in God," it does not say that people believe in humans. . . . If our sisters cannot go to colleges with headscarves, there is oppression in this country. This won't continue. Sooner or later the truth will reveal itself. Are we obliged to be with this religion? Yes, we are![146]

Although Erdoğan's imprisonment lasted only four months, there are many signs that attest to the enduring impact the sentence had on the JDP leadership and organization. During his postprison years, Erdoğan and the party purged their rhetoric of any Islamic symbols and discussions of Islam. Instead of using religious terms, the party conveyed messages that were limited to the importance of freedom of speech and the real meaning of secularism, state disinvolvement in religious affairs.

Yet while Erdoğan's profile represents an important component of the party, the JDP's other founder, Abdullah Gül, epitomizes a different group very active in the party's core leadership, one that never adopted a confrontational rhetoric. Gül was born in Kayseri, a town famous for its skillful tradesmen. Instead of engaging in trade, he studied it. Like many other elite members of the JDP, Gül was born into a blue-collar family and worked to support his university studies. From 1983 to 1991, Gül worked for the Islamic Development Bank. Unlike Erdoğan, whose political views were shaped in local politics, Gül had significant international experience and joined the WP only after receiving Erbakan's invitation. Gül's father was an active member of the NV, and he, like Erdoğan, did not need to prove his ties to the NV parties and Islam. Despite their differences, Erdoğan's and Gül's backgrounds capture the dominant profiles of the JDP leadership. The JDP's upper echelon has an average age of forty-eight, and many came from families with rural backgrounds.[147] More often than not, they were the first ones in their families to obtain higher education. The mélange of traditional background and higher education has created a hybrid lifestyle for all the leaders.[148] According to Akif Gülle, another active member of the elite, their contribution to Turkish politics was to show traditional people that they do not have to compromise their values and forgo upward social and economic mobility because of their background. Their family environment and involvement in political Islamic movements has familiarized them with folk Islam and Islamic tradition, while their formal and informal education has equipped them with unique communications skills and venues. Their relationship to the traditional segments of society is complicated, as they seek to represent and change traditional practices to make Islam more consistent with original customs and main political forces in society and with free market liberalism.

The JDP's commitment to the transfiguration of Turkish politics through institutional reforms and the transformative forces of the economy seems to be reflected in its leadership structure. The engineers and lawyers that dominated the NV parties have been replaced with experts and academics in business, trade, finance, and communication. Although the party seeks to represent a wide spectrum of citizenry, ranging from the observant religious to nonobservant secular voters, the leaders are all observant Muslims. The broad spectrum of ideological positions the leadership represents raises the question of how the party addresses diversity among its own cadres and party institutions.

As the party is one of the youngest in Turkey in terms of its institutional age, and its ideological framework is still in the making, its internal democracy is especially important in order to preserve the variety of opinions it has come to represent. In fact, the JDP's original party statute, which was effective only from August 14, 2001, to February 2, 2003, distinguished the JDP from other Turkish parties. It provided its delegates with extensive powers for controlling the Central Executive Committee. Most notably, for the first time in Turkish politics, a political party set a term limit for its leadership. Likewise, the JDP was the first Turkish party to establish a council of referees on internal democracy, *parti içi demokrasi hakem kurulu.*[149] Notwithstanding its initial promise and innovative institutional design, shortly after Parliament adopted a constitutional amendment that allowed its charismatic leader, Recep Tayyip Erdoğan, to hold public office, the groundbreaking party statute was altered, in a top-down fashion, without approval from the rank-and-file, giving the leadership the right to hand-pick the twelve members of the central decision-making body.

The central executive and decision-making body of fifty is chosen via competitive elections, but, as opposed to the originally envisioned system, competition is by list instead of by individual. The current system gives unmatched power to the list supported by the party leader. Thus, in striking contrast to its initial form, the party's internal democracy has been increasingly limited, and venues for dissenting voices within the party have been tightly restricted. The party now mirrors the highly hierarchical structure of the secular parties of which it has been critical. Even a cursory review of the party's short institutional history reveals a clear disconnect between the party's commitment to internal democracy and its elimination of official, bottom-up feedback channels. The lack of internal debates and collective decision-making mechanisms, as well as the increasing autonomy of the party leadership, marginalizes more and more of its party members. One can find various expressions of growing discontent directed toward the party's authoritarian structure. Ersönmez Yarbay, a former member of Parliament who was not placed on the party's ticket during the 2007 elections, described the party's internal workings as "brush off" democracy, as all those who dissent were swept away by the leadership. Others confirmed that Erdoğan's charismatic leadership has marginalized other members and has led to decisions that violate not only the basic principle of democratic deliberation within the party but also the official nomination requirements for critical positions.[150] The JDP's rather unique candidate selection method reveals the central role that the core leadership plays and the party's increasing exclusion of new elite members not approved by the top leadership. The JDP selects its candidates based on the results of local polls (i.e., popularity of the leader in the region), the interviews at the party centers conducted by five members of the central decision-making body and the approval of the executive committee. This process creates a list from which the top elite handpicks the nominees. As a result, the party did not nominate 150 existing members of Parliament for reelection in 2007; instead it included a significant number of invited candidates who did not have previous ties to the party. Changing 40 percent of the members of Parliament attests both to the party's renewal of its profile and to an increasing monopolization of political power by Erdoğan. Thus, the JDP's leadership structure and the transformation of its party organization raise the question of whether the JDP, even though its initial success was built upon progressive ideas and inclusive leadership, is becoming leader-centered and exclusive in order to maintain the upper echelon of its leadership structure.

CONCLUSION

The NAP, NV parties, and JDP paint their ideal polities in different shades of Islam as they try to question and complement Kemalism. Placing these parties in a multidimensional framework shows that, despite their common questions, pro-Islamic parties differ markedly in their answers. The NAP's treatment of the state and the unity of the national community as unquestionable contrasts with the NV's and JDP's constant discovery of Islam in Kemalism and its resultant transformation of Islamic politics. When we broaden our comparison, it becomes clear that despite their distinctive institutional contexts and doctrines, the politics of religion in Turkey and Israel have spawned two genres of religious parties: sacralizers that imbue their hegemonic nationalism with religious meanings and internal secularizers that bring secular constructs to their political doctrine in order to preserve the power of their respective religious doctrine.

As has happened in Israel, the sacralization of the state and the nation made it initially easier for sacralizer religious parties to accept a hegemonic ideology. Forging what we can call a "Kemalist-Islamist" ideology, which is another contradiction in terms in Turkish politics, the NAP views the state as a modern embodiment of institutions that emerged to enhance the Islamic community. For the party, a moral community grounded in Islam provides the stable foundation of a strong state (see table 4.1). The nation-state's redistributive role in the economic social sphere and its ability to empower individuals as moral agents not only guarantees domestic justice, it also makes it an important global actor. However, the NAP's treatment of many issues as unquestionable poses a strong challenge to its assumed role of accommodating a diversity of ideas under the umbrella of national unity. Despite its claim to an inclusive rhetoric, the NAP accepts all identities, including those of the Kurdish and Alevi groups, only as inherently integral to the Islamic-Turkish identity, not as separate identities in their own right. In other words, for the NAP, claims to be different can only be recognized if the groups do not seek to define themselves beyond the parameters of Turkish Muslimness.

Thus, the NAP's sacralizing policies' initial acceptance of secular and religious actors as a unified entity comes at the price of narrowing the scope of politics and taking skeptical positions vis-à-vis open-ended negotiations in the public sphere. Despite its national outlook the party successfully ties the local to the global while leaving some thorny domestic issues unattended; it ultimately relegates the solution of critical problems to the commitments of individuals towards ensuring that the national community will not be swept away but contribute to and alter the course

TABLE. 4.1

A comparison of the ideological premises of NAP,
the Prosperity Party, and JDP

	NAP	The Prosperity Party	JDP
Main process	Sacralization	Internal secularization	Internal secularization
Hegemonic nationalism	Supportive; Kemalist secularism as an inherently religious project	Rhetorically confrontational; request a redefinition of Kemalism to include public expressions of Islam	Avoids confrontational rhetoric; request redefinition of Kemalism
Nation	Ethnic territorial	Religious community	Pluralistic religious community
State	Supported as sacred	Indifferent to the state as long as it supports the Islamic community	Advocates limited state
Individual vs. community	Individual is ultimate unit	Community is ultimate unit	Value-centered community serves as main reference although balance is shifting toward individual
Inclusive vs. exclusive	Inclusive regarding ethnic Turkish, Islamic-Turkish communities; exclusive regarding non-Turkish groups	Inclusive regarding the Islamic community and non-Turkish Islamic groups; exclusive regarding unorthodox Islamic groups	Inclusive regarding ethnic-cultural groups as long as they do not challenge religious orthodoxy; exclusive to unorthodox Islamic groups

of global processes. Furthermore, and analogous to Mafdal's positions, the NAP's policies show that the sacralization of the state does not translate into full cooperation but, instead, increases the tension between the state and the party. With its sacralizing policies and Kemalist-Islamic ideology, the NAP elevates the state and the unity of the national community to the level of the absolute and broadens the area of politics by viewing individuals in concentric circles that stretch from local to national to global moral communities. However, the NAP often finds itself trying to save the state at the expense of the state's opposition when the nation-state's idealized historical role and policies seem inconsistent or under threat.

Parallel to Shas, Turkey's internal secularizer parties, the NV parties and the JDP, voice common criticisms of hegemonic nationalism as an exclusive ideology, a misapplication of European Enlightenment, and a misconstruction of modernity. To become a democracy, political communities need to have autonomy from the state and be given the latitude to sustain their own presence and values. The NV parties' policies amounted to some contradictory practices. The parties viewed politics through the lens of the state whose legitimacy they challenged on account of the state's batil, or heretic, ideology, yet the parties assigned the state a major role in their emancipatory policies. Furthermore, while they sought to liberate Islam from tradition and the state, the group itself acquired a traditional structure and became a sect-like group by asking unconditional loyalty and political support. Yet in their conflict with the state, the NV parties created not an insular but an accepting and engaging political discourse that has sought to make their policies relevant to the secular world. Thus, the JDP's divergence from the NV reflects a new phase of Islamic politics, which attends not to the tension between Islam and the West, but to the local and global forces of change that can be used to enhance and be enhanced by Islamic beliefs. While the JDP's new Islamic politics incorporates individualism, the free-market economy, and a limited state into its rhetoric, it merely trusts that other conflictual and persistent issues, such as the status of heterodox groups or the political leadership of women, will be resolved through the trickle-down effect of the changes that it introduces.

While the NV parties questioned the legitimacy of the state, the new genre represented by the JDP shifted the fulcrum of the politics of Islam from a community-centered to an institutionally centered focus. In contrast to its predecessors, the JDP adopted the new paradigm of political decentralization, a paradigm that requires less stateness than before.[151] Ironically, the JDP's "conservative democracy," just like Kemalism, justifies its goals by drawing on a market economy to—this time—expand rather than limit the role of Islam. The NAP and the NV parties both endorse the state's presence in the economic sphere and recognize the importance of its redistributive role. The JDP goes further and assigns an almost unquestionable corrective and restrictive role to the forces of the market. Neoliberal market policies promise not only to improve the economy but also to free the public sphere and Islam from state control.

The politics of Islam in Turkey bring to the fore the critical role of the party-sponsored networks. Each party's central organization coordinates its local groups, and in the process, creates a novel political space between the public and the private domain. These networks play critical roles in embedding the party into society in a way not possible via formal venues and in instantaneously disseminating the parties' ideas to the masses in remote parts of the country. These local private-public organizations promote the idea that their community-based politics are not only the panacea for the perennial ills of failing state policies but also that they cushion individuals in competitive market economies from new issues. Even though these parties are more inclusive at the local level than at the national one, their penetration of society faces challenges and self-imposed barriers. For instance, irrespective of its strong local organizations, the NAP has consistently failed to establish vibrant women's branches. In contrast, women are very active in the NV parties and the JDP, yet efforts to include them in the parties' upper echelons and political cadres remain limited. While women as religious students or mothers have a role in these parties' appeals, women stripped of their conventional roles and who are merely participants of the political community remain absent. Likewise, all parties' mobilization efforts seem to be hampered by their understanding of a religious or ethnic religious community as homogeneous; that is, they do not extend unqualified support to the notion of diversity.

Finally, although the NAP, the NV parties, and the JDP successfully highlight different exclusive and authoritarian aspects of the state and the polity, their emancipatory models take a mixed form: their emancipatory ideas are offset by authoritarian and exclusive ones. For instance, in fear of a Hobbesian anarchy, the NAP's policies focus on the responsibility of the state to protect political rights, whereas the NV parties and the JDP center their demands on rights derived from the state against the domination of an antireligious Leviathan state. Both sets of policies often translate into increasing demands for group rights (i.e., rights of cultural, religious, or ethnic groups) at the expense of individual rights, although all parties seem to center on the individual. Their successful critique of the state opens up more room for mainstream religious publics while marginalizing some of the more unconventional religious groups. Thus, despite their varied and overall increasing electoral gains, a closer look at these parties' policies from the perspective of state, community, and individual shows that they bring the symbolic world of Islam and the assumed Kemalist world together in distinctive ways. They address the failure of the existing practices by sacralizing the role of certain institutions or presenting solutions via Islam, thereby transforming both so-called Kemalist laicist and Islamic outlooks at the same time. The combination of their emancipating and restrictive ideas and unique blend of sacro-secular rhetoric makes the question of why people turn to these parties important to analyze.

PART THREE

The Popular Roots of Religious Parties

Between Zionism and Judaism?

Religious Party Supporters in Israel

We don't have primaries and don't need endorsement. We have what no other party has. Our merchandise is unique: values, tradition, father's house, Judaism.[1]

When the Shas Party (*Hit'akhdut ha-Sephardim ha-Olamit Shomrey Torah*, International Organization of Torah-Observant Sephardic Jews) first appeared on the Israeli political scene in the 1984 elections, it was seen as a parochial, ethnic, ultra-Orthodox party and was expected to be a short-term spark in the Israeli political scene. After all, none of the preceding ethnic or ultra-Orthodox movements, let alone a combination of both, had succeeded in expanding its electoral support in Israel's highly volatile political environment. Although religious parties have been part and parcel of Israeli politics since before the establishment of the state, their electoral share has been stable and limited. In fact, prior to Shas no ultra-Orthodox party had ever captured more than 4 percent of the vote in a general election. The meteoric rise of Shas, as a brand-new ultra-Orthodox party, and its ability to raise its electoral support to 13 percent—attaining the third-largest plurality in the parliament—was seen as a "stunning development," and provided evidence that Israeli politics were swept up in the rising tide of religious politics in the world.

The bewildering rise of Shas and the declining electoral fortunes of Mafdal embody many questions that are central to understanding religious-party support, not only in Israel and the Middle East, but in the world in general. Given that religious parties have played an essential and relatively stable role in Israeli politics since the nation's inception, it remains to be answered whether and how these parties have reinvented their roles and attracted a wider segment of the electorate in recent years. Who in the political community responds to religious parties' messages? Are religious parties modern, sect-like organizations that turn their religious messages into political ones? Do individuals endorse religious parties out of conviction? Or do they vote for religious parties for instrumental reasons? Is it the charismatic appeal of religious leaders that sways people to vote for these parties? Underlying these questions is once again the main enigma of modernity, the unexpected re-enchantment with the world, to use Weber's term. Why do a growing number of individuals support religious parties in a global context when the ideas of modernity (e.g., autonomy of individuals and open-endedness of history) and its political model, liberal democracy, are more salient than ever? How does the individuals' growing support of religious movements affect democratic capital in their polities? The increasing eminence of religious politics is particularly perplexing and analytically promising in the case of Israeli politics because, just like their counterparts in Turkey, Israeli voters are inundated by political choices. Twenty-seven parties were listed on the ballot and vied for support in the 2003 Israeli election. Given the large number of options available, why do so many people in Israel and Turkey increasingly give their mandate to religious parties as opposed to others? (See figure 5.1.)

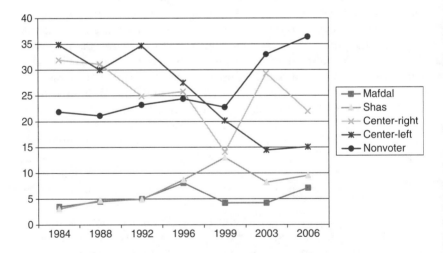

FIGURE 5.1

Vote shares of party blocs and nonparticipants in Israel

SOURCE: Knesset

The explanations of religious party support in Israel present a microcosm of the ongoing conceptual debates in the social sciences in general, and political science in particular. Competing accounts run the gamut from deterministic, structuralist macroaccounts to anecdotal microapproaches. Perhaps due to the rapidly increasing interest in religious parties, there is a growing genre of research that implicitly treats religious parties as electoral accidents and offers ad hoc, or retrospective, explanations for their success. In this genre, one often finds accounts that cover a set of disconnected factors and/or emphasize the constellation of a unique set of circumstances. For instance, the trial of Aryeh Deri prior to the 1999 elections has been identified as one of the primary reasons, if not the primary one, for Shas's success in the 1999 election. Mafdal's withdrawal from the historical coalition with the Labor Party has often been seen as the beginning of its electoral decline. More systematic explanations of Shas's and Mafdal's electoral appeal are informed by three models that attribute the rise of religious parties to (1) a *conflict of values* (i.e., religious parties gain strength in response to a secular threat), (2) a *crisis* of hegemonic policies (i.e., religious parties capitalize on the masses' reactions to the failure and dislocating effects of the dominant socioeconomic policies), and (3) the *choices* of individuals who turn to these parties due to mobilization efforts or the charismatic political appeal of the leadership.

Despite the differences in conceptual assumptions, a review of the way in which the varying accounts analyze religious partisans indicates that their conclusions come from similar sources. More often than not, they glean their arguments from macro-level assessments that show religious partisans reacting to the economic and social transformation of their environment. As a result, central to many accounts are broad structural changes, such as increasing income distribution gaps, changes in the labor market, or the outcomes of local elections. In part due to the difficulties in obtaining empirical data on the leaders and supporters of religious parties, microlevel inquiries are mostly based on anecdotal evidence and selective observations of religious partisans. Missing in these studies are the perceptions of the religious partisans themselves. Opinion surveys, for example, are one of the least-used tools in these analyses. Their absence is especially striking given that opinion polls constitute a major venue for empirical information on the electorate elsewhere and inform the electoral analyses of political parties in general. In part due to the empirical observation deficit, there appears to be a substantial methodological limitations in understanding these parties in their immediate domestic and comparative contexts. More importantly, the dearth of empirical studies of religious partisans ultimately reinforces the widely shared idea that religious parties are sui generis parties and exceptional cases to the overall patterns of electoral competition. As a result, whether and how the perceptions of religious partisans affect religious parties and are affected by the leadership remains one of the important unknowns in our knowledge of religious parties. Many analyses rely on anecdotal evidence to discuss whether supporters of religious parties confirm or refute contending assumptions regarding their motivation. Devoid of empirical evidence, many of the existing arguments reinforce the premises of the clash-, crisis-, and choice-centered accounts and risk creating parallel, self-confirming explanations.

Against this background, the next two chapters are guided by the following goals: At the theoretical level, they illustrate the application of competing paradigms to Israel's Mafdal and Shas and Turkey's NAP, Prosperity, and JDP supporters. They inform us about each model's contribution to understanding and normalizing these parties. By highlighting the models' own raison d'etre as well as their identification of factors that explain religious parties' existence they also alert us to the analytical areas they leave uncharted. At the conceptual level, they draw our attention to the promises and limits of conventional frameworks and markers (Left vs. Right, Ashkenazi vs. Sephardi) that are used to demarcate political positions of religious parties. Our own application of these markers illustrates how a contextualized use of these terms might not only fatally limit our political discussion, but also prevent us from tapping into the analytical potential of already-limited empirical data. Given the changing contours of world politics in general and Israeli politics in particular, we question the analytical cost of an uncritical application of theoretical paradigms, deductive voting models, and conventional political markers.

At the broad methodological level, these chapters present opinion surveys as distinctive analytical venues not only to understand the self-assessment and characteristics of religious partisans but also to demonstrate how this empirical venue is susceptible to challenges, such as sampling bias or high nonresponse rates. The final section offers probabilistic models of religious party choice that take us to the intersection of theoretical arguments and the self-assessment of religious partisans. Viewing the parties from the electorate's perspective alerts us to the importance of two aspects of religious partisans that are sorely neglected in social science research, namely, the supporters' own rationale and their perceived positions within the political system vis-à-vis other parties. In this section we also explore the analytical potential of alternative explanations of party support, such as the one offered by a spatial model of political competition. Spatial analysis recovers the relative ideological positioning of the parties from the assessment of their platforms by the voters. The model draws on the political assessment of the electorate and lets the electorate define the number of ideological dimensions latent in competition. By depicting electoral contests in a new light, the section brings together (1) the perception of religious partisans themselves and (2) the political platforms of the parties.

The broad scope of the goals adopted here serves to highlight the repercussions of deductive, deterministic explanations and the persistent exclusion of the views of religious partisans. In the course of our analysis, we show how inside-out accounts and the inclusion of religious partisans on their own terms can both question and help to deepen our conceptualizations. Approaching religious partisans, who are usually studied en masse, as individuals with choices, and incorporating their rationales and the broader context of their voting into our analysis invites us to revisit and expand the limits of our conceptual and research tools simultaneously. In the following two chapters, we seek to achieve both by delving into the Israeli context first, and then the Turkish one.

COMPETING FRAMEWORKS

Politics of Conflict Between Secular and Jewish (Ultra)-Orthodox Values

When viewed from the perspective of the conflict model, the growing support for religious parties provides evidence of the same widening ideological distance between religious and secular groups in Israeli politics as seen elsewhere. Politics, in this approach, surfaces as an authoritative distribution of values. This often translates into the view of Israeli politics as a zero-sum game, where secular and religious groups have mirror images of each other. Each emphasizes the other's potential for imposing their religious or antireligious rulings in the public sphere. When placed in its historical context, the conflict framework brings to the fore the status quo agreement of 1947, which contained, but did not resolve, the conflict between religious and secular groups. The religious-secular divide remained "the only rift within Israeli society of great social, cultural and political importance." This rift has gained increasing salience, especially as dominant traditional cleavages such as ethnicity (Ashkenazi vs. Sephardi) or commitment to different social models (socialism vs. capitalism) faded away.[2]

At the individual level, conflict models draw our attention to the clash between, using David Ingram's characterization, two competing transformative and preservative collective identities. As such it is Labor Zionism's failure to forge a common syncretist-transformative identity (i.e., open and attentive to different identities rooted in secular values) that strengthened the political appeal of separatist-preservative (exclusionary religious) identities.[3] The growing emphasis on individualism and personal success tarnished Zionist collectivist maxims in Israel's political map, thereby undermining what Charles Liebman and Eliezer Don-Yehiya have called Israel's civil religion, which might have neutralized the secular-religious divide.[4] The cultural transformation begun by Israeli zionism has resulted, not in social integration, but in growing differences in lifestyles and cultural consumption patterns between the Orthodox and non-Orthodox communities, forging diametrically opposed perspectives that serve as political currency for religious parties.[5] Due to the growing estrangement of the secular sector from traditional values and Jewish culture, some scholars have declared that "Israel today is in the midst of a *Kulturkampf* (culture war), [which] has the potential for developing into an unbridgeable rift."[6]

The roots of the current politics of religion, according to the conflict paradigm, are (1) the failure of the state and its adopted policies to successfully mediate between the different demands on the Israeli polity; (2) the shifting and transformative forces of world politics, such as the reconfiguration of regional balances and the intensity of the Arab-Israeli conflict, which makes the dividing line of domestic conflict more salient; and (3) the weakening consolidation of a civil religion that could have superseded the religious-secular divide. These factors are interrelated. For instance, the regional political balance increases the pressure toward withdrawal from the settlements, which aggravates the political differences between secular and religious groups and their view of the territories, which in turn increases the political relevance of religious parties. As the previous chapters discussed, Mafdal and Shas have come down on opposite sides of many issues. This schism between religious parties immediately complicates the implicit premise of the conflict approach, where politics occurs as a contestation between religious and secular values.

Nevertheless, proponents of the conflict approach can easily find evidence to support their view, especially in the case of Shas. On many occasions, Ovadia Yosef has questioned the legitimacy of the political system in Israel:

When the people of Israel dwell in their land, and judge according to foreign laws, it is a thousand times worse than an individual or a community of Jews who use the gentile legal system, for is there no God in Israel? . . . This is as they said, before them and not before idolaters [gentiles], for since they do not recognize the Torah's laws, and since they state that the religion of Moses is no longer valid, therefore they judge according to the laws of their false prophets. One who goes to them [secular courts] for judgment is as one spurns the teaching of the living God, as we have accepted it from generation to generation back to Moses our teacher. The results of this situation are embarrassing. . . . Chazal said (Shabbat 139a) that whenever punishments come upon Israel, go check the Jewish judges. . . . And we, unfortunately, see how difficult the security and economic situation is now; there is no day without its curse, greater than the last.[7]

Overshadowed by such statements, however, are the Shas's unique approach and more conciliatory positions, especially when viewed from the perspective of the ultra-Orthodox world. Despite Shas's denunciations of the secular courts through their criticism, the leadership implicitly legitimates these institutions by recognizing them and equating their rulings to those handed down by non-Jews. The rulings, therefore, grant them a certain amount of authority—a revolutionary step in the ultra-Orthodox world.

Although Shas lends itself to the premises of the conflict model, Mafdal's role obscures any clear-cut distinctions. Mafdal defies the boundaries of two different camps: those who oppose the secular Zionist structure and those who want to keep it intact and declare its authority. The conflict model's own explanation, namely that the religious parties' confrontational policies fuel their power, is starkly contradicted by Mafdal's attempts to establish itself as a bridge between secular and religious groups to achieve internal unity, and as a defender of religious territories. This overarching goal manifests itself in the party's popular election slogans. "Zionism with soul" captures the party's desire to complete, not contradict, the Zionist ideal. Other mottos, like "Let Mafdal deal with Meretz," maintain the language of conflict, which tries to position Mafdal as the main opposing force against secular parties, of which Meretz is one of the most radical.[8] Reflecting the mixed legacy of these policies, Mafdal attracts highly disparate groups of voters who are linked not only by their opposition to territorial concessions but also their old and in some cases newly found adherence to the Biblical definition of the nation, *Am Kadosh*, a holy and separate nation.

The New Mafdal voters were quite varied in terms of party backgrounds, ideological persuasion and ethnic origin. They formerly supported right wing parties such as Tehiya and Moledet, but also the Likud and Labor. While many of the new Mafdal voters were political hardliners, there was also a significant number of centrist and moderates among them. Most of these voters were religious Zionists who were returning to the fold, and a few secular Zionists who were concerned about the Jewish nature of the State of Israel. While many of these new voters were Ashkenazi Jews, Mafdal also increased its electoral share among Sephardi Jews.[9]

Politics of Crisis: Ultra-Orthodox Parties and the Politics of Resentment and Political Alienation

In crisis models, religious parties emerge as magnets for people who react to the perpetual problems inherent in the institutions and policies of the nation-state. Despite its goal of creating an egalitarian society and a unified citizenry, the Israeli nation-state has failed to establish an all-inclusive concept of citizenship and economic equality among diverse ethnic groups. Central to these accounts are institutional, ideological obstacles that limit the redistribution of symbolic and economic power in the state, for instance, the dominant Ashkenazi nature of the Israeli state—which created built-in biases in its policies—and the persistent failure of social and economic policies to ameliorate socioeconomic inequalities among different ethnic and cultural groups. Aaron Willis's early and very comprehensive analysis of Shas includes a summary of the views elicited mostly from the crisis framework that are often referred to when scholars attempt to make sense of Shas's enigmatic rise.

In the 1950's and 1960's when Jews from the Middle Eastern Countries immigrated to the nascent Israeli State, they encountered a variety of ideological and institutional possibilities for assimilation. While many Middle Eastern Jews adopted the secular socialist values of Mapai Zionism, a great number came to support . . . a religious Zionism. Mafdal offered these immigrants both ideological and material support for their absorption [but] Mafdal had a distinctly European (Ashkenazi) flavor, and many immigrants viewed successful absorption into mainstream society as necessitating the abandonment of traditional "ethnic" customs and norms in favor of Ashkenazi cultural models. . . . More than a generation later, the political party of Sephardic Torah Guardians (Shas) has risen to power with the claim that the material and spiritual needs of the Middle Eastern communities have been neglected. They blame the secular, and national-religious, Ashkenazi establishment.[10]

At the heart of the crisis framework is the idea that the socioeconomic disparities between ethnic groups have continued unabated since Israel's founding, despite overall general improvements in education and human capital. This continuing disparity, neglected by the center-left and center-right parties, opened a political window of opportunity for religious parties to develop a class party wrapped in religious discourse, namely Shas. Much research concurs that the structural impediments to a redistribution of power are extremely tenacious. An unhindered social transformation would have reduced the income gap by 19 percent if the Sephardim's level of education had not improved since 1975. The census data from 1999 documents that for the Sephardi community, the overall inequality in income distribution grew by 32 percent from 1975 to 1999, despite the diminishing differences in educational capital between Ashkenazi and Sephardim.[11] Given the pandemic of inequality, crisis models attribute Shas's electoral power to its ability to capitalize on the socioeconomic and cultural grievances of its constituency. In fact, some scholars would argue that without the income inequality suffered by Sephardi communities, there would not be a Sephardi religious party.

Despite their prevalent use, crisis explanations often avoid explaining Mafdal's fluctuating power. After all, for the crisis model, Mafdal is a product of the containment policy of the Israeli state. The political seclusion of ultra-Orthodox communities conferred upon Mafdal the role of forming religious institutions and managing the state's religious pillar. The party became responsible for state-sponsored religious schools and religious courts. Under this system, Mafdal's leadership agreed to narrow its focus to religious issues and accepted socioeconomic policies as external to its agenda in return for the unfettered power to introduce laws, as well as other formal and informal rules, in areas important to its religious constituency.

The Politics of Judaism as a Choice

The question of why individuals turn to religious parties, when answered without referring to structural macro changes, turns our attention to individual choices, which are often linked to three approaches: individuals' attempts to declare their differences (politics of recognition, or identity politics), the parties' effective mobilization of voters (political mobilization), and the attraction of the party leadership (charismatic appeal).

The Politics of Recognition   The politics of recognition views politics in general as a contestation over the allocation of power and pays special attention to symbols and values that grant different power positions in a given society. Thus, attempts for recognition challenge the existing hierarchies and serve as means for more "egalitarian" policies. In this perspective, religious partisans appear as agents who demand acknowledgement in areas previously denied to them. While structural accounts attribute the success of religious parties to failed economic policies, others see religious parties as venues to mobilize marginalized religious groups, assert the groups' distinctiveness, and escape characterizations by outsiders.[12] For the student of identity politics, Mafdal's ideology represents a strong adhesive and a powerful magnet for those who do not want to split their loyalties between the state, the Biblical lands, and their religious community. Nevertheless, the party's embrace of a settler identity has been a mixed blessing, as it shifts the party's focus from the unity of national community to territorial unity, thereby creating internal tensions. The party faces the dilemma of advocating the settlement at the expense of alienating its moderate electorate, fueling a nationally divisive issue, and thus desecrating the unity of nation.

Shas, on the other hand, offers a prime example of the diversification of the Israeli public sphere as well as the emergence of new counter-hegemonic identities. In fact, the party's own 1996 electoral slogan, "Shas is not a platform but an *identity*," directs our attention to a new trend among religious parties: their efforts to present themselves as mass movements and as articulators of a new identity rooted in the old. The self-classification adopted by Shas indicates that the party not only emerged in an environment where the national identity was questioned but that it also embraced this identity as the core of its political program. A statement from this political program repeats the premise that the party does not represent another temporary, ethnic reaction, but a shift in the way the Sephardi community defines itself. In this way, the party challenges how the Sephardi community has been defined by others. The central role of Sephardi identity in Shas is not random political maneuvering, but a result of the historical legacy of policies perceived as exclusive by the Sephardim. Shas's identity politics is attractive to many, as the party redefines the Sephardim's relationship to the state, free from the modernizing and pioneering pressures of Labor Zionism. Shas enables the Sephardim to reassert a dominant role by reemphasizing their traditional, religious foundations, especially those marginalized by the Labor Zionist definition of Jewish Israeli identity groups.[13]

A less-recognized aspect of Shas's identity, discussed in Chapter Three, has drawn our attention to what this identity means in religious terms and its position vis-à-vis the Ashkenazi religious leadership. Within the religious bloc, the statement of Lithuanian Rabbi Schach, who was once Shas's spiritual leader, that "Shas is not yet ready for a leadership role in Israel's ultra-Orthodox world" caused a storm within party circles and further colored the vision of Haredi ultra-Orthodox communities in ethnic terms. Comparable statements about Shas reinforced the idea that, despite their best efforts to emulate Ashkenazi ultra-Orthodox traditions, the Sephardim were likely to be marginalized even in the ultra-Orthodox world. This peripheralization of the Sephardi identity in both secular and religious worlds provides the key to understanding the forces that brought Shas to the forefront of Israeli politics. The success of religious parties expands even more due to the continuing failure of secular center parties, which opens more room for religious parties to consolidate their counter-hegemonic identities.

However, missing in these studies is why certain groups are more receptive to these messages and why Shas's alternative identity appeals not only to the first generation who were subject to exclusionary policies but also to Israel's second-generation Sephardim, who are assimilated and integrated in many regards.[14] Perhaps more importantly, these analyses fail to answer the questions of why and how religious parties establish themselves as crafters of new identities, and what these identities entail.

The Politics of Mobilization From the lens of Politics of Mobilization, religion's return to politics in general stems from its unique ability to mobilize people, especially in Israeli politics. At the broader context of this success lies the failure of major parties to reach out to their constituency, a failure exacerbated by the religious elite's ingenious capabilities for organizing the masses. Religious parties are distinguished from others by not only the number of individuals they mobilize but the ways in which they manage to break through the political apathy of the masses. Research conducted, especially in the field of American politics, tells us that more often than not cost and resources, not motivations, determine whether citizens engage in politics and vote.[15] Diminished individual resources for some groups make political involvement contingent on whether and how party organizations or party elites facilitate their participation. Accordingly, political involvement of resource-poor people is tied to the subsidization of the cost of participation through the provision of information or psychological benefits.

When political participation is seen as a question of mobilization, it directs our attention away from isolated, individual thought processes to the collective dimension of voting decisions. Regardless of how it occurs, mobilization serves as a catalyst for political participation and thus is vital for maintaining a liberal democracy. In their assessment of Israeli politics from 1977 to 2003, Asher Arian and Michal Shamir show that the shifting of conventional party allegiances was accompanied by a significant decline in political participation, mobilization, and party competition, three mainstays of an electoral democracy. Israeli politics adopted a new form during the transition: "with the failing bonds between parties and voters, volatility, the ongoing criticisms of political parties as institutions of government, the declining status of parties in the eyes of voters, the changing calculus of voters, it appears that achieving [political] dominance is a mission impossible."[16] The intertwined processes of political realignment (i.e., shifts in traditional political alliances) and de-alignment (i.e., defection of political parties without forming new political bonds) created an important void not only in party identifications but also in political mobilization, thereby generating an environment conducive to the political outreach of religious parties.

In this context, religious parties are distinguished from others by the ability of their leadership to forge social networks that provide strong horizontal links and, thus, coherence around a core identity.[17] From the perspective of the Israeli system as a whole, the distinction between religious parties and others in general, and between Shas and Mafdal in particular, seems to be their embeddedness in existing communities, their ability to form new communities, and their development of political alliances and identities, thereby mobilizing the electorate in more comprehensive and durable ways. In the case of Mafdal, its electoral power stemmed from its control of the modern ultra-Orthodox bloc. In Israel's highly compartmentalized system, Mafdal forged organic ties with various institutions from schools to religious courts. Due to the existing "religious division of labor," Mafdal maintains an increasingly challenged monopoly over state-affiliated religious schools, the religious state schools, independent religious institutions like Bar Ilan, and the religious higher education institutions, as well as the Office of Ashkenazi Chief Rabbi. Through these institutions, the party has imprinted the socialization of citizens, especially those who attended the religious state schools. Its overall institutional position within the Israeli polity allowed Mafdal to attract a heterogeneous group of people with diverse socioeconomic, geographic, and ethnic backgrounds. The party's ties with movements such as the Young Guard and *Gush Emunim* also permitted it to penetrate socioreligious movements and groups who support redemptive Zionist beliefs. The party's commitment to the settlements, and the ties it established with settlers, also enhanced its presence in settlement areas.[18] Mafdal's mobilization efforts are, therefore, not sporadic but institutionally based, under the tutelage of the state, or rooted in the party's ideology and groups with which it developed organic ties.

Shas, on the other hand, spans the entire spectrum of mobilization venues described by Jan E. Leighley. In Leighley's model, mobilization can be initiated by (1) the elite, through providing information and knowledge that motivates participation, or (2) the party organization's distribution of relational goods, ranging from intangible benefits such as group social interaction to more tangible ones such as employment. In fact, a closer look at Shas's organization shows that Shas penetrated Israeli Sephardic society mostly through its organizational capacity and the services it has delivered. The party is not only a master at spreading motivating knowledge but also creates exclusive membership benefits, such as school and unemployment support.[19]

Ironically, Shas appears to be the party that has inherited the capacity of Israel's first secular Zionist parties by making itself relevant to all different segments of society. In some respects, it has revived Zionism's now feeble collectivistic spirit using its ethnic ultra-Orthodox ideology. The party put itself at the center of a separate and dynamic web of educational and welfare organizations that address the needs of religious Jews but also help disadvantaged communities in general. As such for some observers "Appealing especially to voters who are lower class, less edu-cated, and have large families, Shas fills the functions Mapai had filled in the past, but abandoned when many social services were transferred to the state."[20] Through its service organizations, Shas has managed to ap-peal to a wide range of groups, from those attending its schools and party-affiliated groups, *Avrechim* and *Elhamayaan,* to broader groups who found employment opportunities and a sense of solidarity in the party-sponsored network.[21] For many, these institutions have gradually created a vested interest in the party's electoral success and also serve as a dense political communications network that explains to its beneficiaries the salience of the issues and takes a stance on their solutions.[22]

The Politics of Charismatic Appeal According to Panebianco, "charis-matic parties" represent a total symbiosis between the leader and the or-ganizational identity. These parties differ from others in that they appear as a cohesive coalition held together by loyalty to the leader.[23] They can successfully continue to exist if they engage in (1) an objectification and reutilization of charisma, (2) a transfer of loyalties from the leader to the organization, or (3) a shift from a solidarity system toward a system of in-terests.[24] In the case of Mafdal, the party maintained its presence in Is-raeli politics after reusing the charismatic father Kook's conciliatory ideas and charisma. Nevertheless, during this transformation the party moved away from being the broad religious Zionist party that Kook had envi-sioned to a more narrowly defined party, a party of territorial nationalism and settlement movements, appealing to a different set of constituencies during each phase of the transformative process.

In the case of Shas, Ovadia Yosef's charismatic appeal remains one of the compelling explanations for the party's unexpected popularity. Ac-cording to some observers, Shas appears as a religious, leader-centered party and its institutional organization is simply a tool for the hegemonic appeal of Yosef's ideas, rather than vice versa. In order to "beat the Ashkenazim," Rabbi Yosef has built a strategy based on two pillars: his intimate knowledge of the Torah and Halakha on the one hand and the Shas Party on the other.[25] In fact, descriptions of Yosef by Shas support-ers provide strong evidence for arguments that Shas is Yosef's party. Sto-ries among supporters about Yosef's unique skills, Torah knowledge, and political wisdom create an almost mythical personality. One of the most popular stories recounts that "Yosef's eagerness to learn Torah despite his poor circumstances was so powerful, he had such a photographic mem-ory, that he would climb a ladder with a book, flip through the pages, and grasp the content instantaneously." [26]

Unquestioning loyalty to Yosef reveals itself not only in his widely dis-tributed pictures and writings but also by supporters shielding Yosef against any criticism. Party advocates attribute any unfavorable assessment of Yosef's statements to the audience's lack of understanding or to the decontextualization of his *responsa*. For instance, loyal supporters argue that there are as many phrases to describe sinners against the religious law as there are for those who trespass against secular laws.[27] When Yosef uses Torah terms, the semiotic or symbolic gulf between the secular and the religious publics prevents secular Jews from fully absorbing the meanings. Many descriptions point to the masses' enchantment with Yosef as the only source of Shas's political appeal. In fact, for many Shas supporters Yosef's brilliance is the very reason for his misunderstanding; thus, they disregard the negative assessments. After all, "the Rabbi's written oeuvre and his stunning output in breadth and depth appears in dozens of carefully argued volumes of Halakhic writings. One is reminded of Mozart who composed divine music, while his correspondence often contained scatological expressions."[28] His nuanced explanations could not be grasped by average observers and lead to some misidentifications. When viewed through the lens of a charismatic party model, Yosef is the reason Shas supporters turn to the party. Thus, it is not a coincidence that many declare their unconditional support for him first and the party second:

> As long as Rav Ovadia recommends a vote for Shas, then I will vote for it. Because Shas is Rav Ovadia, all of it. Ovadia created Shas and devoted himself to raising the level of the Sephardim, not only them, but for Judaism and Torah here in the Land of Israel. What Shas has done in just a couple of years, no one, not the Mafdal, and not Agudah, was able to do in the past forty years.[29]

MISSING PERSPECTIVES

Notwithstanding their different rationales, how the contesting frameworks view the role of ideology for the voting decisions of religious partisans points out an inconspicuous area of consensus. For instance, the conflict and crisis models contend that political ideologies of religious parties are molded by their respective religious doctrines. Differences between religious parties are therefore inconsequential. Notwithstanding their variant loci, models resting on the politics of recognition, mobilization and charismatic appeal, ultimately view religious ideologies as merely novel *venues* for the voices of marginalized groups. What matters is the overall *function* of religious parties; thus, the content of religious ideologies is of secondary importance. The assumptions of competing models see religious ideologies uniformly as mirroring religious doctrines or as instrumental, which relegates them to the background of the analyses. Structural factors explain the voting decisions of religious partisans, and a closer look at the interactions between the parties, their ideologies, and partisans is not needed. Those who view quests for recognition as the foundation of religious politics tend to treat religion as a rather homogeneous set of beliefs that inspires comparable political demands among those who share them. Religious values in themselves become markers of the identities who uphold them. Such an approach, regardless of how critical it is of essentialist views, rhetorically perpetuates an understanding of religion as an intrinsically defining core of identities.

In an effort to understand who the religious partisans are and why they turn to religious parties, the following discussion questions the prevailing analyses and attends to the elements they leave unexplained: We first describe how the conventional yardsticks fall short in describing the political positions of religious party supporters and then turn to analyze the supporters as agents of the conflict between the sacred and profane, as alienated masses and articulators of the politics of resentment. In order to explore the analytical expediency of approaches that allow more room for the partisans' perceptions, we then evaluate the ideological spaces from the perspective of the electorate and show that the way we study religious politics produces some anomalies. Our discussion draws on survey data, an extensively used tool in electoral studies, but one that has not received much use in studies of religious parties; instead, religious partisans have been relegated to the category of reactionary voters. What religious partisans react to is perceived to take precedence over how they decide. The following analyses expand on other arguments as well and illustrate that religious partisans, more often than not, defy our initial deductive expectations.

Silent Voices? The Question of Data

In accounts based on either a clash of values, identities, or socioeconomic crises as the main driver of religious party support, religious partisans are referred to as a group, left in the background as silent masses, or viewed as isolated voters consumed by their daily struggles. Accordingly, the empirical evidence for studies of Mafdal and Shas comes in three different forms: ethnographic studies, anecdotal evidence, and macroanalyses of 482 localities, the main units of the election process. Anecdotal evidence supplies us with thick descriptions, even though they are sometimes located in an analytical vacuum, not contextualized or systematically related to other observations. Ethnographic studies offered by anthropologists have proven most helpful, as they effectively introduce us to the symbolic worlds of the movement's participants and leaders. One might argue that despite their opposing foci, both analytical windows tend to emphasize a certain aspect of religion and politics that subtly reinforces the idea that religious parties are sui generis parties that do not lend themselves to broad comparisons or generalization. Some of the most useful analyses suffer from ecological or reverse ecological fallacies, that is, making inferences about individuals based on aggregate data and vice versa respectfully.[30] Despite their shortcomings, it is important to note that analyzing single geographical units is especially useful in Israel, given that the settlements with small populations are ideologically more uniform, not easily accessible, and generally not included in national representative surveys.[31]

It is important to note that our identification of missing components rests on adopting a broader perspective; yet that does not mean that specific accounts are fallacious. On the contrary, pointing out gaps also highlights the studies' strengths and the need for diverse empirical foundations in order to enhance our inquiries. As indicated before, the absence of individual voices from existing analyses leaves an especially important void and deprives our efforts of critical analytical input. Macrolevel or group-level assertions by themselves can create a discourse of their own, without allowing the conclusions to be deepened or questioned by the insight offered by individual-level empirical observations. The difficulties in gathering individual-level observations are discussed in detail below. They occasionally force even choice-centered models, whose premises rest on individuals, to view individuals en bloc. Our analysis draws upon a total of nine different data sets: the first six include the 1992, 1996, 1999, 2001, 2003, and 2006 Israeli Election Studies data. Each is based on representative national samples of Israeli citizens eligible to vote, with sample sizes of 1,091, 1,168, 1,225, 1,417, 1,234, and 1,919 voters, respectively. In order to have a closer look at Shas supporters, three additional surveys are used: the 1999 Dahaf Institute's special survey of 568 Israeli citizens, 261 of whom are Shas supporters; a national election survey conducted by Abraham Diskin in 1999 (referred to as the 1999 Election Study) with a sample size of 900; plus a 2003 religious party supporter survey conducted by the author as a representative national sample of 308 voters, 150 of whom were Shas supporters.[32]

The promise of survey data as a unique venue to look at religious party support is accompanied by some challenges. As all of the surveys are nationally representative surveys, they allow for a comparison of Israel's religious and nonreligious parties. Given that religious party support increased in importance in the early 1990s, these surveys help us probe the nature of the shifts in Mafdal's and Shas's electoral bases. Notwithstanding these benefits, some puzzles remain. With the exception of the 1999 election data collected by Abraham Diskin, all national surveys underrepresent the supporters of religious parties. Especially in the case of Shas, its supporters are significantly fewer among the survey respondents than expected, posing some intriguing questions about both religious partisanship and the ability of surveys to capture these new partisans.[33] Nevertheless, specialized surveys, such as the Dahaf Institute Survey and the 2003 religious-party support survey compensate for this lacuna. Despite their limited sample sizes and the use of different questionnaires, their findings allow us to offer an in-depth analysis of Shas supporters and probe into the findings of national representative surveys.

The consistent underrepresentation of Shas supporters introduces the broader question of why otherwise very reliable national representative surveys underrepresent a certain group and how we can use existing findings to study religious partisans effectively. Surveys are valuable tools in social inquiries for their capacity to bridge conceptual approaches and empirical trends by fusing the abstract and the observed. Even those concepts that appear to be the most straightforward turn out to be complex in the empirical world, and measuring them through survey questions offers a valuable tool to tap into their meanings and gauge their continuing relevance in understanding political practices. For instance, partisanship and party identification, two of the most popular political science concepts, can be applied and probed via survey data. Such applications quickly warn us that what is often assumed to be a simple relationship of party identification, party support, or partisanship to their empirical reference, such as actual votes, do not follow a uniform relation. As Campbell once showed, even simple conceptual constructs get highly complicated once one takes them to the empirical world. Party identification, Campbell argues, helps citizens locate themselves and others on the political spectrum: people use it as a heuristic device, irrespective of whether they vote like a partisan, or think like a partisan, or someone else thinks they are a partisan. An important component of partisanship and its relation to party identification is a matter of self-definition and needs to be treated as such not only in surveys, but beyond surveys.[34]

Consequently, analyzing surveys means not only applying but also constantly questioning our concepts, as data are not always cooperative, and our terms tend to become elusive unless the link between their meanings and empirical domains is constantly reviewed. For instance, the insufficient representation of religious party supporters might stem from (1) a built-in bias in the sampling design or (2) the high nonresponse rate among religious partisans.

The first possible cause of underrepresentation reminds us that even a perfectly random sample can yield biased results if certain segments of society systematically refuse to participate (nonresponders). To eliminate this potential source of bias, even random sampling designs often use mixed strategies of stratification and ultimately rely on households as the final unit from which to select interviewees. Given the significant differences between the households of ultra-Orthodox families and others, the systemic differences may be introducing bias. In fact, Israel's leading pollsters often acknowledge how Israel's large families are not particularly well represented, especially in telephone polls. "In such families, there are usually several people who are eligible to vote, but only one takes part in the survey. Given that large families are either Arab, ultra-Orthodox, or poor, their voices are not heard that clearly in the polls."[35] If this is indeed the case, who the nonrespondents are, and how they are replaced in the sample, becomes a crucial question. Yet at the same time, political orientations generally do not vary much within these large families, so our findings can still speak to overall patterns.

The second factor for underrepresentation in the data directs our attention to the impact of the environment on party identifications in the survey results. The already complex nature of party identification in Israel was exacerbated by the institutional experimentation mandated by the 1992 law. This electoral reform introduced the direct election of the prime minister in order to strengthen the office and reduce the negotiating power of small parties.[36] The dual election strategy aimed at providing a counterweight to the impact of the very low national threshold (2 percent) for national representation, which results in a multiplicity of small parties in Parliament.[37] The two-level competition introduced a unique and unexpected dynamic to the Israeli electoral system, which unleashed complex strategic political calculations. The expectations of the law's originators were dashed by "ticket splitting" when large numbers of voters chose to support different parties for the office of prime minister and for parliamentary representation. The rule, in fact, enhanced the share of small parties in parliament instead of undercutting their power, making them a second choice to balance the power of the separately elected prime minister. Although the electoral system was changed back shortly after the 2001 election, it created complicated electoral calculations and political identities. As a result of this split-party identification, some respondents are likely to report their primary party choice—for prime minister—as their party identification rather than the small parties they are supporting for parliament, bolstering the likelihood that some parties might be underrepresented in surveys.

If underrepresentation results from a reluctance to reveal one's political identity directly, or from the complexities of political identity, then hidden supporters can be recovered by a careful analysis of the existing surveys. For instance, questions such as those about the assessment of the parties on various policies and the ranking of the leadership can help identify Shas supporters who are not revealing their support for Shas in response to questions about party identification. They may hesitate to be direct because of dual party identifications, strategic voting, or stigmas attached to Shas and the like. In fact, the feeling thermometer questions (e.g., how much you like a certain party or party leader) in the existing surveys yield strikingly accurate approximations of Shas support for the 1996 and 1999 elections. In the 1996 election, 8.6 percent of respondents felt very positive about Shas, compared to the party's electoral share of 8.3 percent. Similarly, in the 1999 survey, 13.3 percent of the survey respondents named Shas and Deri as their most-liked party and party leader, and the party received 13 percent of the votes in that election. The high correlation between party identification based on the feeling questions and the real election results suggests that alternative approaches to party identification are possible, but they still serve only as proxies and cannot be treated as declared party choices.

It is also important to note that the National Election Survey questionnaires are not designed to probe the nexus of religion and politics. For instance, instead of probing whether and to what extent people experience and perceive the presence of religious and secular conflict, the 1998 survey asked for the *reasons for such conflict*. Likewise, questions refer to dichotomies such as democratic versus Halakhic forms of state as *alternatives*. Given the surveys' overall aim of tapping into as many issues as possible while taking into account more salient cleavages, such simplifications are unavoidable, yet they still yield significant information. The 2003 religious party support survey was designed to address some gaps and capture the nuances omitted by the National Election Survey. Thus, the analysis below answers theoretical questions by drawing on the rich empirical evidence offered by the available, yet limited, data and illustrates that the data limitations, when they are explored carefully, can have their own merits. Sometimes it is the absence of data or responses that sheds more light on religious partisans. Conventional problems, such as underrepresentation, encourage us to evaluate the existing questionnaires critically.

The questionnaires themselves serve as an important venue for studying the political contexts the surveys have sought to capture. Some questions alert us to how the main political issues and groups have been debated. Others point to issues salient to the Israeli political culture. For instance, all surveys include a question on whether respondents prefer "a socialist or capitalist system," a choice between "private or state interest" that attests to, among others, the effect of the Mapai (Labor) dominant political culture and that would not readily travel to different political systems elsewhere. At the same time, some significant questions such as "whether respondents experience ethnic discrimination in their personal lives" or whether "respondents support more expenditures for public ritual baths" became important in some elections, but were not salient enough overall to be repeated in others. Finally, it is important to note that beyond the specific challenges faced in the implementation of surveys in Israel, capturing religious beliefs, ethnic identities, religiosity and their effects on political beliefs and political choices is a difficult endeavor in its own right.[38] Recognizing these challenges does not undermine the analytical purchase of the data. On the contrary, when limitations are well understood and addressed, surveys serve as unique windows into the world of religious partisans and as indispensable means for systematic information on religious party support. Even skeptics can gain insight from surveys, not by treating them as definite snapshots, but by approaching their formulations, applications and findings as a rich ground to both tackle and elicit further questions.

The Interface of Theoretical Constructs and Empirical Findings: Understanding Religious Party Supporters

Religious Party Supporters and the Politics of Secular-Religious Conflict   From the standpoint of the conflict model, religious party supporters view politics as a constant power struggle between competing worldviews rooted in the secular and the religious. Religious partisans coalesce around the common goal of asserting the role of religion in the public sphere. In these accounts, religious partisans appear on the ideological peripheries of their respective politics and form coherent groups that seek to desecularize their respective politics. In order to thoroughly assess the analytical purchase of the conflict of values thesis to the Israeli context, we need to examine how religious partisans perceive themselves and the extent to which their religious beliefs define their political positions. More specifically, two distinctive, yet intertwined, analyses are needed to (1) understand to what extent religious partisans cluster around common identities and values and how they challenge hegemonic identities and policies and (2) establish whether our markers (e.g., the religious-secular, the Left–Right, and Sephardi–Ashkenazi spectra) are nuanced enough to capture the novel positions of religious partisans.

A quick glance of the religious identifications from the outside often introduces a polarized picture that juxtaposes its secular majority against the ultra-Orthodox minority. In Israel's daily parlance, however, four categories of religious orientations circulate to define its political terrain: ultra-Orthodox (Haredi), religious (*Dati*), traditional (*Masorati*), and secular (*Hiloni*). The same terms are used in the opinion polls to identify respondents' positions vis-à-vis the religious-secular cleavage. Notwithstanding their common use, a closer look at what these terms entail and how they relate to certain political behaviors shows that their meaning is anything but straightforward. Haredi, which literally means "those who tremble in awe of God," refers to the strict adherence to religious rules and describes groups for whom religious tradition is the only source of social order and reality. The Haredi are treated as a coherent unit, irrespective of the competition between different traditions within their ultra-Orthodox bloc. Religious, on the other hand, refers to those who observe Halakhic rules and are conscious of constituting a separate sector within Israeli society. In contrast to the Haredi, the religious reject acculturation and engage actively in the public sphere to ensure religion's central role. Traditionals are perhaps the most significant group because they deliberately distinguish themselves from religious and secular groups by selectively observing religious traditions. While traditionals observe religious rules, *mitzvoth*, their observance is partial and selective. Yet their observance is not completely "random, individualized, or unsystematic, nor is it without intent."[39] Interestingly enough, this group is often neglected in studies of religious politics, as Liebman and Susser have found. They attribute the lack of attention to the group's practice-centered, folk-religious, inarticulate character, which never justifies itself in principled, creative, or rebellious terms. What makes this group especially important for religious parties is that, although their intent may not be "proper" from a religious perspective, they are not without belief. Traditionals are aware of their "deviations," and are unperturbed by them.[40] Therefore, while traditionals are elusive as a group, they are perhaps the key to understanding religious party support.

Given the importance of religious identities overall, extrapolating political views from broad religious identifications needs to be approached cautiously. For instance, do all secularists endorse a complete restriction of the role of religion in the public sphere? If not, what role do they assign to Judaism? How do traditionalists see the role of religion in the public sphere? When we look closely at the political activities of each category, the variation within each group suggests that when and how religion matters to political decisions cannot be deduced from religious identities abstracted from the frequency of religious observance. The key for understanding religion's relevance, especially in the case of groups like traditionalists, is the *meaning* attached to religious rituals and not the broader title of religiosity. The Guttman Report, one of the most comprehensive studies of religious views conducted in Israel, suggests that when the religious-secular spectrum is presented as religious and antireligious on a

7-point scale, 15 percent of the population state strongly antireligious positions (i.e., scores of 1–2), suggesting they view religion's role in the public sphere as a zero-sum game. Yet 50 percent state a qualified religious identity (scores of 3–5), leaving their position on the role of religion in society open to further questions. Given this dispersion, we do not know for sure if traditionalists necessarily support a religious party or what makes a traditionalist support a Haredi party as opposed to a religious party. Do religious parties become more popular as they attract traditionals? Do religious parties capitalize on the private religiosity of individuals or their religiously rooted public expectations? In other words, what is the relationship between religious observance, religious identity, and political position?

If politics are driven by competing values, one would expect the rise of religious parties in world politics in general, and in Israeli politics in particular, to be accompanied by a sudden increase in the religious and Haredi blocs. The assumption is that religious parties do better as individuals become more religious. An analysis of self-reported religious identities contradicts this deductive conclusion, as the distribution of reli-

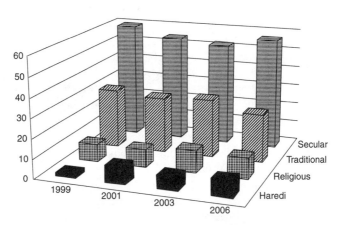

	1999	2001	2003	2006
■ Haredi	1.9	8.7	7	8.4
⊞ Religious	8.8	8.9	11.3	10.6
▨ Traditional	29.9	28.1	29.6	24.4
⊟ Secular	59.4	54.2	52.1	56.6

FIGURE 5.2

Religious self-identification of Israeli citizens

SOURCES: The 1999, 2001, 2003, 2006 Israel Election Study data

gious and secular identification has remained relatively stable from 1992 to 2003 (see figure 5.2). Notwithstanding these findings, one can still argue that it is not the overall change in religious-secular identifications, but the ability of religious parties to mobilize the religious and Haredi publics that explains the parties' electoral fortunes. Although the conflict model tells us that religious partisans come more from among religious ideologues, a closer look at Mafdal and Shas supporters reveals that such deductive accounts need to be approached cautiously. From the standpoint of the conflict model, it is puzzling that Shas's ultra-Orthodox Sephardi supporters are located at different points on the secular ultra-Orthodox continuum. While approximately 50 percent of Shas's voters identify themselves as religious, 32.3 percent choose to be identified as traditional. Dahaf and the 2003 Religious Party Support Survey confirm that a significant, though limited, part of Shas's support comes from those who identify themselves as secular. More intriguingly, fewer traditionalists support Mafdal, popularly known as a moderate party, than Shas. The Haredi presence among Mafdal supporters also remains limited. Hence, Mafdal appears to be more a party of self-reported "religious people," since they consistently constitute the main party support (e.g., 63 percent in the 2001 election data). Shas, though widely considered a Haredi Sephardi party, is supported by voters from the entire religious-secular spectrum.

Shas's ability to appeal to secular groups brings to the fore the intricacy of the connection between personal religious identifications and political views. While religious identities serve as the repository of political positions and ideas, they matter only when they are translated into political demands. Modernity, after all, is based on the idea that the religious beliefs of individuals can be compartmentalized and do not necessarily amount to public demands. Thus, the religiosity of individuals does not unavoidably affect their political calculations mechanically. They can be contained in people's private and immediate social milieu. But the reverse question has rarely been asked: Can religion have a presence in the public sphere without a radical change in the individuals' religiosity? A possible discrepancy between personal identification and political demands grounded in religion refocuses attention on other venues and reasons for religious demands on the public sphere. The intriguing question at the individual level is whether the relative stability of religious identifications is linked with increasing religious demands on the public sphere.

In fact, the religious partisans' expectations of the state vis-à-vis religious affairs introduce another unexpected notion. Despite some minor fluctuations since 1992, more than half of the public (on average 52.5 percent) expresses either opposition to or endorsement of the government's involvement in the observance of religious rules in the public sphere. The percentage of those who strongly favor a Halakhic state increased from 14.1 percent to 29.3 percent from 1992 to 2003; despite the sudden jump in 1999 the number of those who strongly oppose a Halakhic state remained relatively stable (nearly 30 percent) in the same period. The finding at first suggests a rise in ultra-Orthodox beliefs among Israeli citizens. When this conclusion is assessed in the light of insights gained from other results, however, it warns us that the composition of religious parties, which attracts people from different religious orientations, might be reflecting altered political expectations more than the changing environment of sacrosanctity. The relative stability of the level of religious practices and their demands on the state shows that, more than changing the lifestyle of individuals, religious parties have been successful in changing the political demands of individuals.

Religious Party Supporters and the Politics of the Extreme Right? Whether and how the ideological terrain of Israel has changed and how these changes relate to the increasing salience of religious parties can also be explored through the lens of the Left–Right spectrum. In fact, analyses embedded in conflict explanations often resort to the Left–Right spectrum to demarcate and gauge the "extremity" of the positions of the religious parties and their supporters. Understanding the interface of politics and religion in an ideological space defined by a Left–Right spectrum requires that we revisit the roots of the terms. In Israel, as in Turkey, the Left has historically represented, and continues to represent, the policies that assign a central and pioneering role to the state in redistributive policies and in protecting the public sphere against what it perceived to be "anti-democratic forces." The Right emerged as a reaction to the dominance of the state-constitutive ideology. In this dichotomous representation of the Israeli case, Left denoted views derived from Labor Zionism and its collectivistic and transformational policies. The Right articulated the need for more liberties to and greater authority over religious expressions and sought the decline of state dominance in social and economic policies. The strength of the Left–Right spectrum, its ability to subsume various positions under simple categories, has increasingly become its weakness. Using the terms *Left* and *Right* often obscures the emerging hybrid political positions. Some scholars have already warned that the way the Left–Right spectrum is used in Israel is unique to Israel and cannot travel easily elsewhere. The terms have come to represent one's position vis-à-vis the peace process. Although the positions on peace are far from being dichotomous, the Left label currently describes dovish voters, and the Right label expresses hawkish, antipeace positions.[41]

In recognition of the overextended nature of the Left–Right spectrum, the 1992 and 1996 Israeli election surveys created a highly unusual ideological spectrum from Left to religious. In these years, around 8 percent persistently placed themselves beyond a Left–Right identification, defining themselves as religious instead. The 1999 election data collected by Abraham Diskin further exemplify the positioning changes when the multilayered spectra subsumed under the Left–Right spectrum are peeled back and analyzed individually. When respondents were asked in the 1999 election survey to focus on the economic meaning (free vs. controlled economy) and the foreign policy/security-related meaning of the Left–Right spectrum, only 46 percent placed themselves in the same location as their average ideological standing. Twenty-five percent regarded their position as farther to the right, while 39 percent saw themselves as farther left. The results confirm that the voters' Left and Right identifications are not always tied to their abstract and consistent ideological commitments, but to the clustering of specific policy positions in relation to other stances.

Although the meanings attached to the 1999 election data's Left–Right spectrum are not fixed, the self-placement of the respondents on this continuum demonstrates that over the last ten years, there has been a shift toward the ideological extremes. Those who placed themselves at both polar ends (i.e., 1 and 7 on a 7-point spectrum) rose from 15.3 percent in 1992 to 31.4 percent in 2003. Interestingly, the weak center (20 percent) remained stable. Comparing the placement of religious partisans on the conventional Left–Right spectrum to the 1999 Election Study's distribution shows that 65 percent of Shas supporters placed themselves on the Far Right (i.e., 1–2 on a 7-point scale) in 1999, rising to 74 percent in 2003. Twenty-eight percent of Shas supporters see themselves at the center and left of the ideological spectrum. Despite this overall shift, the survey results also confirm there has been limited yet consistent support for Shas among those who view themselves as Left. Overall, 54.2 percent of Shas supporters identified themselves as Right (not extreme Right) and 30 percent at the center, when the categories range from extreme Right to extreme Left. Shas supporters spread even farther along the Left–Right spectrum with regard to the economic issues: 87.2 percent of them identified themselves at the center-right as opposed to the far Right, while a small number (4 percent) identified itself on the left.

Regardless of the ambivalence inherent in the Left–Right designations, it is important to note that significant numbers of Shas supporters come from the opposite pole of the ideological spectrum. This result may be attributable to the respondents' lack of political knowledge, but the consistency suggests that it is more likely to be a direct reflection of Shas's complex political positions. The political identification of Shas supporters is intriguing, not because they cluster around the center and the right, but because of the broad range of their ideological identifications. Given the traditional boundaries between the Left and the Right and the popular image of Shas as a Haredi party, this range of ideological orientations among Shas supporters attests to the party's ability to traverse ideological blocs. According to the Dahaf Institute Survey, a comparison of the Shas supporters' perceptions of their own positions on the Left–Right spectrum with those of the rest of the public reveals an enormous difference. While an overwhelming majority of Shas supporters consider the party as moderate Right, the majority of the other party supporters see Shas as extreme Right. The self-placement of Mafdal voters on the Left–Right spectrum shows, on average, that more than half of them consider themselves as Far Right or Right.

When foreign policy and economic meanings of the Left–Right spectrum were differentiated, Mafdal's perceived ideological homogeneity disintegrated: only 30 percent of Mafdal supporters viewed themselves at the same ideological location on the Left–Right spectrum. A significant number of Mafdal supporters (53.3 percent) are centrists and leftists with respect to economic issues. The apparent contradictions of these findings can be explained by the party's state-centered ideology. After all, Mafdal links the concept of a strong welfare state in domestic issues with the importance of territorial issues. Although the party seems to be moving to the right fringes of the Israeli political sphere, the party's effective election motto, "Mafdal to the Right," resonates with less than half of the supporters when it comes to economic issues. All these findings suggest that it is necessary to develop a multidimensional description of Israel's political space in order to make sense of the ideological diversity absent in the Left–Right spectrum.

Religious Party Supporters and the Politics of Ethnicity?   Another dimension of the conflict models applies uniquely to Israel: the mutually reinforcing effect of ethnic and religious cleavages aggravates the conflict between religious and secular groups. According to common perception, Sephardim are traditionally more religious than Ashkenazi and critical of Ashkenazi secular policies. Given the emphasis on national unity and continuing immigrations from a wide range of countries, ethnicity itself has been both a blind spot and a driving force in Israeli politics. The Israeli polity, as with Turkish nationalism, subsumes all ethnic cultural identities under one national identity, yet latent ethnic issues have always caused important political debates and changes. Some observers argue that Israel's two-party system came to an end in 1977 only when Sephardi populations aligned themselves with Likud. When the hegemony of the Zionist Labor identity started to erode, identities once marginalized by the state became more visible as independent political forces. In fact, evidencing the increasing salience of competing identities, the Israeli election surveys in the 1990s included questions about identity for the first time. An analysis of how Israelis view their primary identities in terms of "Israeli" and "Jewishness" shows that the number of those who identified themselves as Israeli has been on the decline, while Jewishness is on the rise. Those who define their identities beyond the dominant categories of Jewishness and Israeliness constituted on average 9.7 percent of the respondents from 1996 to 2001. The surveys suggest that the size of this group increased significantly in 2001—shortly after the ethnic Haredi party Shas received 13 percent of the votes.

As explained in previous chapters, in Israel ethnic identities have often been reduced to two major groups: Ashkenazi and Sephardi. Each name originally represented two distinctive cultural-regional traditions in Europe: Ashkenaz Germany and Sepharad Spain. As cultural-religious terms, they have become major ethnic identifiers in Israel and divorced themselves from their literal and original meanings; Sephardi came to denote Jews with family origins in the countries of the Middle East, North Africa, and Asia, whereas Ashkenazi came to portray Jews whose families originated in the European countries before immigrating to Israel. The recent immigration wave created new categories, such as immigrants from the former Soviet Republics or Ethiopia. These new citizens are in the process of establishing themselves as new ethnic blocs. The roots and continuing dominance of the Ashkenazi and Sephardi dichotomy raise the question of to what extent the wide array of geographical origins, cultural traits, and political experiences can be captured by these two terms. What common traits do these groups share in today's Israel, how do their differences manifest themselves in the political arena, and what do these divisions mean for religious party supporters?

Comparing the respondents' birthplaces to their ethnic self-identifications reveals a significant divergence between ascribed (i.e., ethnic identity based solely on countries of origin) and self-perceived ethnic identities. Given the increasing number of Israelis born in Israel and the intermarriages among Israelis of different national origins, self-claimed ethnicities gain more significance than those based on geographic formulas. Nevertheless, many surveys still use the respondent's birthplace or the father's birthplace to define ethnicities. Such indirect identification promises to yield statistically significant results about the ethnicity of the people surveyed. Yet it glosses over important questions, such as how ethnic identities are understood by their members, or why some members with the same origin accept a Sephardi ethnic identity and others do not. The conflict models often juxtapose the Ashkenazi secularist elite against the Sephardi religious periphery. This perpetual binary treatment begs the question of how Sephardim, who have their roots in a wide range of geographic areas from Georgia to Yemen, have similar positions vis-à-vis the role of religion in politics. What does their common ethnicity entail? Why is it that 34 percent of Israelis born in Asia choose not to identify themselves as Sephardi, whereas a significant number of Asian Israelis born in Israel (29 percent) embrace it, even though the identity of being a *Sabra* Israeli (a popular name for Israeli-born citizens, or those whose father was born in Israel) is available to them? (See figure 5.3.)

The approaches grounded in the ethnic division of values thesis explain how the religious-secular conflict has been exacerbated by Ashkenazi and Sephardi ethnic differences. Shas is in essence a political movement at the intersection of religious and ethnic conflict: it is seen as an ethno-religious Sephardi protest movement against the Ashkenazi secularist core. The defection of the Sephardi leadership from Mafdal consolidated the image of Mafdal as an Ashkenazi religious party. A detailed analysis of the origins of the respondents suggests, however, that Mafdal cannot be limited to an ethnically homogeneous Ashkenazi party. The 2001 election survey results indicate that around 40.8 percent of Mafdal's supporters have origins in regions regarded as Sephardi. When ethnicity is based on birth-

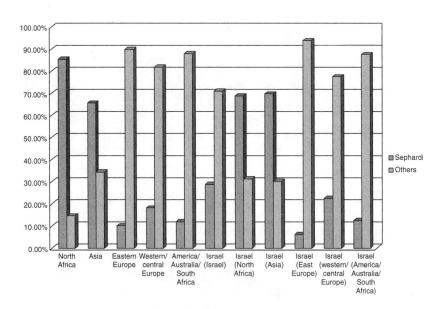

FIGURE 5.3

Birthplaces and self-defined ethnic identities in Israel

SOURCE: The 1999 Israel Election Study data

place, it cannot substantiate the argument that there has been a radical shift in the ethnic profile of Mafdal voters. Rather than becoming another exclusively ethnic religious party, Mafdal appears to have attracted different ethnic communities. According to the 2001 survey, however, the party seems to draw less support from among Sabra (10.2 percent) than Shas (25.3 percent), perhaps due to its sharpening focus on the settlement movement and redemptive Zionism, which finds more supporters among the non–Israeli born.

Likewise, a review of the ethnic backgrounds of Shas supporters sheds light on how Shas has broken the mold of being an ethnic party and emerged as a mass party by gaining the support of those whose votes are determined by their ethnic identities. While the Shas supporters came exclusively from the Sephardi population in 1992, in 1999 a significant number of Shas supporters were non-Sephardim. According to the 2001 election data and the 1999 election study, 54.5 percent and 67 percent of Shas supporters, respectively, were Sephardim (i.e., defined as those who themselves or whose fathers were born in Asia and North Africa). Around one-fourth of Shas supporters were Sabra. The party's Ashkenazi support came more from Jews born in Eastern Europe, South Africa, and America than Western Europe. This inclusion of Ashkenazim does not undermine the central place of ethnicity in Shas rhetoric, but raises the significant question of how a party defined as parochial and ethnically based makes itself relevant to groups with disparate ethnic religious backgrounds.

The sum total of the political, ethnic, and religious identifications of Mafdal and Shas supporters calls into question the pervasive holistic characterization of these parties as cohesive antisecularist, antinationalist, or ultra-Orthodox parties. The assumed polarization between religious and secularist groups does not manifest itself in the views and self-identifications of Mafdal and Shas supporters. Neither does such conflict appear to take the simple form of an identity clash between religious versus secular, Left versus Right, or Ashkenazi versus Sephardi. These individual-level clashes are reflected in various macrolevel studies, which wrestle with the question of why, despite its ultra-Orthodox image, Shas's success increases in communities where religious Jews account for only between 30 and 50 percent of the population. In comparison, the presumably moderate Mafdal party seems to gain support in communities where 50 to 65 percent of citizens are religious.[42] Such findings suggest that religious parties' political positioning and their constituencies cannot be captured through single-dimension identifiers.

One of the major challenges for students of religious parties stems from the conventional conceptual lenses used to define these parties: more often than not, the success of religious parties lies in their ability to question and redefine conventional political positions. Thus, analysts are left with the difficult task of both using and capturing the shifting meanings of these conventional markers. The defiance of religious parties' conventional markers points out that the political fortunes of religious parties do not lie in their ability to capitalize on existing cleavages, but in carving new niches beyond the conventional ideological pockets and conflict lines that once characterized Israeli politics. Accordingly, our analyses of religious party supporters need to allow space for ostensibly contradictory postulations. Shas's electoral fortunes are perhaps not rooted in its ability to draw on established communities, as common explanations suggest, but its capacity to form new communities that attract individuals who are not obvious candidates for membership.[43] The persistent ideological coherence of Mafdal's supporters shows that understanding Mafdal requires a critical assessment of what the party's ideology means to its constituencies. The predominant conceptual lenses perpetuate the conflict arguments at the expense of trivializing intriguing questions, such as, if it is not cohesive religious identity and ethnicity or clustering on the Left–Right spectrum, what other factors and new political markers can help us understand religious party support?

Religious Party Supporters and the Politics of Crisis   If religious support in Israel cannot be attributed simply to polarized groups clustered around Left–Right, secular-religious, Ashkenazi and Sephardi identities, do they come from among politically alienated and disaffected groups as the politics of resentment theses suggests? Do they support religious parties in protest against the main parties, or are they sincere voters who only seek to enhance religion's role in public affairs? Are religious partisans socially and economically displaced masses trying to restore their socioeconomic status? In response to these questions, variants of the crisis explanation argue that religious parties only reflect the absence of political and economic policies responsive to popular expectations. Marginalized groups use religious ideologies and religious parties as instruments for demanding an alternative social and economic order. If socioeconomic or political crises lie at the heart of religious party support, we can expect Mafdal and Shas supporters to come from certain socioeconomic groups (representing certain collective interests) and exhibit signs of political and economic marginalization and alienation. Political apathy often discloses itself in the negative assessment of existing parties or the lack of interest in politics. A portrayal of Israel's issue space can verify these assumptions by identifying specific issues salient only to religious partisans who feel that the system is failing to address them.

A compartmentalized review of the different factors used to explain religious party support illustrates that competing explanations can claim some limited validity due to the capacity of religious parties to traverse the conventional cleavages and heterogeneous profiles of their supporters. Unpacking some of the terms gives us a more nuanced, yet increasingly complicated, perspective. Precisely due to the multifaceted nature of religious party support, however, we need to resort to a more systematic assessment of rival accounts, not only to probe their relevance and weigh their relative explanatory power, but also to avoid the infiltration and dominance of unidimensional depictions of religious parties into our accounts. To this end, a multidimensional and multilayered analysis permits us to identify what factors play key roles and how they interact in attracting diverse groups to Shas's banner. A probabilistic model of religious party support allows us to assess the extent to which the factors singled out in the competing approaches reviewed so far contribute to the explanation of religious parties' support. The models offered here do not present law-like explanations. Neither do we assume that the models give us conclusive results. Rather, they raise new questions and deepen our understanding of religious partisans. Using multinomial logit estimations, we can assess the premises of the politics of resentment and deprivation theses by examining how religious party supporters differ from others with the same demographic and socioeconomic characteristics, describe their reasons for supporting these parties, and evaluate the main actors of the Israeli political system. The specialized 2003 surveys contain the data to question the influence that Shas's mobilization efforts (e.g., the assessment of its school system) and the supporters' shared ethnic identity have had on Shas voters. This survey also brings to the fore issues often neglected in the current analytical debates, such as how Shas supporters view Shas's approach to religion, and the effect of Shas's discourse on the secular public.

Before discussing some of the key findings derived from rarely asked questions and statistical analyses to understand religious partisans, it is important to remember that probabilistic models are a conditional simplification of a complex web of social interactions; they inform our inquiries effectively when we take into account some critical points. One, ceteris paribus, perhaps one of the most precarious assumptions in social science, challenges the applications of statistical models and requires great caution; if they are divorced from their broader political context, they seriously thwart our conclusions. Two, the survey data contain a set of repeated questions that allow us to delve into the patterns behind respondents' votes. However, as our preceding discussion showed, reference points we apply consistently might take different and contradictory meanings over time or when they are applied across parties. For instance, the main determinants of voting decisions, such as the role of parties and the nature of political support, have been shifting in Israel since 1977. In this era, voters' identification with political parties seems to be on the decline, creating a situation in which voters focus on issue positions or ideologies without forging strong ties to the party. The electorate's emphasis on issue positions as opposed to ideologies, especially among religious partisans, can be the reflection of a growing reaction to the inconsistent clustering of issues under ideologies. To complicate the matter further, there are also early signs of an emerging trend that indicates strategic considerations, such as whether postelection calculations (i.e., whether the party will be in opposition or in power) serve as an important component of party choice. As a result, amidst these shifts and new modes of political decisions, trends gleaned from the surveys' results can offer us a critical, yet also a puzzling, mixed picture.

In fact, the direct and often repeated survey question of what determines a person's parliamentary vote opens a window to the complexity of voting decisions and allows us to review the relative impact of issues, party identification, candidates, and postelection calculations in the voters' own declared (electoral) reasoning. Table 5.1 reveals that the explanations of Mafdal and Shas supporters and others have shifted away from party identification toward the dominance of issue positions. Especially in the case of Mafdal, the 2003 survey shows that the voters' identification with the party decreased steadily, while voting based on issues increased dramatically.

The trend for voters to base decisions less on party identification and more on specific issues suggests that the ongoing ideological realignment benefits religious parties. Religious partisans might turn to religious parties not due to reflexive reactions or the party's appeal, but due to their policies and ideas.

The question repeated in every national election survey, "What are the most important issues on Israel's political agenda?" complicates the findings, as Israelis are significantly in consensus about which are the most pressing issues. This finding not only contrasts sharply with the large number of parties competing in the political sphere but poses the question of whether religious parties share a different issue space. The open-ended nature (i.e., the question provides no categories for respondents, thus allowing for answer without any a priori constraints) of the "most important issue" question indicates that despite the striking consensus on primary issues, different publics emerge when nonprimary issues are considered. The categorizations used in table 5.2 show that some issues salient to Shas and Mafdal supporters seem to have less priority for supporters of other parties. For instance, although education is an issue of persistent salience to both parties' supporters, when the findings of the specialized

TABLE 5.1

Main determinants of party choice in Israel

	1992			1996			1999			2003		
	Shas%	Mafdal	Others	Shas	Mafdal	Others	Shas	Mafdal	Others	Shas	Mafdal	Others
Issue positions (ideology)	50	46.3	56.4	45.8	44.9	43.1	56	54	54.3	71.1	66.7	56
Party identification	30	41.5	28.7	41.7	32.7	34.5	20	24	28	16.7	9.5	24.6
Candidate	15	9.8	12.1	8.3	18.4	20.1	24	18	15.3	10	14.3	12.9
Coalition/opposition	5	2.4	2.8	4.2	4.1	2.3	—	4	2.4	2.2	9.5	6.5

SOURCES: Israeli Election Study 1992, 1996, 1999, and 2003

surveys' results are taken into account, Shas voters consistently report education as one of the most urgent issues, while Mafdal supporters attend more to issues creating internal and external tensions. The findings of the 2003 survey that oversampled Shas voters confirm that the issue space of Shas supporters differs from that of other respondents. Similar specialized surveys consistently report that the settlement issue is not high on their agenda; instead, they pay closer attention to problems of ethnic discrimination, religious and secular tension, and socioeconomic inequalities.

The relative consensus among Israeli voters on major important issues begs the question of why religious parties seem to be gaining an advantage in a well-defined issue environment where other parties are historically favored. Is it the result of the nonreligious political parties' declining capacity to resolve issues or their deteriorating image as problem solvers or policy makers? Or is it due to the increasing marginalization of non-primary issues on the center parties' agenda? In fact, the politics of resentment thesis suggests that religious parties rise in reaction to a deadlocked political system. Growing political apathy and the perception that "all parties look alike" make religious parties more appealing in the eyes of a disaffected public. However, assessments of the differences between major parties from 1992 to 2003 portray a mixed picture. Depending on the issue, the public sees increasing policy convergence or divergence among major parties. For instance, more than 80 percent of Shas and Mafdal supporters see irreconcilable differences among the major parties' approaches to Jerusalem, compared to 68 percent of those who support other parties. The disparities become less prominent for other issues, such as religious-secular tensions. The smallest disparity occurs with regard to economic policies (34 percent), the most salient issue for a sizable public.

Politics of Judaism as a Choice   From this broad background of political competition and issue space, we can turn to more specific questions, such as whether and how political positioning, socioeconomic characteristics, or the political assessments of religious partisans affect the voters' party choices. The analysis below uses theoretically significant variables available from the surveys with the highest representation of Shas voters, the 1999, 2001, and 2003 election studies. The findings presented draw on different types of logit estimations that evaluate the effect of factors ranging from demographic characteristics to assessments of major parties. Readers who are not familiar with multinomial logit concepts can still follow the basic findings based on the following information: Multinomial logit models explain the influence of a set of factors on categorical choices, such as political parties. A "multi" model allows for the explanations of decisions that have more than two choices. In our model, the choice is "party support," which consists of three selections:

TABLE 5.2

Most salient issues for religious party constituencies in Israel

	1999			2003			2006			2006
	Mafdal	Shas	Others	Mafdal	Shas	Others	Mafdal	Shas	Others	Shas
	Socioeconomic problems (30.4%)	Socioeconomic problems (27.1%)	Socioeconomic problems (23.4%)	Security general (54.6%)	Security general (53.2%)	Economy (39.1%)	Security general (25%)	Economy (20.6%)	Security general (22%)	Education (46%)
	Education (23.9%)	Security general (17%)	Economy (18.1%)	Economy (27.2%)	Economy (23%)	Security general (42.1%)	Economy (12.5%)	Security general (16.2%)	Economy (15.6%)	Torah Related Issues (19%)
	Security general (13%)	Economy (14.3%)	Peace Process (14.5%)	Internal affairs (13.60%)	Internal affairs (7.7%)	Foreign policy negotiations (7.1%)	Palestinian terror (10.4%)	Social policy, poverty (14.7%)	Social policy, poverty (10.4%)	Welfare Related Issues (18%)
	Internal tensions (13.0%)	Education (8.6%)	Security (8.9%)	Foreign policy negotiations (4.5%)	Education (6%)	Internal affairs (5.1%)	Territories (10.4%)	Interior problems (10.3%)	Interior problems (8.2%)	Security Hamas (5%)
	Territories (5%)	Internal tensions (4.3%)	Internal tensions (5.0%)	Religious character of the state (2%)	Reducing social gap (2%)	Corruption, civil rights, poverty (2.6%)	Social policy, poverty (10.4%)	Education (7.4%)	Education (7.4%)	Withdrawal (1%)

SOURCES: The 1999, 2003, 2006 Israeli Election Study data, The 2006 Malas Institute Findings

NOTE: The questions are open-ended. Answers with the highest frequencies are reported in the table; therefore, the totals do not equal 100 percent. The original survey labels "Interior tensions," "Interior problems," or "Internal affairs," which primarily refer to religious-secular tensions, are used here. For the Malas Institute findings see *Yom Loyom*, March 16, 2006.

support for Shas, Mafdal, or all other parties. Maximum likelihood estimation is used to expand the model's ability to predict party choices as accurately as possible. To evaluate the results of the estimation, analysts think in terms of odds; that is, what are the odds of making a specific selection as opposed to another (e.g., supporting Shas and not the other parties). The odds ratio measures both the strength and direction of the relationship between the factor and the choice we seek to explain. An odds ratio includes two probabilistic statements at once; therefore, the interpretation is not intuitive. The base category within the model and the factor being estimated serve as the point of departure for all interpretations.[44] Another helpful multinomial logit statistic is the standardized parameter estimate, which allows us to better compare the relative weight of the parameters.[45]

Using a model consisting of only demographic characteristics to predict party choices explains approximately 25 percent of the variations in the voting decisions. The explanatory power of the model is enhanced when political assessment variables are added, suggesting that political beliefs and assessments, and not simple, individual-level demographic characteristics, play a critical role in determining party choices. A comparison of the factors that are assumed to attract support for Mafdal or Shas shows that Mafdal's and Shas's supporters are prompted to support their parties by completely opposite triggers. Everything being equal, a favorable assessment of the state's involvement to enhance the role of religion does not appear as the key determinant of Shas support. Therefore, the premises of the conflict model are not readily supported empirically. In contrast, a respondent who is likely to be identified as Sephardi by conventional measures and who has a lower position on the educational ladder is more likely to vote for Shas than other respondents. Identifying oneself as Sephardi increases the odds of voting for Shas by a factor of 5.59. This profile at first supports the politics of deprivation thesis, as it is not the expectations to reconfigure the public sphere according to religious rules via the state, but the voter's ethno-educational position and related policy expectations that define Shas support.

One's negative assessment of the evacuation of the West Bank or a territorial compromise increases the odds of voting for the Shas party by a factor of 1.64. This finding is especially important given that many observers have questioned whether a gap exists between the positions of the Shas elite and the Shas constituency. Considering Ovadia Yosef's unconventional, yet conditional, endorsement of territorial compromise, the findings suggest that there is a disconnect, albeit one that is not as vast as originally presumed. Increased support for Shas seems to be linked to respondents' disagreement with the statement that "evacuating Judeah,

Samariah (West Bank) and the Gaza strip for security would be worth-while." Given that the value of the coefficient is relatively low, and that Yosef's pro-peace position is conditional on preventing the loss of lives, more specific questions are needed to reliably establish the gap. The low coefficient does suggest that Shas supporters, compared to other religious partisans, are likely to have a less hawkish position on the peace process. In fact, specific questions on peace-related issues confirm that Shas supporters do not base their vote on the issue of peace. Likewise, one's religious identification does not emerge as the main predictor of a person's support for Shas. Despite its own strong welfare system, the odds of supporting Shas increase when respondents favor not a state-centered, but a free-market economy. Together, these findings portray religious partisans driven by many forces and whose decisions to turn to religious parties come from an accumulation of various factors.

In striking contrast to the multifaceted nature of Shas supporters, Mafdal supporters are more homogeneous and coherent in their ideologies. As a result, the three most important determinants of Mafdal's support include (1) one's identification as religious or secular, (2) the extent of the expectation that the state will maintain the role of religion, and (3) the respondents' position on the settlement issue. Affirming the importance of party-affiliated educational institutions, education appears as a statistically significant determinant of the party's support. Thus, Israel's moderate religious party, Mafdal, fits the clash model better and questions Mafdal's self-image as self-conscious modern Orthodox. In fact, the consistency of the parameters over time indicates that Mafdal is part of a more uniform ideological movement than Shas, and that respondents' party choices are more directly tied to their ideology. In these findings, however, looms another puzzle: unlike Shas supporters, Mafdal's supporters favor a state-controlled economy. In contrast to other issues, they seem to continue supporting the state's central role in the economic sphere.

The role of gender for party support presents another division of labor between the parties. Mafdal gains more support from men than women. By contrast, Shas is able to appeal to women more effectively. This gender division is confirmed by the specialized 2003 election survey that identifies ultra-Orthodox women as Shas's main loyalists. Shas's ability to liberate women from the traditional socioeconomic structure by providing employment as teachers, as well as the principles that underlie Shas's social welfare system, might help explain this unconventional electoral affinity between the religious parties and female supporters.[46] On the other hand, despite Mafdal's typically modern and inclusive look, the odds of voting for the party increase significantly as we move from women to men.

The 2001 data include fewer Shas and Mafdal supporters but more factors than the 1999 survey, and they allow us to broaden the perspective of our model. For example, we can uncover the effect of the respondents' assessment of Shas's charismatic former leader Deri, or how much respondents follow the polls prior to elections. Consistent with the 1999 findings, the 2001 data again show that demographic factors alone explain only 20 percent of the variation in the vote choice.[47] In contrast to the popular explanation that Aryeh Deri's trial explained the reason for Shas's success, the respondents' evaluation of Deri emerges as only the second-most-effective vote-choice predictor (the second-highest standardized estimators), along with ethnicity. It is important to note, however, that the conviction of Aryeh Deri in 1999 created broad reactions among Sephardim. The 1999 campaign used videos and advertisements entitled "J'accuse," comparing Aryeh Deri's conviction to the infamous ethnic-religious persecution of the Jewish Alfred Dreyfus in France in 1894.[48] Thus, one can argue that the Deri effect is not only a combination of skillful leadership and ethnic support but also the confluence of broader factors marked by an institutional setting where individuals could split their votes due to electoral rules. Irrespective of the "Deri effect" and consistent with the 1999 data, the odds of voting for Shas increase by a factor of 3.66 if a voter is young and has roots in regions designated as Sephardi. Deri's significant role for Shas voters raises the question of whether this leadership effect would increase further if Ovadia Yosef, Shas's spiritual leader, had also been assessed in the survey. If so, it might have further substantiated the charismatic movement explanations. The findings of the 2003 survey tell us, however, that Ovadia's impact is limited when all the other factors are taken into account. Therefore, it seems that it is not a coincidence that despite the extent of the Deri effect, the party survived the end of his leadership without losing its relevance to the electorate. Thus, it is not Deri's leadership per se, but the values and political tensions it symbolized that seemed to be driving people to the party. Shas seems to be institutionalizing itself effectively by maneuvering through Israeli politics with different political leaders. (See table 5.3.)

The common interpretation of Shas supporters as disaffected and alienated or reactionary is challenged by the data: the odds of voting for Shas also increase as one pays closer attention to election polls. Factors that do not have a major effect on Shas support include ideological distance from and reactions to the Labor party. Given the historical and continuing strong affiliation between the Labor party and Secular Zionism, a person's approach to the Labor party can be seen as a reflection of how he or she evaluates Labor Zionism, the state-constitutive ideology. Together, the emerging pattern suggests that instead of being reactionary (to the Labor party and Labor Zionism), Shas supporters appear to be responsive to other changes. How an electoral competition unfolds, as shown by opinion polls, has more influence on their party choice than an ideological template. The findings suggest Shas supporters can be better portrayed as proactive than reactive, as they pay attention to polls and are not simply attracted to Shas as a result of their negative feelings toward the dominant secular party.

Mafdal's supporters reveal rather different features. Support for Mafdal is determined by one's identification on the religious-secular spectrum and an increasing expectation that the state will maintain the central role of Halakhic rules in the public sphere. The assessment of other actors and parties plays a more important role in Mafdal's support than in Shas's. For instance, a respondent's negative assessment of Deri increases the odds of voting for Mafdal noticeably by a standard parameter estimate of 2.58. Thus, despite its moderate look, Mafdal seems more reactionary than Shas. A negative assessment of Labor improves support for Mafdal, making the standardized impact of voting significant (2) in comparison to other triggers. Mafdal supporters are also less attentive to election polls, which depict electoral competition more as a horse race. Considering that Mafdal supporters are more responsive to other actors than to polls suggests that their voting decisions are likely to be more ideological than strategic. The ideology's overall success drives their support. In fact, in one of the most comprehensive analyses of Mafdal support, Asher Cohen defines the complex relationship between nationalist Zionists and Mafdal by describing Mafdal as a rare party that most of its supporters do not vote for—despite or perhaps due to their strong ideological ties, nationalist Zionists criticize the party profusely, yet they still ultimately feel attached to it. Those who do vote for it seek to enhance the party's ideological commitments, for example, to issues such as the refusal to withdraw from settlements.[49]

The 2003 election data further demarcate the main trends that surfaced in previous years, suggesting that they prevail over specific contextual factors. Opposition to Shinui, a party that defines itself as a secular-Zionist party and singles out Shas and Mafdal as its main opponents, increased support for Shas by a factor of 2.21. Shinui's agenda includes a limited role for religion in the public sphere and the launching of a free-market economy. More significantly, the party declared that in order to prevent the funding of Shas's welfare system, it would not join any coalition, including Shas. Therefore, opposition to Shinui carries meaning beyond the simple secular-religious conflict and is perhaps more related to the rivalry over government resources. Based on the respondents' own evaluations, the increasing importance assigned to religious issues raises the respondents' tendency to vote for Shas by a factor of 2. Strikingly, the effect of

TABLE 5.3

A multinomial logit model of Shas and Mafdal support

	Shas 1999	Mafdal 1999		Shas 2001	Mafdal 2001		Shas 2003	Mafdal 2003
Sephardi	3.51** 3.21	0.607 –1.34	Ethnicity	.398*** –4.88	1.029* 0.2	Sephardi (North Africa-	.485*** –4.15	0.985 –0.08
Education (lowest/highest)	.352** –4.83	1.23* 1.56	How much like Deri (hate/love)	1.251*** 3.93	.841*** –2.58	Halakha	.461*** –3.48	.436*** –3.76
Gender (male/female)	2.23* 2.22	0.896 –0.36	Secular religious self-identification (secular/Haredi)	1.63*** 2.89	2.60*** 4.34	Age	0.562 –2.34	1.81*** 2.08
Age 18–29 / 69+	0.953 –0.41	0.98 –0.19	State should enforce Halakha (certainly/certainly not)	.713*** –1.86	.585*** –2.54	Religion's importance for vote (very great influence/none)	.580*** –2.13	.510*** –2.20
Jewish nature of state; every effort to protect Jews (agree/disagree)	.062** –2.68	.587** –2.42	Follow polls (not at all/great extent)	1.277* 1.71	1.163* 0.96	Distance from Shinui (very far/close)	.841** –2.18	.872* –1.46
Left–Right economic mean-ing Right–Left	.868* –0.660	1.152 0.83	Gender (male/female)	1.39* 1.07	.455*** –2.21	Economic issues importance for vote (great/none)	1.29** 1.36	1.16 0.64

(continued)

Table 5.3 (continued)

	Shas 1999	Mafdal 1999		Shas 2001	Mafdal 2001		Shas 2003	Mafdal 2003
Land for peace; give up settlement (agree/disagree)	1.73** 3.09	1.251* 1.69	Education 1–8 16+	.815* −1.04	0.781 0.38	Gender	.551* −1.74	.475** −1.75
Political interest general (very interested/not interested)	.549** −2.97	0.939 −0.42	How much like Labor (hate/love)	0.968 −0.52	.851*** −2.09	Negotiation vs. military solution	1.55 1.2	2.28** 1.66
Religious/secular self-identification (very secular/very religious)	1.44** 1.94	2.39*** 6.28	Income (much higher/much below average)	1.046 0.4	.781** −1.86	Income (much higher/much below average)	1.195* 1.34	819 −1.23
Income (less than $4,000/more than $11,000)	.601** −1.40	1.38 1.19	Age Group 19–29 70+	.688*** −3.66	1.07* 0.58	Education (lowest/highest)	1.051 0.09	2.39*** 2.37

SOURCES: 1999 Election Study; 2001 and 2003 Israeli Election Study Data

NOTE: Each cell shows the odd ratio, standardized parameters. ***, **, and * indicate the coefficient is significant at 0.01, 0.05, and 0.10 levels respectively.

economic issues on voting choices is limited, according to the supporters' own perceptions. In fact, "economic voting" does not distinguish Shas supporters from others. Given that a majority of the Israeli population (87.93 percent) reported economic issues as very important in their voting decisions, the sweeping effect of economic factors occurs across all parties. Shas's voters do not radically differ from others, as economic considerations are part and parcel of political calculations for many. Each decreasing level of income (i.e., from above average to below average) increases the odds of voting for Shas by a comparatively small factor (i.e., by a standardized estimate of 1.22). Once again, the question is, why do these people turn to Shas to express their grievances?

The question of whether conflicts can be prevented via increased military power or through negotiations shows that although support for increased military power is not significant in determining a Shas vote, it is significant for Mafdal's support. Interestingly enough, Shas's and Mafdal's support are inversely related to a favorable evaluation of Shinui, although the distance from Labor is not decisive for either party. Shinui, which advocates the elimination of rabbinical courts and the enforcement of national religious restrictions, for example, appears as the political "other" of both Mafdal and Shas instead of other center-left parties. Shinui has a relatively smaller effect on Shas supporters than on Mafdal's, confirming Shas's proactive, rather than reactionary, nature.

The 2003 religious support data allow us take a closer look at Shas support. Due to the limited number of Mafdal supporters in the survey, this is a binominal logit model that focuses on the question of why people support Shas as opposed to other parties. Stepwise modifications of the data show that when we add variables that characterize the individuals' political beliefs and their evaluation of Shas's service and leadership, the model becomes very effective in predicting Shas's support at the polls, while the originally important predictors, such as education or socioeconomic status, lose their significance. If we focus on the demographic variables alone, they agree with the overall pattern elicited from other surveys. A self-assessment of socioeconomic conditions does not appear as one of the main predictors of a Shas vote; as such Shas supporters come from all different social strata. However, the lower stratum plays a more prominent role. In fact, when asked to compare their income to 9,300 shekel, the average monthly expenditure for a family of four, 42.29 percent of Israelis describe their income as below or much below average. Ninety percent of Shas supporters and 78 percent of other voters rank closing the disparities in income as one of the country's most pressing issues.[50] The quest for alleviating socioeconomic disparities is a concern for most voters, not just Shas supporters. In contrast to other voters, Shas supporters do not seem to question *if* issues posed by their socioeconomic standing in society should be addressed, but are focused on *how*.

The respondents' positions in different issue areas are significant predictors of Shas support. For instance, the odds of voting for Shas increase by a factor of 2.6 when respondents see ethnic discrimination as a significant problem. To place this finding into its broader context, it is critical to note that the Israeli public disagrees about whether and to what extent ethnic discrimination exists. Like other surveys, the 2003 Shas survey shows that Israeli society is perfectly divided: 45 percent believe there is overt discrimination, 43 percent believe that such discrimination does not exist, and the remaining 12 percent are undecided. Other survey results paint comparable pictures. Israeli society often reflects deep schisms over how people assess its inequalities rooted in ethnicity, and a large group of Israelis view ethnic discrimination as an urgent problem. The second issue that differentiates Shas supporters from other voters is the importance they assign to immigration issues. Among other facets of immigration, they question the decisions that allow immigrants to enter the country and how funds are distributed to different immigrant communities. The frequent public controversies around the Jewishness, and therefore the immigration status of some Sephardi groups when combined with the limited public resources available to Sephardim to help them integrate, turn immigration into a hybrid issue. It is not rare to find various groups in Israel contesting the definition and recognition of the Jewishness and ethnicity of certain immigrant groups, which often has bearing on ethnic relationships. Not surprisingly, the more respondents perceive the other parties to have similar immigration policies, the more they support Shas. With the ethnicity debate in Israel strongly tied to the debate on immigration, an individual's position on immigration influences other issue areas. In fact, extant studies neglect to probe how Shas's ethnicity and political agenda are formulated as a result of competition with immigrants from the former Soviet republics over limited state funding. Shas leadership takes the fact that the authenticity of Jewishness is questioned more frequently when immigrants come from Middle Eastern or African countries, such as Yemen and Ethiopia, as a sign of a historical, deeply ingrained anti-Sephardi attitude among secular Jews and the state. Its belief that immigrants from former Soviet republics are subject to more flexible immigration standards prompted the party to sponsor an amendment to the Law of Return that limits the immigration of non-Jews.[51]

Perhaps one of the most intriguing findings of the binomial model is that respondents vote for the party because they see Shas as a lenient and not strictly Orthodox party. Shas's ultra-Orthodoxy seems to amount to a "popularization of Orthodoxy" rather than the spread of ultra-Orthodoxy, which corroborates one of the main theses of this analysis, namely that Shas is an agent of internal secularization. The party has indeed succeeded in its efforts to make the Haredi identity more accommodating. What attracts supporters to the Shas movement is not the acceptance of a strict Haredi version of Judaism, but Shas's redefinition of haredization as a process with important social consequences. Other related findings, such as how Ovadia's sermons are seen as one of the main determinants of Shas support, need to be seen in relation to his role in making Sephardi ultra-Orthodoxy both accessible and popular. To approach Ovadia from the perspective of charismatic leadership obscures his role in redefining the ultra-Orthodox world from within. The relative weight of the "Ovadia effect" shows that, although critical to the party's success, Shas supporters do not appear to be swayed merely by the charismatic influence of another ultra-Orthodox leader. While the party's unconventional position vis-à-vis the peace process makes that a central piece in the party's debate, interestingly, the more respondents view the peace process as not important for Shas's success, the more they support the party. Once again, in Israel's overcrowded political space Shas does not appear to be a party that centers its agenda on peace, unlike many of its political rivals.

Using the results from our binomial model, we can compare various voter profiles and their propensity to vote for Shas. The probability that our median voters (see the median values in bold in table 5.4) will vote for Shas is 8 percent as opposed to other parties. The application of the models to different profiles gives us the likelihood that different demographic groups will vote for Shas. Let's take a voter who is a female, a high school graduate, Sephardi, identifies herself as secular, believes that there is no ethnic discrimination, regards income inequality as an important issue, is below the average income, views Shas's understanding of Judaism as strict, sees Ovadia's messages as important, views Shas's position on the peace process as not important, and comes from the youngest group of the electorate. The likelihood that such a person will vote for Shas is 4 percent. However, if the same person comes from a religious background, the probability goes up to 22 percent. If we look at a voter from the youngest age group with a Yeshiva education, who is ultra-Orthodox and believes that discrimination and inequality are very important issues, who questions that the parties do not differ in their immigration policies, who sees Shas's version of Judaism as lenient, and who assigns great importance to Ovadia, the probability that this person will vote for Shas as opposed to other parties is more than 80 percent. The chance that an Ashkenazi with the same profile will vote for Shas is more than 50 percent. Even more revealing is the fact that the probability of someone voting for Shas who has the same profile yet not responsive to Ovadia's teaching goes down to 30 percent. On the other hand, the probability of a male voting for Shas who defines himself as secular and who possesses a master's degree is less than 10 percent. Among those who define themselves as traditional, this likelihood increases 14 percent.

If we include in our analysis the impact of the Shas network and a comparison between the Shas school system and other schools available for the respondents, the network becomes one of the main predictors of a Shas vote, as important as ethnicity. Shas's welfare system, along with its educational services, attracts the most votes for Shas. Education is one of the most controversial aspects of the Israeli state system, with schools ranging from state-sponsored secular to private ultra-Orthodox. Religious groups play a crucial role in maintaining the autonomy of religious schools. As explained in the previous chapter, Nissim Zeev, one of Shas's founders, has attributed the origin of the Shas movement to the reluctance of the religious bloc to open schools for Sephardi girls. Education in this regard is not a tool of acculturation, but a power leveler that has been the single-minded focus of the party since its inception. Shas and other groups are asserting competing claims on the national identity through the different school systems, and even a cursory review of the schools' budget allocations demonstrates that there has been a striking shift in Israeli politics with respect to education policy. In 2002, for instance, the government reported that 20.4 percent of the country's Jewish schoolchildren attended Haredi, ultra-Orthodox elementary schools as compared to 7.6 percent in 1992. This corresponds to an increase from 35,000 students in 1990–1991 to 112,000 in 2001–2002.[52] Thus, the emergence of Shas's schools reflects a broader trend in the Israeli polity. What makes Shas's institutional approach novel is its ability to appeal to both ultra-Orthodox and non-ultra-Orthodox Israelis at the same time. In Israel's compartmentalized educational system, Shas has successfully used the existing institutional structure to place itself at the center of not only a separate but also a novel pillar of education. A few broad historical analyses show that Shas's success did not occur in an institutional vacuum, beyond the decision-making power of other political actors, or at the expense of the state policies. Some observers argue, for instance, that Shas's efforts to establish a school system have been directly or indirectly supported by the state's policies. From the state's point of view, Shas-like political formations were preferable to its alternatives: the militant Zionism of Gush Emunim and the oppositional, Left-leaning ethnic identity promoted by secular

TABLE 5.4
A logit model of Shas support

Support Shas	Odd ratios SEP	Descriptive (median values are highlighted)	Marginal effects (all other values kept at the mean values)	Marginal effects (all other values kept at the mode values)
Age		Min 18–25		
	1.45*	26–35		
	1.40	**36–45, 36–45**	.022	.0295
		46–55, 56–65		
		Max 66+		
Ethnicity	.201***	Sephardi	−.097	−.1298
	−2.64	**Ashkenazi**		
		Mixed		
Religious		Secular		
		Traditional	.1189	.1595
	7.055***	Religious		
	5.45	Ultra-Orthodox		
		Traditional		
Ethnic discrimination	2.638**	No discrimination	.0590	.0792
	2.52	**Some**		
		Overt discrimination		
Income inequality	.3562**	**Very important issue**	−.0628	−.0843
	−1.71	Undecided		
		Not important issue		
Social condition	1.27*	Way above average	.0150	.0201
	0.66	A bit above average		
		Like average		
		Below average		
Party differences immigration	2.484**	No difference	.0554	.0743
	2.31	**Moderate differences**		
		Very different		
Shas Judaism	.2468**	Flexible	−.0852	−.1143
	−2.26	**Very strict =2**		
Ovadia's messages	1.67**	Not very important	.0313	.0420
	2.6	**Very important**		
Shas position on peace	.4178**	**Not very important**	−.0531	−.0713
	−2.35	Very important		

SOURCE: 2003 Religious Party Supporter data

NOTE: ***, **, and * indicate the coefficient is significant at 0.01, 0.05, and 0.10 levels respectively.

mizrahi political movements. Clearly, Shas's ability to establish its educational pillar is a product of Israel's party system, where coalition bargaining hinges on the allocation of state funds. Due to its successful bargaining, the budget for Shas institutions grew from $21 million in 1985 to $104 million in 1995 and $1.5 billion in 1997.[53] Comparing the increase to that of other schools shows that Shas consolidated its place in Israel not as an autonomous entity but as another state-sponsored education bloc, which makes the party dependent on the electorate's support for votes and on the state for funding.

In light of the role and the funding of the Shas schools, the respondents' assessments of the school system show that the relevance of Shas's welfare and education system sits at the intersection of the party's ideology, the lack of alternative services for the system's beneficiaries, and the party's declared goal of reinforcing traditional practices. For instance, individuals who view the Shas system favorably also find its teaching more lenient than that of other religious and ultra-Orthodox groups. The party is reluctant to publicize the exact number of Shas schools, but according to figures released in 1999, Shas supported 146 elementary schools nationwide, 682 kindergartens, 50 junior high schools, and 86 day-care centers.[54] Shas also claims to employ a total of twenty-four hundred school teachers, principals, and supervisors, and an additional twenty-two hundred kindergarten teachers and teachers' aides. Although these numbers are contested, they still provide evidence of the significant scope of Shas's educational network and the range of people it affects by offering them employment as well as educational opportunities.[55] The schools offer religiously grounded education as well as social services, and appeal especially to low-income families. Among their characteristics are longer hours than other schools, lower tuition rates, free or low-rate transportation services, and hot meals. They also promise to protect students against the ills of modern society. State funding and donations allow the party to offer one of the lowest tuition rates ($250 per month) of any school system, while offering three hours more of education per day. The party-sponsored services are diverse in order to meet the needs of all segments of society. For example, the party offers services ranging from immigrant integration programs to scholarships for yeshiva students to adult training classes. Shas schools embody a microcosm of the party's symbolic world. Students come from diverse backgrounds, and their learning takes place in an environment decorated with pictures of famous Sephardi rabbis, sages, Ovadia Yosef, or cabbalist Yitzhak Kedouri, along with quotations from the Old Testament.

A favorable assessment of Shas's school system, however, cannot be taken as the respondents' wholehearted support for all party policies, as

TABLE 5.5

Assessment of Shas's performance by its supporters

Issue areas	Contributed to great extent %	Contributed to certain extent %	Did not contribute %	Made worse %	Made much worse %	No response %
Improving the conditions of the poor	59	34	3	2	1	1
Promoting the religion	54	37	5	2	1	1
Enhancing education	33	37	24	4	1	1
Promoting economic welfare development	19	21	50	3	1	6
Defense of country	16	21	57	2	2	2
The reduction of the tension between religious and secular	15	27	36	16	5	1
Decreased the tension between Ashkenazi and Sephardi	14	26	39	14	4	3

SOURCE: The 1999 Dahaf Survey

the 1999 Dahaf survey results demonstrate. Table 5.5 conveys that party supporters do not always view the party's performance as effective (high). On the contrary, partisans assess the party's performance on different issues critically, and their support is not automatically reflective of their perceived core identities or religious convictions or an affirmative, across-the-board endorsement of Shas's policies.

SEARCHING FOR ALTERNATIVES:

THE IDEOLOGICAL POSITIONING

OF RELIGIOUS PARTIES

The self-reported profiles of Mafdal's and Shas's supporters indicate that these voters cannot be reduced to devoted flag bearers of the sacred against the secular, or to instrumentalists who turn to religious parties simply to alleviate their political, economic, or ethnic resentments. Understanding the meaning and the full spectrum of linkages requires us to analyze religious party support in relation to other parties. The shortcomings of the Left–Right spectrum for describing Israel's ideological space emphasize the importance of alternative descriptions that can accommodate the multidimensionality of the country's ideological space. The party assessment questions in the existing surveys and the ideological statements of their leaders show the changing contours of Israeli politics, which are dominated by the diametrically opposed positions of the major parties with regard to the peace process. A different picture emerges with respect to socioeconomic policy, however, which Israeli voters consider one of the most pressing issues. Likud's adamant support of a liberal market economy once defined the main fault line of Israel's economic policies; that is, the major parties were divided over the state's redistributive policies. Recently, the traditional differences between the Labor and Likud parties, which ranged from domestic to foreign issues, seem to have merged as both parties overtly or tacitly accept market-based policies. From the standpoint of the voters, the weakening of the ideological center in Israeli politics in general and the decreasing relevance of the popular markers make the positioning of religious parties vis-à-vis other parties critical.

In order to offer a multidimensional ideological space, a factor analysis will elicit the primary latent dimensions from the individual assessment of the parties, the issues, and the main political figures. Factor-analysis results are best understood when they are elaborated on by methods such as spatial analysis. The spatial approach argues that what matters is not how political scientists or experts view these parties, but how they make themselves relevant to the electorate. The method links the individuals' assessment of their positions to the positions of parties in a multidimensional ideological space.[56] When such methods are used to interpret the available survey data, more often than not the resulting dispersions are unexpected. This brings to mind Campbell's point that the ideological coherence we expect from partisans does not always happen. What matters is how the parties' symbolic capital, policy positions, and other relevant practices are regarded by the electorate. The relative positioning of the parties suggests that voters first consider the parties' different positions on socioeconomic policies, and second, base their choice on peace-related issues. Irrespective of the meanings of the ideological dimension, the results present a consistent picture. Shas does not appear at the ideological fringes; in fact, on some dimensions, Mafdal is located farther away from the center than Shas.

The relative positioning of Mafdal and Shas shows that their electoral support cannot be understood in an ideological or contextual vacuum. These parties' successes need to be seen in relational terms within the broader spectrum of the shrinking political space in Israeli politics as elsewhere. While moderate Mafdal has been losing its centrist position, Shas's ultra-Orthodoxy seems to be rather deceptive since, for the first time in Israeli political history, it has adopted policies on economic issues and foreign policy that place it in the expanded center. This is a revolutionary positioning, given that the ultra-Orthodox parties have deemed these policies irrelevant and refrained from taking any position. None of the other religious parties in Israel's religious bloc takes a position on broader economic issues. Not only the United Torah Judaism, but also Mafdal were and remain silent on many issues, including economic policies. In this context, Shas not only incorporates these issues into its platform, but also creates practices that become relevant to the discussion of issues, such as income inequalities and pervasive poverty.[57] What makes this inclusion especially important is that the role of state involvement in economic issues loses relevance in distinguishing the ideological Left from the Right. All center parties converge on the necessity of the market-oriented reforms, and their disagreement is limited to questions of how. In this narrowing ideological picture, Shas stands out by its commitment to a set of issues ignored by other parties.[58]

Ironically, for some observers of Shas, Shas's active involvement in politics is reminiscent of the approaches adopted by the Zionist Mapai. Instead of rejecting them, Shas both appropriates and transforms the position of the center parties. Shas has been seeking to establish a close organic relationship with Histadrut, the labor union movement, which is another unique move for a religious party. It is important to note that many have questioned the party's ideas and policies as attempts to build "machine politics." In reaction to such descriptions, former Shas leader Deri contended that the party is not an agent of pork-barrel politics, but instead promotes a comprehensive vision that is not merely concerned with reallocating Interior Ministry budgets to help "his people," but with reforming the whole of Israeli local government and administration.[59] Although these statements sound only rhetorical within the Haredi (ultra-Orthodox) world, Shas's adherence to a form of *mamlakhtiyut* (statism) in the economic sphere amounts to another innovative position.

In many areas, Shas consistently forms policies that are not easily embraced by others. A case in point is the party's attempt to question the ultra-Orthodox position on territorial issues. Shas's policies, despite their limits, suggested the position of "an ultra-religious pro-peace party," a position that is a contradiction in terms. Pro-peace positions have traditionally been reserved for secular Left-wing parties. Shas's novel and disputed positions do not solely rely on Ovadia's responsa and his sporadic hawkish statements. Shas leaders emphasize various ideas that can serve as foundations for more engagements, since Shas claims a unique vantage and cultural capital point to relate to the Arab "others," based on the Sephardi group's acquaintance with social practices of Middle Eastern

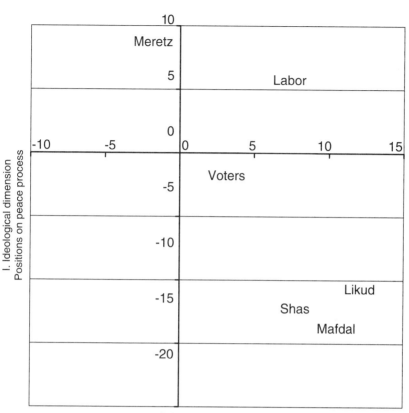

FIGURE 5.4

Political positioning of parties on two ideological dimensions

NOTE: Meretz is a pro-peace party that endorses the state's involvement in the market to eliminate social and economic disparities.

countries.[60] It is not rare to hear Shas leadership statements that illustrate the party's cultural affinities with Arabs and add a new dimension to the party's position on peace negotiations beyond the religiously grounded explanation of Ovadia.[61]

Regardless of the exact ideological location of Mafdal and Shas and the meaning of the ideological dimensions, these maps (see figure 5.4) show that the parties' appeal needs to be understood in relation to each other and other parties and actors. In fact, Shas's ideology, which incorporates Sephardi–ultra-Orthodox–Labor-like features, is a synthesis that is seen as a contradiction in terms in Israeli politics. But it is precisely because of this odd position that the party is able to resist its position as a political outlier. For instance, instead of a wholesale acceptance of Zionist ideology as a sacred movement, as in the case of Mafdal, or a complete rejection of it, as in the case of Agudat Israel, Shas both accommodates and challenges the characteristics of Zionism. Thus, both Shas and Mafdal distance themselves from the ultra-Orthodox parties by opposing their use of religion as a tool of counter-acculturation. They also distance themselves from secularist parties by describing them as antireligious. In the case of Shas, which sits at the intersection of ethnic and ultra-Orthodox policies, this distancing becomes crucial, because the party views the other parties as ethnocentric. In Deri's view, Shas must be approached carefully because "Shas is a Sephardi, but not an ethnic party, open to a mass membership and based on the premise that every Sephardi in Israel, whether observant or not, has a positive regard for traditional values and religion."[62] As a result, when the dominant ideological dimensions of Israeli politics are taken into account, it is not surprising to find that Shas's political location reflects a median position, while Mafdal increasingly diverges from the median position it once occupied.

CONCLUSION

An inside-out analysis of Mafdal and Shas indicates that the conceptual and empirical tools we use to study these parties are part of the conundrum. If we look at religious parties without confining our analysis to the traditional dichotomies, it becomes obvious that religious parties are not simple reactionary movements against the secular world. In their peculiar form, both parties express novel ideological syntheses and serve as transformative movements within Israel's religious blocs and also partially its secular blocs. Despite their common status as "religious parties," the constituencies of Shas and Mafdal differ diametrically with regard to their characteristics and political positions. One can talk about a division of labor in the religious bloc. Mafdal's outward policies (i.e., policies that focus on territorial issues, the nature of the state, and overall national community) and its self-consciously religious partisans contrast with those of Shas. Despite commonly being described as ultra-Orthodox, Shas supporters are not strictly ideological and come from traditional, religious, and ultra-Orthodox voters alike.

The Shas case suggests that it is the party's successful strategy of what can be called adaptive protest that secures it a unique position in the Israeli political space. Both Mafdal and Shas successfully challenge the ideological boundaries within the Orthodox as well as the secular worlds. This strategic positioning appeals to many, especially new generations of voters, who look for novel political positions within the narrowing sphere of political competition. By the same token, both Mafdal's and Shas's main recruitment tool appears not to be the religious conversion to Orthodoxy, but the mobilization of the traditionals and moderates through well-connected national organizational structures and lenient interpretations of their respective religious doctrines. Mafdal's institutional network seems to be on the decline, while Shas fills an important void in Israeli politics by embedding itself in communities. The religious parties are in transformation; thus, a thorough assessment of their contribution to their respective democracy requires an understanding of the broader trajectory of their policies. Shas's transformation to an increasingly inclusive party from its ultra-Orthodox roots and Mafdal's shift toward more exclusivist positions from its moderate foundations manifest themselves in the profiles of their constituencies. Yet these transformations can only be understood when we look at the parties, leadership, constituency, and ideology holistically.

Both parties' changing yet effective roles remind us again that in Israel, where a cultural nationalism served as the state's constitutive ideology, religion has emerged as a symbolic sphere to legitimize political views. This allows different groups to declare their differences without being considered antisystemic, questioned on the authenticity of their political motivations or their Jewishness. Mafdal and Shas represent two different parties for which religion and religiosity are experienced and become relevant to politics in distinctive ways. Placing religious parties into their political contexts through self-assessments of religious party supporters illustrates that religious parties (1) redefine religious ultra-Orthodoxy from within, (2) use religious discourse to transform the public sphere and alter status-quo public policies without radically transforming them, and (3) fill a gap in their respective political systems created by two contradictory processes: polarization of major parties on a few nationally salient issues (e.g., national security) and convergence of main political actors on a large set of socioeconomic and cultural policies and the political void left by these processes. Only when these parties are placed under nondichotomous conceptual lenses do they show that instead of disenchantment with the secular world, supporters turn to these parties for various reasons. However, once they have joined the movements, these supporters form and become part of new powerful political communities, which in turn form their political learning and influence their decisions. The paradox of religious parties is the fact that their political success rests on their inclusiveness, which appeals especially to traditionals. The ongoing transformation of their ideologies and the central role of educational services, especially in Shas's case, suggest that their closely knit networks may turn the traditionals into more religiously oriented participants.

CHAPTER SIX

Between Laicism and Islam?

Religious Party Supporters in Turkey

Our religion is infallible. But political parties and their leaders are not—they make mistakes. So, we have to separate the two.[1]

Any attempt to understand how individuals make their political party choices assumes that there are some underlying patterns that determine specific election results. A review of the recent elections in Turkey initially suggests that such an assumption could be rather tenuous. Since the early 1990s, it has not been rare for a party to gain a significant plurality and establish itself as a pivotal actor in one election, only to fall below the minimum required vote total for parliamentary representation in another.[2] Along with these sporadic changes, there has also been a steady increase in the number of party faithful who have withdrawn from politics.[3] Beneath its ostensible random oscillations, Turkish politics has been marked by the steady decline in support for the center-right and center-left parties (i.e., a collapse of the center) and the disengagement of a significant segment of the electorate from politics (i.e., increasing political apathy). The coexistence of these processes makes the application of conventional explanations about party support highly questionable. Against this background, it is not surprising that the analyses of the elections often speak of the "unique" and "surprising nature" of each election and also the reactionary and unpredictable nature of voting, especially in explaining the bewildering success of pro-Islamic parties. While the collapse of the market in 1994 is seen as the reason for the Welfare Party's victory, in 1995 the rising tide of nationalism with the capture of Kurdish guerilla leader Abdullah Öcalan and the military's 1997 February ultimatum have been presented as tipping events that changed election results in favor of national religious parties in 1999.

Nevertheless, beyond the extreme swings and waves of unpredictable shifts in electoral fortunes, certain patterns exist. For instance, when we look at the support for the NAP, the Prosperity Party, and Justice and Development Party together as a bloc, we see that it has increased dramatically, despite their different vote shares (see figure 6.1). This secular expansion in pro-Islamic conservative support for the entire bloc makes the politics of Islam an intriguing conundrum of Turkish politics. Consistent results that emerge from Turkey's volatile electoral map raise the question of why the NAP, the Prosperity, and the JDP emerged as the main beneficiaries of the politically debilitating processes of the 1980s and 1990s, which included strong political reactions, disengagements, and disaffections. The presence of a similar duality in Israeli politics poses not only the question of whether and how the overall context of political competition matters to the politics of religion, but also whether religious parties are another manifestation of the existing, fluid political situation or a reflection of deeper changes from which new trends are emerging.

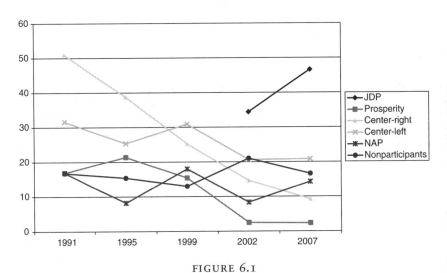

FIGURE 6.1

Vote share by party blocs and nonparticipants in Turkey

SOURCE: Yüksek Seçim Kurulu

NOTE: The rate of nonparticipants reflects the ratio of nonparticipants to the overall number of the electorate. In the 1991 election results, both the NAP and the PP's vote share is reported as 16.8 percent, the total vote for their coalition.

The rise of religious party support in Turkey has occurred in a political atmosphere in which early republican ideals, despite their initially contested nature, have also taken hold. More importantly, Islam has also been transformed from within, becoming more diverse and making the formation of a coherent Islamic agenda very difficult. In this increasingly pluralistic environment, the questions of why the masses turn to the NAP, Prosperity Party, and the JDP get intriguing, especially in light of the continuous fluctuation of support among the parties and the political risk posed by the potentially destabilizing effect of endorsing pro-Islamic parties in Turkey's strictly secular system.

Echoing the global trend, the contradictory role of religious parties sustain ever expanding interest by causing both fear over the expansion of Islamic movements and their authoritarian ideas, as well as excitement regarding its counter-hegemonic nature and liberalizing positions within their respective regimes. Given the domestic and global significance of this conundrum, a substantial amount of literature has emerged on the foundations, contents, and threat posed by the politics of Islam. More often than not, however, the new accounts remain within the boundaries of the dominant paradigms and emulate their methodological foundations. At the conceptual level, like their counterparts in Israel and elsewhere, these accounts attribute the increasing appeal of the politics of Islam to (1) the zero-sum relationship between political Islam and secular Kemalism, in which the rising political power of one requires the decline or annihilation of the other (conflict model); (2) Turkey's macroeconomic policies, which continually seek to improve its weak economic structure and launch redistributive projects, yet their implementations often falter and thereby foment massive destabilizing shocks, resulting in an environment that consistently sustains support for reactionary political parties (politics of crisis and resentment); (3) the unavoidable global wave of political liberalization and the increasing demands for recognition of ethnic-religious identities (politics of recognition); and (4) religious parties' institutional ingenuity in creating social networks and the allure of their charismatic leaders who seem more credible than their failed conventional counterparts.

Politics of Conflict Between Secular and Islamic Values

From the perspective of the conflict model, contested claims over a polity's core guiding values lie at the heart of political competitions. The rise of pro-Islamic parties is seen as an inevitable result of political processes set out by the terms of Turkish nationalism and the state's founding ideology. Accounts embedded in this perspective stress how the universal clash of religious and secular values takes a unique form in Turkey, one of few countries that seeks to authoritatively purge its public sphere of Islamic expressions via its official ideology, *laiklik*. What makes the politics of Islam in Turkey paradoxical is that Kemalism, the state's founding ideology, intentionally sought to discontinue the Ottoman polity's tradition that generated the sharp disconnect between political center and ruled periphery. The inherited detachment between the political center and periphery was present in every aspect of the society and created constant cultural tension that prevented hybrid formations and progress in certain areas. As such, for some scholars it was not an accident that "no Ottoman composers like Beethoven or Schubert" emerged who made "use of peasant themes in music."[4]

Within the conflict paradigm, Kemalist nationalism fell victim to the paradox of nationalism: during the process of reinventing their respective traditions, nationalisms also become susceptible to the influence of traditional forces. Although its integrative national project necessitated the opening up of a new political role for Islam, the Kemalist elite ended up containing the role of Islam at the expense of reinforcing some practices it had sought to alter. Instead of treating the Islamic traditional values as a repository of political ideals and foundations for appropriate social institutions, Kemalism relegated Islamic values and their most devout believers to a marginal role and invented a whole new cultural framework.[5] The drastic reforms adopted to accomplish this end resulted not only in an institutional disjuncture within the country's political foundations but also within its cultural traditions. The first organized Kemalist elite not only constrained Islam's political capacity but also tried to alter conventional Islamic practice in the public sphere. Changing the call for prayers, *ezan*, from its original Arabic to Turkish and outlawing all religious orders became issues that symbolized not only the suppression of Islam in its habitual form but also the suppression of its practitioners.[6] It is not a coincidence that the first opposition party, the Democratic Party, based its agenda on reactions to the RPP's strict secularism. The current picture from the lens of the conflict model is another manifestation of this opposition. In essence, the politics of Islam in Turkey rest on the perpetual tension introduced by the Kemalist quest to have a popular democratic regime without giving Islam a public role.

From the outset, the Kemalist state had reacted severely to all pro-Islamic and civil organizations. Its attitude toward Islam remained unchanged, albeit in a more moderate mode after the transition to multi-party government. The key reason for this is the ideological orientation of the Republican state, which, from the beginning, has been hostile to Islam. The state viewed Islam as the principal cause of Turkey's underdeveloped status. In fact, in the first two decades of the Republic the power elite tried to destroy Islam and its culture as a force in Turkey. After the transition to a multi-party government, the Kemalist elite continued its enmity to Islam, and even in the so-called "constitutional periods," based on the 1961 and 1982 constitutions, did not give up that policy. Everything Kemalists did originated from the dictates of secularism.[7]

When viewed from the perspective of the conflict model, secularist policies' universal contradictions repeat themselves in the Turkish case. The state enforces the policies that confine the public appearance and role of religion to the political sphere in order to ensure its freedom. The internal contradiction of Kemalism stems from its aims to be a popular state ideology while superseding the popular traditions and religious beliefs of the people, thereby falling into the pitfall of what Rousseau calls "forcing people to be free" and adopting authoritarian reforms to liberate people from the restrictive practices of their traditions. Although the new secular republic required loyal citizens who would forge ties beyond the bonds of their religious convictions, secularism's failure to create a strong civil religion prevented this relationship from forming. The forced removal of Islam from the new secular public imagery deprived the incipient regime of some vital assets, namely political consensus on critical issues as well as its source of popular legitimacy.[8] The more the republican elite failed to create an integrative national culture, the more it resorted to authoritarian assimilatory policies of Turkification and secularization, thereby trapping itself in a vicious cycle. As a result, from the inception of the republic, religiously grounded movements acquired countervailing roles, ranging from questioning the legitimacy of the state to opposing (or in some cases justifying) certain social changes, thereby becoming the driving force of political competition in Turkish politics.

Turkey's secularism project remains at the heart of the Prosperity Party's and the JDP's political discourses, which reiterate that "laicism is a foreign term and imposed practice" and needs to be localized and liberalized. Such statements underline the sense of political alienation and foreign intrusion in the conservative groups' deep-seated reactions to the state's uprooting of Islam from both political and social practices. People are drawn to religious parties when official policies appear to cut individuals' ties to their moral religious communities for the sake of modernization and a strong state. Limiting the role of Islam depletes not only the country's religious-spiritual capital, but also its democratic economic capital. In other words, "cutting the Turkish people off from the Islamic faith results in the destruction of its moral fabric, which, in turn, condemns people to perpetual underdevelopment and social unrest."[9] By voting for religious parties, the electorate tries to open the political center to the presence of Islam, to express the increasing political power of traditional masses in the state, a process that some have called the "peripherilization of the center," namely the ability of Islamic values and agents to make inroads into the political arena conventionally reserved for the secularist elite.

Viewed from the focal point of the conflict model, religious claims cannot constitute mere instruments but ends in themselves; religious values' ability to transcend other mundane differences explains why a broad coalition of supporters, sometimes with contradictory economic interests, turns to these parties. In some analyses, the supporters of the Prosperity Party and the JDP are categorized into three separate constituencies which at first seem disparate but are brought together through their shared proximity to Islam albeit an Islam that takes different forms in each. One group is regional and mostly located in the Black Sea region, where both rural and urban residents are more inclined to use religious discourse in their daily lives and thus in politics. In the southeast, voters are attracted to religious parties because *medreseler* (theological schools) and *seyhlik* (religious sect leadership) were long dominant and because the ethnic Kurdish identity has maintained its distinctive Islamic aspect. The internal Turkish migration from rural areas to the cities has displaced the traditional strongholds of Islam, thereby creating a support base for religious parties in big metropolitan areas such as Istanbul, Ankara, and Izmir. The backbone of religious-party support in urban settings comes mostly from among Black Sea conservatives or migrants from the central Anatolian and southeast regions. What keeps these otherwise contesting groups together and motivates their support for the Prosperity Party and the JDP is their Islamically derived shared value system, and thus, their political position, which in one way or another endorses limiting the secularism of the state.

In fact, the quest to redefine the relationship between the secularist state and its estranged public appears in the programs of all religious parties. For instance, according to the JDP:

Our Party shall prepare a completely new constitutional bill to allow freedoms, responding to the needs of the entire society, conforming to the principle of laws and standards in democratic countries, aiming at establishing a new "social contract" between society and the State. . . . Turkey's biggest problem is the lack of confidence. When the State's confidence towards the people, and the people's confidence towards the State are restored, when the people's demands coincide with the agenda of politics, Turkey's walk to the summit in the international race shall definitely be realized.[10]

While the Prosperity Party and the JDP serve as prototypical cases, at first the NAP appears as more of an anomaly from the standpoint of the conflict model. The model still remains relevant, however, in that it perceives the NAP's platform as one that rests on the fear of conflict. After all, the NAP's political positions are rooted in the party's reaction to the tension between Kemalism and Islam. Its understanding of politics, very much analogous to Mafdal's redemptive politics, results in a political view that considers any action or belief that challenges the sacred nature of the state and the unity of the political community as a politically destabilizing force. Thus, for the NAP, politics becomes an area not for the clash of differences but for their organization or elimination. As a result, the party presumes a national-religious identity through which allegiances become more important than negotiations and conflicts. Paradoxically, at its core the NAP's view of politics is still consistent with the premise of the conflict model in that it perceives politics as a contest of values and builds its policies to avoid conflict. Engaging in a process of a sacralization of politics, the NAP treats the Kemalist state not as a suppressor of Islam but as the instrument for containing the divisive effects of politics without undermining the continuity of the polity and the *Muslimness* of community. It opens a venue to express Islam in the public sphere without relegating it as counter-state or antisystemic.

In the end, the constituencies of the Prosperity, JDP, and the NAP form competing blocs within the same ideological neighborhood. Due to their overlapping platforms, the supporters of these parties may vote for any one of them in a given political contest, depending on whether they prioritize religion over nationalism. Yet in the end, the parties seek to carefully distinguish themselves from the other parties and present their role as a direly needed corrective force against the secularizing policies of the state.

Politics of Crisis: Pro-Islamic Parties and Politics of Resentment and Political Alienation

While intrinsic differences among Islamic and secular values inform the analyses derived from the conflict model, Islam appears to be more of a *venue* to express political economic reactions in the crisis approach. The raison d'etre and increasing popularity of religious parties, according to the crisis model, is a series of failed macroeconomic policies that have perpetuated the existing broad social and economic inequalities. Destabilizing economic reforms undermine the middle class, worsen the conditions of the urban poor, and generate a new wave of migration from the countryside to urban squatter neighborhoods or shantytowns. These dislocated and marginalized groups form the backbone of the radical parties, Islamists and nationalist-religious parties alike. As the state has opened the Turkish economy more and more to global forces, the number of those who feel excluded and lost has only increased. Among many others, small merchants, businessmen, artisans, and "the little man in the bazaar working his copper plates, all lost out."[11] It is not a coincidence, therefore, that Islamic parties increased their electoral fortunes rapidly from 1990 to 1996, during a period when the disposable income of families declined by 45 percent in real terms.[12] However, along with the casualties of its failed mechanisms, such as the expansion of urban poor, the market reforms also created "new wealth" for conservative groups that had been previously excluded from the resources available to the secular business elite.[13]

The center parties' perpetual failures in addressing the strikingly skewed and persistently uneven income distribution exacerbated the average person's feeling of exclusion and reinforced the image of religious parties as a remedial agent. For example, in the bastion of religious party support, urban Istanbul, a mere 1 percent of the city's population (18,000 families) earned 30 percent of its $20 billion income.[14] These striking income discrepancies were not limited to metropolitan areas but also occurred across the less urban regions. The expanding regional income disparity between Turkey's western and southeastern regions further increased the sense of relative deprivation, thus heightening the popularity of pro-Islamic parties as proponents of "just order."[15] The incessant crises caused by the government's neoliberal socioeconomic policies (e.g., decrease in disposable income, declining social security benefits) or the destabilizing effect of the Kurdish problem prompted 30 percent of the region's population to migrate to metropolitan areas. The constant influx of people to shantytowns established groups that rely on their Islamic values to create more stable social and economic environments and who, amid overwhelming political and economic turmoil, are not shy to express their desire for more egalitarian and redistributive policies.

While massive structural changes in the economic and political sphere are seen as the cause of religious party support, they are assumed to have contradictory effects on the NAP, the Prosperity, and JDP supporters. For some scholars, the NAP's electoral success stems from the electorate's reactions to the instability and uncertainty associated with globalization. The *Ülkücüs*, the NAP party supporters, come more from those who feel they belong to a "risk society."[16] They view the stable social order as increasingly dented, especially in the central Anatolian provinces where well-entrenched societal ties have been challenged by the destabilizing economic reforms.[17] A review of the history of the NAP from the crisis perspective shows that the party has always capitalized on reactions against subversive forces. For this reason, the NAP's policies often focused on heterodox groups, such as Alevis, who challenge the orthodox beliefs and the unity of Islamic groups and welcome political and economic restructuring.[18] With the same protective, reflexive muscle facing the increasing influence of international forces, the party shifted its focus to the necessity of a selective integration into the world economy and the safeguarding of national industry. Without the preservation of Islamic nationalism, the party suggested, the forces of globalization would not only make Turkey a peripheral state, but further marginalize its existing peripheral groups.[19]

When viewed from the perspective of structural effects, the support for the pro-Islamic Prosperity Party and the JDP has two different and potentially rival groups. Both parties attract the losers of the rapid socioeconomic liberalization by offering explanations of the injustices embedded in the government's macro policies. This discursive appeal is cushioned by the party's social networks, which offer moral and material help for replacing what has been swept away by the disruptive effect of economic liberalization policies.[20] As a result "among the urban poor, buffeted by subsidy cuts and 100 percent inflation, there appears this party [WP] which talks about a just order, which employs a Marxist analysis without employing a Marxist discourse, which denounces the exploitation of the working man by anonymous market forces. This was the message of the Islamic party, and it appealed to many people."[21] Along with the anticipated losers, the Prosperity Party and the JDP also appeal to unexpected winners—those who moved to big cities, could not find jobs in the formal sector, and instead became "petty entrepreneurs." Although these individuals were vulnerable to market fluctuations and political instability, they still managed to achieve a relatively high, while varying, amount of success. Other unexpected winners, popularly known as Anatolian tigers, represent small- or middle-scale family enterprises in Anatolian towns whose worldviews are imprinted by Islam. Tigers successfully undertook business ventures and established themselves as competitive actors in both domestic and global markets. MÜSİAD (*Müstakil İş Adamları Derneği*, or Independent Industrialists and Businessmen's Association), which represents these conservative yet free-market-oriented entrepreneurs, declares its goal as *morally responsible growth* "which ultimately aims at creating a country with advanced high-tech industries in a highly developed commercial environment, but without sacrificing national and moral values, where labor is not exploited and where the distribution of the national income is just and fair."[22]

What keeps these two groups together, the expected losers and unexpected winners, is not their shared conservative values but the political capacity of these values to alter their social positions. At the end of the day, Islam maintains its relevance as its social capital becomes instrumentally critical for securing financial solidarity and reciprocal trust beyond the tutelage of the state. The need for a financial security network became especially critical when the salience of the traditional working class faltered and the state's role in the economy declined. Ironically, the state's disinvolvement with the economy triggered an increasing reliance on social networks built via shared Islamic values. As a result, the Prosperity's and the JDP's popular support has gained from their role in enhancing informal and formal alternative institutions that protect not only the losers but also the winners of the globalization game from the immoral liberalism taking hold in Turkey. Both parties attract voters who have not been able to leverage the economic reforms for more power and status in society. As in the case of Shas, the Prosperity's and the JDP's ideologies offer visions of moral and material equity that respond to the voters' social and economic needs and aspirations by grounding them in religious discourse. In the religious parties' appeal, instead of serving the core idea of maintaining "order," religion and religious ties are seen as facilitators of change, especially in undertaking macroeconomic adjustments. The coalitions behind the religious-nationalist parties have been formed due to the centripetal forces of socioeconomic change in domestic and global markets. The parties' support bases are therefore neither homogeneous nor united. "Factional rivalries were potentially fierce, but subdued and subordinated to an iron discipline in the pursuit of attaining political power."[23]

The Politics of Islam as a Choice

The commonly shared idea that decisions based on beliefs are at odds with decisions based on reason precludes many from viewing the support for religious parties as a careful selection from among different choices. As explained in Chapter One, *choice,* the core term of many political analyses, is not frequently used in the discussion of politics of religion. Religious beliefs or reactions that instigate pro-Islamic party support are believed to counteract decisions that require the acknowledgement and assessment of alternatives. As a result *options* and *selections,* the main pillars of political decisions, are often treated as irrelevant in religious party support at the individual level. Choice-centered approaches claimed analytical purchase in part as a reaction to macrolevel inquiries that reduced the role of religious supporters to passive recipients of religious ideas or reactionary agents mobilized by changes in their stable environment. Guiding these choice-centered studies is the question of why and how religious partisans, given the availability of other sources of political attraction, choose religious parties in competitive democracies. Many disparate responses that reclaim the primacy of choice draw attention to different processes and actors in the politics of religion, for instance:

1. People turn to religious parties to express their identities. The foundation of religious support lies in its ability to make identities that have been pushed to the peripheries by the coercive modernization project of the center parties both more visible and more salient (politics of recognition).

2. Religious parties make themselves plausible choices for broader constituencies by reducing the cost of political involvement and offering them tangible and intangible benefits provided via their elaborate party apparatuses (politics of mobilization).

3. Religious party supporters come mostly from those swayed by the charismatic appeal of leaders (charismatic appeal).

The Politics of Recognition   While politics is often described as the authoritative allocation of values or scarce resources, this description omits a simple yet crucial point: the distribution of values is not always done by taking into account the differences that might be pertinent to all members in a polity. Politics privileges the rights of officially recognized identities; therefore, the struggle over the definition of politically relevant categories constitutes one of the most critical aspects of politics.[24] Under this approach, Islamic politics, in opposition to authoritative secularism or assimilative nationalism, appears as a struggle to attain recognition and as a contest to redistribute values.[25] Despite its ideological utopia, Kemalism, just like its Israeli counterpart, Labor Zionism, fell short of forming a syncretistic-transformative identity (i.e., inclusive and attentive to different identities) and could not prevent the creation of separatist-preservative (exclusionary) identities.[26] The lack of a consensual identity or social contract became more pronounced with the disengagement of the state from the economic sphere and the liberalization of the political sphere.[27]

Attesting to the growing visibility and plurality of identities once subsumed under the national identity, a range of studies emerged to explore these new claims, the people who responded to them, and what their political goals entailed. In the exploration of these identities and the perceived ambiguities within them, some assessments of Turkish politics, reminiscent of publications in Israel, are titled "Turkey in Search of Identity" or "Intricacies of Turkish Identities; Turkey at the Crossroads."[28] In this new post-Kemalist milieu, Islam gained salience as a springboard for articulating locally grounded and empowering identities. In the end, Islamic beliefs and traditions form for many a foundation for their social imagination within which they reconstruct a sense of belonging to Islam and an anchor in new and challenging surroundings.[29] The NAP, the Prosperity Party, and the JDP are unique choices for the electorate because these parties represent not only the reaction of the peripheries to the center but also the socially mobilized groups' challenges to the recalcitrant power structure, both in the religious communities and in the state.

When Turkish politics is seen as a battlefield of identities, the Prosperity Party and the JDP appear as contenders for power over identities grounded in Islam, whereas the NAP articulates the demands of those whose identity is tied in with a "loss of genuine national identity." The NAP views the politics of recognition, in its untamed form, as a step toward disintegrating existing cultural-ethnic unions.[30] As a result, what motivates the NAP most is resistance to what the party perceives to be an "identity threat." In fact, the NAP has coined the term "politics of responsibility" to counter the growing interest in "politics of difference," the belief that irresponsible claims of difference weaken the overall strength of the polity. The party's emphasis on destructive global forces has led some scholars to describe the NAP as an agent instrumental in the "securitization" of identity issues, which ultimately promotes a reified all-embracing sense of Turkishness as a panacea. This discursive approach makes the party appealing to a range of groups, from former military recruits who suffered the consequences of the Kurdish problem to those attentive to the opportunities of global integration, such as the independence of new Turkish republics. In essence, according to the politics of recognition, the NAP receives support due to the party's defensive political reflex "based on the existence of an enemy, fictitious or real, which has to be challenged and destroyed."[31]

Conversely, the Prosperity Party and the JDP represent quests to accommodate the diversity of identities in the political sphere through a redefinition of the monolithic secular Turkish identity. The lack of political liberties and the enforcement of other restrictive state measures manifest themselves in policies that perceive the expansion of civil society and popular parties as a threat. Thus, both parties strengthen their central role as promoters of the right to be free from the state's control. A division of labor emerges in this picture. While the NAP views the increasing claims for recognition as a challenge and an opportunity to redefine Turkishness, the Prosperity Party and JDP support officially unrecognized groups who, via Islam, seek to legitimize their public demands. Put differently, the NAP capitalizes on the fear of sociocultural polarization along ethnic (Kurdish vs. Turkish) and religious (Alevi Islam vs. Sunni Islam) axes. The Prosperity Party and the JDP, on the other hand, benefit from the fear of limited diversification and liberalization due to the resilience of hegemonic nationalism.[32] For many observers, the role of Islam as the main currency in the politics of identity makes it a liberating force. The shared Islamic values and beliefs generate an area located between traditional practices and official doctrines. This area enables the masses to imagine their social position and relationships to other groups in unprecedented ways.[33] Terms such as Islamist business elite or Islamist feminists exemplify how Islam informs and breeds identities that can be seen as contradictions in terms. These groups came into being as the choices of individuals and describe new identities, not those lost:

Islamic women hurt the feelings of modern women and upset the status quo; they are playing with ambivalence, being both Muslim and modern without wanting to give up one for the other. They are outside a regime of imitation, critical of both subservient traditions and assimilative modernity. One can almost twist the argument and say that they are neither Muslim nor modern. The ambiguity of signs disturbs both the traditional Muslim and the secular modernist social groups.[34]

Thus, religious parties gain support due to their ability to articulate the distinctive positions of the newly noticeable political actors whose views have been left outside the scope of the conventional terms of politics. The existing contracted definition of citizenship explains why religious parties capitalize on the antagonistic relationship between the hegemonic identity and other identities. Likewise, it is not surprising that the pro-Islamic parties in general, and the Prosperity, JDP, and NAP in particular, define their mission as "making peace" *(barıstrmak)* between the secularist state and the Islamic public. Religious parties ultimately strive to carve out more space in the public sphere for the marginalized masses, yet this struggle, in an ironic way, rests on and thus reinforces the presumed divisions between the authoritarian secular state and suppressed Muslim citizens.[35]

The Politics of Mobilization Since the mid-1980s, Turkish politics has experienced an increasing wave of political apathy that has manifested itself in unprecedented rates of nonvoting. Many observers attribute the NAP, Prosperity Party, and JDP's political victories to their ability to alleviate the epidemic of mistrust and disaffection. Using Jan Leighley's terms, the parties provide individuals with an information subsidy, participation-facilitating knowledge, or relational goods (e.g., solidarity, support) that altogether make politics a worthwhile practice. In many cases, the parties form ad hoc election committees whose members go door to door to ensure that individuals vote and who also watch the activities of the other parties to prevent election fraud and assure accurate vote counting. In addition to the parties' election-centered mobilization drives, they have more permanent networks that distribute relational goods: that treat the members as a community and offer help ranging from intangible benefits, such as solidarity, to more tangible ones, such as heating assistance during the winter.[36] Students of political mobilization maintain that the parties offer a solution to the voting paradox not by making political participation a one-time voting exercise but by offering a range of tangible and intangible benefits that trivializes the conventional calculations of costs attributed to political participation.

Overall, pro-Islamic parties differ from others as they build their organizations from the bottom up based on *mahalle*, neighborhoods, the main units of society. The parties draw on existing communities where traditional values and Islam play a critical role. Unlike the RPP, for instance, which lacks a strong connection to local groups and common cultural practices, the pro-Islamic parties imbue their political messages with the daily Islamic rituals and practices, thereby making them easily accessible to ordinary people. As such, some concluded that these networks are nothing more than shelters of value-centered political processes rooted in local culture, interpersonal relations, and community networks and generators of religious parties' political capital. Yet for some they are self-sustaining and well-entrenched political movements that are critical for these political parties' success. In other words, Islam as the facilitator of political debates and interactions between otherwise disconnected actors provides religious parties with a unique type of political currency.[37]

By any account, the NAP, Prosperity, and JDP differ from others by their social connectedness. In the case of the NAP, *ülkü ocaks*, neighborhood organizations for young people, offer mentor relationships between elder and younger members and emerge as key institutions. Each ocak serves as a tuition-free school with centralized training programs in all branches.[38] Likewise, the Prosperity Party and the JDP created two parallel, well-connected organizations based on volunteer services and party-sponsored initiatives. Both parties have street representatives active in their community, who not only organize various activities but also provide the party with essential information regarding the composition and needs of the community by visiting and collecting data from each household. The parties use polls extensively in their own organizations to ensure the popularity of party activists at each level. Just like the emphases in Judaism, Islam's emphasis on charity, social solidarity, and helping out those in need, when coupled with the party's political messages to weed out the institutional roots of social ills, makes the party institutions not only habitual places where traditional roles are not challenged but also political spaces in which various interpersonal exchanges can form new ties. Instead of being limited to charitable engagements, the exchanges and interactions, either implicitly or explicitly, actually help to facilitate political learning through their teachings and activities. Even though the parties do not sponsor religious schools directly, Qur'an schools, which teach basic prayers and how to read the Qur'an, are often supported and attended by party volunteers. Throughout the range of their sacro-secular engagements, party activists, one way or another, mention the parties' message of expanding moral solidarity and the relevance of Islam in Turkey's increasingly individualistic, changing, and religiously hostile environment. All these activities provide various material as well as emotional goods that allow the parties to further recruit people from different socioeconomic backgrounds. The party volunteer networks mitigate the high cost of services, for instance, by providing tutoring for the centralized university entrance exams, annual exams that determine whether students go to college and to which one they will be assigned, or by distributing coal to low-income families for heating. They create a cadre of volunteers along with a vibrant, yet in some cases increasingly dependent, set of political communities.

The core proposal of the mobilization theory can be summarized as, "no mobilization network, no support." People turn to the NAP, the Prosperity Party, and the JDP not on election day, but through a more gradual and comprehensive process. Just like the NAP and Shas, these parties reduce the distance between political party and society. With their formal and informal institutional web of relational organizations, these parties are well entrenched in their societies. Conversely, conventional parties rely on other intermediary organizations and maintain loosely connected and sparsely attended local organizations, thus severing the link between the party apparatus and society. One of the paradoxes of the religious party support hinges on the precarious role of their networks: The parties' electoral strengths depend on their networks' ability to serve as the grounds for political learning and distribution of their benefits. However, these networks are meticulously scrutinized and coordinated by the religious parties thereby undermining their autonomy as a civic political force. Therefore, although the parties are relatively well entrenched in society due to these networks, perhaps the intriguing question is exactly how entrenched these networks are in serving as long-term breeding grounds for participatory and democratic practices, and what would happen if the parties failed to perform their role as organizers, enablers, and providers. Or more importantly, given the pervasive political apathy, do these networks base their power on a small number of activists? Do they attract the disaffected temporarily with short-term benefits, or do they forge lasting political affiliation?

The Politics of Charismatic Appeal   For charismatic party models, religious-party supporters are not ad hoc coalitions of socially displaced voters, nor are they attracted to these parties out of a feeling of estrangement from the system. The political attraction of the leadership is decisive for the voters. The application of the charismatic model to religious parties is somewhat puzzling in that not only religious parties but all of Turkey's political parties—just like their Israeli counterparts—are leader-centered and lack internal democracy. In fact, many observers agree that the most typical feature of all Turkish political parties has been the unquestioned authority of the leader, unconstrained by party structures.[39] "No political faction or actor can act autonomously against the will and actions of the leader. Overall the charisma of the leader, reinforced by a lack of internal democracy, attracts the voters' support, rather than the party's ideology."[40]

In the face of these leader-centered parties, some observers unavoidably conclude that there would not have been an NAP if it had not been for Türkeş, if Erbakan had not led the NV Parties it would not have scored its historical victory, and that the JDP is simply Erdoğan's party. Their leadership and innovative roles as originators of the parties' ideologies and organizational structures distinguish the NAP, the Prosperity Party, and the JDP from other parties. In fact, the three parties fit Panebianco's model of charismatic parties with their highly centralized organizations that attract people from various backgrounds, begging the question of to what extent these parties are capable of surviving and routinizing their charismatic appeal.[41]

As explained in Chapter Five, the first head of the NAP, Türkeş, was given the title of *başbuğ*, leader commander, thereby signifying his critical position as ultimate ruler within the party. His manifesto, *Dokuz Işık*, formed the ideological foundation of the party. Türkeş's central role convinced some observers that the NAP could not survive without him. In fact, his successor, Bahçeli, failed to match Türkeş's charismatic appeal. He came across as bureaucratic and consumed by real politics. Ironically, these traits may have helped Bahçeli to successfully complete the second stage of a charismatic party's development, namely, as Panebianco has phrased it, the reutilization of charisma. Bahçeli not only maintained the party's institutions, he applied Türkeş's ideas to the changing political and economic context by focusing on the process of globalization and offering a nationalist perspective on it.[42] In the end, Türkeş's efforts to place ideology at the center of the movement may have prevented the party's demise after his departure.

In comparison to the NAP, the Prosperity Party and the JDP remain in the first stage of charismatic party development. Erbakan and Erdoğan continue to play critical roles in their parties, inspiring loyalty and attracting support from the masses directly. Due to his central role in the NV movement, some scholars speak of *Erbakanism* to describe the NV, Turkey's first openly Islamic political movement. In addition to being called *mücahid*, warrior for Islam, by NV supporters, a pledge of allegiance to Erbakan marked the beginning of party meetings. This organized solidarity around Erbakan revealed itself best in the shifting core of the center from a civil society movement to a more hierarchical structure. It is important to note that while Erdoğan's charismatic appeal may have surpassed Erbakan's, the nature of their respective popularities differed dramatically. As stated in Chapter Four, Erdoğan graduated from a state-sponsored religious school, and in contrast to Erbakan, can claim doctrinal knowledge of Islam. His wife and daughters suffer from secularist restrictions; thus he claims an innate understanding of religiously oppressed groups' problems. As a result, he does not use religious symbols and expressions as overtly and frequently as Erbakan to claim legitimacy among Islamic circles.[43] Ironically, both the trials of Erbakan and Erdoğan vastly increased their popularity. Similar to the impact of Aryeh Deri's imprisonment, Erdoğan's sentence boosted his support, not only among those who viewed his prosecution as a suppression of their brave Islamist challenge against the secularist state, but also among groups who interpreted it as the state's reaction to dissenters.

When viewed through the lens of charismatic appeal, the JDP's meteoric rise draws on Erdoğan's profile as an ordinary man with extraordinary commitment and skill. His decision to continue living in a middle-income neighborhood, his visits to poor families, and breaking his fast in the *iftar* tents (tents set up for serving meals to poor people during Ramadan) depicts him as a pious Muslim, a self-made leader who understands the concerns of common people. The stories about his leadership emphasize his authority, his intolerance of corruption, and his commitment to his religious principles. When faced with difficult policy choices, the JDP leadership argues that Erdoğan's special ties to the common man will offset any attack on the party.[44] Erdoğan built his reputation as an effective service deliverer and problem solver within the existing governmental system: "His populist flair and 'language of the people' set him apart as one who could shake up the way business was done in Ankara while still playing by the constitutional rules of the game."[45]

Like other models, used in isolation, the charismatic model gives us a compelling account of the appeal of religious parties. Many questions arise, however, once analysts go beyond the popular arguments that religious parties, at their core, are charismatic-leader parties. If charismatic appeal is the driving force of party support, why do the parties' electoral gains fluctuate significantly over a short span of time? Given the continuing splits within these parties, when and how does the charismatic appeal wear out or get challenged by others? Given the overall leader-centric structure of party politics in Turkey, what sets apart the leaders of pro-Islamic parties? Perhaps the more vexing question is whether and how the charismatic leadership of religious parties differs from nonreligious parties and how their impact aligns with other important factors.

As is the case elsewhere, the quest to understand the popular roots of the politics of Islam in Turkey has generated an ever-growing body of analyses. Behind their increasing diversity, many of these studies either privilege structure (institutional conditions and political constraints) over agents or overemphasize how shared Islamic values connect pro-Islamic party supporters en masse. Regardless of their immediate foci, the explanations, one way or another, refer to how fault lines separate Islamic and Kemalist values or Turkey's strong state and its official ideology of secularism. In a political environment defined by Islam and its ideological other, Kemalist secularism, people turn to religious parties to express their religious convictions. The diverse analyses of Islam are united by the shared assumption that the secularist elite committed one cardinal sin: it launched policies that did not acknowledge the masses' values. Instead, the elite sought to dominate these values in order to fulfill a modernist vision. It is not a coincidence, therefore, that despite their different starting points, many researchers at the end rely on data from *gecekondu* (shantytowns), which literally means houses that are built overnight. Gecekondus have mushroomed around and in the urban centers since the 1950s. For many, these towns serve as a microcosm of Turkish politics, as they embody the rapid transition from rural to urban communities, and the clash of religious and secular, traditional and modern.[46] Studies that adopt this view illustrate how traditional values prevail and how Islamic beliefs are reinvented to give meaning to religious partisans' experiences. Thick descriptions of the conditions and overall beliefs of these communities explain how Islamic values remain relevant and are reinvented, often rendering the party structure and the interactions between parties and their constituencies of secondary importance.[47]

Many studies question why Islam shapes political movements or why individuals are attracted to Islamic groups. They depict religious partisans as amorphous groups united both by a deep discontent with the existing system and by common Islamic values not shared by other factions. The presumed broad coalition of supporters, consisting of the young, the urban, the poor, conservative entrepreneurs, Islamist intellectuals, Islamist women, and other ethnic groups, is often broad enough to justify multiple and frequently contesting arguments. Not addressed in these sweeping accounts is the question of how this extensive coalition, which represents the majority of the Turkish electorate, selects one party over the other. More importantly, given the overall voter volatility, how is it that the same coalition remains as the empirical reference point to explain changing electoral decisions? What do we gain analytically from such accounts?

Silent Voices? Questions of Data

Irrespective of their theoretical foundations and immediate focus of interest, many accounts converge in how they study religious partisans. They elicit their conclusions from the analysis of macrohistorical transformations, as manifested in structural factors, with selective references to individuals and based on in-depth interviews with targeted party activists. While these studies successfully demystify certain aspects of pro-Islamic party supporters, religious partisans as individuals and specific groups beyond the religious-secular divide fall into the cracks between macroprocesses and agent-based thick descriptions.

A systematic relational understanding of the interactions between context, individuals, and ideology is lacking in these accounts. Our emphasis on the systematic analysis of religious partisans by no means suggests that regularity-seeking statistical analyses are preferable over others. Neither does it suggest that the existing studies should privilege agents over structure or search for different forms of generalizable results. Rather, it argues that when research acknowledges its assumptions, applies its terms consistently, and refrains from extending its results without ensuring its external validity, it can better equip us in identifying and precluding potentially essentialist studies. Otherwise random and slanted research selections, when repeated enough, create their own dominant discursive spheres that can be perilously limiting, especially in areas where there is overwhelming interest and intellectual anxiety. Keeping the conceptual frameworks and empirical tools that we rely on as part of our analytical discourse helps prevent us from concentrating on selected characteristics of the supporters and the political context. As stated in our introductory chapter, theory-neutral observations and methods cannot exist. It is important to remember John Dryzek's warning against becoming too comfortable with the normalization of our assumptions and methods, thereby confusing the view defined by our instrument with the universe we seek to explore.[48]

We draw attention to simple, yet often neglected facts when we place our inquiries at the nexus of the broader national setting of political decision making and the microconstraints and latitudes of the individuals' decisions. The politics of Islam are not a unique decision-making universe based on beliefs and reactions. Nor are the politics of Islam in the Turkish case an exceptional phenomenon or a completely new political beast. The political decisions of religious party supporters cannot be triggered merely by structural factors or self-enforcing value clashes. Rather, how individual beliefs and systemic and ideational factors interact and, more significantly, what they mean to voters are critical and need to be accommodated in our analyses without privileging one dimension over others.

When viewed from this perspective, the absence of a consistent and wider range of the religious partisans' own assessments signals an important methodological void and disconnect between theoretical and empirical studies. This lacuna requires that more attention be given to the individual beliefs, characteristics, and decision-making processes of the silent supporters of Islamic parties. The section below ventures into this analytical space. It takes a closer look at the self-assessments and demographic characteristics of religious partisans to address the electoral puzzles posed by religious parties. Four groups of data sets provide the observations on which our analysis is based: (1) the World Values Surveys of 1990 and 1994 for Turkey, with a sample size of 1,030 and 1,907 individuals, respectively;[49] (2) the Turkish Socioeconomic Research Foundation's (TÜSES) 1996 and 1998 surveys, administered to representative national samples of 1,800 and 2,224 Turkish voters, respectively; (3) the 2001 Turkish election data set, which includes 1,201 face-to-face interviews conducted in twelve provinces;[50] and (4) the 2005 Religious Party Support data, a data set collected by the author and based on a national representative survey of 1,016 Turkish citizens eligible to vote.[51]

The data collected in Turkey do not have the underrepresentation problem that plagues the Israeli surveys, but other challenges remain. Three caveats need to be laid out to better evaluate the conclusions drawn from these surveys: the identifications of (1) ideological positions, (2) ethnic and unorthodox religious identities, and (3) actual versus reported income pose several challenges.

Echoing the complexity in Israel, additional caution is needed for any discussion using ideology and Left-Right terms in the Turkish case. After all, Turkish political culture has been permanently marked by the polarized politics of the 1970s, when political conflicts often escalated into violent confrontations. The 1980 military intervention stabilized the system by outlawing and radically suppressing various left- and right-wing groups. The conflict-ridden politics of the 1970s have imbued the word *ideology* with a negative connotation and equated its meaning to dogmatic convictions and the propensity to use violence for promoting a political cause. As a result of this legacy, one can speak of a lingering effect of the fear of the word *ideology* in Turkey. Likewise, the terms *Left* and *Right* became loaded with meanings that are associated with specific factions and have therefore been used very cautiously in Turkey. Unsurprisingly, especially right after the 1980 coup, voters placed *themselves* in the center rather than at the margins of the ideological spectrum. Although one can speak of a normalization of the terms *Left* and *Right*, they are not widely circulated or easily claimed terms in the Turkish context. An observable shift away from the center, therefore, highlights a significant transformation of the political sphere.

Another area, ethnic-religious identities, poses similar problems. The emphasis of the hegemonic discourse on ethnic-religious unity may lead the electorate to shy away from identifying with unorthodox religious and politicized ethnic identities. The contested status of Alevis and Kurds makes their identities especially difficult to express publicly. To exacerbate the problem, the official census data do not include questions on religious or ethnic identity. Therefore, the sizes of various ethnic and religious groups remain disputed, making it difficult to estimate whether and to what extent these groups are underrepresented in data collection projects. As direct questions are often avoided, surveys typically use proxy questions to demarcate these identities. For instance, the 2001 Turkish election survey uses the questions, "What language is spoken at home?" and "What symbols does your household contain?" as proxies for ethnic and religious identities, respectively. Given the deficiency of efficient data collection, especially on self-identifications, the direct and open-ended questions of the TÜSES surveys offer the most detailed accounts. The responses to the TÜSES surveys yielded more than forty identity groups, indicating the insufficiency of dominant labels for capturing the existing diversity. In the absence of census data and detailed direct questions to define identities, one of the most popular explanations of religious party support, "identity politics" lacks clear empirical references and support. Nevertheless, despite their shortcoming, survey data provide a wealth of much-needed information, especially given the shortage of large-scale observations and the limited knowledge of existing religious and ethnic identities.

The prevalence of unregistered economic activities in Turkey poses another challenge. The main difficulty is how to obtain the real income of respondents instead of the officially reported one. Any analysis of economic indicators needs to take into account that the state's ability to collect taxes is limited, especially among self-employed voters. To compensate for this shortcoming, data collection efforts often use other measures related to income (e.g., average consumption and saving) that do not require divulging confidential information and might give better estimates of the real earned income. Perhaps more important is people's assessment of their socioeconomic status in society. Even though they are only personal estimates, these assessments are the ones that affect the individuals' political decisions. The individuals' assessments of their personal economic standing allow us an important venue for obtaining socioeconomic data at the individual level that cannot be derived from other macrolevel sources and income-specific-based descriptions.

Finally, it is important to note that opinion surveys are effective research tools, but neither the sampling methodology nor the actual questionnaire can be mechanically produced via the application of certain rules. Both require a deep understanding of the political culture that they seek to represent and analyze. More importantly, as long as the data limitations are taken into account, survey data can be invaluable instruments in addressing research questions. For instance, some ideological markers are used consistently in repeated and similar surveys (e.g., World Values Surveys) and therefore allow us to capture over-time and across-space variations. The challenge in using survey data in the Turkish context, or any other context for that matter, is to ensure that they are not used selectively to perpetuate a priori ideas held by researchers. The survey findings, when used in conjunction with other analytic tools, offer us a broad and unique window into the voters' views. Some survey findings appear to be inconsistent and incoherent. This is precisely one of the reasons survey data can be helpful. Theory-defined observations might preclude the contradictory data to the extent that they create, in Thomas Kuhn's sense, paradigm-dominated explanations. Using an approach similar to the one adopted in Chapter Five, the following section questions both our conceptual tools and the commonly used markers (e.g., primary identities and placement on the Left–Right spectrum, etc.), as well as patterns identified by them, in order to tackle the questions of why and how a significant segment of the electorate, despite a plethora of political options, consistently views pro-Islamic parties as a more viable choice than other parties.

The Interface of Theoretical Constructs and Empirical Findings: Understanding Religious Supporters

Accounts of an Islamic resurgence, which reverberate through explanations of religious movements in general, focus on reactions to Turkey's authoritarian secularism and persistent economic and social crises. Somewhat normalized, analytically reductionist ideas often manifest themselves in the simplified, yet powerful formula for pro-Islamic party supporters: the deeper a person's religious commitment, combined with a lack of social and economic resources in the face of the challenges of modernity, the more he or she is likely to turn to proreligious parties.[52] Groups united by the fear of losing Islamic values and motivated by the resentment of inegalitarian policies constitute the backbone of the pro-Islamic constituency. Commonly accepted reifications become more elaborate under different frameworks. For instance, those who view religious parties as "protest movements" contend that the electorate votes retrospectively based on the party's performance. The disaffected voters punish center parties by turning to political outsiders, such as pro-Islamist parties. The promises of Islamic values and the protestors' fear of reverse mobilization or the further deterioration of their socioeconomic status only add to the popularity of Islamic parties.

A review of the existing opinion polls and the distribution of election results alerts us that some compelling accounts can obscure the differences between religious parties, hide their transformation, and overlook the heterogeneous electoral coalitions behind them. As explained in a prior section, repeated applications and confirmations of these formulas reify religious party supporters as passive recipients and ignore their role as active constituents of transformation. If the electoral appeal of religious parties indeed originates from their dual call for a return to Islamic values and fair socioeconomic policies, the supporters of these parties should come overwhelmingly from among the economically vulnerable of the believers. More specifically, we should expect to find that supporters of the Prosperity Party and the JDP, which represent traditional values against secularist elites, strongly oppose the institutions, ideas, and identities forged by Kemalist secularism. For example, in comparison to supporters of other parties, the JDP and Prosperity Party constituents should perceive *Muslimness* as their primary identity (traditional *millet* identity) as opposed to their Turkishness (construct of modern Turkish Nationalism). More importantly, the JDP and Prosperity Party supporters can be expected to espouse *Sharia* (Qur'anic rule) and be more critical than others of existing institutions, especially those that are deemed to be representative of secular establishments, such as the military.

Religious Party Supporters and the Politics of Conflict   The Kemalist secularist dictum that religion needs to be a matter of conscience (private beliefs) informs not only many state policies, but many analyses as well. In its strict form, Turkey's constitutionally protected laïcité lends itself to an easy and popular explanation, namely that supporters of religious parties are devoted believers who want to restore the role of religion in the public sphere. Despite their differences, religious partisans gather under religious party banners to contest the domination of secularist values. As a result, a limited terminology exists in the public sphere to capture the multiplicity of Islamic ideas as well as the contradiction between Islam's actual and expected roles. In the absence of a finely tuned public debate and terminology, diverging positions on the public expression of Islam are often subsumed under the terms *secular* and *antisecular*, *religious* and *not religious*. Consequently, the question of religiosity, "how religious are you?" serves to identify religious identities in Turkish politics. Direct questions like these offer broad assessments about the role of religion in people's lives. These wide-ranging categories fail to differentiate how the beliefs of individuals affect their expectations of the public sphere.

A review of the religious identities and positions on the religious–secular spectrum warns us against conflating different identities, creating empirically meaningless constructs and, more importantly, ascribing a set of

political behavior to each group. In contrast to the widely shared and reified secular-religious divisions, one's religious, self-identified beliefs and
position on laicism do not determine each other. In fact, a closer analysis
turns the essence of the clash of values argument upside down. Even a
simple chi-square test (an estimate of whether knowledge of one characteristic increases or decreases the accurate prediction of the others) suggests that personal assessments of religiosity and support for laïcité are
not systematically related (see figure 6.2).

   In fact, support for laicism has acquired a meaning beyond mere opposition to a public role for Islam. For instance, politically moderate
Turks have one of the highest rates of opposition to laicism. They avoid a
self-definition of secular and do not oppose or support laicism as a bloc.
More importantly, they adopt different positions on laïcité for religious
reasons. Open-ended, unconstrained explanations of individuals' positions on laïcité confirm that opposition to laicism can be rooted in values
not informed by religion, such as political liberalization. Likewise, many
support laicism not for antireligious reasons, but to help foster a pluralistic political structure in Turkey without also establishing domination by
one of the groups. The interaction between laicism and religiosity there-

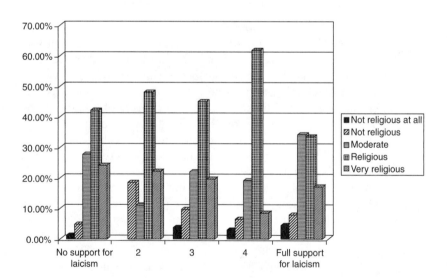

FIGURE 6.2

Support for laicism and religiosity

SOURCE: 2005 Tepe-Religious Party Support data

NOTE: Distribution of religiosity within groups is based on their declared level of support for laicism.

fore is not a deterministic one, and those who are not on the extremes, "moderate" and "not religious," are likely to play a more decisive role for religious party support than others.

Embracing common identities based on Islam does not necessarily translate into endorsing a religious regime informed by Islam. The sporadically heated, continuing debate about Sharia, and the electorate's positions on it, permits us to tackle whether and to what extent individuals want to alter the role of religion in the public sphere or reorganize the public sphere according to their religious beliefs.[53] *Sharia* literally means a set of Islamic rules. In Turkey's daily political parlance, being for or against Sharia has come to represent the support for a religiously grounded regime, so much so that in many public protests secular groups use the slogans "No to Sharia" and "Turkey won't be a Sharia rule" to declare their opposition to religious groups. Due to its role as an ideological marker in Turkish politics, surveys usually include a question on whether the respondent supports Sharia. The opinion polls reveal that, in general, Sharia is a divisive but not a polarizing issue: 20 percent seem to be undecided, 60 percent oppose it, while 20 percent support it.

In this fragmented picture, the NAP, Prosperity, and JDP supporters' endorsements of Sharia, while remaining at levels above the national average, vary over time. (See figure 6.3.) Around one-fourth of the NAP supporters and around 40 percent of the JDP and its predecessors' supporters view Sharia as a more desirable regime.[54] This relatively stable pattern broke down in 1996 when 61 percent of Welfare and 31 percent of the NAP supporters declared a Sharia regime as a better rule for the country. The 1996 survey was implemented the year after the Prosperity Party had achieved the hitherto highest level of support. Thus, the jump in support can be attributed to the party's successful mobilization and legitimization of its political project, whereas the decline can be attributed to the electorate's disenchantment with the form of Islamic rule envisioned by the party and the authoritarian turn in politics that resulted from the military's ultimatum. Regardless of its rationale, oscillations in the support for Sharia indicate not a firm theological conviction but the fact that variant political reckonings lie beneath its endorsement.

An open-ended question in the 1998 survey, "why do you support Sharia?" sheds some light on the paradox posed by the continuing relevance of Sharia as a political alternative in general and to the supporters of the NAP and the JDP and its predecessors in particular. A relatively limited percent of the supporters of the NAP and the JDP's predecessors support Sharia as a requirement of Muslimness: Only 29.1 percent of the Prosperity and 10 percent of the NAP voters are primarily motivated by religious convictions in their support of Sharia. Varying rationales cluster

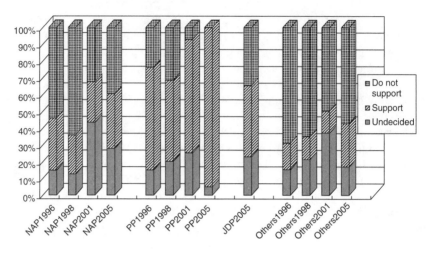

FIGURE 6.3

Endorsement of Islamic (Sharia) rule

SOURCES: 1996, 1998 Turkish Socioeconomic Research Foundation (TÜSES) data; 2001 Turkish election data; 2005 Tepe-Religious Party Support data

NOTE: Each column summarizes the proportion of support (or lack thereof) extended for Islamic rule by the supporters of the Nationalist Action Party (NAP), Prosperity Party (PP), Justice and Development Party (JDP), and Others (other parties).

around the statement "because Sharia will bring more moral values and thus honesty to the system." The rather mundane and instrumental justifications offered by a significant percentage of respondents indicate that they view Sharia not as a sweeping regime change or antisystemic challenge to the existing state but as a way to reform the system or establish a moral shield against sources of social decay. When the respondents were asked in the 2005 Religious Party survey what laicism meant to them, a broad spectrum of competing definitions emerged. They ranged from interpretations that associated laicism with the official state policy to those that saw laicism as a means to achieve social peace. Thus, regardless of the reasons, shifts in the voters' support of Sharia alert us to the fact that we cannot speak of a well-entrenched and uncompromising Islamic opposition rooted merely in the politics of values. Understanding the public demands of the pro-Islamic groups requires us to assess how Sharia is defined by the political elite, by the voters, and by the context of their assessment.

As in the case of Israel, the surveys from 1996 to 2005 lack the ability to properly categorize religious identities, but they do signal an overall increase among those who see themselves as religious. According to the 2005 survey, the average religiosity is 6.56 on a scale of zero to 10, where the majority of people assigned themselves to scores between 4 and 9.12. The electorate's avoidance of extremes, that is, secular and very religious, points out the critical role of "moderates," not as a rhetorical category, but as an important identification for those who selectively observe religious practices (equivalent to Israel's "traditionals"). Like their Israeli counterparts, Turkish religious parties seem to attract voters who place themselves in different locations on the ideological and religious spectrum. To complicate the picture further, the JDP received one of the highest percentages of votes in Turkish politics (34.21 percent), while its supporters were characterized by the highest average religiosity score (7.34), with one of the highest standard deviations (2.08). The average religiosity of NAP supporters is not very different, 6.98, with a standard deviation of 2.05. Yet despite the perceived central role of Islam in the NAP and the Prosperity Party rhetoric, the majority of NAP and Prosperity Party supporters consist of those who consider themselves moderately religious or religious, rather than very religious (see figure 6.4). "Very religious" voters constitute only 38 percent of the Prosperity and 12 percent of the NAP voter base. These trends seem to confirm the high level of religiosity among the party supporters, yet despite the central role of Islam in the Prosperity's and the JDP's rhetoric, 62 percent and 88 percent of their supporters, respectively, do not consider themselves very religious.

The detailed questions used in the 2005 survey draw our attention to neglected aspects of religion where private and public religious beliefs can interact in different ways in defining one's political positions. For instance, when we use a new continuum ranging from folk Islam to individual Islamic practices, a different picture emerges than the one presented by a religious-secular one. Folk Islam includes traditional religious practices such as shrine visits or giving alms. Individual Islam, on the other hand, describes attendance to rituals that are regularly performed alone and require daily commitments (e.g., praying five times). This nuanced understanding of religiosity draws our attention to the discrepancies between private experience and public expectations of Islam. Although the JDP supporters score much higher on the different practices of Islam, this difference gets less accentuated when respondents assess the impact of their religious values on their social decisions. For instance, less than half of the NAP supporters report to follow individual Islamic practices regularly as opposed to 70 percent of the JDP supporters. Notwithstanding this difference more than half of the NAP supporters indicate that their social decisions are affected by their religious values (see table 6.1). These patterns substantiate arguments, such as the one offered by Nikkie Keddie, that religious

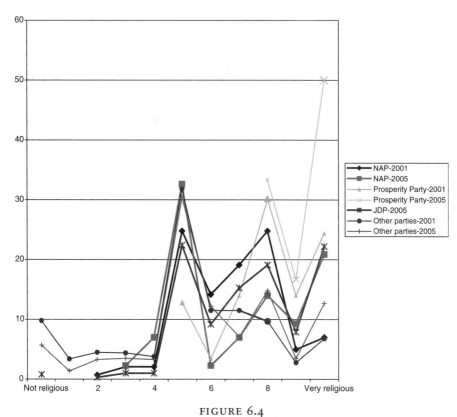

FIGURE 6.4

Dispersion of religiosity and party support in Turkey

SOURCES: 2005 Tepe-Religious Party Support data and the 2001 Election Data

NOTE: The religiosity of supporters denotes their self-identification on
a 0–10 spectrum where 0 indicates not religious at all and 10 indicates
very religious.

nationalism is more a communal identity or a question of public religiosity
than a private practice.[55] Yet when the question is asked to what extent individuals apply religious ideas to their decision-making process, it appears
that the JDP's and Prosperity's individualized Islam also translates into
greater demands on the public sphere.

However, as the 2005 results show, these overall more religious yet
also mixed profiles of the party supporters attest to these parties' ability
to transcend a strict secular-religious division, but they do not allow us to
confirm that it is the ideological tension between Kemalist and Islamic
values that motivates voters to support pro-Islamic parties. Therefore, accounts that assume "competing identities" or "irreconcilable" views of

TABLE 6.1

Religious practices and religious party support in Turkey

		JDP	NAP	Others
Folk Islam	Usually	1.1%		.7%
	Sometimes	12.8%	4.7%	9.5%
	Rarely	68.4%	60.5%	59.7%
	Never	17.9%	34.9%	30.1%
Communal	Usually	27.5%	7%	10.7%
	Sometimes	44.1%	55.8%	31.3%
	Rarely	27.0%	37.2%	43.7%
	Never	1.3%	14.3%	
Individual Islam	Usually	70.9 %	41.9%	34.2%
	Sometimes	25.5%	46.5%	33.6%
	Rarely	3.6%	11.6%	20.3%
	Never			11.9%
Religious values and social decisions	Does not affect	34.7%	42.8%	63.1%
	Affects significantly	65.3%	57.2%	36.9%

SOURCE: 2005 Tepe-Religious Party Support data

idealized public spheres fall short in explaining why pro-Islamic parties appeal to such a broad ideological spectrum of voters.

Religious Party Supporters and the Politics of Ethnicity? Self-identifications of citizens' primary identity give us a broader foundation for probing to what extent the well-entrenched claim that counter-hegemonic identities (i.e., identities that challenge the official national identity) lie at the root of religious support. When we group the 1996 TÜSES survey's findings into broad categories, those who consider their most important identity to be Turkish made up 33.7 percent of the total population, whereas 36.1 percent reported their religious identity as primary. When the entire list of identities rooted in Muslimness (including the hyphenated ones) is taken into account, Muslimness reached a total of forty-one percent, exceeding the proportion of those who identified themselves with Turkishness. The total share of hybrid identities exceeded the most cited identity, Turkishness. The vocal expression of diverse, less visible identities beyond the dominant Turkish nationalist discourse and its "other," *Kurdishness*, might come as a surprise considering the existing literature's lopsided focus on these two main identity groups. The persistent pluralistic picture warns us that ethnically and religiously grounded identities continue to serve as sources of primary public identities, even (or perhaps more so) in countries where national identity has been promoted and firmly protected as a hegemonic official ideology.

What is still surprising, however, is not so much the spectrum of these identities, but how they fluctuate significantly over a short period of time. One would expect that these identities would be pluralistic yet relatively stable, considering their deep roots and the long processes needed to mobilize them politically. The results suggest that the identities might be a driving force behind religious parties, but in return the parties' policies seem to shape identities by defining their public and political expressions; therefore, the relationship is a more reciprocal one and cannot be reduced to a simple chain of causality. For example, high levels of Kurdishness (10 percent) were reported following the 1995 election when Turkey's overtly Islamist Welfare party won in a landslide with a platform that publicly professed support for the Kurdish identity. The 1998 survey findings showed that *Turkishness* (the term emphasizes the official ethnic description of national identity) was named as the primary identity for 58.8 percent of the population, while another 25.8 percent chose to be identified as Muslim, a counter-hegemonic identity; the once popular Kurdish identity, however, became significantly less salient (3 percent). The remaining 12.4 percent of respondents reported the religious identities of Alevis and various other ethnic groups, including Cherkessians, Laz, and Bosnians.

Given this plethora of identities, the supporters of neither the Prosperity Party, nor the JDP, nor the NAP are anchored in one predominant identity. The 2005 Religious Party survey at first confirms that JDP supporters come more from those who see religion as the main source of their public identity (40 percent). Nevertheless, 47 percent of those Turkish voters who view Islam as the main reference point of their identity did not vote for the party. Neither did 74 percent of those who identified themselves with some ethnic group (see figure 6.4). This finding is significant, given that the JDP is often described as the party with a very high level of support among ethnic Kurdish groups. Yet the election results indicate that this high support rests not on an expression of marginalized identities alone, but on a range of institutional and ideational factors. For instance, many of the votes have stemmed from the fact that the Kurdish party has been unable to pass the minimum national threshold. Kurdish backing seems to be directed toward pro-Islamic parties more due to the confluence of the parties' Islamic values and critical position vis-a-vis the state than their explicit inclusive rhetoric on ethnic rights.

The absence of clear alliances along the lines of party preferences and identities, coupled with the sporadic shifts in the declared identities, suggests that including identity politics in religious party explanations opens a Pandora's box. More questions arise than are answered when religious parties are viewed as polar opposites of the Kemalist state and its secular Turkish identity. For instance, "other identities which include a wide spectrum from Laz, Kirmanci, Bektashi, to Georgian" are consistently reported at a significant level (around one-tenth of the supporters). The 2005 religious party support survey indicates there has been a significant shift toward "local identities," a term that summarizes identification with one's place of birth or ethnic traditions (see figure 6.5). All in all, a review of the self-descriptions suggests that primary identities are not only resilient and plural but malleable and, depending on the political context, politically relevant. It is not their suppressed essence but the combination of these factors that makes identities an important aspect of political rivalries in Turkish politics. Nevertheless, instead of treating these identities as in conflict, we might see that competing reference points for political choices often exist in the same individuals. In other words, it is not an intrinsically incompatible value system that separates the secular national discourse from the Islamic one. Instead, Kemalist secularism and Islamic

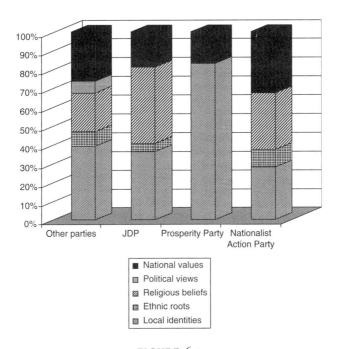

FIGURE 6.5

Sources of primary identifications and party choice in Turkey

SOURCE: 2005 Tepe-Religious Party Support data

NOTE: JDP is Justice and Development Party.

identities are capable of endowing different groups with a broader identity that extends beyond the realm of local identities. Their capacity to form overarching identities seems to position them as political rivals in an environment where the risk of polarized pluralism exists.

Religious Party Supporters and the Politics of the Extreme Right Defining religious party supporters using the conventional political markers Left and Right further introduces us to the increasing hollowness of such terms, the shifting contours of political competitions, and the elusive location of religious parties in Turkey. As explained in Chapter Four, the term *Left* acquired a rather unique meaning in Turkey's new polity and came to signify advocates of policies that sought to forge national cultural unity as well as state-sponsored socioeconomic development projects to ensure equality. In the eyes of right-wing supporters, "the Left allowed limited space for individuals and defined them as unidimensional secular citizens, opposed to alternative conceptions of citizenship."[56] In this ideological division of labor, the Left is seen as the political vision that opened the door for authoritarian policies to secure the welfare of the citizens, while the Right represents traditional cultural values and more freedom for individuals and nonstate market initiatives. Yet these distinctions have been in flux, posing the question of to what extent the political map of Turkey, its extremist tendencies, and more importantly, the politics of Islam can be captured by these terms.

The shifting placements on the Left–Right spectrum with respect to different issues are by no means unique to Turkey. On the contrary, as explained earlier, similar discrepancies urged scholars like Bobbio to argue that Left and Right remain relevant as they represent relational, not absolute, signifiers. In essence, Left and Right help us to place parties on two issue dimensions: (1) ensuring overall liberties at the expense of some inequality or (2) endorsing authoritarian policies for the common good by sacrificing some freedoms.[57] Overall, the Left views equality as the final product of politics, whereas the Right focuses on liberty as politics' main input and accepts natural inequality. If we accept Bobbio's argument and assume that despite its changing meanings and its narrowing range, the Left–Right spectrum still matters, then we must tackle the vexing question of where to locate religious parties in relation to other parties. After all, it is not only how the NV parties or the JDP position themselves on the left or right but also where the other parties stand in the country's ideological spectra that affects the electorate's voting decisions.

Since the 1980 coup, political parties have used the Left–Right terms to prove that they are center parties and not extremists. This galvanization of the center has complicated the use of the spectrum in Turkish politics. For instance, in reaction to its characterization as the radical Right, the NAP declared itself the "least understood party in Turkish politics," a portrayal that now serves as a powerful slogan in party circles.[58] Recai Kutan's explanation of the Prosperity Party's stand on the Left–Right spectrum captures the position of pro-Islamic parties in general:

We are often asked if we are on the Left or Right, or if we are trying to become a center party. First, we do not accept the conventional definition of Left and Right. But if you ask who represents the center, the reasonable answer should be the center defines whoever represents the beliefs, world views, visions and desires of the nation. The most essential criterion [to decide which party is at the center] is the nation's views. Whichever party distances itself from the desires of the nation becomes a fringe party. We believe that we represent our people's views and beliefs best. Therefore, the Virtue Party must be the center party.[59]

The rhetorical orientation of the parties toward the center reflects the parties' deep-seated fears of being punished for holding strictly ideological positions. It also ushers in the emergence of a new mode of politics in which it becomes an arena for competition, not over different policy objectives, but over electing efficient executors of agreed-upon policies to ensure political stability and growth in the market. Against this backdrop, any reference to ideology suggests the possibility of dogmatic commitment, thus risking political instability. As a result and perhaps more so than for nonreligious parties, the NAP, the Prosperity Party, and later the JDP have tried to define themselves ideologically as center parties.

A comparison of the self-placement of these parties' supporters along the Left–Right spectrum suggests that the party leadership's disassociation from the polar markers is not merely rhetorical. According to the 1996 World Values Survey, the number of NAP supporters who considered themselves at the center or left of the center ironically increased at the same time that the prevalent image of the NAP as a Far Right party grew even more. In 1995, 16 percent of the NAP supporters and 25 percent of the Prosperity supporters identified themselves as at the center or left of the center respectively, in contrast to their characterization as anti-Left. As the NAP reached the apex of its power in 1999, the number of NAP voters who identified themselves as left of the political center climbed to 29 percent. In the same year, as support for the Prosperity Party eroded, so did the number of center or left-of-center supporters. The swings suggest that the increasing popularity of the pro-Islamist parties results not only from an increasing Islamization of the public but also from growing voter volatility among the center and the center-left electorate.

Instead of using a scale, the 1996 and 1998 TÜSES surveys asked respondents to identify themselves using three main groups: left-wingers, right-wingers and others. In 1996, 66.4 percent of NAP and 55.6 percent of Prosperity supporters defined themselves as right-wingers. In this simplified and contracted ideological space, 26.2 percent of the NAP and 28.8 percent of the Prosperity Party supporters viewed their ideological position *beyond* the Right-Left divide. Parallel to the transformation of the Israeli public, the total number of nonidentifiers increased as well, so much so that they constituted almost one-third of Prosperity Party supporters. The overall percentage of those who did not want to place themselves on the left or right climbed dramatically to 19.7 percent nationwide in 2001. The percentage of those who viewed their political position beyond the left and right was highest among JDP and Prosperity supporters, indicating the emergence of the *critical electorate,* a new genre of voters who evade conventional labels.

The 2001 and 2005 surveys show that the Kurdish ethnic party, DEHAP, the Democratic People's Party, and the NAP, define the Far Left and Far Right end of the Left–Right spectrum, respectively. These parties differ from each other in many regards. The former is an ethnic party whose ideology is rooted in a class struggle and that subscribes to political decentralization. The latter is a religious and nationalist party that promotes political centralization and the unifying role of ethnic-religious identities. What makes this spectrum more intricate is that other parties who are placed on the right, such as the Prosperity and JDP parties, share many political positions of the DEHAP and also strive for political decentralization. In fact, in Turkey's southeast region, the Prosperity and the JDP parties successfully established themselves as viable political alternatives to the DEHAP.[60]

Putting politics under the lenses of the Left–Right spectrum draws our attention to several contradictory trends. The ideological markers defy the conventional dividing line where the positions of extreme Left and Right converge on a set of issues. An increasing number of people declare that their views are not accommodated by the Left–Right spectrum, whereas those who do place themselves within that framework increasingly choose the right side of the spectrum. This seemingly inconsistent picture can be described as an era of massive political reconfiguration, where generally successive processes of realignment and dealignment unfold at the same time. They form parallel to the transformation of Israeli politics: while the electorate dissociates itself from existing parties and political positions (i.e., the initial stage of realignment), voters do not form new political alliances, but increasingly disengage from politics (i.e., de-alignment) and look for alternatives to spur the policies in the right direction by assigning roles to actors other than the state (i.e., the conventional Right position). Amid these changes, a swing toward right-wing positions (from 5, the average placement score on the Left–Right spectrum in 2001, to 6 in 2005) indicates that the Left cannot present itself as a viable option.

The puzzling result, however, is the electoral collapse of center-right parties, despite political forces that favor the Right. The gap raises the question of why the electorate shied away from center-right parties that appeared to be closer to their ideal position than the far-Right parties. After all, both directional and proximity models of voting tell us that the ideological affinity between voters and parties defines how the electorate decides on its party choice. Under the directional voting model, voters support parties that are likely to change government policies in the direction they prefer. In contrast, the proximity model proposes that the electorate votes for parties closest to their ideological positions.[61] When viewed from these conventional models of voting, the 2002 election is a conundrum, empirically as well as conceptually, since the electorate voted for the JDP, a party without a policy-making record and not clearly different from far-Right parties.

A review of the ideological positions of the existing parties offers a solution to the enigmatic rise of the JDP. First, the location of political parties from the electorate's perspective draws our attention to a possible disconnect between some scholarly and public placements of the parties and the importance of what we can call the compensatory factor—the confidence in the party's capacity to enforce or execute policies evenhandedly, making it more appealing than those that appear to be weak enforcers. It is not the position per se, but the extent to which people find the position coherent and reliable that makes a difference. Ideological homogeneity (i.e., the standard deviation around a given party's average ideological score), or the degree to which individuals agree on a party's position, also indicates that the electorate favors parties with clear ideological views. On the right side of the map, the JDP and NAP occupy opposite locations: the higher ideological complexity attributed to the NAP contrasts with the ideological homogeneity of the JDP (see figure 6.6). The NAP creates a sense of ambivalence among the electorate, possibly due to its Turkish-Islamic idealism. Considering the ultrapragmatism of the other parties and their inability to deliver on their political promises, one can argue that this placement needs to be seen in relative terms. It is also important to note that being a political unknown and striking a delicate balance between being an anti-status quo without being an anti-systemic party might have been a political asset for the JDP in the 2002 and 2005 elections. In fact, many participants in public debates described "not a tested party" as a positive quality, especially during the period of economic and political crises, when the "tested" center parties seemed to be failing and deadlocked.

The ideological Left-Right dispersion of the main parties suggests that such unidimensional spectra alone are weak tools for understanding the position of individuals. The JDP has, in fact, carefully positioned itself at the center of the Right parties as opposed to the far Right. The inability of all center parties to pass the national threshold in the 2002 elections

suggests that an ideological position per se cannot account for their electoral fortunes. A noticeable gap exists at the ideological center of Turkish
politics, and it represents not the presence of parties, but rather a void,
created by the voters' lack of trust in the solidity of the center parties'
ideological commitments. In Turkey's crisis-ridden political context, pro-
Islamic parties present themselves as more viable candidates with a clear
message, a record of service delivery, and direct ties to the electorate.

The Left–Right spectrum does not capture the credibility of the parties'
messages and the individuals' belief in the extent to which they can enforce their policies. In fact, when respondents were asked in 1998 which
party represented the rights of individuals against injustices, 45.5 percent
argued that there was no such party in Turkish politics. By the same token,

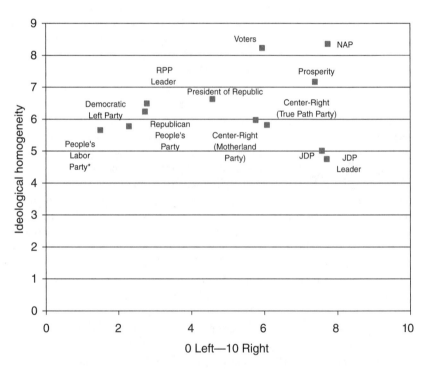

FIGURE 6.6

*Political positioning of parties and leaders on the Left-Right
spectrum, 2005*

SOURCE: 2005 Tepe-Religious Party Support Data

*The People's Labor Party is the predecessor of DEHAP.

when asked which party could solve Turkey's problems most effectively, 46.5 percent of the supporters of other parties stated that none of the existing parties could solve the issues salient to them. Around one-third of the Prosperity and NAP supporters declared that they believed that their party would resolve the problems. The lack of confidence in the parties increased to such a level that in 2005 the main party representing the political Left, the RPP, was identified as one of the least-trusted political institutions in Turkish politics. Pro-Islamic parties, in general, rank higher on the trust ladder, while the JDP appears as the most-trusted political party (see table 6.2). This trust is both crucial and relative, given the overall mistrust in political institutions and the trend of disengagement from politics. In fact, only 40.5 percent of the 3,400 respondents in the 2001 World Values Survey for Turkey agreed that politics is an important venue for changing existing policies. By the same token, 66 percent stated that they are not interested in politics. This stunning disengagement explains why more than 20 percent of eligible voters abstained—illegally—from voting in the 2002 election, an election marked by the preceding economic and political crises.

Religious Party Supporters and the Politics of Crisis   As discussed earlier, the crisis model views pro-Islamic party voters as "vulnerables" who seek refuge from socioeconomic crises under the shelter of religious parties. Facing resilient external factors that threaten to consign them to permanent loser positions, the electorate turns to pro-Islamic parties that promise change and economic justice in contrast to traditional political practices and irresponsible economic growth. The pro-Islamic identities of these parties are instrumental, as they promise economic improvements without radically changing the social and cultural rubric of society. The parties' core promises are successfully captured in the NAP's once very popular electoral slogan "change without alienation." More nuanced explanations draw our attention also to those who have benefited from Turkey's economically liberalizing macropolicies, but who still feel that they have not had a fair opportunity to enhance their resources and socioeconomic status. The crisis argument states that those who are more vulnerable to the negative impacts of socioeconomic reforms, as well as those socially mobilized yet handicapped by the existing system, form the natural constituencies of religious parties. Thus, the main political currency for religious parties, beyond their religious appearance, is political apathy triggered by discrimination and persistent exclusion.

In fact, the 2005 survey shows that 61 percent of JDP supporters define themselves as economic survivors who barely make ends meet, but who also see themselves, paradoxically, as middle class. Similar findings at first strongly corroborate crisis explanations, yet, as in the Israeli case, they need to be broadened to include the relative positioning of supporters.

TABLE 6.2
The state of political trust in Turkish politics

	JDP supporters			Prosperity supporters			NAP supporters			Others			Overall trust (0–10 scale)
	Don't trust	Uncertain	Trust	Don't trust	Uncertain	Trust	Don't trust	Uncertain	Trust	Don't trust	Uncertain	Trust	
Justice and Development Party	5.6%	13.3%	81.1%	33.3%	—	66.7%	37.2%	23.3%	39.5%	40.9%	21.6%	37.6%	6.07%
Republican People Party	72.2%	17.1%	10.7%	100.0%	—	—	88.4%	11.6%		57.0%	20.2%	22.8%	2.89%
Turkish National Assembly	12.2%	13.5%	74.2%	16.7%	33.3%	50.0%	23.3%	18.6%	58.1%	28.5%	20.9%	50.6%	6.47%
State	9.4%	9.9%	80.6%	16.7%	33.3%	50.0%	18.6%	9.3%	72.1%	24.3%	19.7%	56.0%	7.01%
Military	7.9%	7.9%	84.2%	16.7%	33.3%	50.0%	4.7%	9.3%	86.0%	13.4%	9.2%	77.4%	8.09%
Constitution	12.2%	13.5%	74.2%	50.0%	16.7%	33.3%	20.9%	11.6%	67.4%	17.4%	13.9%	68.7%	7.24%
European Union	33.9%	23.7%	42.3%	66.7%	16.7%	16.7%	53.5%	16.3%	30.2%	33.2%	20.9%	45.9%	5.06%
International Monetary Fund	62.8%	24.0%	13.3%	100%	—	—	88.4%	11.6%	—	68.5%	20.2%	11.3%	2.46%

SOURCE: Tepe 2005 Religious Party Support data

NOTE: All questions asked the respondents to indicate their level of trust in a given institution by using a 0–10 scale. The percentages indicate the distribution of trust among each party's followers listed in the columns. Overall trust scores indicate the average rating of the institutions or leaders.

Turkey's remarkably uneven income distribution relegates around 59 percent of nonreligious party followers to the "economic survivors" category
as well. Perhaps far more striking is the consistent finding that about one-
fourth of JDP supporters come from economically better-off voters, and
that the NAP is supported by an even higher share of this group (37.1 percent). The Prosperity Party maintains a core consistency of supporters
that is perfectly divided between the economically vulnerable and those
who are better off. Thus, the self-identification of economic status of
religious-party supporters disproves some overemphasized correlations
that highlight conceptually consistent and convenient explanations, yet
whose cumulative effect can nonetheless be misleading.

Other demographic factors, such as age and the location on Turkey's
geographical peripheries, reveal some intricate patterns that cannot easily
be subsumed under the politics of crisis or resentment. For instance, one
would expect that the "vulnerables" would come from older, less competitive age groups. Likewise, those with fixed incomes or those at the lower
end of the socioeconomic ladder would seem to be the most likely proreligious partisans. However, the demographic characteristics of the NAP,
the Prosperity Party, and the JDP illustrate that while each party has some
base of support in all age groups, the rate of support declines with increases in age. This persistent pattern is reminiscent of Beck's political socialization thesis. Perhaps a new mode of political socialization breeds
new trends, such as disengagements from politics or shifts in the existing
political alignments, preparing voters to see proreligious parties as more
appealing or strategic choices.[62]

The politics of resentment and the peripheralization theses are often
translated into the regional division of labor among parties, where religious parties represent traditional segments of society or rural, semiur-
ban groups. Pro-Islamic parties seem to be better connected with the religious symbols and ideas that dominate public life in these settings. Some
of these rural supporters have recently moved to big metropolitan areas.
An analysis of the local elective offices won by the JDP in the March
2004 municipal election shows that the JDP succeeded in areas where the
politics of resentment thesis would have predicted the party's failure. At
the regional level, the JDP was able to penetrate West Marmara and
southeastern Turkey, the bastion of the secular RPP and a predominantly
Kurdish area. For instance, in East Marmara the JDP won 23.2 percent
of the votes as opposed to the RPP's 24.1 percent share, and in southeastern Anatolia the JDP garnered 26 percent of the votes as opposed to
the Kurdish DEHAP's 28.8 percent. Thus, the pro-Islamic parties' successes might result not from being the most preferred party, but the
second-best choice for those who find voting for their primary preference

too costly for various reasons. The NAP's growth mirrored the JDP's pattern of electoral expansion and repeated its increasing success in regions not previously considered its strongholds, such as the south and west (25.3 percent and 22.5 percent respectively). Thus, the ascendance of religious parties seems to stem not exclusively from the reactions of traditional groups in the periphery but from the support of the traditionals or moderates who see the parties as viable alternatives to their competitors.

The increasing heterogeneity of the urban setting has reduced the urban/rural dichotomy's analytical purchase. For instance, the nearly equal level of support for the NAP and Prosperity in rural and urban districts indicates that these parties are neither urban- nor rural-based parties. The NAP enjoys a slight advantage in rural areas, while the Prosperity Party and JDP maintain a similar slight advantage in urban areas. A closer look at the municipal offices won by the JDP reveals that the JDP emerged as the top vote getter in those regions that ranked highest in economic development and average level of income, attesting to the transformation of the Islamic constituency and disproving the thesis that its support is based in economically marginalized municipalities.[63]

The issue space (i.e., the identification and distribution of issues) defined by the electorate indicates that there appears to be a significant consensus among voters. For example, the electorate's overwhelming concern with economic issues such as unemployment has shown to cut across ideological divides. As a result, neither the broad issue of the economy nor the economic self-assessment of individuals can be used any longer to decisively differentiate religious party voters from others. The detailed questions asked in the 1996 and 1998 surveys allow us a closer look at how religious party supporters select and rank pressing issues (see table 6.3). The Prosperity Party supporters diverge from others with their attention to systemic issues, such as "how the country is run" and institutional ones pertaining to education. The most pressing issues reported for JDP and Prosperity supporters indicate that they avoid some of the issues that dominate the national agenda. The "terror" issue, for instance, is often used as a proxy for the Kurdish problem and appears as the third most prominent topic after the economy and unemployment. NAP supporters are more responsive to unemployment, foreign policy, and terror-related problems, reflecting the party's ties to male youths through ülkü ocaks. Although important, the issue of unemployment is less urgent to Prosperity supporters. JDP and Prosperity supporters consider systemic issues such as corruption, religious issues, human rights, and education more salient. It is important to note that the "other" category (i.e., issues that cannot be accommodated

TABLE 6.3

Salient issues for NAP, Prosperity, and JDP supporters

2007	NAP (% distribution within the party)	Prosperity	JDP	Others
Economic issues/poverty	39.2	47.4	42.1	36.5
Corruption	25.2	33.3	26.6	22
Activities against laicism	11.9	1.3	6.1	20.1
Activities against democracy	7.9	6.4	9.0	9.7
Social security system	13.3	6.4	11.6	9.2
Others	2.0	5.1	4.2	2.2

1998	NAP	Prosperity	Others
Economy	48.3	34.7	47.9
Unemployment	15.2	8.9	10.5
Terror	15.2	12.4	11.4
Corruption	7.3	11.6	7.6
Others	7.9	15.1	16.0
Religious issues	1.7	7.3	1.5
Human rights/democracy	1.1	5.0	2.0
Education	1.7	3.9	2.0
Foreign relations	1.7	1.2	1.1

1996	NAP	Prosperity	Others
Economy	39.3	43.6	47.8
Unemployment	18.9	14.3	10.8
Terror	24.6	14.4	16.6
The way the country is run/corruption	.8	6.25	3.9
Others	9.1	17.5	13.5
Human rights/democracy	2.5	1.1	2.5
Education	0	.8	1.9
Foreign relations	4.9	2.1	2.1

SOURCES: 2007 Konda Survey (the results draw on a nationally representative survey of 3,189 Turkish voters conducted in July of 2007) and 1996 and 1998 TÜSES data

under the main groupings) appears as the second most pivotal issue classification among Prosperity supporters in 1996 and 1998. The popularity of "other" can be seen as one reason pro-Islamic party supporters have become estranged from the center parties, which, by coalescing around the same issues and adopting similar policies, narrow their shared political space. Regardless of the reasons, an important segment of the JDP and Prosperity supporters seem to question the rules of power sharing.

The Politics of Islam as a Choice   As in the case of Israel, proreligious NAP, Prosperity, and JDP supporters are characterized by their diversity not by their homogeneity. The broad differences that characterize the coalitions of supporters defy reductionist theories and open a space for the emergence of other explanations. The relative importance of various voter characteristics for religious party support, such as gender, education, age, and primary identity, among others, are best addressed in a multinomial model. Such a model offers analytical leverage over others as it allows us to review the individual, the relative, and the cumulative impact at the same time. As noted earlier, radical shifts in voter support occurred across the 1995, 1999, and 2002 elections. The 1995 election was marked by the success of the Prosperity Party; the NAP captured the highest plurality in its history in 1999; and the JDP transformed itself from an opposition movement within the Prosperity Party to the most popular national party in 2002. Given these shifts, the multinomial models based on 1996 TÜSES data, 2001 Turkish election study, and 2005 Religious Party Support data allow us to probe into the shifting terrain of voting decisions during the decisive periods when the politics of religion dominated the political scene.

Party preference, in all models, describes the respondents' propensity to vote for the NAP or the Prosperity Party as opposed to their competitors. The 2005 data focus specifically on the JDP and NAP votes, as the Prosperity Party almost disappeared from Turkey's political map after receiving only around 2 percent of the total votes. The demographic and attitudinal characteristics included in the multinomial models include gender, education, age, primary identification, socioeconomic standing, trust in parties, income, and a general assessment of economic and ethnic policies and level of participation. *Primary identification* denotes how individuals describe their main political and cultural identity on a continuum from particularistic ethnic and religious groups (i.e., Alevi, Kurdish), to religious identity (Sunni, Turkish/Sunni), to secular national Turkish. *Perceived socioeconomic standing* is used here to report the 1996 overall assessment of a given individual's status in society, from lower to higher (the coding in the 2001 data used the opposite order [from national to local]); *trust in parties* captures whether a respondent felt confident that parties, in general, can resolve the major problems facing the country. The inclusion of trust enables us to explore whether respondents feel alienated from the political system or believe the existing political institutions have the capacity to improve the system (external efficacy). *General assessment* determines whether the respondents believe that their overall situation has improved or not.

Participation is an index variable that ranks the respondents' involvement in politics from minimum (only voting) to maximum involvement (attending meetings and taking part in campaign activities). In the model based on the 1996 TÜSES data (1996 model), the assessment of ethnic policies (*ethnic liberalism*) is defined as a tripartite variable. In this model 1 denotes the respondents who consider ethnic demands a reflection of ethnic separatism and favor more restrictions on ethnic cultural rights; 2 indicates that respondents are content with the status quo; and 3 includes those who consider the current practices repressive and seek further liberalization of ethnic rights.

The 1996 model confirms that the crisis and conflict models find some support when we explain individual choices. Yet conclusions devoid of an inclusion of other factors and broader context of decision making simultaneously can lend themselves to some confounding generalization (see table 6.4). In fact, their ostensibly contradictory accounts complement each other, effectively revealing the complexity of *why* people turn to pro-Islamic parties. For instance, consistent with the politics of resentment, when individuals report a low social and economic status, it increases their propensity to vote for either one of the pro-Islamic parties instead of their rivals. However, the relative effect of perceived socio-economic status is higher for the NAP than for the Prosperity. It is striking that, when all other explanatory factors for pro-Islamic party support are included, socioeconomic standing as a predictor of support for the Prosperity and the NAP ranks low. Support for the Prosperity Party seems to be most affected by income level and changes in social position. Economic status variables constitute a secondary vote trigger (i.e., their coefficient is not as high as the others) for NAP supporters. The higher level of political participation of the younger male age group and their reaction to political diversity (e.g., the extension of further rights to ethnic groups) help us to better explain the NAP's support.

Likewise, the differential yet very close impact of education blurs the dichotomy introduced by the tension between center and periphery and blunts the idea that higher education alleviates reactions to the secular Kemalist creed. Support for pro-Islamic parties would be expected to decrease with higher levels of education due to the state monopoly on education exposing young people to secular values. In a striking parallel to the differences between Mafdal and Shas backing, the educational and primary identities of voters have opposite effects upon NAP and Prosperity support in every year but 2001. If we look at the overriding pattern, the tendency to vote for the NAP rises with increasing levels of education, while decreasing levels of education seem to raise the odds of voting for the Prosperity Party. The primary identity of voters (ethnic, religious, or national) turns out to be one of the least effective predictors of a religious party vote. However, the more a person accentuates his or her Turkishness, as opposed to other ethnic or religious particularistic dimensions of identity, the more likely this person is to support the NAP. Conversely, the more individuals emphasize the ethnic particularistic dimension of their identity, the more they tend to support the Prosperity Party.

Competition between national unity as part of the Islamic "religious community" and the ethnic historical "national community" differentiates JDP, Prosperity, and NAP supporters from others. Less visible in the relationship of pro-Islamic parties to identity is the fact that diverging meanings are increasingly attached to Muslimness, especially among supporters of the Prosperity Party and the JDP. Muslimness at first appears to serve as a broad melting pot of competing identities. JDP and Prosperity partisans view Muslimness not in conjunction with local identities, but as an overarching classification that transcends local identities rendering them irrelevant as competing sources of political loyalties. This is why the ethnic liberalization variable, which asks individuals to assess the existing policies regarding ethnicity, diffuses the differences between the NAP and Prosperity supporters. Despite their differences, support for both organizations rises as respondents support restrictions on parties with a strictly ethnic (read ethnic non-religious or in some cases anti-religious) platform.

Given the capacity of Muslimness to declare competing identities politically secondary and its ability to couple itself with the national identity, the central role of Muslimness in NAP's support seems consistent with the party's opposition to ethnic liberalization. Perhaps more perplexing is that those who view their primary identities in *ethnic* religious terms are more likely to support the Prosperity Party, while their political attitudes indicate that they are likely to oppose ethnic liberalization. These seemingly paradoxical patterns stem from the ability of Islam to espouse opposing messages concurrently. What seems to be Muslimness's attraction to opposing reasons alerts us to the possibility that the political demands rooted in distinctive public identities in isolation are not at the heart of pro-Islamic party support. While both Muslimness and Kurdishness play important roles in supporting the Prosperity Party, the party's ability to reach Kurdish voters stems neither from (1) its platform of enhancing ethnic diversity per se, nor (2) its commitment to contain existing value-plurality rooted in different traditions, nor (3) its assumed role in accommodating individuals' distinctive cultural practices and beliefs. It is instead linked to the pro-Islamic parties' emphases on Muslimness as a common identity, which deems other latent identities as secondary to politics and allows the electorate to bring to the fore other issues. In the final analysis, these results seem to suggest that underlying the National View parties' and the JDP's pluralist projects and ethnic appeals is not an effort to recognize distinctive identities on their own terms, but a reductionist approach that presumes that a national identity defined in religious terms will cease to be a political problem.

The patterns elicited by the self-assessment and demographic characteristics of the voters warn us that political alienation theses are not readily tenable. The multiplicity of ways in which the trust-in-parties variable affect voting decisions questions the description of the politics of Islam as politics of reaction and resentment. One's trust in parties can be captured by the degree to which voters endorse the belief that "major parties can solve the problems facing the country." The wording of the question lumps "one of the major parties" together as a broad range of parties without specifying names. This wholesale approach might complicate the assessments, yet the results still warn us against the janus-faced nature of the confidence in institutions and the overall assessment of parties. For instance, in 1996 the propensity to vote for both parties increased as the voters stated that one of the parties would be affective in addressing the main problems afflicting their lives. By itself this finding partially refutes the political alienation thesis, which tells us that the depleted confidence in political parties and the resulting political disengagement triggers reactionary voting and support for religious parties. However, the trust variable had a differential impact after 1996. For instance, the 2001 results show that the skepticism about the parties increased the odds of voting for NAP. Although still very limited, the trust in parties' ability to solve problems increased JDP support. Alas, the impact was reversed again in 2005 when mistrust in the system triggered JDP votes while trust in the system evoked NAP support. The results indicate that the assessment of parties does not have a uniform effect, suggesting that the electorate does not turn to religious parties due to their chronic apathy. "Trust in political institutions and parties" needs to be evaluated in tandem with other patterns, especially against the low trust environment of Turkish politics. The findings also encourage us to approach confidence in institutions and trust not only as exogenous (i.e., external) to religious party support but also as endogenous.

When we broaden our analysis to include a detailed participation index, political participation, rather than political disaffection, surfaces as the main trigger of support for both parties. The participation index includes political activities beyond the compulsory act of voting, from frequent involvement in political discussions to taking an active part in a political party. Religious party supporters differ from others in their political activities since they do not merely limit their engagement with politics to what can be called "habitual involvement," such as legally required voting. Voting for pro-Islamic parties is not a one-day-at-the-ballot-box activity. In contrast to the NAP, the JDP and the Prosperity supporters are efficient players in politics. Their political endeavors are more numerous than those of other party followers, which contradicts the assumption that political alienation and overall loss of confidence in politics is responsible for religious party support. The high degree of political participation of religious party supporters may foster their dichotomized perception of politics: high levels of trust in selected parties and in politics at the local level contrast with increasing skepticism about institutions and politics at the national level. The centrality of participation reflects the pro-Islamic parties' successful mobilization of the electorate toward creating political communities, not in conventional, limited patronage terms, but as a way to create political ideas.

Any assessment of religious parties quickly reveals that they are masters of political communication. Their inventiveness, however, results from several factors. These parties not only disseminate ideas but create new practices both through drawing on and altering traditional settings. For instance, religious gatherings or home visits serve as "habitual" traditional venues for political communications, but they also acquire new meanings due to the parties' organizational efforts. The party-sponsored networks blur the strict distinction between home and street, private and public. Blending the old way of interacting with new ways of relating and forming communities, party activists are able to effectively answer the questions of potential recruits. These communications are highly structured, however, and it is not rare for activists to take communication lessons. Extensive use of religious allegories and symbols eases the communication gap, and in the first visits, party representatives resolve any questions the individual might have and collect the relevant information to effectively integrate the person into the network. This personal connections-based approach is infeasible for conventional parties, whose symbolic spheres do not allow them to penetrate into private domains and whose organizational networks fail to forge continuous interactions. Thus, religious parties might draw individuals into their realm of politics on the basis of their disillusionment with existing institutions and agents. However, those who turn to religious parties do not limit their political engagement to "voting" and therefore do not dwell on their negative assessment of institutions; instead, they actively participate in politics to develop interaction-based political capital, which can be used toward fixing the game of politics. For this reason, political mistrust and formal schooling emerge as important, yet relatively poor, predictors of religious party support. Pro-Islamic parties are able to transform the initial mistrust of their partisans into trust. Supporters learn to have faith in the parties' ability to deliver political results effectively.

The high level of engagement of pro-Islamic party supporters points out the importance of the "informational subsidy," "political learning,"

TABLE 6.4

A multinomial logit model of religious party support in Turkey

1996	NAP (odd ratios standard coefficient)	Prosperity	2001	NAP	Prosperity	2005	NAP	JDP
Socio-economic standing	.89* (−1.19)	.91* (−1.72)	Age group	.68** (−2.01)	.86 (−0.65)	Age	1.29*** (2.52)	1.27*** (4.92)
Income	.87** (−2.10)	.77*** (−6.55)	Education	.98 (−0.15)	.79* (−1.42)	Education	1.16 (0.79)	.97 (−0.33)
Education	1.24** (2.00)	.89** (−1.78)	Gender	2.25*** (2.77)	1.88** (1.84)	Gender	.5220* (−1.52)	.939 (−0.34)
Age	.451*** (−4.90)	.790*** (−2.85)	Religiosity	1.73*** (3.45)	2.27*** (4.12)	Individual Islam	1.34 (1.21)	1.97*** (6.25)
Perceived socioeconomic position	.912** (−1.72)	.887*** (−1.19)	Primary identity	.744* (−1.60)	1.032 (0.19)	Social Islam	.678* (−1.35)	1.153 (1.16)
Assessment of change in socioeconomic standing	.697** (−2.0)	.615*** (−4.96)	Income groups	970 (−0.26)	1.061 (0.46)	Laicism	.756** (−1.84)	.774*** (−3.6)
Primary identification	1.068* (1.23)	.949* (−1.75)	Trust in parties	.845 (−0.79)	1.037 (0.17)	Change in socioeconomic status	1.186 (0.77)	.653*** (−4.05)

(continued)

TABLE 6.4
A multinomial logit model of religious party support in Turkey (continued)

1996	NAP (odd ratios standard coefficient)	Prosperity	2001	NAP	Prosperity	2005	NAP	JDP
Evaluation of ethnic policies	.652*** (-3.59)	.792** (-3.46)	Trust in military	1.271*** (3.58)	.857*** (-3.09)	Income	1.002 (0.02)	.873*** (-2.13)
Participation	2.409*** (6.09)	2.081*** (9.60)	Political knowledge	1.105* (1.40)	.949 (-0.72)	Headscarf	.446*** (-3.08)	.739*** (-3.02)
Trust in parties	1.407*** (0.92)	1.1508*** (0.95)	Ethnic rights	.914 (-0.51)	.828 (-0.84)	Trust in state	.919 (-0.32)	1.433*** (2.89)
Gender	3.304*** (4.73)	1.250* (1.94)	Change in economic conditions	.890 (-0.46)	.503* (-1.96)	Trust in military	1.9521* (1.66)	1.102 (0.68)
			Religious leader	1.004 (0.09)	1.583*** (6.37)	Political participation	1.113 (1.13)	.945* (-1.22)
						Party effectiveness	.904 (-0.49)	1.216** (2.06)
						Ethnic rights	.428*** (-3.76)	.912 (-1.03)
						Religious rights	1.0 (0.66)	1.0 (1.01)
						Identity	1.07	.924 (-1.45)

SOURCES: 1996 TÜSES Data; 2001 Turkish National Election Data; 2005 Religious Party Support data
NOTE: ***, **, and * indicate the coefficient is significant at 0.01, 0.05, and 0.10 levels respectively.

and "trust building" activities—main ingredients of political engagement that are generated and reinforced among the voters through their involvement with party institutions. The unofficial political learning and transformation that supporters gain through party-affiliated institutions and the ideas forged during their mobilization need to be included in the analysis of both parties' support.

The multinomial logit model based on the 2001 survey includes some variables not available in the 1996 and 1998 surveys (see table 6.4). Their addition enables us to explore more deeply how religious parties in general, and the NAP in particular, bring together seemingly opposite perspectives. The patterns identified provide further evidence for the argument that the conflict and clash explanations do not offer alternative approaches; instead, the processes they build on are intertwined at a deeper level. As opposed to looking for a silver bullet or randomly mixing different factors, we need to ask how the main traits of the political context, the efforts of the parties and the views of the electorate, interweave and seek to tease out the dynamic processes they unleash. Unless reciprocal interactions and alterations are recognized, a static model can fail to identify significant transformations and amplify the importance of short-term dispositions. For example, the 2001 model reveals the first signs of a new pattern that becomes more pronounced in the 2005 model. For instance, backing for the NAP intensifies as people both put more trust in the military, the guardian of secularist ideology and the state's unity, and see themselves as more religious than others. This emerging voter profile could be translated into a new political position such as "Kemalist-Islamist voter," or, "authoritarian Islamist." Both, however, are oxymorons in Turkey's political landscape. Not only do these two seemingly contradictory positions have a mutually reinforcing and positive influence on the NAP, they also emerge as two of the most important determinants for NAP support. Such unexpected results attest to the parties' ability to conduct a dual discourse. They not only blend clashing commitments rhetorically, they make them relevant to the electorate. The NAP expresses the political option of collectively subscribing to status quo nationalism and anti–status quo religious communalism as a congruous position. In a striking contrast, Prosperity supporters come from those who are religious, but who are also critical of the status quo nationalism and the role of the military.

The declining impact of education on the NAP votes challenges the patterns revealed in earlier models. Considering that the 2001 survey was taken after the party reached the apex of its power in 1999, the growth of support seems to be related to the party's ability to attract a more hybrid voter profile. Another intriguing change in the characterization of pro-Islamic party voters is the general shift in the relative importance of their ethnic and primary identity. The increasing tendency of NAP supporters to emphasize their local and religious identities might be a reflection of the efforts of the party leadership to promote a more inclusive discourse on diversity. The party's 1999 motto, "We are a party of determined men, not like those hesitators [cowards]," embodied the party's discourse that appealed not only to the young, male electorate, but also to disaffected pro-Islamic supporters who had become increasingly critical of Prosperity's inability to address the issues pertaining to the public role of Islam.

In the 2001 model, the Prosperity and NAP supporters are distinguished from other parties by their trust in the political stewardship of a religious leader. Behind this convergence, once again, lie disparate reasons. The two parties differ on how much their confidence is related to the ability of a religious leader to govern the country. Votes for the Prosperity Party increase dramatically with the respondents' growing confidence in the national leadership skills of a religious leader. NAP supporters seem to limit their ideas only to an approval of moral values of such leaders. Without making their positive assessment a main determinant of their voting decisions.

By the same token, it is important to note that while the 2005 results show NAP supporters applying religion to their social decisions more than we expect considering their lower level of individual Islamic practices (in comparison to the JDP supporters), this social application remains limited. When we expand the scope of social Islam (i.e., one's tendency to decide on social issues using Islamic principles) to include the reconfiguration of the public sphere according to Islamic practices (e.g., allowing for the rules on inheritance and marriages guided by Islam) NAP and JDP supporters differ significantly from one another. When social Islam is conceptualized in its broadest sense, a person's propensity to apply Islamic rules to their social practices increases their tendency to support the JDP while decreasing the tendency to vote for NAP.

To this end, the variable *ethnic rights* in the 2005 model estimates to what extent the respondents want to grant further rights to ethnic groups. A one indicates the respondents are against the extension of cultural and political rights while a 3 indicates full support for ethnic diversity. The respondents' positions on the headscarf issue captures whether they (1) oppose the ban on the use of headscarves in state institutions or (3) support it. The *religious rights* variable assesses whether voters approve the expansion of the rights to heterodox religious groups; a 3 represents the demand for more rights and 1 a demand for more restrictions. *Individual Islam* is an index variable that measures the extent to which individuals observe Islamic commandments, with a ranking from none to complete observance. *Social Islam* gauges to what extent individuals use religion as a basis for social and political decisions. *Laicism* allows us to gauge the extent to which respondents support laicism. The *party efficiency* index is based on the respondents' perceptions of whether the major parties can address Turkey's problems effectively: a score of 1 tells us that the respondents find the parties effective, while 3 records that they believe the opposite. *Participation* is another index variable that describes respondents' level of engagement in politics, ranking their activities from none to frequently. *Change in socioeconomic status* ranges from much better, 1, to much worse, 7.

The inclusion of these factors in a model enables us to further question the theses that portray pro-Islamic movements either as indigenous local quests for, or hindrances of, further democratization of their respective regimes. Many such arguments, without looking deeper at the nature or scope of the demands, view religious parties' calls for the expansion of individual rights vis-à-vis the state as a critical step in the opening up of the public sphere to different views thus ultimately tantamount to the liberalization of the public sphere or the increasing domination of religion. Questions that share the common theme of rights, and especially religious rights, introduce us to the largely neglected aspects of respondents' positions, not only vis-à-vis the state's authoritarian policies, but also vis-à-vis other groups in the polity. Supporters of both the NAP and JDP converge in their positions on the headscarf issue: support for both parties grows with increasing objections to the turban ban. A different trend and a mixed picture emerge when we expand the scope of rights horizontally by shifting the focus from the state to groups, thereby attending more to the relationship between individuals. The findings show that the positions of individuals (1) on the expansion of the rights to allow all groups to pursue their rituals or beliefs and (2) the rights protecting individuals from the state do not overlap. In contrast the effect of the rights from variable one's support for expanding religious rights to heterodox and non-Islamic groups does not emerge as a significant determinant of the decision to vote for either JDP or NAP.

The growing convergence of the Prosperity Party and the NAP supporters shows that the coalition of believers in 1991 was formed due primarily to the electoral constraints but, nevertheless, was not merely a political convenience. The supporters came from a similar pool of citizens, and the coalition further reinforced the ideological affinity among them. The expansion of cultural rights to ethnic groups does not seem to play a significant role in the decision to vote for the JDP. However, opposition to the extension of ethnic rights surfaces as the main impetus for support of the NAP. The odds of voting for the party decrease drastically among those who advocate more rights for minorities. It is important to note that, perhaps due to the confluence of the heightened political apathy that helped define the 2002 election and the exponential increase in JDP's supporters, the 2005 data reveal an overall declining impact of political participation, but more so for the JDP than the NAP. Still, NAP voters come more from those with a high level of engagement in politics, while JDP supporters more accurately match the average profile of the Turkish electorate. In other words, the record high support for the JDP is partially attributable to the exponential increase of support among individuals only loosely connected to the party and whose participation is limited to a minimum level, that is, voting; thus the party's electoral support cannot be attributed to its organic growth (i.e., the grassroots expansion of its network) but successful electoral appeal to different groups.

The 2005 model brings several other anomalous patterns to the surface. For instance, the conventionally accepted antagonism of religious party supporters toward the military, the *trust in military* variable, does not have a substantial effect on the decisions of JDP supporters, nor does a negative assessment of the state. The odds of voting for the JDP increase by a factor of 1.43 when voters have higher confidence in the state. On the other hand, a negative assessment of the state seems to be associated with NAP supporters' tendencies to vote for the party, although its impact is rather limited. To complicate the picture further, support for both parties increases with the respondents' declining support for laicism. This finding seems inconsistent with the NAP's state-centered policy position.

It is important to note that the survey was held at a time when the JDP had reached the apex of its power and reconfigured and reinvented many institutions by passing an unprecedented number of bills in parliament. Considering that the NAP focuses on the historical mission of the state and not on its current, specific embodiment, the result suggests that NAP supporters perceive the JDP's radical reforms and control of the state as a crisis of stateness, that is, the legitimacy, capacity, and policies of the state. The lack of confidence may have been the result of the adopted reforms, rightfully described as the silent revolution by the JDP. The same reforms, and the JDP's political dominance of the state, not only convinced JDP supporters to trust the party, they also created a group of skeptics. The indifference of JDP supporters to the military, their opposition to laicism, and their elective quest for religious freedoms challenge value-centered politics and defy the monolithic sense of the tension between groups built around value politics. Pro-Islamic party supporters do not challenge the state as a whole but compartmentalize it. The policies of the state become more important than the state as an institution. The state and the military are not perceived to have uniform but changing impacts, and their defining role for pro-Islamic voters needs to be treated as a variable, rather than a constant. To assume the existence of a uniform, invariant opposition to the "establishment" obscures our understanding of pro-Islamic voters.

Overall, the multinomial model draws our attention to the presence of many atypical ideological couplings that remain undetected by the conflict and crisis explanations and/or obscured by their derivatives, such as the political alienation theses. Each approach needs to be carefully recalibrated by incorporating the gray areas that they have overlooked. For instance, the voters' lack of confidence in the effectiveness of political parties attests to the important dual role of religious politics: on the one hand, pro-Islamic parties are backed because of a lack of trust in the main parties, but on the other hand and more importantly, they are supported because they generate trust in politics. In effect, JDP supporters appear to be reacting to a crisis of political representation and policy making rather than to issues of stateness. When the religious issues are separated out, the model shows that increasing age and a longer practice of Islam enhance the odds of voting for the JDP. This support is not necessarily an opposition to secularist institutions; in fact, it is more situational.

Any attempt to treat Islam as a categorical group needs to take into account the individualization of Islam. This process can be seen as the individuals' regular practice of Islamic rituals as opposed to sporadic observances of folk Islam or communal practices. Folk Islam requires less effort and does not result in the deliberate creation of parallel, yet isolated life spheres (i.e., strict compartmentalization of religious and secular beliefs and practices) as the theories of secularism envision. In the individualization of Islam, we observe an increasing tendency to make decisions by relying on religious terms while still imbuing them with secular meanings and vice versa. In contrast to the Prosperity Party's once highly popular slogan, "We are the party of the oppressed," those who have experienced an improvement in their economic status tend to shift their support to the JDP. The JDP supporters, despite their lower income, come more from among those who have experienced a positive change in their socioeconomic status, while NAP supporters fall into the opposite category. Considering that the JDP's success represented an exponential expansion, it is not surprising that some of the earlier patterns got lost or became less visible. Taken together, the findings signal a transformation of the politics of Islam in Turkey: the growing importance of an individually grounded Islam as opposed to one that emphasizes and is experienced as a community. While other explanations, such as retrospective economic voting (i.e., voting based on the past economic performance of dominant parties), appear to be relevant, pro-Islamic parties seem to base their initial appeal on skepticism; they quickly replace it with trust based on political mobilization embedded in both traditional (e.g., coffee house meetings) and innovative, novel practices (e.g., public deliberation meetings led by activists who often get training in persuasive political communication) and forge forward-looking decisions that assign a positive role to the party.

Pro-Islamic or not, an important aspect of multiparty politics is not only the party's claimed position but the political meaning of this position vis-à-vis that of others. Especially in Turkey's competitive system, none of the parties can be understood in isolation from each other. As exemplified in Chapter Five and the discussion above, a one-dimensional political space cannot capture the main contours of political competition. The 2001 and 2005 surveys allow us to elicit the ideological standing of the parties as seen through the eyes of the electorate. The relative location of the parties describes the cognitive organization of voters and may lack the analytical consistency we expect. It is important to remember that the term *space* refers to the latent dimension that underlies political competitions.[64] While the voters' assessments of the parties may change, the model assumes that the latent space remains the same for each party. A spatial analysis is not a universal and decisive analytical portrayal, but rather a particular analytical representation of the political arena that permits us to consider alternative ways of thinking about political contestations. It is a valuable tool because it draws our attention to how voters make political selections based on their own position and the assessments of the parties' ideological stances in reference to their own point and with respect to other parties. The two-dimensional representation and the emphasis on the electorate's perception together may result in findings that show parties in "extreme" locations in a one-dimensional space and "centrist" locations in another. The distribution of the variations shows that the differences can be captured by either two or three ideological dimensions simultaneously and that to rely solely on one seriously impairs explanation.[65]

The positioning of the parties presents a fairly consistent dispersion compared to the one that emerged in figure 6.6. Relative location of the parties suggests that Turkey's ideological space can be seen as consisting of at least two ideological continua. The first continuum appears to represent competing positions spanning from a centralized, collective political identity to a pluralistic political identity. The second continuum summarizes the parties' positions regarding the form and degree of state involvement, especially in the economic sphere. Notwithstanding their popular description as Right or far-Right parties, the pro-Islamic parties appear in the expanded center of

Turkey's ideological space. The ideological positioning indicates how the pro-Islamic parties acquired political capital through their versatile roles and bivalence, making them relevant to both secular and pro-Islamic publics and representing an emerging new form of right-wing party in Turkey.

Despite its popular image as a radical ethnic, sometimes neofascist party, the NAP positions itself in the same ideological neighborhood as the True Path Party and the Democratic Left Party. The NAP's position is strategic in that its treatment of the state as a sacred institution aligns the party with the adamant supporters of the Kemalist secular state, the Democratic Left Party, as well as with neoconservative parties. Thus, the NAP is able to fuse two contradictory views successfully, not only discursively but also in the public's assessment, by adopting a collectivistic nationalist approach in its cultural policies and an individualistic liberal stance in its economic policies. Taken together, the party appears as the polar opposite of the Kurdish People's Labor Party (in its 2007 reincarnation, Democratic Society Party) by taking an extreme position on the collective identity end of the first dimension. However, the party takes a moderate position on the degree of state involvement by endorsing a limited state presence in the economic sphere. This amalgamation of two different positions shows that the party has managed to distance itself from its pre-1980, ethnically exclusive image and has successfully relocated itself closer to the center-left and center-right parties. At first glance, this positioning seems inconsistent. In fact, a review of the NAP's ideological positions with respect to these two dimensions illustrates that this is the exact position the party's rhetoric aims for. The NAP's ideology, which the electorate perceived to be the most incoherent of any religious party, brings together distinct conceptions of national identity ranging from religious membership to racial kinship under an Islamicized and ethnic construction of Turkishness, while simultaneously adopting a new economic vision that endorses the establishment of a free market economy without deregulating the market altogether, not as a challenge to the state but to strengthen it.

The neglected aspect of the NAP's policies places the party at the expanded center of Turkish politics: the NAP advocates a limited economic role for the state and the establishment of a liberal market economy, but endorses a strong secular state in the cultural sphere.[66] In the views of the NAP leadership, a free market system is not antithetical to a strong state, but serves as a means for a more competitive national economy and a more unified collective identity. Thus, many of the party's policy projects combine tenets of laissez faire and statism: "The failure of privatization stems from excessive loans given to the public enterprises. This is obvious. For an effective privatization process, we need to keep the bureaucratic and political influences out. The inefficient use of resources interrupts the accumulation of capital and corrupts state policies in general." Thus, privatization becomes a tool to save the state.[67] Despite its nationalist tone, the party's statements regarding economic issues reiterate the idea that "we cannot compete in a global economy by nationalizing our policies and closing our doors."[68] For the NAP, opening the door should not undermine the national community and the state's control.

Overall, the NAP's political position needs to be seen in light of its popular motto: "We are as Turkish as the Tengri mountain (the mythical homeland of the original Turkish race in Central Asia), and as Muslim as the Hira mountain (located in the Muslim holy lands in Saudi Arabia). Both philosophies are our principles." In its current rhetoric, the NAP places Turkish Islam, or "Anatolian Islam," in the center of its appeal as a unitary commitment in order to accommodate dual loyalties to a secular state and an Islamic nation. The fluctuating yet persistent electoral support for the NAP shows how its historical claim to bivalence, that is, inhabiting the secular and Islamic symbolic world at the same time, allows it to endorse competing secularist and Islamist positions. In the words of Devlet Bahçeli, "Nowhere in the world have democracy and social solidarity flourished through privileging ethnic and religious differences. In none of these countries have social order and political competition been maintained by neglecting national culture and common values."[69] Despite its integrationist approach, the NAP believes that "irresponsible" or "absolute" multiculturalism undermines national unity and the consolidation of democracy, thereby precluding the possibility of a liberal pluralist conception of the nation and introducing a conditional one.

In contrast, the perceived locations of the Prosperity Party and the JDP in Turkey's political universe seem to embody a transposition of conventional commitments amid the unfolding ideological realignment. Although their justifications differ, the placement of the parties reflects the progressive convergence of the political positions of the conventional center parties. For instance, while the Prosperity Party recognizes the Kurdish people as another Muslim group, the RPP tries, with limited political success, to accommodate the Kurds within an inclusive definition of citizenship based on the secular principle of multiculturalism. Despite their different rationale their overall stance places both parties in the center of the continuum ranging from a stringently unified collective identity to a decentralized particularistic one. Put differently, in the changing political center both parties are proponents of a pluralist national identity. In fact, the careful shift in the JDP's discourse from a focus on Turkishness to Turkish citizenship captures the growing emphasis on the diversity of identities. Erdoğan argues that "Turkish citizenship is the common denominator of various identities, but Islam serves as cement to keep these identities together." Instead of presenting these ideas as alternatives to Kemalist citizenship, Erdoğan substantiates the party's views by referring to the core idea of Ataturk's *Speech* which, after all, presents Islam "as the essential unifying factor in the Turkish nation."[70]

Given the gamut of competing ideas that seek to define the direction of change in Turkey's ongoing political liberalization, the Prosperity Party and the JDP differ from the NAP in the sense that their cultural policies do not assume the ethnic and cultural homogeneity of Turkishness and/or the intertwined nature of Turkishness and Islam. For both parties, the idealized global Islamic community serves as an ultimate cultural frame to accommodate different ethnic groups excluded under the secularist nation-state ideologies. Recognition of this underlying Islamic community eliminates the artificial divisions imposed on people through imported ideologies. The central role of Islam in a community does not oppress, but rather unites, its members around common moral values and treats the commitment to these values as the *only* criterion of inclusion. Although the practical application of such a project entails various complications, the ideal of an Islamic community as a congruous society accommodates many groups excluded by secularist ethnic policies and serves as the linchpin of the religious parties' projects on political and social stability.

The positions of the Prosperity Party and the JDP on the second dimension of Turkey's ideological sphere explain how these parties endorse a mixed form of etatism and free market economy to assure Turkey's social and economic development. Etatism refers to the strong role of the state in building the economy, and is the counterpart of *mamlakhtiyut* in the Israeli context. As detailed in Chapter Four, while the Prosperity Party has set as its goal the provision of minimum welfare for all citizens (to be accomplished with an economic model that allows the citizens' economic enterprises to resist Western domination), it needs appropriate state policies to support their efforts. The party's rhetoric opposes the concentration of capital in a few hands, especially those of the state-supported secularist business elite, and calls for a decentralization of wealth, ultimately seeking liberal and egalitarian redistributive policies.

Unlike the NAP, the JDP and the Prosperity Party endorse the state's redistributive role as transitional, to strengthen the effectiveness of free enterprises and morally and socially responsible nongovernmental institutions. In essence, the role of the state is reduced to that of an agent for reallocating critical resources, but it does not become an indispensable institution in its own right. Both parties oppose state policies that seek to promote the state as the foundational institution of the Turkish polity. This is why both parties' programs are filled by statements such as "the state exists only to serve its people" and "the social state provides for the needs of all people without discrimination and takes the steps necessary to ensure an equal distribution of minimal social welfare." The parties object, however, to a strong regulatory state in the cultural realm.

The Prosperity Party's and JDP's bifurcated vision of a strong state in the economic sphere and a limited state in cultural affairs explains the parties' odd commitments and political locations. Underlying the political positions of both parties is the view that for a nation to secure a stable liberal polity and succeed in an increasingly competitive world economy, it is necessary to empower moral individuals, who need the freedom to express their beliefs, and to require a heightened degree of state coordination. These are not separate goals; on the contrary, the free market can function without destroying the social fabric of a society only when individuals are equipped with a strong work ethic and act in accordance with moral responsibilities informed by Islam. In their search for balance between a morally responsible and a free market economy, the JDP's and Prosperity's economic rhetoric takes a hybrid form: an aggressive commitment to the deregulation of the market is accompanied by the need to protect the economically vulnerable population by promoting low-income housing projects and community-based services.

The increasingly critical role of the free market economy suggests that the politics of Islam entered a new phase with the JDP's policies. As discussed in Chapter Four, the Prosperity leadership advocated the idea that the state's involvement in the economic sphere needs to be limited to areas in which the private sector would not invest. Such areas have often included infrastructure projects in the less-developed areas of southern and eastern Turkey. While the NAP sees market policies as a means to strengthen the state, according to the JDP, the state only offers tax benefits and land in order to strengthen private sectors and agents. Thus, the JDP differs from all other parties with its unequivocal emphasis on increasing economic freedoms as a critical step forward in empowering individuals and in strengthening the exercise of society's religious rights. Although the JDP's predecessors shared the party's economic vision of a balanced development program led by morally responsible producers and consumers, the JDP seems to be accepting the market as the main driving force of social transformation. The JDP envisions a *Homo Islamicus*, who eliminates the unfair structure of the market economy through an Islamic ethic, which serves as the impetus to transform Turkish politics. This moral market approach emphasizes a morally regulated market model and a type of self-interest that ultimately seeks to serve the public interest and thus promotes social cohesion rather than class conflict.[71] It is this idealized economic structure that entrusts its mechanisms to moral individuals and to the Islamic market community, thus creating the party's reconciliatory position, which makes the JDP appealing to those who want to increase their share of the benefits from free-market-oriented policies and to advance from their positions of "vulnerables" to main beneficiaries.

CONCLUSION

A review of the voters' characteristics, from simple descriptions to more elaborate multinomial estimations, calls into question the various straw men proposed in the beginning of this chapter. The findings do not substantiate models that assume religious parties can be understood as battlegrounds of a secular-religious conflict. Neither the NAP nor the Prosperity nor the JDP supporters tightly cluster around certain religious values, nor do they universally support political projects derived from Islam. On the contrary, in each party's political platform and in the assessment of individuals, Islam takes on varying political meanings. The very political Sharia project is one of the most striking examples of the interface between religious and secular meanings. Only a limited number of people endorse Sharia rule as an exclusively religious regime; instead, most divorce Sharia from its theological meaning and assign it an instrumental value. The different meanings assigned to Islamic beliefs and constructs such as Sharia warn us against adopting any form of essentialism where the use of religion is seen as a counter position vis-à-vis the state, or a stance for the expansion of rights in civil society. Understanding pro-Islamic support requires us to focus on the gray areas highlighted in our analysis more than on the accentuated edges of sacro-secular constructs. Only then can we fully grasp new ideological positions that are likely to define the direction of the existing political transformation of Islam. We can also discern that growing numbers of people support the military, the guardian of the secular republic, but at the same time express opposition to secularism. Likewise, the pro-Islamic parties' support for religious rights cannot be taken as indicating their role in promoting religious rights per se; it needs, rather, to be contextualized prior to any generalization. We need to acknowledge and actively incorporate the diversity of positions under Islam in general and Turkish Islam in particular.

Also, opposition to the state in itself cannot be taken as a sign of the antisystemic or liberating nature of these movements. It is important to note that, despite their substantial contribution to democracy in challenging the authoritarian nature of state policies, even in the midst of the reforms launched by the JDP, the Prosperity Party, and the NAP, these parties' supporters seem reluctant to (re)distribute rights and liberties evenly across different groups. Thus, if pro-Islamic groups challenge the establishment, the existing power sharing structure, the challenge remains limited or selective. Pro-Islamic groups unite around the goal of extending rights against the state and do not veer far away from the official hegemonic ideology when it comes to public identities and rights that cannot be reduced to religious beliefs. Horizontal rights, rights between citizens that are not directly derived from or opposed by Islam, and which are currently low on the list of prior-ities for these parties, will eventually be critical for defining how democratic these parties' policies really are. When placed under competing conceptual lenses, the universal pattern that emerges indicates that the Prosperity Party and NAP supporters are active participants in the political community and that they treat politics as a tool for bettering their conditions rather than simply as a tool for contesting existing economic conditions. It is important to note that political mobilization, the main political capital of pro-Islamic parties, is also in the process of transformation. A review of the trends con-firms the presence of resilient, but also shifting forces. Perhaps most strik-ing is that although the JDP benefited from the Prosperity Party's massive 1980s mobilization drive, its increasing emphasis on social transformation from the top down and on individual responsibility changes the relative im-portance of political mobilization. The spatial representation of Turkish political space reinforces the proactive and unconventional role of pro-Islamic parties. It directs our attention to the overall array of parties, which shows a gap that new and unconventional religious parties can fill, thereby contributing to the overall support for religious parties. The positioning of these organizations does not reflect simple political maneuvering, but in-stead points to deeper and more convoluted undercurrents. The success of religious parties is not only due to the decline of center parties or their competitors' inability to respond to change, but also to their own capacity to introduce novel social networks and political positions.

The NAP, the Prosperity Party, and the JDP are not parochial movements or reactionary reflections of the global surge of Islam. To the contrary, they have successfully positioned themselves as parties that link local, national, and global issues. They reconcile opposing political stances within frag-mented political contexts increasingly defined by processes of realignment and de-alignment. Pro-Islamic parties not only oppose policies but also of-fer positions beyond the bifurcated image of the state in the economic and cultural sphere. Although perceived as eclectic or pragmatic, these parties forge highly complex and multifaceted ideologies that distance themselves from traditional Left and Right politics. A comparison of the use of reli-gious beliefs and ideas in these parties' rhetorical arsenals illustrates that their very success needs to be seen, not as a holistic rejection, but as a unique set of ideas through which they defy the distinctions between secular-national and local-religious loyalties. It is their ability to carve an ideological position beyond the conventional schism that lies at the root of their suc-cess. Although the presence of this new space makes these parties indispen-sable agents for consolidating the game of democracy as the only game in town and in empowering citizens vis-à-vis state, the overall democratic cap-ital of these parties depends on how they approach their fellow citizens.

Sacro-Secular Encounters

A Comparative Model of Religious Parties

The resiliency and continuing success of religious parties continues to puzzle us by unleashing a growing anxiety about religion's threat to liberalism as well as an unprecedented hope about religion's ability to sow the seeds of locally grown democracies. Compelling terms such as "the paradox of modernity" have become common parlance in any discussion of religion's new role. The reenchantment with the world, the return of religion to world politics—a belief system modernity believed it had once defeated—leaves us with the sense that we face a social force displaced from its proper location and time, with some of its manifestations more perilous than others.[1] Attempts to unravel this paradox have created the dominant yet incongruous analytical currents that shape today's efforts to grasp the interface of religion and politics. Overarching issues, such as why a religious canopy is re-covering politics in many parts of the world or whether the return of religion amounts to the end of liberalism, have generated broadly conceived discussions (i.e., metanarratives). Other vexing questions, such as whether the policies of a given Islamic movement obstruct liberalism or whether Jewish ultra-Orthodox groups challenge Israeli democracy, are often relegated to narrowly defined research areas (i.e., particularistic narratives). Scholarly debates set off by these countervailing narratives successfully open up new intellectual spaces that enhance our understanding, but also create formidable analytical hurdles that thwart our current inquiries.

Against this backdrop, our inquiry into the politics of Judaism and Islam locates itself at the interface of globally (homogenizing) and locally (compartmentalizing) grounded studies. The conclusions of our research demonstrate that meta- and particularistic discourses generate an increasing analytical entropy, as critical questions like "why religion?" or "why now, and with what implications?" cannot be answered through broad deductive exercises. An unchallenged assumption that the impact of distinctive religious doctrines on politics is unique to those doctrines deprives us of knowledge that can only be gained by inquiring into how different religious doctrines can mold comparable political positions and how seemingly sui generis positions are actually shared. Failing to relate particularistic analyses to each other, and to the existing metanarratives, risks generating self-affirming conclusions and parallel research communities. Habitual decisions not to mix seemingly different social processes and movements—not comparing apples and oranges—can obscure critical, analytically parallel processes, which become apparent only when comparisons are made that include the multiplicity of their traits. Although social scientists are rightly concerned about conceptual stretching, our research efforts can be susceptible to conceptual contraction or analytical parochialism, which generate yet another set of fallacies in our analysis. The more we treat the uniqueness of movements embedded in different doctrines as a "given," the more we situate ourselves in a broadening, yet fragmented analytical map. Thus, the paradox of the return of religion is perhaps more a paradox of our own creation and the product of analytical approaches that result from our inability to balance the countervailing trends.

Our comparative inquiry into the politics of Judaism and Islam illustrates that it is precisely the commonalities of religious parties based in different religions that help us to better understand their uniqueness. Putting the politics of Judaism and Islam under the same analytical lens enables us to engage with the broader question of "Why religion?" and the specific question "In what forms?" without limiting ourselves to a specific research community. Although simplification is unavoidable in any inquiry into complex social realities, oversimplification, especially that imposed by conceptual binaries devoid of empirical foundations, needs to be avoided. Revealed in our analysis is the conclusion that the politics of religion, and any movement associated with it, cannot be grasped thoroughly without defining (1) religion's overall position within its state structure and politics (i.e., the historical and political vantage points and constraints facing religion) as well as the conceptions of the main institutions and terms of politics within religious movements, (2) the relative ideological positions of political parties engaged in electoral competitions (political situational opportunities and limitations), (3) the specific content of beliefs and practices that inform the religious parties' ideologies (symbolic capital, ideational and internal constraints), and (4) the way in which religious parties ground themselves in their communities (e.g., network capital, the vertical and horizontal organizations of religious parties), which explains their ability to link local organizations nationally and internationally by forging a system of mutual support and new common identities (communal and organizational opportunities and limitations).

The aspects of the politics of religion that we addressed here by no means exhaust all the factors that define the political appeal of religious parties. Nor do the listed dimensions have a simple additive effect on religion's political manifestation. Instead, the distinctive aspects of the politics of religion altogether form a heuristic venue that draws our attention to areas that vanish in the polarized world of dichotomies. More importantly, the distinctive components when viewed together help us to better grasp the incongruous tendencies and structures contained in religious ideologies. The inclusion of separate components identifies a reciprocal chain of interactions among them and points out the shortsightedness of analyses that privilege one component over others. The critical consequences of the interplay of structural, situational, and value-centered dimensions show that the analytical cost of conflating them is rather high. Peeling away each dimension and recognizing the wealth of modes through which religion and state can interact free us from the firm grip of ubiquitous accounts that pit secularist agents against religion and turn a deaf ear to too many voices that are atypical or nonconforming. The multifaceted nature of religious movements makes it especially important to develop models that center on the dynamic nature of these movements and take into account the scope of their sometime inconsistent aspects. Only such models can withstand the tendency to either marginalize or overemphasize two important factors: (1) what makes a religion a religion, namely its sacred ideas and symbols, and (2) what turns religious movements to political movements, namely their interaction with other actors under the rules of a given socioeconomic milieu.

THE POSITIONING OF RELIGION IN A POLITICAL SYSTEM

The myth of pure religious and secular domains penetrates many analyses. Such compartmentalization one way or another juxtaposes religious movements against the secular public, agents, and the state. Despite their initial robustness, these depictions not only have limited analytical purchase, they also often prevent us from probing into the crucial areas where critical engagements of secular and sacred occur—beyond the neatly divided world of the separation myth. As explained in Chapter Three, models based on a dichotomy between contestation and accommodation ignore the full spectrum of power-sharing modalities between state and religion. Power, after all, is not only institutional but relational (i.e., it abides in relations). Thus, approaches that envision suppressed religious groups vis-a-vis the state use a minimalist definition of power and emphasize conflicts as opposed to less visible but more pervasive compromises. Israel and Turkey offer perfect examples of how religion can take on multiple, contradictory roles at the same time in the same polity. More importantly, the relationship between the state and religion, between secular and religious publics, is not necessarily one of antagonism. Instead, at the nexus of state, secularism, and religion, we observe various modes of confrontation, mutual dependence, and transformation. More intriguingly, official state doctrines do not always translate into political practices, and religion, as a resilient force, has the capacity to evade official restrictions and mold institutional practices.

As we detailed in Chapter Three, the state-founding ideologies of Israel and Turkey have been marked by internal dilemmas, as they relied on Judaism and Islam respectively to define a common denominator for their national identities even as they worked to contain religion's ability to challenge state policies. The power-sharing arrangements between state and religion in Israel and Turkey, respectively, illustrate that institutions do not resolve the conflicts in favor of only the secular or only religion. Rather, the arrangements more often than not deepen the symbolic, political, and financial dependency between religious and secular groups. The manifestation of complex and reciprocal relationships in both polities urges us to think in broader, relational categories, such as "dependent autonomy" or "controlled dependency." Only such terms allow us to differentiate between the ideational and institutional aspects of the relationship between religion and secular groups and institutions. For instance, under a *controlled dependency* model the state claims control over religion (i.e., institutional separation) at the same time that it remains dependent on religion for its legitimacy (i.e., ideational dependence). Conversely, in a situation of dependent autonomy the religious and secular each claim autonomous ideational or institutional spheres, but in the end they remain dependent on each other for their survival.

The institutional arrangements in Israel and Turkey exemplify the importance that an understanding of the current role of religion has in any polity. It requires a reassessment of the political-historical role of religion within the state, without being constrained by the assumption that each always seeks to claim full authority over the other. In many other polities, religion serves as the main source of nationhood, and religious demands play a critical role in either justifying or discrediting secular public demands. Many institutions that rest on the presumed ideational divisions between the religious and the secular remain tenuous. One of the most revealing examples of such compromise is Israel's Status Quo Agreement of

1947, which continues to offer the blueprint for the existing multilayered sharing of authority between religious and secular groups within and beyond the state structure. As a result of the Status Quo, religious authorities maintain broad autonomy over their own educational and community matters. Yet this power exceeds the limits of the religious community as there are areas regulated by religious rules and officials; for example, religion defines the main civil ceremonies and religious conversions that are critical for citizenship. More importantly, the delegation of extensive power to the religious bloc does not result in full-fledged autonomy from the state, but rather in a mixed form characterized by an ingrained institutional and financial dependence of religious institutions on the state for their existence. The Orthodox groups enjoy nationwide authority over a wide range of issues but also depend upon their state status and state funds to maintain their presence. At the ideational level, the state continues to refer to religion implicitly and explicitly to justify its policies. Questions over the scope of the public authority of Judaism and how to treat the exemptions granted to observant religious publics remain and continue to create divisions, not only between the religious and secular, but also within the religious bloc. It is not the *absence* of full religious autonomy and control, but rather its *implausibility* that lies at the root of the continuous political negotiations.

Likewise, the current politics of Islam in Turkey cannot be understood without taking into account what lies beneath its stringent secularism and its presumed unified secularist opposition to Islam. As explained in Chapter Three, it is not accidental that only fourteen years after the establishment of the state, when the state centralized political power, the constitution was amended to define the Turkish state as secular, *laik,* instead of *Islamic.* The state's effort to promote an Islam more compatible with the premise of a nation-state *limited,* but also *consolidated,* the role of religion in the polity. Due to Islam's presence in the public imaginary and its potent political power, official policies and practices regarding the role of Islam are not always congruous. Just like religions in other polities, Islam assumed multiple roles in Turkey's politics by legitimizing state power and providing the source for allegories and beliefs that have informed political ideologies and communication. Religion becomes an especially important political asset at times when the state needs to justify its presence and policies. For example, despite its staunch secular outlook, the 1980 military regime relied to a great extent on Islam to justify its political agenda and restore political stability in Turkey.[2] The fact that the government's financial support for Imam Hatip schools has grown significantly, regardless of the ideological orientation of the ruling governments, attests to the Islamic public's irresistible attraction to political parties.[3]

Looking at and beyond the existing institutional arrangements invites us to pay closer attention to not only how symbols and beliefs can assume multiple meanings and endorse contradictory positions, but also how the institutions that draw on them can do so as well. Religious movements and parties emerge from within the political historical system, not independently of it, or against it. Trying to understand the interaction between institutions and religious and secular beliefs requires us to delve into the not easily discernible process of "adaptive transformation." Some secular institutions, such as the state, and other carriers of secular values are capable of appropriating religious symbols, beliefs, and institutions for their own survival and interest. The multiplicity of ways in which adaptive transformation occurs, and in which the symbolic repertoire of "religious" and secular beliefs merge, is critical to how religious politics manifests itself. Of the expressions of adaptive transformation, which characterizes many religious movements, "compliant protest" or "dissension" indicates how religion and the state, religious and secular values, find venues to coexist (i.e., compliance) while continuing to confront each other at the same time (i.e., dissension). Consequently, it is important to tease out the shape and direction of the transformative convergences, thereby highlighting the gray areas glossed over by dichotomous categories. Binaries suggest that religious and secular can cohabit, but cannot be merged. Yet the political reality shows that they (i.e., religious and secular) often blend and tend to alter each other; thus our understanding of politics of religion hinges on our ability to revisit conceptual tools that perpetuate religion's and secular's assumed antithetical presence. To emphasize the mutual permanency of religious and secular institutions and terms, we need to identify the presence of sacro-secular, Janus-faced practices and terms that have meaning both in and beyond the religious and secular worlds. Recognizing them as such provides us with a constant reminder of the porous wall between the secular and sacred, while also indicating the centrality of the osmotic process that takes place between them.

Abandoning binary approaches does not deter us from understanding religious movements in a structured way. Instead of taking us to relativistic words, our efforts to build a dynamic conceptual language better prepare us to capture the elusive political capacities and limits of these movements. As Weber explained the structural and ideational processes are intertwined and it should not be our "aim to substitute for a one-sided materialistic an equally one-sided spiritualistic causal interpretation of culture and of history" to understand social political process. After all "each is equally possible, but each, if it does not serve as the preparation, but as the conclusion of an investigation, accomplishes equally little in the interest of historical truth." Likewise, in our inquiries, strict compartmentalization does little in promoting much needed understanding of religion's political presence.[4]

POLITICAL SITUATIONAL OPPORTUNITIES
AND LIMITATIONS

The politics of religion is nested in the broader game of politics, and its manifestations need to be analyzed in relation to its political setting. Religious parties are constrained by and adapt to the formal and informal rules governing electoral competition. Like other political actors, in the end they seek to expand their appeal and seize political power. One of the less addressed puzzles surrounding the "return of religion" is the question of how religious parties can make themselves relevant in spite of the unique sets of institutional rules they operate under. The configuration and resiliency of religious parties under the Israeli and Turkish systems indicate both the power and the limits of institutional rules. Perhaps most revealing is the constant failure of electoral engineering intended to limit the power of small and religious parties. In Israel, the Knesset adopted the direct election of Israel's highest legislative and executive positions as part of the 1992 coalition negotiations. This experiment to increase the negotiating power vested in the prime minister, which meant curbing the power of small parties (read religious parties) not only failed, but further enhanced their power, as increasing numbers of people split their tickets and supported religious parties. The law's revocation in 2001 has not substantially decreased the percentage of votes cast for religious parties in elections since then.[5] In 1983, the Turkish parliament adopted a 10 percent national threshold for parliamentary representation, essentially voiding any ballots cast for losing parties by transferring them to winning parties. Yet the high threshold has led to an increasing number of preelection coalitions in general, and an infamous "holy coalition of religious parties" in 1991, which marked the first decisive appearance of religious parties at the national level.[6] What is striking, however, is that once they became nationally salient and credible, pro-Islamic parties were able to successfully circumvent both the overt and the built-in hidden constraints of Turkey's electoral system with significant sucess.

Although the *rules* of the electoral competition are indispensable for understanding the forms and quantities of religious parties, the ways in which people make their political decisions cannot be understood by using institutional reductionist approaches alone. Along with the position of the individual in each respective community, we need to attend to the strength and composition of the main political parties and the nature of the presumed political center. The voters' assessment of the game of politics indicates that they often contradict the main parties' own claims and require identifications that go beyond the official positions. In fact, our findings draw attention to a widening discrepancy between public perceptions and claimed party positions in part due to (1) the overcrowding of the political center, (2) the declining trust in political parties, and (3) the overall shrinking of the "mainstream" political arena. Politics in many countries has been marked by the increasing dominance of just a few issues (e.g., the form and place of privatization, security-related issues) at the expense of a broader issue scope that might include topics deemed important by traditional and religious publics. In other words, the reduction in policy differences among the main parties, at a time when the public's issue domain is expanding, amounts to a crisis of the political center and its representation. The crisis is exacerbated by the declining trust of the public in the ability of all centrist parties to advance and implement effective policies. Therefore, although the political actors remain the same, the main parties' roles as occupiers of the center of the political competition seem to be getting increasingly weak.

One of the largely ignored aspects of religious parties is that at the end of the day they are political parties and susceptible to the same ideas and competition from other agents, secular and religious alike, as other parties. Therefore, the engagement of a religious party in politics, like that of any other party, cannot be viewed independently from the position of other political actors. Nor is their position vis-à-vis their main secular opponents alone sufficient to expose the full spectrum of the ideas of religious parties. Neglected in many analyses is the recognition that despite their convergence to ensure political survival, the competition between religious groups is as intense as and sometimes more critical for democracy than their competition against secular groups. Despite their agreement on the need to promote religious values and transfer resources to religious groups, questions regarding how these values will be defined and how resources for the religious groups will be allocated set religious groups against each other. This is why, for instance, we fail to understand the very genesis of Shas unless we address in our analysis the relationship between the religious bloc and the state, the competition within the religious bloc, and the easy entrance rule in Israeli politics.

IDEATIONAL (INTERNAL) CONSTRAINTS
AND RELIGIOUS IDEOLOGIES

Prevalent inquiries often treat religious parties and their ideas as merely expedient *vessel*s to express the political frustrations and economic dissatisfaction of the masses. Islam becomes the language of anger and ultra-Orthodox Jewish ideologues serve as venues of resentment. Alternative views that assign a central role to the ideologies of religious parties promote the idea that these ideologies *mirror* the fundamental beliefs of their respective doctrines. Ironically, in the final analysis, both approaches suggest that the specific ideas adopted in religious ideologies are inconsequential. The doctrines in general (Islam and Judaism) or the functions (e.g., promoting communications, protest) of the ideas matter most for politics. Thus, our frameworks either overvalue doctrinal beliefs (i.e., essentialist accounts) or trivialize them (i.e., reductionist-structuralist accounts), thereby making it especially critical to offer an inside-out analysis of religious beliefs, values and ideas.

Attending to the diversity within and across the politics of Judaism and Islam shows that essentialism and reductionism at any level, especially in the understanding of the ideologies of religious parties, render exceptionally powerful, yet often misleading, verdicts. As our comparative analysis detailed, religious party ideologies are neither vessels of resentment nor untainted mirrors of religious doctrine. Instead, religious ideas serve as both reflective and constructive means. They represent and redefine the ideas embedded in their respective religious doctrines when they address mundane issues under the guidance of spiritual knowledge and address spiritual issues in the face of mundane challenges. Different extrapolations from the same religious symbols lead to vast discrepancies in the way the parties perceive the political world. Avoiding the trap of both reductionism and essentialism requires the inclusion of the symbolic world of religious parties, not simply in opposition to the dominant value system, but within their respective political and religious discursive worlds.

Including the *internal* (ideational) constraints of religious parties enables us to approach religious movements without reducing their position to our own a priori postulations and often alters how we look at the relationship between religious parties and democracy. We can then delve into the beliefs and symbols that inform the religious parties and their partisans' decisions via inductive analyses that understand the leaders and supporters of religious parties on their own terms. Such an inside-out look quickly establishes that the strength of religious parties does not lie in their pragmatic religious discourse, but in a carefully interwoven set of values that tie the religious ideas and symbols to newly emerging questions and issues. It is the religious parties' ability to imbue religious symbols with meanings relevant to today's politics that makes them so important for crafting new ideas. Our two-layered comparison within and across religions and polities repeatedly shows that religious leaders have often taken diametrically opposed positions on the hegemonic state ideology and the boundaries between individual and community and that reductionist ideological coherency is not always delivered in a given doctrine. What seem like trivial disagreements on religious principles to outside observers serve as deeply divisive issues among the religious publics, often preventing religious groups from acting as a unified religious bloc.

The cases of Mafdal, Shas, the NAP, and the Prosperity Party indicate that, more often than not, religious parties not only focus on different parts of their respective doctrines but also glean different meanings and positions from the very same religious symbols or texts. Due to these differences, religious parties compete with each other as fiercely as with secular agents, and this competition amplifies their differences. In fact, both internal competition and the effort to maximize their votes in the broader electoral game have significantly transformed religious parties since the early 1980s. It is noteworthy in this context that even the most inward-looking, ultra-Orthodox parties (for example, Israel's United Torah Judaism [UTJ]) can change their political position. UTJ, which has traditionally declined to participate in governing Israel, started taking a more active role in Israeli politics in order to safeguard its state funding. However, the change in UTJ's political participation did not affect its ideology. The UTJ's recent involvement simultaneously confirms and questions the conventional thesis that an open and diverse religious marketplace will eventually motivate quiescent groups to take part in power-sharing arrangements.

The content of the ideologies of religious parties covered in our analysis lends itself to categorization as parties that (1) imbue their nationalist discourse with religious symbols and (2) continuously challenge secular nationalist ideas, but open religious ideas up to secular diffusion. The first group of parties, *religious parties with nationalist foundations*, not only refrains from challenging the existing secular institutions, such as the state, but also assumes that they have a significant religious essence or role. As discussed in detail in Chapter Four, in the ideology of Israel's Mafdal, a national religious party, history needs to be seen as the unfolding of the divinely ordained process of redemption. In this view, secular institutions and actors have an intrinsic divine essence, and thus it is the national religious party's duty not to alienate but to cooperate with them.[7] In other words, when placed under the sacred canopy, the secular institutions of the state and the religious public become, not competing groups, but intrinsically interdependent instruments in the unfolding of a religiously defined history. The unity of the nation and the territory are necessary steps in preparation for the promised divine redemption, which will achieve the promised stable society. Likewise, Turkey's NAP does not question the secularist political system and refuses to see secular national ideologies as antithetical to religious ones. For the party, Turkey's secularism, which appears to be anti-Islamic, actually eliminates destructive forces and serves as the cement that keeps the Turkish-Muslim community stabilized. Thus, the state and its secularism are not inimical to "Muslimness."[8] What makes the NAP's position intriguing is that it justifies secularism with its Turkish Islamism. Under the shelter of its secular state, Turkey's Muslim community can prevail against threats from within or from outside that imperil its existence. In the NAP's own terms, Turkish Islamism, the key ideology for the party, is not an eclectic ideology, but an acknowledgment of the mutually dependent relationship between the secular state and the Islamic community.

It is important to note that by assigning religious functions to secular national institutions, these parties view engaging in politics as something of a religious ritual and altruistic exercise. The national religious party leaders often remind their constituency that "Anyone who believes and who wants to have a life according to his beliefs, needs to engage in politics. Otherwise politics becomes an area for a minority to rule another minority, neither one respecting the other's values or beliefs."[9] Although such statements suggest that national religious parties are content with the status quo and the state, they are not only capable of adopting a highly critical language but often confront the state to restore its assumed nature. For instance, in response to religious groups' critique of Turkey's strict secularism, the national religious party leadership strips the state's of its endeared sanctity and argues that "any state rule that places social pressure on people due [merely] to their religious beliefs cannot be acceptable."[10] Nevertheless, in the end, nationalist parties are united in the belief that individual political rights cannot be allowed to undermine the unity and sanctity of the state and its nation.

The way in which they simultaneously question and embrace secular ideas connects parties assigned to the second group, the *religious expansionist and revisionist parties*. The parties maintain their dissenting positions, but they also adapt their respective doctrines to the constraints of the secular political world, thereby providing the catalyst for its transformation. As we explained in Chapters Four and Five, Israel's Shas Party and Turkey's JDP and Prosperity Party claim to be Zionist and Kemalist, respectively, while at the same time constantly debating the meanings of these hegemonic national ideologies and the policies derived from them. This dual rhetoric enables them to cross the conventional social divisions between the secular and the religious. Attesting to the party's remarkable ability to adapt, Shas quickly distanced itself from its parent ultra-Orthodox party.[11] On the other hand, Shas's leadership successfully advocated the idea that the Sephardim entered the game of politics at a great disadvantage and made itself relevant to secular Jewry. The party's core constituency, Sephardim, was portrayed as confined to an isolated social role and cultural place when the founding ideology of the state denied the pluralistic, multitribal nature of the Israeli nation and disregarded the peculiarities and special needs of groups who had their roots in the Middle East, North Africa, and Asia. The religious blocs did not ameliorate, but rather exacerbated, the political exclusion of Sephardim in religious terms. Shas, however, serves to reverse the marginalization of Sephardim under the state's ethnic policies. What is remarkable is that the party's dissenting language actually promotes a pluralistic political project, integrating otherwise loosely connected Sephardi groups, while promoting the idea that the Israeli nation *halachically* is a society consisting of different cultural communities.

Turkey's Prosperity Party and the brand-new JDP can be characterized as examples of these religiously *expansionist and revisionist* parties. The parties share the idea that the marginalization of Islam depleted Turkey's social capital and turned its social and economic ills into chronic problems. Given Turkey's constitutional constraints, the JDP's and the Prosperity Party's dissent is muted, but still powerful. They consider their partisan involvement in Turkey's politics as a reflection of their duty to protect Turkey's Islamic identity, which allows them to address its broader social problems.[12] These parties' adaptive transformations sometimes appear as overt policies. Their quest for a redefinition of democratic, secular practices to better accommodate religious agents and perspectives manifests itself in a compelling plea for the decentralization of the political and economic systems. By allowing more room for Islam and newly emerging entrepreneurs, the parties envision that the "Muslimness" of citizens, when freely expressed, will create moral order in their immediate social and economic surroundings. The way in which the JDP has distanced itself from the legacy of Turkey's first pro-Islamic leader, Erbakan, and his confrontational policies exemplifies these religious parties' internal struggles, which are often directed at finding leaders who are consistent in a religious paradigm and who are also capable of effectively engaging with the conditions and opportunities in the existing political and social context.

A review of the internal dynamics of religious parties reveals that their success lies not in their dormant hierarchical structure but in their intense political debates and search to develop better political ideas. This is why in the views of the JDP leadership, which governed Turkey when this study was conducted, Erbakan's disciples defected from the old party. The defectors wanted to pursue "more consistent and realistic policies" to strengthen the role of Islam without "fighting with the system."[13] In fact, the party disassociated itself from confrontational policies, refused identification with the existing political terms, and coined *conservative democracy* to represent its new ideology. In the formation of these new approaches, we can observe how these parties' bivalence, their ability to exist in and transform the religious and secular worlds, characterizes their ideologies. The party defines conservative democracy as a venue to inform the state's policies with "common values," a term the party uses as proxy for Islamic values.[14] As an example of the process of appropriation of common terms and the transformation of them from within, the JDP designated human rights, one of the key terms of Turkey's secular political liberalization policies, as the main currency of its agenda. However, rights are more often than not narrowly defined as "freedom from the state's control," not individual rights in broadly defined terms as an end in themselves and in relation to other individuals. The party's commitment to reforms that promise to redefine key political institutions not only reflects its efforts to challenge the secular institutions from within the system by opening more of the public sphere to religion, but also captures an exposure to and involvement with the key terms of the secular world that it tries to shape. Ironically, the party's newly adopted conservative ideology—centered on "rights" and "traditional values"—and its increasing commitment to decentralization via market reforms and individualism bring the party actually closer to the dominant symbolic system it is critical of and in which it tries to exist.

THE VERTICAL AND HORIZONTAL ORGANIZATION OF RELIGIOUS PARTIES

While endemic political apathy and weakening political ties mar many polities across the world, religious parties defy the global curse of political alienation with organizations that are firmly grounded in local communities. The religious parties' successes among local groups cannot be reduced to the restoration of traditional communities or the creation of brand-new ones. Neither can the vitality of these groups be solely attributed to their fulfillment of economic needs or commitment to religious, conservative ideas. Rather, religious parties differ from others by leading the creation of what we can call new-old or traditional and modern communities. These political communities are unique in their ability to draw on existing old, traditional interactions, yet they also expand and transform these groups into tightly knit, broader communities. Through their network of grassroots institutions, they constantly blend and remold political ideas, religious beliefs, and economic interests. These groups help religious parties to connect otherwise separated communities and also to forge new ties across local groups, both nationally and internationally. As detailed in Chapters Four and Five, the parties' ideas do not only serve as the guideline for future expectations, but have immediate relevance to the parties' existing local roots (horizontal expansion) roots and their organizational decisions and relations to other institutions (vertical foundations). When the parties' overall organization is taken into account, we face a striking contrast between the religious parties' inclusive, transformative, responsive horizontal foundations and other parties' hierarchical, exclusive, administrative, political organizations. Generally speaking, these parties become resilient forces by including elements of traditional society, transforming old practices into new ones, and fostering a common group identity with new ties and the interdependence of its members.

Despite the groups' common characteristics, the political communities forged by these parties differ significantly with respect to their constituents and the manner in which they are sustained. For instance, the compliant relationship between the state and national religious parties makes them less reliant on traditional communities. After all, along with their local organizations, state religious schools serve as durable places for the parties to cultivate their values and ties to different communities. The national religious-party-affiliated youth centers remain important attractions, especially for youngsters who are looking for an intense political education, solidarity, and the power of an organized community. In the case of Turkey, for instance, *ülkücü* communities create a microcosm of the party's ideal polity. Recruiting mostly among young, socially and politically active members, ülkücüs emphasize social responsibility and regard it as their mission to be an altruistic watchdog for the national community. Their highly hierarchical organization often transforms itself into an economic solidarity group, where the party identity serves as an essential factor in conducting business and seeking government employment. More importantly, the link between the party's local groups and the party center is a rather direct one. Those who excel in the party's local institutions can later climb the party's hierarchical, internal career ladder.

The organizations of national religious parties in general exhibit two unique characteristics. The central and stable role of the party-affiliated institutions in the formation of the national religious parties makes them less dependent on services provided via local associations. Due to the central role of futuristic ideas and the unity of the national communities, the advocates of the parties' ideologies can mobilize the formation of brand-new communities. A striking example of this is Mafdal's successful appeal among those who promote the settlement movement in Israel. Mafdal's ideology emphasizes the land, and the party positions itself as the natural representative of the people who settle in the disputed territories. In fact, many settlers who have an elective affinity for the party often form close, partisan ties based on concerns for their political and economic survival.

Within the spectrum of religious parties, Shas, the JDP, and the Prosperity Party emerge as the ultimate masters of communally grounded organizations. As reviewed in Chapter Four, Shas owes its electoral success to its ability to organize a network of communities through a common party identity and the provision of social services. In the case of Shas, the party-centered welfare system includes day care, elementary school education, and adult training services and competes successfully with its secular counterparts through affordable school tuition rates. In the case of Prosperity and JDP, vibrant communities exist as well, but with less pronounced ties. All of these services are delivered in an environment where political ideas remain in the forefront.[15] Nevertheless, what makes all of these expansionist-revivalist parties unique is that they make their services available to anyone, unlike other ultra-Orthodox parties for whom ultra-Orthodoxy or being religious is a prerequisite. For instance, the way Shas combines its lenient, neo-Orthodox Sephardi approach with its ubiquitous organizations enables it to reach out to groups beyond the Sephardim or ultra-Orthodox Jews.[16] This national network translates the party's religious ideas into a novel, nationwide communitarian practice and gives credibility to its political rhetoric.

The JDP and the Prosperity Party stand out as the most organized and community-grounded parties in Turkey's political arena, reminiscent of the Shas model. Both parties use street-level representatives who regularly collect a wealth of information from individual households and forward that information to the party. The parties' entrenchment in their respective communities makes them the most effective ombudsmen in the country. Exchanges between the party and its constituency are not simple patron–client exchanges: the very nature of the interactions and the way they occur in habitual settings makes the party's political community a resilient one. Although face-to-face relations played the key role after the JDP took over the government, there has been an effort to institutionalize these relationships, often using very innovative means of communications. The JDP opened a toll-free line to enable citizens to make direct requests from the party center, while Shas solicits for donations to its construction and charity projects via Internet and satellite broadcasting. The JDP-sponsored local organizations, like those of Shas, established easily accessible community centers, which help to make the JDP's policies more comprehensible and acceptable to a wider range of citizens. Like Shas's activities, the political engagements of the JDP and Prosperity blur the distinctions between private households and the public and local and global. Home visits by party activists to hear and resolve problems are a common practice. An environment such as this easily transforms average housewives into public activists without affecting their social positions.

Religious parties seem to create a political sphere in which households expand to the world of politics instead of the world of politics contracting into households.

The religious parties' local effectiveness does not amount to the revival or creation of reactionary, inward looking communities that are confined regionally or nationally. On the contrary, religious parties transform traditions to forge new, locally rooted and inventive organizations that are also linked internationally. It is important to note that through ideas transmitted via their solidarity network, these parties reach out to communities located beyond their national boundaries. Shas's recent inclusion of "international" into its name is not a misnomer but reflects the party's internationally oriented policies. The pronouncements of Shas's spiritual leader, Ovadia Yosef, are transmitted regularly via satellite, and the party receives continuous support from Diaspora Sephardic communities. The party's messages have been popular among Sephardic communities in countries ranging from France to Argentina. Likewise, despite the critical role of the land for Mafdal, "People of Israel" is a territorial category not limited to Israel proper. As a result, the party's messianic view defines its political project as encompassing not only Israel but also the Jewish community elsewhere. The party receives important support from Diaspora communities and links local political communities to international ones. The NAP's activities treat the Turkish republic and world politics as their ultimate reference point for their political community, to the extent that members are encouraged to host and visit people from the other Turkic republics. The JDP and Prosperity draw remarkable support from Muslim communities in Europe and to a certain extent from Asia. The National View foundation in Western Europe played a critical role in the NV parties' success not only by transferring ideas and financial support but also in terms of real votes. The foundations in Germany launched political pilgrimage trips, voting trips to Turkey, to ensure the NV parties' electoral success. Thus, these parties' political communities are locally grounded, but globally oriented. Their strong ideational and institutional connections between private domains and local, national, and global politics distinguish religious parties from others.

Yet the parties' well-connected horizontal local and international networks and their electoral successes generate some mixed results. This is clearly exemplified in the case of Shas; on the one hand, the party's increasing electoral success makes Shas more dependent on the government budget in order to support its welfare network. On the other hand, as its political power grows, the party strives to achieve more of a self-sustaining religious community. These dual processes motivate the parties to embrace existing institutions but also to become increasingly critical of them, and as a result, Shas is caught between the demands of religious communities and the policies of existing institutions. In Turkey's political milieu, the ubiquitous surveillance by secular institutions tones down the demands of the religious publics, but ironically this scrutiny also legitimizes the parties' raison d'être. One of the most important implications of this environment is that in order to prevent the pro-Islamic parties' closure as antisystemic and thus unconstitutional, Turkey's vibrant local political communities refrain from putting full-force pressure on their religious parties, especially on issues pertaining to the public expression of Islam. Nevertheless, the supporters' self-censorship of political expectations is likely to become less common as the continuous political successes of pro-Islamic parties increase their grassroots expectations. The more pro-Islamic parties gain political power and circumvent the systemic constraints, the more we can expect this grassroots pressure. Such demands are likely to challenge the parties' conciliatory policies and affect their political capital. How the local communities' pressure will affect the parties remains to be seen. What is certain, however, is that without a party network sustained by multiple community groups, no religious party would exist.

The horizontal, local organization of religious parties differs from their vertical party organization. Without exception, all of the religious parties are highly hierarchical and centered around a small group of leaders. In cases where religious parties have a well-known powerful spiritual leader, such as Shas, the internal controls are even stronger. In parties that have internal mechanisms in place to propose and elect candidates to leadership positions, the final appointments are still controlled by the spiritual leader or the upper echelon of the parties. The parties' effort to balance religious currents and reach out to the traditionalists often results in a highly elaborate institutional structure and election mechanism. One of the most striking examples comes from the JDP. The selection of party officials rests on a three-tiered, carefully designed formal selection procedure, which makes the JDP the party with the highest level of democracy among those covered in this study. The party selects its officials through (1) a local popularity poll, (2) approval by the local organization, and (3) approval by the party center. In practice, these three stages result in a list from which the party leadership makes the final selections and sometimes bypasses the local organizations' decisions. It is important to note, however, that internal democracy is not a common currency in either Israel or Turkey, and leadership-centered parties are the norm rather than the exception. Even so, religious parties are still more centralized than other parties, and this fact poses questions about the extent to which they articulate the diversity of demands and opinions in their decisions.

Despite the significance of their leaders, one needs to be very cautious before presenting these parties simply as parties of charismatic leaders or movements. For instance, the Shas party has already survived three political leaders (Peretz, Deri, and Yishau)—including the highly popular, charismatic leadership of Deri. Likewise, Turkey's Islamist parties easily shifted their support from the appealing leadership of Necmettin Erbakan to Tayyip Erdoğan and expanded the movement's power. It is important to note that none of these leaders is an ideologue. Instead of presenting complete, detailed ideologies, they define the main parameters guiding the party's policies. The challenge for understanding religious parties therefore is that we must tease out how these parties benefit from the presence of charismatic leaders. The role of these leaders is especially critical as they are instrumental not only in making some key decisions but also in justifying what could be religiously questionable and unconventional pronouncements. Their contributions become exceptionally critical when party ideology is on trial, as they provide party discipline and minimize the impact of challenges. Nevertheless, given the strong roots of these parties in their respective communities, single-track assessments that suggest that Shas is Ovadia's party or the JDP is Erdoğan's party do not allow us to grasp the depth of these movements.

UNDERSTANDING THE NEXUS OF THE RELIGIOUS, THE SECULAR, AND POLITICS

The diversity of political positions in the politics of Judaism and Islam establishes that doctrinal principles do not translate into ideological positions ipso facto, or reflect on political life directly. But religious hermeneutics, interpreting the meaning of the religious texts, cannot be isolated from how religion affects human conduct in general and politics in particular. At the heart of religious movements lies a transformative, adaptive interaction between the secular and religious, not a clash. In this regard, we may be witnessing a unique era that is marked, not by the defeat of the secular with the "return of religion," but a novel merger of previously separate paradigms. In an effort to understand the nature of this interaction at the nexus of religion and politics, the preceding chapters laid out two broad processes, internal secularization and sacralization. We can classify religious parties as either internal secularizers or sacralizers, depending on which process primarily defines their overall ideology.

Sacralizers are the parties that identify inherent and latent religious functions in secular ideas and institutions and accept their declared positions due to their intrinsic religious meaning. These parties perceive secular constructs under a sacred canopy. Once the underlying religious functions of secular institutions are uncovered, their present manifestations and expressed will are no longer questioned. The acceptance of secular institutions or actors is not based on an acceptance of differences, but a redefinition of secular institutions in a religious paradigm. Therefore, these parties are more likely to, and often do, endorse the authoritarian policies of the sacralized institutions. The term *internal secularization* describes the process engaged in by religious agents that do not sacralize but challenge secular institutions by offering religious alternatives. Through their efforts to separate themselves from the secular, they engage in a process of creating religious ideas equivalent to secular ones. Ironically, as a result of their efforts at separation, these parties are more likely to transform religious ideas from within and, in the long run, accommodate some of the premises of a pluralistic democratic society in their ideology and in their practices.

It is important to note that we do not propose these processes in order to introduce yet another deterministic formula. Rather, they are intended to facilitate broader comparisons by discerning the dominant modes through which secular and religious values, beliefs, and practices are interwoven. It is also important to note that the processes are not mutually exclusive. They only assist our inquiries at the nexus of religion and politics without allowing our vision to be blurred by strict separation of religion and secular. This typology of religious parties is especially important, as it redirects our attention not only to how ideas and ideologies interact but also to what they convey, how they do so, and with what implications.

Placing religious parties under the lens of these processes helps us to better assess not only how but also why religious parties take the positions they do vis-à-vis the most significant components of and agents in their respective democracies. Sacralizers and internal secularizers differ significantly (1) in the way they treat the hegemonic ideology, the state, and the nation, (2) in how they balance the interaction between community and individual, and (3) in the degree to which they are open to other heterodox, ethnic groups or open to altering the traditional social roles. In other words, understanding religious parties' stances in these areas affords us a nuanced depiction of how their political-religious beliefs describe other actors, and whether and how religious ideologies foster coexistence, allow individual differences, and develop a framework that promotes not only the rights of religion in the public sphere but also the expansion of the rights of other actors.

A concerted effort to view religious politics in multiple layers is especially important, as the relationship of religious parties to democracy is often defined on the basis of just one of these areas. In the existing literature, a religious party's acceptance of the secular state, the existing composition of the nation, and the status quo often results in its designation as a "moderate" party, as opposed to antisystemic. When the parties' positions across all areas are viewed together, however, it becomes clear that not all of the positions of religious parties are congruous. Instead, the way in which a party justifies its position given its religious framework introduces different practical restrictions on its support for the existing state and nationalist ideology and its approach to coexistence. As a result, any assessment of how religious parties contribute to or hinder their democracies cannot be based on only one declared issue position or segment of its current praxis without also questioning its ideological justification. The way in which parties confirm their position in religious terms is consequential and has direct bearing on their position on democracy. Only by piercing through the meaning attached to their positions can we address to what extent these parties' policies are inclusive or exclusive and how they stand vis-à-vis the project of liberal democracy.

Understanding whether religious parties' ideologies are marked by internal secularization or sacralization promises a better assessment of their position on democracy by underlining positions to which these processes make them especially receptive. Sacralizers, such as Mafdal and the NAP, infuse secular institutions with religious values and treat them as sacrosanct. For these parties the gulf between the secular nature of the state and the religious nature of society is a fallacy, as each has an intrinsically complementary role in the unfolding, religiously revealed, and progressive social transformation. The views of both Mafdal and the Nationalist Religious Party converge on the role of the state as guardian of the religious community. Both view the national community as pluralistic but also treat this pluralism as transitory, as it stems from the groups' lack of understanding of their common religious essence. It is not surprising, therefore, that Mafdal's motto, "we are the soul of Zionism," reflects its perceived role as complementary to the secular institutions, and not antithetical. Likewise, the statement of Turkey's NAP, "Turkishness is our body, Islam our soul," portrays how Muslimness and Turkishness are constituent of a whole.

What is missing in many analyses is that national religious parties not only accept but also build their political project around modern constructs like the state, which for them eventually becomes *pivotal* for the preservation of religious community. Sacralizers consider secularists as unaware carriers of the nation's religious essence. Ironically, the parties' unequivocal commitment to the unity of the national community enables them to accommodate differences that do not threaten the perceived ethnic and religious unity. The conviction that individual differences are inconsequential and result from a veil of ignorance forms both the foundation and the limits of these parties' tolerance. As detailed in Chapters Four and Five, when the country's territorial or national unity faces a challenge, national religious parties may become intolerant of the state, as they deem the state diverging from the divinely ascribed role. Some Mafdal members, for instance, declare efforts to withdraw from the settlements as a reason for civil war. They distinguish between the ideal and the practice of the state and challenge its antiredemptionist policies. By the same token, Turkey's NAP does not hesitate to publicly demand a military takeover of political power if a ruling government indicates its willingness to accept a national compromise on issues like Northern Cyprus or the Kurdish question.

Overall, sacralizing allows some religious parties to claim a "compromising" position. These parties' assignment of religious essence to existing institutions enables them to accept their present form, making national religious parties especially ideal partners in a procedural democracy, that is, a polity where the process and the institutions of representation exist, and actors do not question the legitimacy of the institutions. This initial recognition of all other agents in politics, this very same sacralization of politics, does not permit the parties to engage in deeply transforming questioning and negotiations. Small aberrations from the expected roles, especially the state's role, initiate authoritarian reactions. What ultimately matters for the sacralizer parties is ensuring the unfolding of redemption and fulfillment of the historically and religiously defined mission of the political institutions.

The second process, internal secularization, differs from sacralization as the former does not discover religious meanings in secular institutions. Instead, internal secularization rests on questioning the very raison d'etre of secular institutions. Despite the initially confrontational language of the parties, internal secularizers do not reject the secular world in toto. Ironically, in their initial rejection they not only implicitly recognize secular institutions but also allow religious ideas to absorb secular ones. For instance, both the JDP and Prosperity challenge secularism as a political project. Instead of rejecting secularism altogether, they argue that secularism has become a regressive project only because "Kemalism did not define *Laiklik* (secularism) thoroughly by remaining loyal to its original intent. Even the very term *'laiklik'* remained a foreign term without a Turkish equivalent and is used as a tool to subdue religious opposition."[17] Lacking a vernacularized equivalent, that laiklik does not allow religious symbols alienates moderate Muslims, which in return, undermines the legitimacy of the Kemalist regime. These parties argue that the real meaning of secularism, namely the autonomy of religious groups is not only consistent with Islam, but is in essence an accepted Islamic practice. Thus, the more the term and other secular constructs reflect their locally supported religious meanings, the better they will serve the country's democracy.

The approach of Turkey's pro-Islamic parties to laiklik captures how the process of transformative adaptation can reveal itself as internal secularization and how at the end even the most tenacious religious and secular ideas prove eventually to be mutually permeable. Turkey's pro-Islamic parties contest many practices that are attributed to a secular idea and institution, such as the effort to create areligious school environments. The rejection does not initiate a disengagement from politics or strictly insular discussions. In contrast, it initiates another level of engagement in an effort to address the contested practice and find its religiously equivalent explanation. Throughout this process a new discursive sphere opens up that explains how the essence of the rejected practice can be reinvented in religious doctrine and in some cases how it can be improved upon. Eventually it becomes an ideationally osmotic process fraught with tensions, but it brings the secular and the religious closer together instead of distancing them. As a result, unlike their sacralizer counterparts who accept institutions and practices and legitimize them through religious reasoning, the positions of internal secularizers are characterized by their initial distrust of the state and the cumulative results of its policies. The parties then introduce religiously grounded alternative policies and practices. The starting point of the dialogical interaction, which includes rejection of the practice, recognition of its essence, and effort toward replacement, opens the door for the invention of unconventional religious and secular positions. As a result, these parties strike a balance between being anti–status quo or antisystemic movements. They challenge the secular pillars of Zionism and Kemalism not because they are modernizing, but because they are not modernizing enough due to their misperceptions and misplaced policies. As a result, their quest for change does not rely on a radical shift in the goals of their ideological other but on their argument that they can deliver the promises of national secularism, social equality, and distributive justice more effectively.

The processes of sacralization and internal secularization draw our attention to the fact that religious and secular do not clash but rather go through a mutually transformative process in which novel appearances hide under old practices and seemingly new practices perpetuate old ideas. This blending does not, however, automatically lead to liberating and congruous fusion of each part, and consequently, it does not always enhance the practice of democratic diversity. For instance, internal secularizers' defense of the religious rights of citizens contributed to the political liberalization of their respective democratic community. Yet a review of these parties' discourse in Chapters Four and Five indicates that their demands for cultural and religious rights do not always extend to other groups whose identities cannot be reduced to religious terms, or who hold heterodox beliefs. Internal secularizers are less open than sacralizers to groups that can challenge the religious community from within. For example, while Shas maintains a tolerant attitude towards Arabs, the party is very critical of immigrants, particularly of recent arrivals from the former Soviet republics who are seen as an internal threat to the purity of the religious community. Similarly, the JDP and the Prosperity Party's willingness to accept the Kurds' cultural rights does not extend to Alevis or Turkey's other unorthodox Islamic groups. Kurds are accepted due to their shared Muslimness, not because the parties adhere to a principled commitment to the right to cultural differences. More importantly, although religious parties mobilize women successfully, all of these parties stumble over the emancipation of women from traditional gender roles. Religious parties are adamant about promoting the rights of observant women in the public sphere, but in their own institutions, they allow women limited, clearly demarcated opportunities to challenge traditional roles and hold leadership positions, thus maintaining traditional practices.

Viewing religious parties via sacralization and internal secularization shows that their democratic balance sheets are mixed (see table C.1). The involvement of religious parties in politics per se assumes a crucial role for legitimizing democratic competition as the only game in town for achieving political power. The parties expand the boundaries of politics by articulating novel political choices in Israel's and Turkey's ever diminishing political space and volatile political climate. They carve a space beyond the habitual one by defying positions assigned to religious and secular blocs. Instead of rejecting secularism categorically, some of these parties reinforce secular nationalist ideas, while others reinterpret religious values and make them more compatible with secular ones. Nevertheless, while they are capable of challenging secular nationalism, religious parties continue to be bound by secular nationalist paradigms. Thus, religious parties are very much a product of their respective political systems and cannot be treated as external to them or as isolated reactionary groups within them. Any account that defines religious parties at a substantial level and labels them as either antidemocratic or democratic must include their positions on various actors in the democratic game, and more importantly, move beyond the parties' acceptance of democratic procedures and secular ideas and analyze in detail their ideational foundations. Omitting this last step can yield highly misleading conclusions.

TABLE C.I

A typology of religious parties

	National Religious Parties	Religious Expansionist and Revisionist Parties
Main Process	Sacralization	Internal Secularization
Hegemonic Nationalism	Sacralization of nationalism as inherently a religious project	Challenges but also adopts nationalism; Requests its pluralization to accommodate ethnic-religious plurality
Nation	Ethnic territorial	Religious community
State	Supportive of the state; treats it as sacred as it supports the religious community	Indifferent to the state, as long as it supports the religious community
Individual vs. Community	Individual as constituent of community is ultimate unit	Community (transcending individual differences) is ultimate unit
Inclusive vs. Exclusive *	Inclusive with regard to differences that remain within the framework of the ethnic-religious community	Inclusive with regard to disparate religious and ethnic groups to the extent that they are inward, cohabit the same polity and do not challenge the hegemonic religious ideas
	Exclusive with regard to unorthodox religious and ethnic groups	Exclusive with regard to unorthodox religious groups especially to those which challenge the orthodoxy from within

*Inclusive and Exclusive categories are used here to assess the boundaries of religious parties' ideal communities, their position vis-à-vis other ethnic and religious groups, and to delineate *the extent to which* these parties accept the extension of basic liberal rights and freedoms to other communities.

RETURN TO RELIGION AS A POLITICAL FORCE

The political history of any polity shows that religion has always been part and parcel of the private practices and public decisions of a country's citizens and therefore an indispensable aspect of politics. As a consequence, the prophecy that religion would grow to be irrelevant to individuals and thus to politics is a conceptual, deductive conclusion, rather than an empirically grounded supposition. The unexpected "return" of religion thesis that marks many studies today appears to be more our return to the once marginalized field of religion and politics, than religion's return to world politics in unprecedented forms. The analysis presented here is an engagement with both "returns" and a reflection of the increasing relevance of religion in political decisions and our effort to capture the ways in which such relevance and decisions occur. By crossing the conventional bridges between the politics of Judaism and Islam, the preceding sections attended to popular questions such as "why religion and why now?" as well as the more crucial, but less popular ones, for example how we can understand religion's new role without subsuming it under various homogenizing labels.

The diversity of positions contained in the politics of Judaism and Islam establishes that the ideological underpinnings of religious parties span a range of positions. Our efforts to describe these parties must allow their multidimensional nature to reveal itself. Given that the relationship of political groups and movements toward democracy forms the ultimate goal of our assessment, it is especially important that we recalibrate our conceptual tools. As the project of democracy becomes more complex and populated with unexpected actors, and our scholarly assessment can obliquely or directly affect their political treatment, we cannot afford to misinterpret their political potential. Generalizing from a single aspect of the movement and defining its relationship to democracy by overvaluing that one component risks creating idealized models detached from the realities of religious parties. For instance, if we try to gauge the positions of religious parties vis-à-vis their country's state and hegemonic discourse, in many cases religious parties have a liberating effect, especially by exposing exclusive government policies. Yet these critical, liberating positions do not automatically translate into the liberation of their party members. Full-fledged support for the project of liberal democracy tends to be missing, particularly for those areas of social interaction where tradition dominates, such as patriarchal decision making. A reliable assessment of these parties requires holistic approaches that include their positions toward other institutions and actors as well as toward their own members. More importantly, it requires an intellectually uncomfortable category of "mixed" characteristics as these parties engage in many liberating, empowering, and regressive practices at the same time.

What makes the interpretations and the positions of religious parties so compelling is their ability to situate their views within a historical continuity and make themselves pertinent not only to religious, but to secular communities. It is not a coincidence, therefore, that the ingenuity of religious leaders is not expressed only in their reaction to social, political, and economic changes but in the extension of religious doctrines to new, nonreligious issues. Not coincidentally, the ideologues of all religious movements covered in this study at some point worked in state positions or occupied significant public offices and have close ties with communities beyond their local and national groups. If Erbakan had not come to know *Gastarbeiter* communities in Germany, and had they not supported Turkey's first Islamist movement with their political and financial capital, perhaps the movement could not have taken the form it did. Without the attention that Sephardi communities directed to Shas, Shas would have been deprived of significant financial and political support. The creativity of religious parties lies in their remarkable ability to reinterpret widely shared beliefs and the political latitude inherent in their founding ideologies and changing local and global environments. Instead of emerging as a movement *against* change, the religious movement serves as a rich platform *for* change. Change via religion comforts the individual, as venturing to the new becomes not an adventure with an open-ended future but a discovery of continuity in (already known) lost ideas, values, and communities. Thus, religious parties gain political support not as reticent and resistant forces against change but as forces to define and alter current practices and direct the course of unfolding processes. As a corollary to this, no religious movement in the post–cold war era is purely homegrown or inward looking. In fact, the opposite is true. Religious movement supporters are locally situated and globally oriented. They understand local needs but attain political power due to their ability to link the local and the global, travel across different religious communities, and immerse themselves in different traditions. Their efforts do not center on reviving traditional religious ideas, but on offering new solutions to recurring problems from within their respective religious paradigms.

The complexity we face with regard to religious parties reaffirms the conclusion that the multifaceted nature of religious parties allows for various explanations. Any quest to understand what their real nature is demands that we take into account the structural and ideational foundations of these movements and the constraints imposed on them by their respective polity, and more importantly, question the transformative interaction between them. After all, religious parties do not rest on ancient doctrinal ideas or already existing communities. Nor are the religious ideas and communities modeled from the lost past. Instead they blend old and new ideas and engage in the process of globalization by carving out places in it for their idealized future. In the face of a state of flux, religion's ability to create a sense of a political community and secure order while legitimizing different social projects to alter society without creating drastic ruptures makes it an increasingly safe domain of transformation in world politics. The NAP's popular slogan "change without alienation" captures the main premise of religious parties regardless of their host doctrine. At the end, the return of religion to politics does not reflect the outcome of some structural, deterministic processes that needs to be dealt with, but the outcome of individual and collective choices that are facilitated by conducive environments and the power of shared symbolic capital, and that in turn shape these environments and symbols.

The way in which religion's appeal, or its political capital, comes into being is crucial. Perhaps more critical, however, is how its political capital is spent in the local and global marketplace of ideas. The main hurdle in front of us is engaging with religion's elusive structure and what often appear to be the "obsolete ideas" or "irrational" practices of its leaders and supporters. Including such inquiries is the sine qua non of enhancing our analytical assessment of studies ranging from electoral politics to conflict resolution. Gaining a solid understanding of the political role of religion is a journey both in and out of the religious symbolic world into the religion's interaction with structural factors. Even if we give credit to the argument that a reenchantment with the world is simply the reawakening of some dormant religious ideas or the simple reaction to structural failures, we need to acknowledge that it is neither the same old religious ideas nor the same reactions that are detached from the very environment from which they emerge. In order to demystify the return of religion to politics, we need to cross the boundaries of sacred and secular and structural determinism to study religion, regardless of its doctrinal form, as a political force not for or against liberal democracy, but as a part of it.

Notes

Introduction

1. William Safran, *The Secular and the Sacred: Nation, Religion, and Politics* (Portland, OR: Taylor and Francis, 2002), 3.

2. Joshua Mitchell, *The Fragility of Freedom: Tocqueville on Religion, Democracy, and the American Future* (Chicago: University of Chicago Press, 1995), 34.

3. Ibid.

4. Benedict de Spinoza, *A Theologico-Political Treatise*, trans. R.H.M. Elwes (New York: Dover, 1955), 47.

5. Ibid.

6. For more details, see Larry J. Diamond, "Is the Third Wave Over?" *Journal of Democracy* 7, no. 3 (July 1996): 20–37.

7. Kenneth D. Wald and Clyde Wilcox, "Getting Religion: Has Political Science Rediscovered the Faith Factor?" *American Political Science Review* 100, no. 4 (2006): 523.

8. Ibid.

9. Thomas Nagel, *The View from Nowhere* (New York and Oxford: Oxford University Press, 1986).

10. http://www.freedomhouse.org/uploads/fiw/FIWAllScores.xls (accessed on December 20, 2007).

11. Thomas Carothers, "The End of the Transition Paradigm," *Journal of Democracy* 13, no. 1 (2002): 5–21.

12. David Collier and Steven Levitsky, "Research Note: Democracy with Adjectives: Conceptual Innovation in Comparative Research," *World Politics* 49, no. 3 (1997): 430–51.

13. For a detailed review of this argument, see Leonard Binder, *Islamic Liberalism: A Critique of Development Ideologies* (Chicago: University of Chicago Press, 1988).

14. This thesis is formulated as the clash of civilizations by Samuel P. Huntington, "The Clash of Civilizations?" *Foreign Affairs* 72, no. 3 (1993): 22–49.

15. Alexis de Tocqueville, *Democracy in America* (New York: Knopf, 1948), 47.

16. Mark Juergensmeyer, *The New Cold War: Religious Nationalism Confronts the Secular State* (Berkeley: University of California Press, 1993).

17. For a rare use of the term, see Norman A. Stillman, "The Judeo-Islamic Historical Encounter: Visions and Revisions," in *Israel and Ishmael*, ed. Tudor Parfitt (New York: St. Martin's Press, 2000).

18. John L. Esposito and John O. Voll, *Islam and Democracy* (New York: Oxford University Press, 1996).

19. Shmuel N. Eisenstadt, "Multiple Modernities," *Daedalus* 129, no. 1 (2000).

20. Modernity generates new forms of malaise (alienation, meaninglessness, a sense of impending social dissolution) as well. Charles Taylor, "Modern Social Imaginaries," *Public Culture* 14, no. 1 (Winter 2002).

21. Scott Mainwaring and Timothy R. Scully, eds., *Christian Democracy in Latin America: Electoral Competition and Regime Conflicts* (Stanford, CA: Stanford University Press, 2003); Stathis N. Kalyvas, "Democracy and Religious Politics: Evidence from Belgium," *Comparative Political Studies* 31, no. 3 (June 1998): 292–321.

22. Charles Taylor, "A Catholic Modernity?" in *A Catholic Modernity?* ed. James Heft (New York: Oxford University Press, 2005), 13–37.

23. Eisenstadt, "Multiple Modernities," 91–118; Göran Therborn, "Routes to/through Modernity," in *Global Modernities*, eds. Mike Featherstone, Scott Lash and Roland Robertson (London: Sage, 1995).

24. Anthony Giddens, *Modernity and Self-Identity: Self and Society in the Late Modern Age* (Cambridge, MA: Polity, 1991).

25. John Waterbury, "The Potential for Political Liberalization in the Middle East," in *Democracy Without Democrats: The Renewal of Politics in the Muslim World*, ed. Ghassan Salame (London and New York: I. B. Taurus, 1994).

26. John Dryzek, "The Mismeasure of Political Man," *Journal of Politics* 50, no. 3 (August 1988): 705–26.

27. Howard L. Reiter, "The Study of Political Parties, 1906–2005: The View from the Journals," *American Political Science Review* 100, no. 4 (November 2006): 617.

28. Sultan Tepe and Roni Baum, "Shas: Likud with Kippa?" in *Israeli Elections Studies—2007*, eds. Asher Arian and Michal Shamir (New York: Transaction Publications, 2007).

29. There are two main ultra-Orthodox parties, *Degel HaTorah* (the Torah of Israel) and *Agudat Israel* (Union of Israel), which represent Israel's Lithunian and Hasidic blocs, respectively, and receive around 4 percent of the total votes. They are not included in this study as they do not strive to be a mass party like the other groups considered in this analysis.

30. Due to the strict secularist feature of the Turkish Constitution, all political parties that explicitly refer to religious norms are banned from participating in the electoral system. The Virtue Party was banned on June 22, 2001, and then adopted the new name Prosperity Party (*Saadet Partisi*). For the purpose of clarity, this study uses the party's most recent name, the Prosperity Party, or the National View parties (*Milli Görüş*)—a broad name that refers to grassroots organizations of Turkey's openly Islamist social movements.

31. The data used in this study became available through the help of those who collected them, including Michal Shamir, Abraham Diskin, Veri Araştırma, Sezgin

Tüzün, Ali Çarkoğlu, Tarhan Erdem, Eren Pultar, and Mina Tsemach. Their generous contributions formed the foundation of the statistical analyses. The 2003 Israeli data and the 2005 Turkish election data, which rest on national samples of the Israeli and Turkish electorates, respectively, were designed and collected by the author with the help of Haifa University Statistics Center and Frekans Field and Data Processing Center. Earlier versions of some of the ideas and analyses developed here first appeared in the *Journal of Democracy, Democratization*, and the *Mediterranean Quarterly*. See Chapters 4 and 5 for more details.

32. Both the surveys and the research to develop the surveys were made possible by grants from several institutions, including American Association of University Women, United States Institute of Peace, University of Illinois at Chicago Campus Research Board, the University of Illinois Office of Social Science Research, Smith Richardson Foundation, the University of Texas at Austin, and the Ford Foundation.

33. Ted G. Jelen and Clyde Wilcox, eds., *Religion and Politics in Comparative Perspective: The One, the Few and the Many* (New York: Cambridge University Press, 2002).

34. Lisa Anderson, "Politics in the Middle East: Opportunities and Limits in the Quest for Theory," in *Area Studies and Social Science: Strategies for Understanding Middle East Politics*, ed. Mark Tessler (Bloomington: Indiana University Press, 1999); Lisa Anderson, "Scholarship, Policy, Debate Conflict: Why We Study the Middle East and Why It Matters," *Middle East Studies Association Bulletin* 38, no. 1 (2004): 1–10.

Chapter One

1. *U.S. v. Seeger*, 380 U.S. 163 (1965).

2. *Welsh v. U.S.*, 398 U.S. 333 (1970).

3. This definition of power is used by Weber, "Macht bedeutet jede Chance, innerhalb einer sozialen Beziehung den eigenen Willen auch gegen Widerstreben durchzusetzen, gleichviel worauf diese Chance beruht." Max Weber, *Wirtschaft und Gesellschaft* (Tübingen: JCB Mohr, 1975), 28.

4. David Easton, *The Political System: An Inquiry on the State of Political Science*, 2nd ed. (New York: Alfred A. Knopf, 1971).

5. Gustavo Benavides, *Religion and Political Power* (Albany: State University of New York Press, 1989).

6. For different definitions of religion see Raymond Firth, "Problem and Assumption in an Anthropological Study of Religion," *Journal of the Royal Anthropological Institute* 89 (1959): 129–48 (cf. p. 31); Jack Goody, "Religion and Ritual: The Definitional Problem," *British Journal of Sociology* 12 (1961): 142–64; Clifford Geertz, "Religion as a Cultural System," in *Anthropological Approaches to the Study of Religion*, ed. Michael Banton (London: Tavistock Publications, 1966), 1–46; Peter Berger, *The Sacred Canopy: Elements of a Sociological Theory of Religion* (Garden City, NY: Doubleday, 1967); Bryan S. Turner, *Religion and Social Theory: A Materialist Theory* (London: Heinemann Educational, 1983); Robert Bocock and Kenneth Thompson, eds., *Religion and Ideology* (Manchester: Manchester University, 1985); Kenneth Thompson, *Beliefs and Ideology* (London:

Tavistock Publications, 1986); Ugo Bianchi, "The Definition of Religion," in *Problems and Methods of the History of Religions*, eds. Ugo Bianchi et al. (Leiden, The Netherlands: Brill, 1972); W. Richard Comstock, "Toward Open Definitions of Religion," *Journal of the American Academy of Religion* 52 (1984): 499–517.

7. Weber, *Wirtschaft und Gesellschaft*.

8. For a critique of the desecularization thesis, see Peter Berger, *The Desecularization of the World* (Grand Rapids, MI: William Eerdmans, 1999).

9. Max Weber, *Essays in Sociology*, eds. H. H. Gerth and C. Wright Mills (New York: Oxford University Press, 1946), 351.

10. Even Auguste Compte, a social theorist who viewed social evolution as a process consisting of three-stages (i.e., the theological stage, the metaphysical stage, and the positive stage), also acknowledged that the last stage did not create a stable order and that the stages could coexist and compete in what he saw as a revolutionary stage. In the last stage, he argued, "between the necessity of observing facts in order to form a theory, and having a theory in order to observe facts, the human mind would have been entangled in a vicious circle, but for the natural opening afforded by theological conceptions." Auguste Compte, *Cours de Philosophie Positive* (Paris: Rouen frères, 1941).

11. Weber, *Essays in Sociology*, 352.

12. Ibid. Also, in *Science as Vocation* Weber argues that "All theology represents an intellectual *rationalization* of the possession of sacred values. No science is absolutely free from presuppositions, and no science can prove its fundamental value to the person who rejects these presuppositions." Max Weber, *Essays in Sociology*, 148–55.

13. Max Weber, *The Protestant Ethic and the Spirit of Capitalism* (London: Allen and Unwin, 1930).

14. Robert Alun Jones, *Emile Durkheim: An Introduction to Four Major Works* (Beverly Hills, CA: Sage Publications, 1986), 115–55.

15. Robert Alun Jones, "Emile Durkheim," in *Major Social Theorists*, ed. George Ritzer (Malden, MA: Blackwell Publishers, 2000), 216–19.

16. Ibid., 219.

17. Robert Alun Jones, *The Development of Durkheim's Social Realism* (New York: Cambridge University Press, 1999), 84.

18. Emile Durkheim, *Suicide* (New York: Free Press, 1897; reprint, 1997).

19. Durkheim defines religion as "beliefs and practices which unite individuals into one single moral community" and as a "source of collective identity consolidating the image of religion as a source of a certain social order." In his view, religion is, like other traditions, the product of collective thinking that creates a set of concepts and abstract thoughts to explain reality. Emile Durkheim, *The Elementary Forms of the Religious Life* (New York: Free Press, 1965), 62–68.

20. Conflations of concepts such as rationalization, modernization, and secularization serve to reinforce certain understanding of social transformation and contradict Weberian and Durkheimian traditions that question the interrelations among them.

21. Talcott Parsons and Edward A. Shils, *Toward a General Theory of Action: Theoretical Foundations for the Social Sciences* (New Brunswick, NJ: Transaction Publishers, 2001).

22. Berger, *The Sacred Canopy.*

23. Alan Aldridge, *Religion in the Contemporary World* (Cambridge, UK: Polity Press, 2000).

24. For a review of religious voluntarism, see Wade Clark Roof and William McKinney, *American Mainline Religion* (New Brunswick, NJ: Rutgers University Press, 1987).

25. Laurence Iannaccone, "Rational Choice: A Framework for the Scientific Study of Religion," in *Rational Choice Theory and Religion*, ed. L. A. Young (New York: Routledge, 1997).

26. For Stark and Bainbridge, compensators are the substitutes for high rewards. As individuals always seek immortality, enlightenment, and the meaning of life, they will accept and choose supernaturalistic compensators. Rodney Stark and William Sims Bainbridge, "Toward a Theory of Religion: Religious Commitment," *Journal for Scientific Study of Religion* 19 (1980).

27. Methodological individualism presumes that all sociological explanations can be reduced to the facts about individuals and individual behaviors. Steven Lukes, *Emile Durkheim and His Life and Work* (London: Allen Lane, 1973).

28. Bryan Wilson and Jamie Cresswell, *New Religious Movements: Challenge and Response* (New York: Routledge, in association with the Institute of Oriental Philosophy European Centre, 1999).

29. Robert Bellah, *Beyond Belief: Essays on Religion in a Post-Traditional World* (New York: Harper and Row, 1970); Peter Berger, *Facing up to Modernity: Excursions in Society, Politics, and Religion* (New York: Basic Books, 1977); Jurgen Habermas, *Communication and the Evolution of Society* (Boston: Beacon Press, 1979).

30. Bryon Wilson, *Contemporary Transformations of Religion* (London and New York: Oxford University Press, 1976).

31. Hans Kohn, *The Idea of Nationalism: A Study in Its Origins and Background* (New York: Macmillan, 1951).

32. Benedict R. Anderson, *Imagined Communities: Reflections on the Origin and Spread of Nationalism* (London: Verso, 1983); Eric Hobsbawm and Terence Ranger, *The Invention of Tradition* (Cambridge: Cambridge University Press, 1984).

33. Oliver Roy, *Echec de l'islam*, trans. Carol Volk (Cambridge, MA: Harvard University Press, 1994).

34. Laurence J. Silberstein, *Martin Buber's Social and Religious Thought: Alienation and the Quest for Meaning* (New York: New York University Press, 1989).

35. Richard Rose and Doh Chull Shin, "Democratization Backwards: The Problem of Third-Wave Democracies," *British Journal of Political Science* 31 (2001): 331–54.

36. For applications and critical assessments of this view, see Binnaz Toprak, *Islam and Political Development in Turkey* (Leiden, The Netherlands: Brill, 1981); John L. Esposito and John O. Voll, *Islam and Democracy* (New York: Oxford University Press, 1996); Sami Zubaida, *Islam, the People and the State: Essays on Political Ideas and Movements in the Middle East* (London and New York: I.B. Tauris, 1993).

37. Francois Burgat and William Dowell, *The Islamic Movement in North Africa* (Austin: University of Texas at Austin Press, 1993).

38. Emile F. Sahliyeh, *Religious Resurgence and Politics in the Contemporary World* (New York: State University of New York Press, 1990), 12–35.

39. Stephen Warner, "Work in Progress toward a New Paradigm for the Sociological Study of Religion in the United States," *American Journal of Sociology* 98, no. 5 (March 1993): 1044–93.

40. Ibid.

41. Among other studies, see Rodney Stark, *Acts of Faith: Explaining the Human Side of Religion* (Berkeley: University of California Press, 2000); Lawrence A. Young, *Rational Choice Theory and Religion: Summary and Assessment* (New York: Routledge, 1997); Roger Finke and Rodney Stark, *The Churching of America, 1776–1990: Winners and Losers in Our Religious Economy* (New Brunswick, NJ: Rutgers University Press, 1992); Nancy Tatom Ammerman and Arthur E. Farnsley II, *Congregation and Community* (New Brunswick, NJ: Rutgers University Press, 1997).

42. James D. Montgomery, "The Dynamics of the Religious Economy: Exit, Voice, and Denominational Secularization," *Rationality and Society* 8 (1996); Mark Chaves and James D. Montgomery, "Rationality and the Framing of Religious Choices," *Journal for the Scientific Study of Religion* 35, no. 2 (June 1996).

43. For example, the leaders of the conservative secular Right in the Republican Party allied themselves in the late 1970s and 1980s with the conservative Protestant movement to expand their electoral support. Kenneth D. Wald, *Religion and Politics in the United States* (Washington, DC: CQ Press, 1992).

44. For a review of such arguments, see Esposito and Voll, *Islam and Democracy*; Nilüfer Göle, *The Forbidden Modern: Civilization and Veiling* (Ann Arbor: University of Michigan Press, 1996); Allan Metz, "Religion and State in Israel," in *The Religious Challenge to the State*, eds. Moen C. Matthew and Gustofsor S. Lowell (Philadelphia: Temple University Press, 1992).

45. Peter Hirschberg, *The World of Shas* (New York: The American Jewish Committee, 2000).

46. Faruk Birtek and Binnaz Toprak, "The Conflictual Agendas of Neo-Liberal Reconstruction and the Rise of Islamic Politics in Turkey," *Praxis International*, July 1993.

47. For detailed discussions of such arguments see Binnaz Toprak, "Islam and Secular State in Turkey," in *Turkey: Political, Social, and Economic Challenges in the 1990s*, eds. Ciğdem Balım et al. (New York: E.J. Brill, 1995); Roy, *Echec de l'islam*; Sami Zubaida, *Islam, The People and the State: Essays on Political Ideas and Movements in the Middle East* (London and New York: I.B. Tauris, 1993).

48. For an analysis that traces the economic foundations of political parties and reactions, see Ziya Öniş and Barry Rubin, eds., *Turkish Economy in Crisis* (London: Frank Cass, 2003).

49. Robert Wuthnow, *Rediscovering the Sacred: Perspectives on Religion in Contemporary Society* (Grand Rapids, MI: William B. Eerdmans, 1992).

50. Clifford Geertz, *The Interpretation of Cultures* (New York: Basic Books, 1973).

51. Burgat and Dowell, *The Islamic Movement in North Africa.*

52. Benavides, *Religion and Political Power.*

53. Berger, *The Sacred Canopy.*

54. Max Weber's account of secularization serves as a generative metaphor in the various conceptualizations by reducing secularism to a monolithic transformation that starts with "disenchantment" with the mystical world and results in the consequent domination of rationality. For a survey of various theses on secularization, see Aldridge, *Religion in the Contemporary World.*

55. See James A. Beckford and Karel Dobbelaere, *Secularization, Rationalism, and Sectarianism* (Oxford, UK: Clarendon Press; New York: Oxford University Press, 1993).

56. Mark Chaves, "Secularization as Declining Religious Authority," *Social Forces* 72, no.3 (March 1994): 749–74.

57. Roberto Cipriani, "Religiosity, Religious Secularism and Secular Religions," *International Social Science Journal* 46 (June 1994).

58. Samuel Heilman, "Modern Jews and Persistence of Religion," in *Religion and Social Order*, ed. David Bromley (Stamford, CT: Jai Press, 1991).

59. Said Amir Arjomand, *The Political Dimensions of Religion* (Albany: State University of New York Press, 1993).

60. The ideas of divine redemption and the unity of the Islamic nation, ummah, exemplify the terms that play out as important allegories in justifying or altering the status quo.

61. Hans Mol, *Identity and the Sacred: A Sketch for a New Social-Scientific Theory of Religion* (New York: Free Press, 1976).

62. From Peter L. Berger and Thomas Luckmann, *The Social Construction of Reality: A Treatise in the Sociology of Knowledge* (Garden City, NY: Anchor Books, 1966), 51–55, 59–61.

63. Ibid.

64. Ruşen Çakır, İrfan Bozan, Hakan Talu, *İmam Hatip: Efsaneler ve Gerçekler* (İstanbul: Turkish Economic and Social Research Foundation, 2004).

65. Max Weber, *Essays in Sociology*, 270.

66. M. Granovetter, "Economic Action and Social Structure: The Problem of Embeddedness," *American Journal of Sociology* 91 (1985): 487.

67. Jon Elster, *Solomonic Judgments: Studies in the Limitations of Rationality* (Cambridge and New York: Cambridge University Press, 1989).

68. Mark Granovetter and Richard Swedberg, *The Sociology of Economic Life* (Boulder, CO: Westview Press, 1992).

Chapter Two

1. Alexis de Tocqueville, *Democracy in America* (New York: Knopf, 1948), 122.

2. Sydney Tarrow, "State and Opportunities," in *Comparative Perspectives on Social Movements*, eds. Doug McAdam, John D. McCarthy, and Mayer N. Zald (Cambridge: Cambridge University Press, 1996), 44.

3. Daniel L. Dreisbach, *Thomas Jefferson and the Wall of Separation: Between Church and State* (New York: New York University Press, 2002).

4. Thomas Jefferson wrote a letter to the Danbury Baptist Association in 1802 to answer a letter from them written in October 1801: "Believing with you that religion is a matter which lies solely between man and his god, that he owes account to none other for his faith or his worship, that the legitimate powers of government reach actions only, and not opinions, I contemplate with sovereign reverence that act of the whole American people which declared that their legislature should make no law respecting an establishment of religion, or prohibiting the free exercise thereof, thus building a wall of separation between church and state."

5. Dreisbach, *Thomas Jefferson and the Wall of Separation.*

6. Joshua Mitchell, *The Fragility of Freedom: Tocqueville on Religion, Democracy, and the American Future* (Chicago: University of Chicago Press, 1995), 37–46.

7. Elisabeth Zoller, "Laïcité in the United States or The Separation of Church and State in a Pluralist Society," *Indiana Journal of Global Legal Studies* 13, no. 2 (2006): 561–94.

8. Ibid.

9. Jean-Paul Willaime, "The Cultural Turn in the Sociology of Religion in France," *Sociology of Religion* 65, no. 4 (2004): 373–89.

10. John Richard Bowen, *Why the French Don't like Headscarves: Islam, the State, and Public Space* (Princeton, NJ: Princeton University Press, 2006).

11. From 1558 onward, a moderate Protestantism provided the foundation of the Church of England (the Anglican Church). The Church of England attempted to consolidate its position as the national religion of England and a distinctive middle way between Catholicism and Puritanism with varying degrees of success.

12. Ranu Samantrai, "Continuity or Rupture? An Argument for Secular Britain," *Social Text* 18, no. 3 (2000): 105–21.

13. Susan Siavoshi, "Between Heaven and Earth: The Dilemma of Islamic Republic of Iran," in *Religion and Politics in Comparative Perspective: The One, the Few and the Many,* eds. Ted G. Jelen and Clyde Wilcox (New York: Cambridge University Press, 2002), 125–41.

14. Theodor Herzl was born in Budapest in 1860. His ideas were greatly shaped by the German-Jewish Enlightenment of the period and its secularist ideas. In 1878 his family moved to Vienna, and in 1884, Herzl was awarded a doctorate of law from the University of Vienna. He became a writer and a journalist, working as the Paris correspondent of the influential liberal Vienna newspaper *Neue Freie Presse.* The first Zionist Congress was held in Basle, Switzerland, August 29–31, 1897, under his leadership. His books *Der Judenstaat* (The Jewish State, 1896) and *The Jew's State, Altneuland* (Old New Land, 1902) introduced a wide audience to the idea of a modern nation-state as the only politically viable solution to the Jewish problem. Herzl died in Vienna in 1904. Mustafa Kemal Atatürk was born in Salonica (located in today's Greece, then an Ottoman city) in 1881. He graduated from the War Academy in Istanbul in 1905 and became part of a group "Homeland and Freedom." He initiated the War of Independence on May 19, 1919, and presided over the first Grand National Assembly on April 23, 1920. On October 29, 1923, the Republic of Turkey was

declared, and Mustafa Kemal became the first president. In his memoirs, correspondence, and speeches, he provided his account of the nation-building process in Turkey. When the surname law was adopted in 1934, the national parliament gave him the name Atatürk (Father of the Turks). He died on November 10, 1938.

15. For a historical review and critique of the perception of Jewish nation as anomaly, see Evron Boas, *Jewish State or Israeli Nation?* (Bloomington: Indiana University Press, 1995).

16. Theodor Herzl, *The Jewish State: An Attempt at a Modern Solution of the Jewish Question,* ed. Jacob M. Alkow (New York: American Zionist Emergency Council, 1946).

17. Hess was a German journalist and socialist who influenced Karl Marx and Friedrich Engels and later became a proponent of Zionism. His most prominent work, the early Zionist *Rom und Jerusalem, die letzte Nationalitätsfrage* (1862; Rome and Jerusalem: A Study in Jewish Nationalism) influenced Theodor Herzl. According to Hess, the Jews would never fully be accepted by others until they had their own country. Moses Hess, *Rome and Jerusalem: A Study in Jewish Nationalism* (New York: Bloch, 1943).

18. Berlin Sir Isaiah, *Life and Opinions of Moses Hess, the Jewish Historical Society of England* (Cambridge, UK: W. Heffer & Sons, 1959).

19. Theodor Herzl, *Altneuland* (Haifa, Israel: Haifa Pub. Co., 1961), 17.

20. Rebuilding of the temple holds an important place in the idea of redemption. Herzl used religious parables and prophecies about redemption to describe the Zionist movement's goals. For a discussion of Herlz's gradual embrace of religion in his public appeals, see Melman Yossi, *The New Israelis: An Intimate View of a Changing People* (New York: Carol Publishing Group, 1992).

21. Nathan Birnbaum, *Confession* (New York: Jewish Pocket Books, 1947).

22. Zion acts as one of the key terms in Judaism, as it denotes the last center of the Jewish state and, at the same time, a holy site.

23. As explained in the following chapters, redemption constitutes one of the most unifying and divisive terms in the Judaic tradition. Two contrasting interpretations of redemption, one through men's labor and the other through divine intervention, coexist within the Orthodox community but also divide it. After the 1967 War, the idea that redemption will come through human labor became more dominant and triggered the split and merger of various religious organizations.

24. Cited in Max Nordau, "Ein Templerstreit," *Die Welt,* June 2, 1897; Shmuel Almog, *Tzionut ve-historya* (Jerusalem: Magnes Press, 1982), 69. Over the course of time, Rabbi Kook was to draw a sharp distinction between Herzl and Nordau: "the latter is the abomination of my soul and of the soul of everyone who has a spark of Judaism," *Iggerot ha-Reiyah,* vol. 2 (Jerusalem: Mosad HaRav Kook, 1990), 294.

25. Herzl declared at the first congress that Zionism "is not intended to impinge upon the religious consciousness of any stream in Judaism." At subsequent congresses, he repeatedly declared "Zionism does not do anything against religion." He thereby sought to bypass the conflict concerning this question. See Alex Bein, *Theodor Herzl: A Biography* (Jerusalem: Hassifria Hazionit, 1976)

185, 193, 213. For more details see Joseph Adler, *The Herzl Paradox: Political, Social and Economic Theories of a Realist* (New York: Hadrian Press and Herzl Press, 1962).

26. Eliezer Don Yehiya, "Zionism in Retrospective," *Modern Judaism* 18, no. 3 (1998): 267–76.

27. According to Gorny, for example, one can identify two distinct models of culture in the early years of Zionism. The first was that of the traditional world of Jewish learning, symbolized by the yeshivah. The second included *Bildung*, the cultural ethos inspired by the Enlightenment, which had decisively shaped the intellectual discourse of Central and Eastern Europe in the nineteenth century. Yosef Gorny, "Thoughts on Zionism as a Utopian Ideology," *Modern Judaism* 18, no. 3 (1998): 241–51.

28. Each of these movements sought to strengthen the foundations of the traditional social order against the threat of assimilation exerted by the appealing ideas of European Enlightenment and the isolationist policies of the Russian empire. The growing appeal of these movements was reflected in the rapid increase in the number of religious schools, yeshivas, in the late nineteenth and the early twentieth century. That growth, according to Luz, was not due to a "growing fervor for Torah Study among the masses but was rather a direct result of the spread of modernist ideas, fear of assimilation, and the decrease in the number of students learning the Torah in informal settings." Ehud Luz, *Parallels Meet: Religion and Nationalism in the Early Zionist Movement (1882–1904)* (Philadelphia: Jewish Publication Society, 1988).

29. The Western European Jewry opposed these religious-traditionalist movements on two grounds. One, by isolating themselves in the narrow world of Torah, the traditionalist movements failed to contribute to a comprehensive modern solution to the "Jewish Question." Two, the rabbis' opposition to the Western democracies and their refusal to modify religion would result in an increasing estrangement of the younger generation from Judaism.

30. Birnbaum, *Confession*.

31. Zionism proved to be an effective international political movement with the gathering of 250 delegates from twenty-four European countries on August 29, 1897, in Switzerland. Sephardi, or non-Western Jews, participated in small numbers, and a limited number supported continental nationalism and Marxism.

32. David Vital, *The Future of the Jews* (Cambridge, MA: Harvard University Press, 1990).

33. Menachem Friedman, "The State of Israel as a Theological Dilemma," in *The Israeli State and Society: Boundaries and Frontiers*, ed. Baruch Kimmerling (Albany: State University of New York Press, 1989).

34. For more detailed analysis of these groups, see Shmuel Almog, Jehuda Reinhaz, and Anita Shaira, eds., *Zionism and Religion* (Hanover, NH: University Press of New England, 1998). Also see Ben Halpern and Jehuda Reinharz, *Zionism and the Creation of a New Society* (Hanover, NH: University Press of New England, 2000).

35. Hamizrahi was set up as the Zionist movement of religious Jewry in Eastern Europe in 1902.

36. The Israeli state adopted a unique educational system through the Ministry of Education and Culture with respect to the *Haredi* ultra-Orthodox community. A separate administrative unit of the state manages the two Haredi educational systems and only employs inspectors from the Haredi community. The educational institutions of the Haredi systems are officially recognized and considered in compliance with the law of compulsory education.

37. Asher Cohen and Bernard Susser, "From Accommodation to Decision: Transformations in Israel's Religio-Political Life," *Journal of Church and State* 38, no. 4 (1996): 817–39.

38. An institution comparable to the Chief Rabbinate, *Hacham Bashi*, acted as the chief Jewish religious authority during Ottoman rule.

39. Norman L. Zucker, *The Coming Crisis in Israel: Private Faith and Public Policy* (Cambridge, MA: MIT Press, 1973).

40. Attesting to the complexity of the process, the rabbinical sector of the electoral body comprises thirty rabbis from the country's largest cities, fourteen rabbis from large towns, two from leading regional councils, eight from large moshavim, four from major neighborhoods (one each from Jerusalem, Tel Aviv, Haifa, and Be'er Sheva), the ten most-senior *dayanim* (rabbinical court judges), the IDF's chief rabbi and his deputy, and ten rabbis named by the government.

41. Although the ministry of religious affairs was dissolved, the center for the development of holy sites will be the responsibility of the Tourism Ministry, the rabbinic courts will be under the control of the Justice Ministry, and the rabbi of the holy sites and of the Western Wall will be under the supervision of the Chief Rabbinate. Zvi Zrahiya, "Religious Affairs Ministry to Be Dissolved," *Haaretz*, March 3, 2004.

42. Amnon Rubinstein, "State and Religion in Israel," *Journal of Contemporary History* 2, no. 4 (Church and Politics, October 1967): 107–21.

43. For an argument that asserts that the Status Quo was not a compromise, but a symbolic movement by secularist Zionists to incorporate religious blocs into the Zionist movement, see Yosef Goell, "Status Quo that Never Was," *The Jerusalem Post*, November 30, 1990.

44. Aviezer Ravitzky, *Religious and Secular Jews in Israel: A Kulturkampf?* (Jerusalem: Israeli Democracy Institute, 2000).

45. Ibid.

46. Lilly Weissbrod, "Religion as National Identity in a Secular Society," *Review of Religious Research* 24, no. 3 (March 1983): 188–205.

47. The archaeological studies of Israel as the Holy and National Land offer an excellent example of religio-national projects which, among others, resulted in the discovery of the Dead Sea Scrolls, and later Yigal Yadin's excavations at Massada (a site of fierce Jewish resistance to the Romans after the fall of Jerusalem in AD 70).

48. For a detailed review of such cases, see Shetreet Shimon, *Between Three Branches of Government: The Balance of Rights in Matters of Religion in Israel* (Jerusalem: The Floersheimer Institute for Policy Studies, 1999).

49. Şerif Mardin, *Religion and Social Change in Modern Turkey: The Case of Bediuzzaman Said Nursi* (New York: State University of New York Press, 1989), 12.

50. Ibid., 112.

51. Caliph literally means "successor"; in this context, the successor of the Prophet Muhammad is a title of honor adopted by the Ottoman sultans in the sixteenth century after Sultan Selim I was recognized as guardian of the holy cities of Mecca and Medina.

52. İlber Ortaylı, "Osmanli Kimliği," *Cogito*, no. 19 (Summer 1999).

53. Kemal Atatürk, *Söylev* (Ankara: Türk Tarih Kurumu Basimevi, 1986).

54. Suna Kili and A. Şeref Gözübüyük, *Türk Anayasa Metinleri* (Istanbul: Türkiye İş Bankası Kültür Yayınları, 2000).

55. Ibid.

56. Ibid.

57. Kemal Atatürk, *Nutuk, Söylev, Vesikalar, Belgeler*, vol. 3 (Ankara: Türk Tarih Kurumu, 1999), 374–76.

58. Şevket Süreyya Aydemir, *Tek Adam Mustafa Kemal'in Hayatı*, vol. 3 (İstanbul: Remzi Kitapevi, 1969), 77.

59. For the English translation of the text, see Elaine Diana Smith, *Turkey: The Origins of the Kemalist Movement (1919–1923)* (Washington, DC, 1959).

60. Abdulaziz Mecdi (Karesi) was a member of the first national assembly. A reference to this speech can be found in Tarık Zafer Tunaya, *Türkiye'de Siyasi Partiler* (İstanbul: Hürriyet Vakfı Yayınları, 1986).

61. For an extended discussion of the second group, see Ahmet Demirel, *Birinci Mecliste Muhalefet: İkinci Grup* (İstanbul: İletisim, 1994).

62. Atatürk, *Söylev*.

63. Ibid.

64. Ziya Gökalp, "Milliyetçilik," *Yeni Mecmua* 2, no. 33 (Şubat, 1918): 122–23.

65. Ziya Gökalp, *Türkcülüğün Esasları* (Istanbul: Remzi Kitapevi, 1997), 56.

66. Nihat Nirun, *Sistematik Sosyoloji Açısından Ziya Gökalp* (Ankara: KTB Yayınları, 1999), 148.

67. Gökalp, *Türkcülüğün Esasları*, 82.

68. Necmeddin Şahiner, *Bilinmeyen Taraflarıyle Bediüzzaman Said Nursî* (İstanbul: Yeni Asya Yayınları, 1979), 236.

69. Cited in Mardin, *Religion and Social Change in Modern Turkey*.

70. Niyazi Berkes, *The Development of Secularism in Turkey* (London: Hurst & Co., 1998).

71. Turkification of Islam included substituting the Turkish word *Tanrı* for the Arabic word *Allah* and introducing Turkish for the daily calls to prayer. As a result of widespread opposition to the Turkification of Arabic prayers, it was decided in 1933 to return to the Arabic version of the call to prayer. For a discussion of the terminology of Kemalism, see Erik-Jan Zurcher, *The Core Terminology of Kemalism: Mefkûre, Millî, Muasır, Medenî*, http://www.let.leidenuniv.nl/tcimo/tulp/Research/terms.htm. Also see Mimar Türksinan, *Türkiye'de Siyasal Sosyalleşme ve Siyasal Sembolizm* (İstanbul: Birey Yayınları, 2000).

72. Berkes, *The Development of Secularism in Turkey*, 460.

73. For more detailed discussion of the population exchanges, see Stephen P. Ladas, *The Exchange of Minorities; Bulgaria, Greece and Turkey* (New York: Macmillan, 1932).

74. Kemal Arı, *Büyük Mübadele, Türkiye'ye Zorunlu Göç 1923–1925* (Istanbul: Tarih Yurt Vakfı Yayınları, 1995).

75. For the institutional deployment of Turkish secularism, see Berkes, *The Development of Secularism in Turkey*.

76. Various institutions were established to explore historical and cultural commonalities, to forge and consolidate the secular Turkish identity. In 1930, the Turkish History Association was established to study the roots of Turkish identity in the pre-Islamic period. This project introduced a new notion of history based on secular, nationalist ideology, contradicting the still-influential Ottomanist approach, which disregarded pre-Islamic Turkish history. As a result of these efforts, new Turkish history was written through the studies of scholars such as Fuat Köprülü (1890–1966). In his *The History of Turkey*, Köprülü, drawing on the findings in archeology, literature, and Turcology, contended that the turning point in Turkish history was the Turkification of Anatolia under the Anatolian *Selçuks*.

77. Mardin, *Religion and Social Change in Modern Turkey*.

78. Şerif Mardin, *Din ve İdeoloji Turkiye'de Halk Katındaki Dinsel İnançlarin Siyasal Eylemi Etkilendirmesine İlişkin Bir Kavramlaştırma Modeli* (Ankara: Sevinç Matbaasi, 1969).

79. For more information, see Mardin, *Religion and Social Change in Modern Turkey*.

80. Yasin Aktay, *Political and Intellectual Disputes on the Academisation of Religious Knowledge* (Ankara: Middle East Technical University, 1993), 49.

81. İsmet Özel, *Üç Mesele: Teknik, Medeniyet, Yabancılaşma* (İstanbul: Dergah Yayınları, 1984), 26.

82. Andrew Davison, *Secularism and Revivalism in Turkey* (New Haven and London: Yale University Press, 1998), 191.

Chapter Three

1. Israel Bartal, "Responses to Modernity: Haskala, Orthodoxy, and Nationalism in Eastern Europe," in *Zionism and Religion*, eds. Shmuel Almog, Jehuda Reinharz, and Anita Shapira (Hanover, NH: University Press of New England, 1998), 18.

2. Bnei Akiva, the religious Zionist youth movement, was founded in Jerusalem in 1929 based on the twin ideals of Torah VeAvoda—a blend of Orthodox observance of religious commandments and Zionist pioneering. The movement became an international movement in 1954. For more details, see Bnei Akiva, *Mazkirut Olamit, Shemitta* (Tel-Aviv: Bnei Akiva, 1965).

3. Especially after the hegemonic rise of the nationalist movement, the religious terms *geullah*, redemption, and *kibbutz galuyot*, ingathering of exiles, emerged to both justify and counter modern nationalism. Michael Lowy, *Redemption and Utopia: Jewish Libertarian Thought in Central Europe; A Study in Elective Affinity* (London: Athlone, 1992).

4. Nathan Birnbaum, *Confession* (New York: Jewish Pocket Books, 1947), 27.

5. Ibid., 45.

6. Unless indicated otherwise, all the references to Kook refer to Avraham Yitzchak HaCohen Kook, who made a permanent mark on Israeli politics (1865–1935). He served as the first chief rabbi in Eretz Israel during Yishuv, the prestate period. He is considered to be the most influential thinker of religious Zionism. His overall ideas are being taught in *Merkaz ha-Rav* in Jerusalem. It is one of few yeshivot whose students serve in the Israeli army.

7. Avraham Yitzchak Kook, *Olat Ha-Reiyah* (Jerusalem: Mosad ha-Rav ha-Miśrad le-inyene datot, 1985), 94–96.

8. Ibid., 236 and *Igrot HaReiyah* vol. II, letter 555 (Jerusalem: Mosad ha-Rav, 1966).

9. Arthur Hertzberg, *The Zionist Idea: A Historical Analysis and Reader* (Garden City, NY: Doubleday, 1959), 419.

10. Avraham Kook, *Ma'amarei Ha-Reiya* (Jerusalem: Mosad ha-Rav ha-Miśrad le-inyene datot, 1985), 403–4.

11. For a discussion of the shift from the idea of "normalization" to "uniqueness," see Boas Evron, *Jewish State or Israeli Nation* (Bloomington: Indiana University Press, 1995).

12. For more on Mafdal's ideology as grounded in attempts to nationalize Judaism, see Gary S. Schiff, *Tradition and Politics: The Religious Parties of Israel* (Detroit: Wayne State University Press, 1977).

13. In his letter to the Rothschild family in 1835; see Jody Myers, *Seeking Zion: Modernity and Messianic Activism in the Writings of Tsevi Hirsch Kalischer* (Oxford; Portland, OR: Littman Library of Jewish Civilization, 2003).

14. Tsevi Hirsch Kalischer, "Derishat Zion" (1862), in *The Zionist Idea,* ed. Arthur Hertzberg (New York: Harper & Row, 1959), 111.

15. Ibid.

16. Gerald J. Blidstein, "Jewish Law Applied: The State of Israel in Halachic Thought," *Magshimon* 23 (June 22, 2003).

17. Rabbi Mordechai Eliahu and Rabbi Avraham Shapira, "A Torah View of the Laws of the State and the Implementation of Takanot Today," *Tehumin* vol.3 (1982), 238–46, quoted in Blidstein, "Jewish Law Applied."

18. Ibid.

19. Ibid.

20. For a summary version of Mafdal's party program (in Hebrew), see www .mafdal.org.il (accessed August 21, 2006).

21. Ibid.

22. Zvi Yehuda Kook, "Mizmor 19" (speech) (Jerusalem: Mercaz HaRav, May 14, 1969), cited in *Torah Mitzion*, no. 87 (May 8, 2005).

23. Avraham Kook, *Ein Aya* vol. 2 (Jerusalem: Mosad ha-Rav Kook, 1994), 186–87; Kook, *Olat Ha-Reiyah* vol. 1 (Jerusalem: Mosad ha-Rav ha-Miśrad le-inyene datot, 1985), 374–77. For more details, see Lawrence J. Kaplan and David Shatz, *Rabbi Abraham Isaac Kook and Jewish Spirituality* (New York: New York University Press, 1995), 196; and Rabbi Chanan Morrison, "Eikev: Two Loves for Eretz Yisrael," in *A New Light on the Weekly Torah Portion from the Writings of Rabbi Avraham Kook* (Jerusalem: Urim Publication, 2006), 303–11.

24. Rabbi Yehudah Shaviv, "Explain a Midrash: The Importance of Unity," *Shabbat-B'shabbato* no. 687 (February 14, 1998).

25. Avraham Kook, "Eitzot Merahok," *HaPeles* (Berlin, 1902), 30; see Ben Zion Bokser, *Abraham Yitzchak Kook: The Lights of Penitence, the Moral Principles, Lights of Holiness, Essays, Letters, and Poems* (New York: Paulist Press, 1978), 389; and Jack Cohen, *Guides for an Age of Confusion: Studies in the Thinking of Avraham Y. Kook and Mordecai M. Kaplan* (New York: Fordham University Press, 1999), 311.

26. Kook, *Ein Aya* vol. 2, 176. For further details see Cohen, *Guides for an Age of Confusion*, 324; Rabbi Chanan Morrison, "Mishpatim: Following the Majority Opinion," in *A New Light on the Weekly Torah Portion from the Writings of Rabbi Abraham Isaac HaKohen Kook* (Jerusalem: Urim Publication, 2006), 142.

27. Avraham Kook, *Ein Aya* vol. 1, 57. For further details, see Rabbi Chanan Morrison, "Mishpatim: Trust in God vs. Self-Reliance," in *A New Light on the Weekly Torah Portion from the Writings of Rabbi Abraham Isaac HaKohen Kook* (Jerusalem: Urim Publication, 2006), 136.

28. Rabbi Yisrael Rozen, "Point of View: Self Centered Leadership," *Shabbat-B'shabbato* no. 734 (January 9, 1999).

29. Mafdal Party Program.

30. Nissim Swed, "Religious Zionism in Action: Unity in the Nation," *Shabbat* no. 686 (February 7, 1998).

31. Ibid.

32. Cohen, *Guides for an Age of Confusion*, 185.

33. Avraham Kook, *Orot* (Jerusalem: Mosad Harav Kook, 1963), 169, paragraph 6; Avraham Kook, *Midbar Shur* (Jerusalem: Orot Publishing, 2001), 110–15.

34. Cohen, *Guides for an Age of Confusion*, 250; Kook, *Ein Aya* vol. 1, 157.

35. Herb Keinon, "Mafdal: Bending to Realpolitik," *Jerusalem Post*, June 11, 1999.

36. A fuller explanation of Yitzhak Levy's ideas on culture war can be found in Asher Wallfish, "Peretz Deliberately Intended to Kindle Fierce Passion," *Jerusalem Post*, July 12, 1991.

37. Ibid.

38. Herb Keinon, "The NRP: Bending to Realpolitik," *Jerusalem Post*, June 11, 1999.

39. Rabbi Yisrael Rozen, "Ashkenazi Supremacy," *Shabbat-B'shabbato* no. 714 (August 22, 1998).

40. Ibid.

41. Ibid.

42. Ibid.

43. Rabbi Levi Nachum, "Balak's Advice: To Evict Us from the Land," *Shabbat-B'shabbato* (DN North Judea, Israel), no. 708:17 (Tamuz 5758/July 11, 1998).

44. Mafdal's Party Program.

45. Shlomo Goren, "Sacred Land and Moral Danger," *Techumin* no. 15 (1995): 13.

46. Avner Hai-Shaki, former Minister of Religious Affairs, in interview with author, June 1999.

47. Cited in Zvi Yaron, "The Philosophy of Rabbi Kook," *Hagshama* 7 (August 2006).

48. Colin Shindler, *The Triumph of Military Zionism* (London and New York: I.B. Tauri, 2006).

49. Ezra Gellman, *Essays on the Thought and Philosophy of Rabbi Kook* (Rutherford, NJ: Fairleigh Dickinson University Press, 1991), 25–46.

50. The term "moderate" needs to be understood within the context of Mafdal. While considered moderate, Hammer still declared, "If the government decides that we will not continue to settle Judea and Samaria, we will regard this as crossing over the red line we have set ourselves on this issue." Cited in Gershon R. Kieval, *Party Politics in Israel and the Occupied Territories* (Westport, CT: Greenwood Press, 1983).

51. Menahem Mor, *Jewish Sects, Religious Movements, and Political Parties* (Omaha, NE: Fordham University Press, 1992), 376; David Ben Gurion, *Israel: A Personal History* (Tel Aviv: Sabra Publications, 1971), 45.

52. Despite the widening gap between various factions—including those under Yosef Burg—Haim Druckman, leader of the Gush Eminum, and Ben Meir Shapira endorsed the idea that domestic compromise-seeking policies were the priority of the party.

53. Haim Shapiro, "NRP Rabbis Forbid Golan Pullout," *Jerusalem Post*, January 5, 2000.

54. The council of Hakibbutz Hadati, the religious kibbutz movement, passed a resolution that rabbis should not determine political issues. *Ha'aretz*, June 26, 1998, and Larry Derfner, "Ideology of Moderation," *Jerusalem Post*, October 4, 1996.

55. For a very comprehensive review of the party's internal conflicts, see Asher Arian and Michal Shamir, *The Elections in Israel 2003* (New Brunswick, NJ: Transaction Publishers, 2005).

56. Bar Ilan University, which has around 25,000 students, holds a unique place in the Israeli educational system by requiring all students to take extensive courses in Judaism regardless of their fields.

57. The average age of the party's members of the Knesset in the last three Knessets.

58. Marx Eric, "Starting a Revolution in the National Religious Party," *Forward*, September 19, 2003.

59. Rabbi Yisrael Rozen, "Men and Women in Local Politics," *Shabbat-B'shabbato* no. 726 (November 14, 1998).

60. Yitzhak Levy was one of the Moroccan political elite who moved to Israel after the establishment of the state. Like all other Mafdal leaders, he served as an officer in the Israel Defense Forces and was active in the establishment of Elon Moreh in Judea.

61. For one of the first introductions of Shas to the Israeli public, see Patricia Golan, "Righting Wrongs," *Jerusalem Post*, August 17, 1985.

62. The coalition of Agudat Israel and Hadegel Torah under the United Torah Judaism ended shortly after the 2003 election. The parties, which cater to

different communities, decided to continue their coalition negotiations independently.

63. For a brief analysis of religious parties in Israel, see Asher Arian, *The Second Republic* (Chatham, NJ: Chatham House, 1998).

64. Eliezer Don-Yihya, "Zionism in Retrospective," *Modern Judaism* 18, no. 3 (October 1998): 267–76.

65. Menachem Friedman, "The Ultra-Orthodox in Israeli Politics," *Jerusalem Letter/Viewpoints*, July 15, 1990.

66. Roni Baum, "A Haredi-Zionist Movement?" in *Shas: The Challenge of Israeliness* (in Hebrew), ed. Yoav Peled (Tel Aviv: Yedior Aliaronot, 2003), 102–25.

67. Ovadia Yosef, *Torah She-be-Al Peh*, no. 16 (1973): 19–20.

68. Ovadia Yosef, *Yabi'a Omer* vol. 6 (Jerusalem: Machon HaMeor, 1986), 41.

69. Omar Kamil, *Von Ben Gurion zu Ovadia Yosef* (unpublished dissertation, Universitätsbibliothek Leipzig, 2003), 157.

70. Yosef states that "If their traditions are in dissonance with Yosef Karo, who is central to Sephardi thought, they also have to go by the board." Cited in Zvi Zohar's talk at http://www.ivri-nasawi.org/shas.html. For more details see Zion Zohar, "Oriental Jewry Confronts Modernity—The Case of Rabbi Ovadiah Yosef," *Modern Judaism* 24, no. 2 (2004): 120–49.

71. Dan Petreanu, "An Enigma Called Der'i," *Jerusalem Post*, November 17, 1989.

72. Ibid.

73. Ovadia Yosef, "Parashat Pekudei: The Bell and the Pomegranates," *Aram Soba Newsletter* (Jerusalem, 1999); Aryeh Deri, "Parashat Ki Tisa," *Aram Soba*, 2001.

74. Yosef, "Parashat Pekudei"; Deri, "Parashat Ki Tisa," 6.

75. Deri, "Parashat Ki Tisa," 6.

76. Aryeh Deri, "Parashat Ki Tisa, The Roar of Aryeh," *Aram Soba Newsletter* (Jerusalem, 2001): 3.

77. Ibid.

78. Ovadia Yosef, "Parashat Vayikra: A Soul That Sins Inadvertently," *Aram Soba Newsletter* (Jerusalem, 2001): 1; and Ovadia Yosef, "We and the Common-Folk in the Fields," *Aram Soba Newsletter* (Jerusalem, 2001): 10.

79. Yosef, "Parash at Pekudei."

80. Yoel Finkelman, "Haredi Isolation in Changing Environments: A Case Study in Yeshiva Immigration," *Modern Judaism* 22, no. 1 (2002): 61–82.

81. Ovadia Yosef, "Parashat Ekev: Allow the Blessing to Abound," *Aram Soba Newsletter* (Jerusalem, 1999): 3.

82. Ibid., 4.

83. Deri, "Parashat Toledot: The Roar of Aryeh," *Aram Soba Newsletter* (Jerusalem, 2004): 1.

84. Yossi Klein Halevi, "Religious Revival," *Jerusalem Report*, July 11, 1996.

85. Jordan Elgrably, "The Shas Phenomenon," *Jewish Journal*, October 13, 2000.

86. Gerald M. Steinberg, "Interpretations of Jewish Tradition on Democracy," *Land and Peace* 439 (October 2, 2000): 17–46.

87. As Yosef defines the concept "it is a basic *halakhic* principle that all commandments are suspended in the face of mortal danger."

88. Shira Schmidt, "What Is a Nice Leftist Like You Doing at the Site of a Right-Wing Demonstration?" *Cross Currents*, July 22, 2005.

89. Shlomo Katz, "HaMaayan," *Bechukotai* 17, no. 33 (May 28, 2005): 10.

90. Ovadiah Yosef, "Parashat Ki Tisa," *Aram Soba Newsletter* (Jerusalem, 2001): 7.

91. Ibid.

92. Ovadiah Yosef, "Torat Ha'moadim," *Parashat Teruma* (September 30, 2000): 12.

93. Ovadiah Yosef, "Parashat Balak," *Aram Soba Newsletter* (Jerusalem, 2004).

94. Avrahim Avidani, advisor to one of the Shas Party founders and Nissim Zeev in discussion with the author, July 1999.

95. Ovadiah Yosef, "Parashat Va'era," *Aram Soba Newsletter* (Jerusalem, 2001): 8.

96. Ovadiah Yosef, *Yabi'a Omer*, vol. 8 (Jerusalem: Machon HaMeor, 1986); *Even Ha-Ezer* no. 11, sec. 2.

97. Aryeh Deri, "Parashat Beresheet," *Aram Soba Newsletter* (Jerusalem, 1998).

98. Ibid.

99. Jacob Lupu, *Can Shas Restore Past Glory?* (Jerusalem: The Floersheimer Institute for Policy Studies, 2004).

100. Amir Horkin, "Political Mobilization, Ethnicity, Religiosity and Voting for the Shas Movement" (master's thesis, Tel Aviv University, 1993).

101. Ibid.

102. Ovadiah Yosef, "Parashat Matot—Mas'ei," *Aram Soba Newsletter* (Jerusalem, 2004).

103. Peter Hirschberg, *The World of Shas* (New York: The American Jewish Committee Publications, 1999).

104. The numbers regarding Shas's educational system vary, as the party does not reveal exact figures. The ministry estimated that the number of children in Shas's school system reached 31,000 in the 1998–99 academic year. For different estimates, see Doron Gideon and Rebecca Kook, "Religion and the Politics of Inclusion: The Success of the Ultra-Orthodox Parties," in *Shas: The Challenge of Israeliness,* ed. Yoav Peled (Tel Aviv: Yediot Ahronot, 2002); and Judy Dempsey, "Small Voices Insist on Being Heard," *Financial Times*, July 3, 1999.

105. Yeshiva Or Hachaim, http://www.orhachaim.org/ (accessed June 1, 2007).

106. According to a 1997 report, the average number of students per class was 29 in the state schools and 23.2 in Shas schools. The average class hours per week was 37.7 in the state schools, 38.8 in the Ashkenazi ultra-Orthodox, and 46 in the Shas schools. For further details, see Varda Shiffer, *The Haredi Education in Israel: Allocation, Regulation, and Control* (Jerusalem: The Floersheimer Institute for Policy Studies, 1998).

107. Due to their religious status, *Cohenim* cannot use hospitals through regular venues. Aryeh Deri, "Parashat Behar-Behukotai," *Aram Soba Newsletter* (Jerusalem, 2003).

108. Ovadiah Yosef and Yabiyah Omer, Part 8, section 38 *Orach Chaim*, quoted in "Parashat Balak," *Daat Emet*, June 2001.

109. Rabbi Ephrahim Avidani, one of the founders of Shas and Shas Knesset consultant, in interview with author, July 1998.

110. Nitzan Chen and Anshel Pfeffer, *Maran Ovadia Yosef: Habiografia* (Jerusalem: Keter, 2004),127.

111. Ovadia Yosef, "The Laws of Blessings," *Aram Soba Newsletter* (Jerusalem, 2004): 7.

112. For a brief account of the rapprochement between Hadash and Shas, see David Zev Harris and Liat Collins, "Barak on Verge of Forming Government. Shas in, Likud out," *Jerusalem Post*, June 29, 1999.

113. Petreanu, "An Enigma Called Der'i."

114. David Tal and Nissim Zeev (Shas members of the Knesset), in discussion with the author, July 1999.

115. Yishuv literally means "sit" or "settle" and is still used to refer to Israel in the ultra-Orthodox circles.

116. For a biography of Ovadia Yosef, see Binyamin Lau, *Mi-Maran ad Maran: Mishnato ha-Hilkhatit shel ha-Rav Ovadiah Yosef* (Tel Aviv, 2005).

117. Yosef brought not only religious but also political capital to the movement. He steadily climbed the ladder of the religious hierarchy in Israel's pillarized state system, assuming critical roles. He was first appointed a *dayan* or judge of the Sephardi *Bet Din* (rabbinical court) in Jerusalem. He later became the head of the Cairo Beit Din and deputy chief rabbi of Egypt in 1947, effectively strengthening its ability to understand Muslim communities. Arye Dayan, *Ha-Ma'yan ha-mitgabe: sipurah shel tenu'at Shas* (Jerusalem: Keter, 1999).

118. Nitzan Chen, "He Put On a Umm Kolthoum Tape, May God Erase Her Memory," *Du Et Magazine*, December 20, 2004.

119. Petreanu, "An Enigma Called Der'i."

120. The fact that Yosef's son failed to be placed on the Shas list after his open critique of the party shows that it is not kinship but reverence to religious leadership and the embrace of Shas ideas that qualify one to be on the party list. The Torah Sage Council usually chooses the party elite from among those already active and senior in its educational system.

121. One of the party leaders humorously said, "We looked at various pictures. Peretz's picture reminded us of Herzl. We thought that he would appeal to the secular public more than anyone else." Others confirmed that Peretz was not part of the original movement when he was invited to lead the party. Personal interview with a Shas leader June 2000.

122. For a description of Peretz's positions, see Thomas Friedman, "Small Party Says It Is Quitting Israeli Cabinet," *New York Times*, December 17, 1984.

123. Peter Hirschberg, "John Travolta Plays the Knesset," *Jerusalem Report*, December 16, 1993.

124. Ovadia Yosef, "Ceding Territory of the Land of Israel in Order to Save Lives," quoted in Ezra Kopelowitz and Diamond Matthew, "Religion That Strengthens Democracy: An Analysis of Religious Political Strategies in Israel," *Theory and Society* 27, no. 5 (1998): 696.

125. Saguy Avi, *Religious Zionism: Between Openness and Closedness* (Jerusalem: Oz Veshalom and Netivot, 2003).

126. Aryeh A. Frimer and Rabbi Dov I, "Women's Prayer Services: Theory and Practice," *Tradition* 32, no. 2 (Winter 1998): 5–118.

Chapter Four

1. T. W. Adorno, *Negative Dialectics*, trans. E. B. Ashton (New York: Seabury, 1973), 133.

2. Prayer rug, *seccade*, is often used as a symbol of Islamic commitments. Heiko Henkel, "Between Belief and Unbelief Lies the Performance of *Salāt*': Meaning and Efficacy of a Muslim Ritual," *Journal of the Royal Anthropological Institute* 11, no. 3 (2005): 487–507. The 1982 Constitution and the Law on Political Parties required the parties to operate in loyalty to the principles of Kemalism (Article 4) and not to pursue policies drawing on differences of sect, race, or language, or to disturb the national unity by promoting languages and cultures other than Turkish. See Bülent Tanor, *Perspectives on Democratization in Turkey* (Istanbul: TÜSİAD, 1997), 27–59.

3. For a review of the takiyye, see Taha Akyol, "Refah Partisi ve Takiyye," *Milliyet*, July 7, 1996; Mehmet Soydan, *Turkey's Reality: Welfare* (Istanbul: Birey, 1994), 56–62.

4. The GUP is an electorally small (it receives around 2 percent of the total votes) but ideologically pivotal party. Various aspects of the GUP's leadership and positions are addressed in this study to explain the extent and the limit of the NAP's Islamization and the broader spectrum of ideas marking Turkey's Islamic nationalist sphere.

5. Öz, in interview with author (May 2000). Öz was a member of Parliament on the NAP ticket and served as a member of the NAP Central Executive Committee and as advisor to the NAP's leader, Bahceli.

6. Aslan Bulut, "Milliyetcilik Kelimesinden Ne Anlıyoruz," *Yeni Çağ*, September 5, 2005.

7. Tanıl Bora and Kemal Can, *Devlet Ocak Dergah* (İletişim Yayınları, 1999); Hugh Poulton, *Silindir Şapka, Bozkurt* (Istanbul: Sarmal Yayınları, 1999).

8. Mustafa Çalık, *MHP Hareketi, Kaynakları ve Gelişimi* (Ankara: Cedit Yayınları, 1996).

9. A national representative survey conducted by Yılmaz Esmer suggested that 40.49 percent of WP defectors voted for the NAP. *Milliyet*, May 6, 1999.

10. Ülkü Ocakları, *1944 Turancılık Davası*, Ülkü Ocakları Eğitim Kültür-Vakfı Genel Merkezi (Ankara, 2002).

11. Personal interview with author Nejdet Sevinç (March 2000).

12. The NAP's Policy Statement, http://www.mhp.org.tr.

13. Ibid.

14. Sait Başer, *Gök Tanrı'nın Sıfatlarına Esmaü'l-Hüsna Açısından Bakış* (İstanbul: Seyran, 1991).

15. Necdet Sevinç, "Türk Müslümanlığı, İslam ve Şamanism," *Büyük Kurultay*, October 21, 1998; interview with Sait Başer, *Büyük Kurultay*, October 28, 1998; Ahmet Güner, "Ümmet Siyasi Birlik Değildir," *Büyük Kurultay*, January 18, 1999.

16. *Al-Hujurat*: 13, Qur'an.

17. Hasan Küçük, "Türk İslam Ülküsü," *Büyük Kurultay*, February 9, 1998; İbrahim Aydemir, "Türk Müslümanlığı," *Büyük Kurultay*, September 21, 1998; Metin Kaplan, "Turancılık Nedir?," *Ülkü Ocağı Dergisi* 66 (October 1999): 17–21.

18. For further discussions on nation as an Islamic construct, see Oğuz Ünal, "Fazilet Millet Kavramını Reddediyor," *Büyük Kurultay*, February 1, 1999.

19. *Ülkü Ocakları* website at: http://www.wkuocaklari.org.tr/bozhurt/index .htm (accessed April 20, 2008).

20. Aslan Bulut, "MHP'nin Yeni Söylemi," *Büyük Kurultay*, October 11, 1994.

21. Ibid.

22. Ahmet Gürsoy, "Dinin Milliyeti," *Büyük Kurultay*, October 13, 1998.

23. Merve Kavakçı's protest resulted in the June 2001 Constitutional Court's decision to bar her from her political rights for five years.

24. *Büyük Kurultay,* September 21, 1998.

25. The NAP's Policy Statement.

26. NAP Party Program (Ankara, 1999).

27. Türkeş, *Dokuz Işık*, 60.

28. Personal interviews with Beşiktaş Ocağı members (June 1999).

29. Personal interviews with Cağlayan Ülkü Ocağı members (Istanbul, 1999).

30. Devlet Bahçeli speech, delivered at NAP Central Decision-Making and Executive Body (September 9, 2005).

31. Personal interviews with a group of ülkücüs in Çemberlitaş Ülkü Ocak in Istanbul (April 2000).

32. After the 1999 election attesting to the NAP's attempt to forge a new image, around two hundred ocaks were abolished.

33. Ülkücüs often refer to leaders claimed by separate movements such as Oğuz Khan, Ahmet Yesevi, the Prophet Mohammed, Fatih Mehmet, and Atatürk. *Alperen, Alperen Gençlik Ocakları* statement (Istanbul, 2000).

34. Unlike the intense indoctrinations in ocaks, the NV members acquired their party identification more as part of a social network that, while without strong ideological commitments, stressed increasing attendance and adherence to Islamic rituals and beliefs.

35. Nizam'i Ocakları *İnançlarımız* (Ankara, 1998).

36. Personal interviews with the Cağlayan Ülkü Ocağı attendants April 1998–May 1999.

37. NAP Party Program.

38. An interview with Devlet Bahçeli, *Milliyet*, April 28, 1999.

39. Özcan Yeniçeri, *Yeniden Türkleşmeler* (Ankara: Ülkü Ocakları Derneği, 2002).

40. Milliyetçi Hareket Partisi, *Kültürel Politikalar* (Ankara: Sargın, 1999).

41. The NAP's Policy Statement.

42. Personal interview with Ali Baykan, who served as the member of the executive board of the NAP Istanbul Organization (May 1999).

43. Bora and Can, *Devlet Ocak Dergah*.

44. Bülent Yahnici, *Büyük Kurultay*, February 23, 1998.

45. With the Islamization of its discourse, the NAP managed to mobilize some Welfare voters on its side. Yılmaz Esmer's findings (*Milliyet*, May 6, 1999) suggest that 40.49 percent of Welfare Party defectors voted for the NAP.

46. Enis Öksüz, "Nation and Nationalism," *Yeni Cağ Gazetesi*, September 16, 2005.

47. NAP Party Program.

48. Personal interview with Esat Öz (May 2000).

49. İsmet İnonü's policies during World War II sought neutrality but also signaled that the country was close to supporting Germany, creating a complex environment for nationalist movements.

50. Abdullah Muradoğlu, "Türkeş'in Gizli Dünyasi," *Yeni Şafak*, September 25, 2005.

51. Muhsin Yazıcıoğlu, *Yeni Şafak*, December 1, 1996. For an evaluation of the GUP movement from an Islamist perspective see İsmail Ceylan, *Milli Gazete*, January 1–7, 1997.

52. The GUP emblem replaced the gray wolf with a rose, which represents the prophet Mohammed. GUP Party Program, available from http://www.bbp.org.tr/program_bolum3.asp (accessed October 15, 2006).

53. Aslan Bulut, "*MHP'nin Yeni Söylemi, Değişen Toplum mu MHP mi?*", *Ortadoğu*, October 11, 1994.

54. *Yazıcıoğlu* was born in 1954 in Elmali, a small village of a central Anatolian city, Sivas. He joined the NAP youth groups during his education at a veterinary school in Ankara. He became assistant secretary general of the NAP in 1987.

55. Devlet Bahçeli was born in 1948 in Adana's Osmaniye district. Coming from a privileged background, he studied at private schools until he started his college education at the Ankara Economic and Commercial Sciences Academy. During his university years he participated in seminars put on by Türkeş and became active in the *Ülkücü Ocakları*. He contributed to the establishment of the new Idealist Clubs and joined the NAP upon the invitation of Türkeş in 1987.

56. For a full text of that declaration see *Büyük Kurultay*, November 3, 1997.

57. The distinction between *ocaklı* and *not ocaklı* remains an important marker among the NAP leaders and activists. Personal interviews with Cağlayan Ocak members (May 1999).

58. A descriptive statistic regarding the parties' candidates can be found in Erol Tuncer, *Seçim '99 Sayısal ve Siyasal Değerlendirme* (Ankara: TESAV, 1999), 17–56.

59. *TBMM Albümü: 21. Dönem, Ankara: TBMM* (Ankara, 1999).

60. For more details see "Ülkü Ocakları," *Hürriyet*, April 29, 1999.

61. Personal interview with Lütfü Esengül, member of the Central Decision-Making Committee of the Virtue Party (May 2000).

62. "Law on the Political Parties," *Official Gazette*, April 23, 1983.

63. Erbakan was born in Sinop, a town in northern Turkey on the Black Sea, in 1926. He received degrees in mechanical engineering from Istanbul Technical University, where he later taught, and the Rhenish-Westphalian Technical University of Aachen, then in West Germany. For an extended biography see Metin Hasirci, *Bitmeyen Mücadele* (Adapazari: Degisim Yayinlari, 1996).

64. Cited in Abdullah Manaz, *Dünyada ve Türkiye'de İslamcılık* (Ankara: Ayrac, 2005), 358.

65. *Official Gazette* 14072 (January 14, 1972).

66. *Ayın Tarihi* (Ankara: Turkish GrandNational Assembly, September 1980).
67. Ümit Cizre, *AP-ordu İlişkileri* (Istanbul: İletişim Yayınları, 1993).
68. Kenan Evren, "Erzurum" (speech), *Milliyet*, October 2, 1982.
69. The WP had increased its votes to 1,717,425 (7.16 percent of the total votes) in the November 29, 1987, elections. In the 1989 local elections the party further expanded its support to 9.8 percent by winning in twenty municipalities.
70. Hasan Ceylan's interview with Dergah, cited in Rusen Çakir, *Ne Seriat, Ne Demokrasi: Refah Partisini Anlamak* (Istanbul: Metis Yayinlari, 1994).
71. It is hard to determine the exact share of the WP in the total vote. Yet with the defection of twenty-two members of the other two parties, the WP held forty-one seats in Parliament.
72. The NCS's "advisory decisions" resulted in tightening the ban on religious sects, stopping recruitment of those who appear to be Islamist for government posts, and keeping tight restrictions on the religious, especially women who wear the türban in government offices and state-sponsored schools.
73. *Selam*, September 26–October 2, 1999.
74. A full text of the indictment can be found at http://www.belgenet.com/dava/rpdava.html. For a detailed description of the court decision in English, see Stephen Kinzer, "Turkey Bans Welfare Party," *New York Times*, January 17, 1998.
75. Jeremy Salt, "Turkey's Military Democracy," *Current History* 28, no. 625 (February 1999): 76. Although the numbers are always contested, the order is estimated to have more than 800,000 regular attendants in Turkey.
76. *Tarikat*, literally path, describes religious groups organized around the teaching of a leader. Each tarikat has a different approach on Islam. The Kemalist reforms' abolition of all formal Islamic organizations did not eradicate the activities of tarikats, many of which survived as informal and underground organizations.
77. M. Yasar, "İskenderpaşa Cemaati," in *İslamcılık*, ed. Yasin Aktay (Istanbul: İletişim, 2000), 325.
78. Ibid.
79. Necmettin Erbakan, *Milli Görüş* (Istanbul: Dergah, 1975), 139.
80. Ibid.
81. Ibid., 146.
82. NOP Party Program (Ankara, 1971).
83. Nurşen Mazıcı, *Belgelerle Atatürk Döneminde Muhalefet (1919–1926)* (İstanbul: Dilmen, 1984).
84. Erbakan, *Milli Görüş*, 47.
85. Necmettin Erbakan, "Düzeltilmesi Gereken Kavram Kargaşası," *Milli Gazete*, March 8, 1997.
86. Ibid.
87. Şevket Eygi, *Milli Gazete*, March 3, 1997.
88. For the NV's views on laicism see M. Kutan, *Turkiye'nin Oncelikleri ve Temel Görüşlerimiz* (Ankara: Bilkent, December 7, 1998).
89. Ibid.
90. Among others, the NV-affiliated newspapers include *Milli Gazete*, *Akit*, and *Yeni Şafak*. *Milli Gazete* can be regarded as the party's official daily and has a cir-

culation of 33,000 in Turkey and of 10,000 in Europe. The readers buy the paper to reveal their political support for the movement. *Akit* has the largest circulation rate in small towns and usually uses radical language compared to the others.

91. Mevlüt Özcan, "Sabir," *Milli Gazete*, February 4, 1997.

92. Ali Aksal, "Gelişigüzel," *Milli Gazete*, March 18, 1997.

93. Asım Yenihaber, "Milliyetçi Partinin Çıkmazı," *Akit*, May 30, 2001.

94. Interview with M. Kutan, *Yeni Şafak*, May 24, 1998.

95. Doğan Duman, *Demokrasi Sürecinde Türkiye'de İslamcılık* (İzmir: Dokuz Eylül Yayınları, 1999).

96. M. Kutan, *Turkiye'nin Öncelikleri ve Temel Görüşlermimiz* (Ankara: Semih Ofset, 1998).

97. The debates centered on whether and how the NV's pluralistic legal system could accommodate multidimensional identities, such as secular-Muslim. For a response to the critiques, see Ali Bulaç, "Medine Vesikası Hakkında Genel Bilgiler," *Birikim* 38, no. 39 (1992), 102–11.

98. Ergün Göze, *Siyasi Ifrat Cinneti*, April 19, 1977, cited in Ahmet Yıldız, "Politico-Religious Discourse of Political Islam," *The Muslim World* 93 (April 2003).

99. Refah Partisi, *Seçim Sloganları* (Ankara: Refah Partisi, 1991).

100. Rasim Cinisli, *Yeni Şafak*, May 18, 1998.

101. A. Aksal, "Gelisi güzel," *Milli Gazete*, March 18, 1997.

102. *Hürriyet*, March 11, 2000.

103. Ömer Ören, *Milli Gazete*, May 15, 1998.

104. Personal interview of Betigul Argun with Yazıcıoğlu (June 1998).

105. Mehmet Eygi, *Milli Gazete*, May 3, 1992.

106. Ibid.

107. M. Kutan, *Yeni Şafak*, August 19, 1998.

108. For a critical discussion of such statements, see Abdullatif Şener, *Milliyet*, January 8, 2007.

109. "Kutan'in Gafi," *Radikal*, October 7, 1998.

110. Personal interview with Naci Terzi. Terzi was the WP's representative from Erzincan, which includes a significant number of Alevis.

111. Many articles in *Milli Gazete* oppose the efforts to Turkify Islam, efforts ranging from using Turkish in prayers to emphasizing the Turkish-Islamic synthesis.

112. Ersin Gürdoğan, *Görünmeyen Üniversite* (Fatih, Istanbul: Seha Nesriyat, 1989).

113. Soydan, *Turkey's Reality*, 536.

114. Leadership change is calculated by taking the proportions of the new candidates to the total. Tuncer, *Seçim '99*.

115. Personal interviews with the women leaders at Çevizlibağ, the NV center.

116. "Soru ve cevaplarla İslam," *Milli Gazete*, September 20, 2005.

117. For a comparable analysis of the party leadership see Ruşen Çakır, *Ne Şeriat, Ne Demokrasi: Refah Partisi'ni Anlamak* (Istanbul: Metis, 1994).

118. While the head of the traditional bloc, Kutan, received 633 votes to ensure the victory, Gül received 521 votes from the 1,236 delegates on May 14, 2000. This date can be taken as the real date of the establishment of the JDP.

119. Personal interview with Lütfü Esengün (Istanbul, May 2000).

120. Personal interview with Cemil Çicek (June 2001).

121. Interview with Tayyip Erdoğan, NTV (October 2003).

122. JDP Party Program (Ankara, 2002).

123. Ibid., 89.

124. Ibid.

125. JDP Party Program (Ankara, 2001).

126. Tayyip Erdoğan, speech delivered at the Parliament, May 5, 2004.

127. Tayyip Erdoğan, speech delivered at Boğazici Universitesi Derneği Dolmabahçe, October 10, 2004.

128. *Temel Görüşlerimiz* (Ankara, 2002), 25.

129. Yalçın Akdoğan, *Muhafazakar Demokrasi* (Ankara: Alfa Basın Yayın, 2004).

130. Ibid., 128.

131. Ibid., 133.

132. Sultan Tepe, "Turkey's AKP: A Model 'Muslim-Democratic' Party?", *Journal of Democracy* 16, no. 3 (July 2005).

133. For instance, the party includes abortion as an important issue, although it never took part in Turkey's moral debate.

134. Yalçın Akdoğan, *Muhafazakar Demokrasi* (Ankara: Alfa Basım Yayın, 2004), 23.

135. Personal interview with Gülle, June 2004.

136. For the text, see www.akparti.org.tr.

137. The speech delivered by Tayyip Erdoğan on August 12, 2005, in Diyarbakır. *Milliyet*, August 14, 2005.

138. JDP Party Program.

139. Tayyip Erdoğan Diyarbakir speech, *AnsesNet*, August 12, 2005.

140. Ibid.

141. Karl Polanyi, "Aristotle Discovers the Economy" in Karl Polanyi et al., *Trade Markets in the Early Empire*s (Glencoe, IL: Free Press, 1957), 139–40.

142. European Commission, *Turkey's Progress Report* (Brussels: August 2006), 34–47.

143. Ali Bardakoğlu's interview at Kanal 7, *Haberturk*, December 12, 2003.

144. Tayyip Erdoğan, *Milliyet*, September 23, 2005.

145. Soydan, *Turkey's Reality*.

146. Tayyip Erdoğan's speech delivered in Siirt, February 27, 1997.

147. The party set the age limit for its leadership as sixty-five. *Dünya*, June 5, 2007.

148. For a detailed background of the JDP's first ministers, see *Yeni Şafak*, November 25–December 18, 2002.

149. Given the low profile of the council, one can argue that it has become a symbolic intraparty institution as well. Personal interview with Nur Topaloğlu, May 2004.

150. In a rare of act of protest, a JDP member signed a petition to have the Constitutional Court determine the constitutionality of Erdoğan's nomination to the position of speaker of Parliament.

151. In the words of Bülent Arınç's (a critical elite member of both the NV parties and the JDP), "We saw a Leviathan state as necessary for Turkey. Yet, the

February 28 decisions changed our perception and only then did we see Turkey as a small state, and therefore the European Union as a politically expedient choice." Cited in Murat Yetkin, "Beni 28 Şubat AB'ci yapti," *Radikal*, June 5, 2005.

Chapter Five

1. *Yom Leyom* (February 2, 2006), 17.

2. Efraim Inbar, "A House Less Divided," *Jerusalem Post*, February 15, 1999.

3. David Ingram, *Rights, Democracy and Fulfillment in the Era of Identity Politics: Principled Compromises in a Compromised World* (Lanham, MD: Rowman & Littlefield, 2004).

4. Shmuel Sandler, Robert O. Freedman, and Shibley Telhami, "The Religious-Secular Divide in Israeli Politics," *Middle East Policy Journal* 6, no. 4 (1999): 137–46.

5. Zion Zohar, "Oriental Jewry Confronts Modernity–The Case of Rabbi Ovadiah Yosef," *Modern Judaism* 24, no. 2 (2004): 120–49.

6. Inbar, "A House Less Divided."

7. Ovadia Yosef, *Responsa Yichveh Daat*, part 4, paragraph 65 (Jerusalem: Or Hamizrah 1981), 308–14.

8. Ibid.

9. Eliezer Don-Yehiya, "Religion, Ethnicity and Electoral Reform: The Religious Parties and the 1996 Elections," in *Israel at the Polls, 1996* (London: Frank Cass, 1998).

10. Aaron Willis, "Redefining Religious Zionism: Shas' Ethno-politics," *Israel Studies Bulletin* 8, no. 1 (1992): 3–8.

11. The research findings of Yinon Cohen and Yitchak Haberfeld, cited in Ephraim Yuchtman-Yaar, "Continuity and Change in Israeli Society: The Test of the Melting Pot," *Israel Studies* 10, no. 2 (2005): 91–128.

12. William Connolly, *Identity/Difference: Democratic Negotiations of Political Paradox* (Minneapolis: University of Minnesota Press, 2002).

13. Gal Levy, "And Thanks to the Ashkenazim: The Politics of Mizrahi Ethnicity in Israel" (in Hebrew) (master's thesis, Tel Aviv University, 1995).

14. Sami Shalom Chetrit, *HaMaavak HaMizrahi Beyisrael, Bein Dikui, Leshihrur, Beib Hizdahut, Lealternativa, 1948–2003* (Tel Aviv: Am Oved, 2004).

15. S. Verba, K. L. Schlozman, and H. E. Brady, "Rational Action and Political Activity," *Journal of Theoretical Politics* 12, no. 3 (2000): 243–68.

16. Asher Arian and Michal Shamir, "On Mistaking a Dominant Party in a Dealigning System," *The Elections In Israel: 2003* (New Brunswick, NJ: Transaction Publishers, 2005).

17. Dieter Rucht, "The Impact of National Contexts on Social Movement Structures," in *Comparative Perspectives on Social Movements: Political Opportunities, Mobilizing Structures, and Cultural Framings*, eds. Doug McAdam, John D. McCarthy, and Mayer N. Zald (Cambridge: Cambridge University Press, 1996).

18. Gregory S. Mahler, *Israel after Begin* (Albany: State University of New York Press, 1990).

19. Jan E. Leighley, *Strength in Numbers? The Political Mobilization of Racial and Ethnic Minorities* (Princeton, NJ: Princeton University Press, 2001).

20. Asher Arian, "Political Parties and the Emergence of Israel's Second Republic," in *Political Parties and the Collapse of the Old Orders*, ed. John Kenneth White (Albany: State University of New York Press, 1998).

21. E.g., Eitan Schiffman, "The Shas School System in Israel," *Nationalism & Ethnic Politics* 11, no. 1 (2005): 89.

22. Amir Horkin, "Political Mobilization, Ethnicity, Religiosity and Voting for the Shas Movement" (in Hebrew) (master's thesis, Tel Aviv University, 1993).

23. Angelo Panebianco, *Political Parties: Organization and Power* (Cambridge: Cambridge University Press, 1988).

24. Ami Pedahzur and Avraham Brichta, "The Institutionalization of Extreme Right-Wing Charismatic Parties: A Paradox?" *Party Politics* 8, no. 1 (2002): 31–49.

25. Omar Kamil, "Rabbi Ovadia Yosef and His Culture War in Israel," *Middle East Review of International Affairs* 4, no. 4 (2000): 22.

26. Personal interview with Avraham Avidani (Jerusalem, June 1999).

27. Shira Schmidt, "To Ignore or Confront Controversy?" *Cross Currents*, March 15, 2005.

28. Ibid.

29. Willis, "Redefining Religious Zionism," 3–8.

30. In one of the most informative analyses of Shas, Peled's findings match the 1983 census data and 1996 election results. Shalev and Levy's conclusions are mostly informed by the Shas supporters available in the 2003 data. Yoav Peled, "Toward a Redefinition of Jewish Nationalism in Israel? The Enigma of Shas," *Ethnic and Racial Studies* 21 (1998). Michael Shalev and Gal Levy, "The Winners and Losers of 2003: Ideology, Social Structure, and Political Change," in *The Elections in Israel: 2003*, eds. Arian Asher and Michal Shamir (New Brunswick, NJ: Transaction Publishers, 2005).

31. Asher Cohen, "Religious Zionism and the National Religious Party in the 2003 Elections," in *The Elections in Israel: 2003*.

32. The author thanks Israel Social Science Data Center for help in gaining access to the data and the University of Illinois Office of Research for support in conducting the 2003 survey.

33. Both the 1996 and 1999 surveys significantly overestimated the support for Likud and Labor while failing to describe Shas's rising support. For a discussion of the difficulties posed by the underrepresentation, see Richard Breen, "Why Is Support for Extreme Parties Underestimated by Surveys? A Latent Class Analysis," *British Journal of Political Science* 30, no. 2 (2000): 375–82.

34. James E. Campbell, Mary Munro, John R. Alford, and Bruce Campbell, "Partisanship and Voting," in *Research in Micropolitics*, ed. Samuel Long (Greenwich, CT: JAI Press, 1986), 100.

35. Personal interview with Mina Tzemah, Tel Aviv, June 1999.

36. The 1992 law (which was replaced in 2001) required voters to cast separate votes for the offices of prime minister and Knesset. It not only failed to curb the power of small parties, it augmented their numbers and reinforced their bargaining position in Knesset. In 1996 Likud and Labor received 53.3 percent of total votes

while nine small parties gained seats in Knesset. Michael Harris and Gideon Doron, "Assessing the Electoral Reform of 1992 and Its Impact on the Elections of 1996 and 1999," *Israel Studies* 4, no. 2 (1999): 16–39.

37. In 2001 Knesset restored the pre-1992 system. *Haaretz,* March 8, 2001.

38. For a detailed discussion of quantifying religion at the state level, see Jonathan Fox and Shmuel Sandler, "Quantifying Religion: Toward Building More Effective Ways of Measuring Religious Influence on State Level Behavior," *Journal of Church and State* 45, no. 3 (Summer 2003): 559–88.

39. Charles S. Liebman, "Reconceptualizing the Culture Conflict among Israeli Jews," *Israel Studies* 2, no. 2 (1997): 172–89.

40. Ibid.

41. Jay Bushinsky, "Left, Right," *Jerusalem Post,* July 11, 1996.

42. Gideon Doron and Rebecca Kook, "Religion and the Politics of Inclusion: The Success of the Ultra-Orthodox Parties," in *The Elections in Israel, 1996,* eds. Asher Arian and Michal Shamir (Albany: State University of New York Press, 1999).

43. Sami Shalom Chetrit, *HaMaavak HaMizrahi beyisrael, bein Dikui, Leshihrur, Beib hizdahut, lealternativa, 1948–2003* (Tel Aviv: Am Oved, 2004).

44. The comparison group is defined as "support for other parties." For logit models, see Scott Long, *Regression Models for Categorical and Limited Dependent Variables: Analysis and Interpretation* (Thousand Oaks, CA: Sage Publications, 1997).

45. A standardized parameter estimate shows the ratio of the importance of the influence of a given parameter on the vote choice relative to other factors in the model.

46. Shalev and Levy, "The Winners and Losers of 2003," 167–86.

47. Twenty-five percent is the lowest of Cox Snell, Nagelkerke, McFadden pseudo R-squares.

48. The tape used Emile Zola's letter of 1898 titled "I accuse" to denunciate authorities for their conviction of an army officer, Alfred Dreyfus, for treason due to his religious identity.

49. Cohen, "Religious Zionism and National Religious Party in the 2003 Elections," 187–215.

50. Israel's economy has witnessed a negative growth (–0.9 percent and 1 percent in 2001 and 2002) for the first time its history, a rise in its unemployment rate (10.8 percent), and a significant decrease (–3.5 percent) in the purchasing power of the real wage from 2002 to 2004. Israel Central Bureau of Statistics, "1999–2004 Main Economic indicators," http://www.cbs.gov.il/new_e.htm (accessed January 18, 2007).

51. Heidi Gleit and Danna Harman, "PM Rips Shas Demands to Amend Law of Return," *Jerusalem Post* (November 29, 1999), 2.

52. Obtained from www.knesset.gov.il.

53. Ricki Tessler, "The Price of Revolution," in *The Challenge of Israeliness,* ed. Y. Peled Shas (Tel Aviv: Yediot Achronot, 2001), 278.

54. Peter Hirschberg, *World of Shas* (New York: Jewish Committee, 1999).

55. Jacop Lupu, *Can Shas Restore Past Glory?* (Jerusalem: The Floersheimer Institute for Policy Studies, 2004).

56. The spatial analysis rests on individuals' ratings of the given candidates and parties. Each rating is assumed to be a function of both policy and nonpolicy factors in addition to an idiosyncratic (error) term. Drawing upon these ratings, the map program projects the basic features of the political space by specifying the number of dimensions of the political competition and the positioning of the actors on each. James Enelow and Melvin Hinich, *Advances in the Spatial Theory of Voting* (New York: Cambridge University Press, 1990).

57. Pinhas Landau, "The Unorthodox Aryeh Deri," *Jerusalem Post*, April 7, 1989. The author thanks Mel Hinich for his contribution to the analysis of Israeli and Turkish political competitions.

58. Shas's protests of budgets in response to the proposed cuts on welfare payments caused some crises. "Prudence vs. Populism," *Jerusalem Post*, December 19, 2001.

59. David Zev Harris, "Shas's Next Move—Control of Histadrut," *Jerusalem Post*, April 11, 2000.

60. Arye Deri's statements attest to Shas's intricate relationship with the Arab population: "I grew up with Arabs in Morocco. The Israeli Arabs say I was the best Interior Minister they ever had. I took their complaints of discrimination seriously. Not that I wasn't tough with them. But I always spoke to them at eye level. If Sephardim were in charge of the peace process, we would have gotten much further." Yossi Halevi, "The Unorthodox Politics of an Ultra-Orthodox Rebel," *New York Times*, July 1, 1997.

61. Rabbi Elbaz, one of Shas's leading rabbis, describes the cultural affinity formed among the communities who lived under the Ottoman *millet* system as an advantage: "We Sephardim are Middle Eastern people . . . we lived with Arabs in the past." Deborah Sontag, " 'Second Israel' Hails First Big Election Triumph," *New York Times*, May 21, 1999.

62. Landau, "The Unorthodox Arye Deri."

Chapter Six

1. Recep Tayyip Erdoğan, "A Union of Civilizations," *New Perspectives Quarterly*, 24. no. 3 (Spring 2007).

2. In 1991 the NAP and WP joined forces and received 16 percent of votes. The WP alone received 21 percent in 1995, while the NAP's share could not reach the national threshold. While many predicted the NAP's political demise, it established itself as one of the leading parties in the 1999 election. The Prosperity Party and the NAP failed to gain access to the National Assembly, while the JDP received 34 percent of the votes in 2002. The NAP made another "surprise" return in 2007.

3. The number of nonvoters reached 21 percent in 2002, a record high since the 1983 election. In Turkey's electoral system nonparticipants enhance the power of parties that manage to pass the 10 percent national threshold, thereby playing an indirect yet decisive role in defining the configuration of parliament.

4. Şerif Mardin, "Center-Periphery Relations: A Key to Turkish Politics?" *Daedalus* 102, no. 1 (Winter 1973): 169–90.

5. Ayhan Akman, "Modernist Nationalism: Statism and National Identity in Turkey," *Nationalities Papers* 32, no. 1 (2004): 23–51.

6. Ahmet Kardam and Sezgin Tüzün, *Siyasi Kutuplaşmalar ve Seçmen Davranışları* (Istanbul: Veri Araştırma, 1998).

7. Mustafa Erdoğan, "Islam in Turkish Politics, Turkey's Quest for Democracy without Islam," *Liberal. Düşünce* 4, no. 14 (1999).

8. Mardin, "Center-Periphery Relations," 169–90; Nilüfer Narlı, "The Rise of the Islamist Movement in Turkey," *Middle East Review of International Affairs* 3, no. 3 (1999).

9. Sam Kaplan, "Religious Nationalism: A Textbook Case from Turkey," *Comparative Studies of South Asia, Africa and the Middle East* 25, no. 3 (2005): 665–76.

10. JDP Party Program, http://www.akparti.org.tr/.

11. Binnaz Toprak, "Religion and State in Turkey," *Middle Eastern Lectures* 4 (2001).

12. The Under-secretariat of Treasury and Foreign Trade, Main Economic Indicators, http://www.treasury.gov.tr/stat/e-gosterge.htm (accessed January 18, 2007).

13. Ziya Öniş and Barry Rubin, *The Turkish Economy in Crisis* (Portland, OR: Frank Cass, 2003).

14. Ümit Cizre-Sakallıoğlu and Erinç Yeldan, "Politics, Society and Financial Liberalization: Turkey in the 1990s," *Development and Change* 31, no. 2 (2000).

15. Per capita income in the poorest cities in the southeast amounts to only one-eleventh of the per capita income in the industrial center in western Turkey.

16. Ziya Öniş, "Globalization, Democratization and the Far Right: Turkey's Nationalist Action Party in Critical Perspective," *Democratization* 10, no. 1 (2003): 27–52.

17. Ali Çarkoğlu, "Geography of the April 1999 Turkish Elections," *Turkish Studies* 1, no. 1 (2000): 149–72.

18. Tanıl Bora and Kemal Can, *Devlet Ocak Dergah* (Istanbul: Iletişim Yayınları, 1999).

19. E. Arıkan, "The Programme of the Nationalist Action Party: An Iron Hand in a Velvet Glove," *Middle Eastern Studies* 34, no.4 (October 1998): 120–34.

20. Haldun Gülalp, "Whatever Happened to Secularization? The Multiple Islams in Turkey," *The South Atlantic Quarterly* 102, no 2/3 (Spring/Summer 2003): 381–95.

21. Toprak, "Religion and State in Turkey."

22. MÜSİAD was a small group of businessmen in 1990 and gradually grew to 3,000 members and thirty branch offices, in all major industrial and commercial cities of Turkey. For more detailed information on MÜSİAD, see http://www.musiad.org.tr/ and Ayse Buğra, *Islam in Economic Organizations* (Istanbul: TESEV, 1999).

23. For instance, the NV Party supporters in central Anatolia were mostly town dwellers who had an affinity with Turkish nationalism and whose religiosity was mixed with anti-Alevi feelings.

24. Patchen Markell, *Bound by Recognition* (Princeton, NJ: Princeton University Press, 2003).

25. Nilüfer Göle, *The Forbidden Modern: Civilization and Veiling* (Ann Arbor: University of Michigan, 1996).

26. David Ingram, *Rights, Democracy, and Fulfillment in the Era of Identity Politics: Principled Compromises in a Compromised World* (Lanham, MD: Rowman & Littlefield, 2004).

27. Nevzat Soğuk, "Traveling Islam: Islamic Identities in Transnational Localities," *Theory and Event* 7, no. 2 (2004): 1–15.

28. Ziya Öniş, "Turkey in the Post-Cold War Era: In Search of Identity," *Middle East Journal* 49, no. 1 (Winter 1995): 48–68.

29. Nilüfer Göle, "The Islamist Identity," in *Islam, European Public Space, and Civility, Religion in New Europe*, ed. Krzysztof Michalski (Budapest: Central European University Press, 2006).

30. Devlet Bahçeli, *Yeni Çağın Eşiğinde Türkiye ve Dünya* (Ankara: Araştırma Geliştirme, 2000), 49.

31. Arıkan, "The Programme of the Nationalist Action Party," 120–34.

32. M. Yavuz, "The Politics of Fear: The Rise of the Nationalist Action Party (MHP) in Turkey," *Middle East Journal* 56, no. 2 (Spring 2002): 200–21.

33. Dilip Gaonkar, "Toward New Imaginaries: An Introduction," *Public Culture* 14, no. 1 (Winter 2002): 1–19.

34. Nilüfer Göle, "Islam in Public: New Visibilities and New Imaginaries," *Public Culture* 14, no. 1 (Winter 2002): 173–90.

35. Niyazi Berkes, *Teokrasi ve Laiklik* (Istanbul: Adam Yayıncılık, 1984), 91.

36. Jan Leighley, *Strength in Numbers? The Political Mobilization of Racial and Ethnic Minorities* (Princeton, NJ: Princeton University Press, 2001).

37. Jenny White, *Islamist Mobilization in Turkey: A Study in Vernacular Politics* (Seattle: University of Washington Press, 2002).

38. See chapter 4 for details.

39. Ümit Sakallıoğlu, "Liberalism, Democracy and the Turkish Centre-Right: The Identity Crisis of the True Path Party," *Middle Eastern Studies* 32 (April 1996): 142–61.

40. Ibid.

41. Angelo Panebianco, *Political Parties: Organization and Power* (Cambridge: Cambridge University Press, 1988).

42. Devoid of Türkeş's charisma, Bahçeli still received all but eight votes in the party's congress in 2000 and established himself as the indisputable leader of the party. "MHP Oybirligi ile Bahçeli dedi," *Hürriyet*, November 2000.

43. For a political profile of Tayyip Erdoğan, see Metin Heper and Şule Toktaş, "Islam, Modernity, and Democracy in Contemporary Turkey: The Case of Recep Tayyip Erdoğan," *Muslim World* 93, no. 2 (April 2003): 157–85.

44. Personal interviews with Murat Mercan (Ankara, January 2005).

45. R. Mecham, "The Ashes of Virtue, a Promise of Light: The Transformation of Political Islam in Turkey," *Third World Quarterly* 25, no. 2 (2004): 339–58.

46. Tahire Erman, "The Politics of Squatter *(Gecekondu)* Studies in Turkey: The Changing Representation of Rural Migrants in the Academic Discourse," *Urban Studies* 38, no. 7 (2001): 983–1002.

47. For a comprehensive study that offers a critical analysis of gecekondu areas, see Cihan Tuğal, "The Appeal of Islamic Politics: Ritual and Dialogue in a Poor

District of Turkey," *The Sociological Quarterly* 47, no. 2 (2006): 245–73; White, *Islamist Mobilization in Turkey*. Intriguingly, White attributes Ümraniye residents' lack of concern about the closure of NV parties to Islamic civil society's expansion, thereby suggesting that Islamic party politics is primarily reflective of civil society's activities.

48. John Dryzek, "The Mismeasure of Political Man," *Journal of Politics* 50, no. 3 (1988): 705.

49. For details on TÜSES surveys, see Erol Tuncer, *Seçim '99: Sayısal ve Siyasal Değerlendirme* (Ankara: TESAV, 1999); Ahmet Kardam and Sezgin Tüzün, *Türkiye'de Siyasi Kutuplaşmalar ve Seçmen Davranışları* (Istanbul: Veri Araştırma, 1998).

50. The survey is based on the "random sampling" method with the objective of representing the urban, nationwide voting-age population. The twelve provinces included Adana, Ankara, Antalya, Bursa, Diyarbakır Erzurum, Istanbul, Izmir, Konya, Manisa, Samsun, and Trabzon.

51. Using the 2000 census findings, 26 percent of respondents were from the Marmara region, 13 percent from the Mediterranean, 13 percent Aegean, 17 percent Central Anatolia, 12 percent Black Sea Region, 9 percent Eastern Turkey, and 10 percent South East Region. The questionnaire was designed by the author and included 120 questions answered in person pertaining to the assessment of the impact of religion on voting behavior. A set of open-ended questions was used, such as "what does laicism mean to you?" and "why do you support or oppose Turkey's EU membership?" For more details, see http://www.uic.edu/sultantepe.html.

52. Birol Akgün, "Türkiye'de Seçmen Davranışlarının Ekonomik Politik'i Üzerine Bir Model Denemesi," *Liberal Düşünce* 4, no. 14 (Spring 1999): 62–83.

53. For competing meanings of Sharia, see Charles Kruzman, "Liberal Islam: Prospects ad Challenges," *Middle East Review of International Affairs* 3, no. 3 (September 1999): 11–19.

54. Both the 2001 and 1998 TÜSES data reveal that around 25 percent of the NAP supporters and 45.8 percent of the Prosperity Party supporters endorse Sharia.

55. Nikki Keddie, "The New Religious Politics: Where, When, and Why Do 'Fundamentalisms' Appear?" *Comparative Studies in Society and History* 40, no. 4 (October 1998): 696–723.

56. For a discussion of the Republican project, see Taha Akyol, "Liberalism, Republicanism, Leftism," *Milliyet*, June 5, 2006.

57. Norberto Bobbio, *Left and Right: The Significance of a Political Distinction* (Chicago: University of Chicago Press, 1996).

58. Personal interview with Ahmet Sevinc, Büyük Kurultay, Istanbul, June 1998.

59. Interview with Recai Kutan, *Yeni Şafak*, May 24, 1998.

60. DEHAP united with another party, and after this study was completed, took on a new name: *Demokratik Toplum Partisi*, Democratic Society Party.

61. James Adams, "An Assessment of Voting Systems under the Proximity and Directional Models of the Vote," *Public Choice* 98, no. 1 (1999): 131; Christian Henning, Mel Hinich, and Susumu Shikano, "Directional versus

Proximity Models of Voting: Different Concepts but One Theory," in *Interdisziplinäre Sozialforschung. Theorie und empirische Anwendungen 17* (2004): 117–38.

62. Paul Beck and M. Jennings, "Family Traditions, Political Periods, and the Development of Partisan Orientations," *The Journal of Politics* 53 (August 1991): 742–63.

63. Ahmet Demirel, "*28 Mart'da ne oldu?*" *Birikim*, no. 181 (May 2004).

64. A spatial analysis method estimates the perceived position of actors in a Euclidian space from the ideological distances reported by the voters.

65. The eigenvalues that define the number of relevant political dimensions indicate that a two-dimensional spatial analysis accounts for 70.85 percent of the variation in individual perceptions.

66. The NAP played a critical role in passing some controversial bills toward securing a free market. For example, despite its core supporters' opposition, the party endorsed the *tahkim* law, which opened the way for an international legal inspection of the conflicts between Turkish and foreign companies.

67. Devlet Bahçeli, *Siyasette Ilke ve Ekonomide Kararlılık* (Ankara: MHP Araştırma Geliştime, 2000).

68. Ibid.

69. Devlet Bahçeli, *MHP ve Gündemi Oluşturan Sorunlar* (Ankara: MHP Araştırma Geliştirme, 1999).

70. Tayyip Erdoğan, "Religion Is Cement," *Milliyet*, December 11, 2005.

71. Ayse Buğra, "Labour, Capital, and Religion: Harmony and Conflict among the Constituency of Political Islam in Turkey," *Middle Eastern Studies* 38, no. 2 (April 2002): 187–205.

Conclusion

1. In "Science as a Vocation," Max Weber wrote: "The fate of our times is characterized by rationalization and intellectualization and, above all, by the *disenchantment* of the world . . . the bearing of man has been disenchanted and denuded of its mystical but inwardly genuine plasticity." Max Weber, "Science As a Vocation," in *Essays in Sociology*, eds. H. H. Gerth and C. Wright Mills (New York: Oxford University Press, 1946), 155; Lawrence E. Cahoone, *Dilemma of Modernity: Philosophy, Culture, and Anti-Culture, State* (New York: University of New York, 1988).

2. As explained in Chapter 4, the leader of the 1980 coup, Kenan Evren, who later became Turkey's eighth president, quoted Quranic verses and religious analogies extensively in his public speeches in order to emphasize the unity of Turks as Muslims. Evren also became the first president to attend the Fourth Islamic Conference Summit. The regime of General Kenan Evren also made religious education compulsory for elementary and secondary school students in the 1982 constitution in order to prevent political conflicts, especially among Turkey's dominant Sunni and minority Alevi groups.

3. The number of students attending Imam Hatip high schools has increased by 45 percent. Disregarding the growing discrepancy between the num-

ber of available jobs and the number of graduates, the ruling parties have established even more of these schools in order to win the support of conservative groups. Çakır Rusen, İrfan Bozan, and Hakan Talu, *İmam Hatip: Efsaneler ve Gerçekler* (Istanbul: Turkish Economic and Social Research Foundation, 2004).

4. Max Weber, *The Protestant Ethic and the Spirit of Capitalism* (London: Allen and Unwin, 1930), 183.

5. For further details of the introduction and implementation of the law, see http://www.knesset.gov.il/elections01/about_direct_eng.htm.

6. "The coalition of believers" brought together three parties, Nationalist Labor Party (later the Nationalist Action Party), Reformist Party, and the Welfare Party.

7. As indicated earlier, readers can find a detailed discussion of redemptive messianic ideologies in Eliezer Schweid, "Jewish Messianism: Metamorphosis of an Idea," *Jerusalem Quarterly* 36 (Summer 1985); Aviezer Ravitzky, *Messianism, Zionism and Jewish Religious Radicalism* (Chicago: University of Chicago Press, 1996).

8. For an analysis of how the NAP seeks to strike a balance between Islamism and Nationalism, see Sultan Tepe, "Kemalism, Islamism, and the Nationalist Action Party," *Turkish Studies* 1, no. 1 (2000); Burak Arikan and Alev Cinar, "The Nationalist Action Party: Representing the State, the Nation or the Nationalists?" in *Political Parties in Turkey*, eds. Barry Rubin and Metin Heper (London: Frank Cass, 2002).

9. The statements popular among national religious party supporters are overtly adopted in the Grand Unity Party Program, a splinter of the NAP whose leader was once the leading figure in the NAP. The program is available at http://www.bbp.org.tr.

10. NAP Party Program, available at http://www.mhp.org.tr/program/.

11. For a detailed discussion of the rise of Shas, see Peter Hirschberg, *The World of Shas* (New York: The American Jewish Committee Publications, 1999). For an analysis of its appeal, see Yoav Peled, "Toward a Redefinition of Jewish Nationalism in Israel? The Enigma of Shas," *Ethnic and Racial Studies* 2 (1998); and Michael Shalev and Gal Levy, "The Winners and Losers of 2003: Ideology, Social Structure, and Political Change," in *The Elections in Israel: 2003*, eds. Arian Asher and Michal Shamir (New York: Transaction, 2005); Etta Bick, "A Party in Decline: Shas in Israel's 2003 Elections," *Israel Affairs* 10, no. 4 (2004).

12. Ümit Cizre Sakallıoğlu, "Parameters and Strategies of Islam-State Interaction in Republican Turkey," *International Journal of Middle East Studies* 28 (1996).

13. Personal interview with Cemil Çicek, Ankara, June 1998.

14. Ed. M Hakan Yavuz, *The Emergence of a New Turkey: Democracy and the AK Party* (Salt Lake City: University of Utah Press, 2006).

15. For a more detailed discussion of Shas's novel discursive appeal, see Yadgar Yaacov, "Shas as a Struggle to Create a New Field: A Bourdieuan Perspective of an Israeli Phenomenon," *Sociology of Religion* (2003).

16. Herb Keinon, "Those Unsinkable Shasniks: Anatomy of a Victory," *The*

Jerusalem Post, May 20, 1999. For a more detailed analysis of Shas's ability to attract moderate Sephardim, see Aaron Willis, "Redefining Religious Zionism: Shas' Ethno-Politics," *Israel Studies Bulletin*, 8, no. 2 (1992).

17. Necmettin Erbakan, "Düzeltilmesi Gereken Kavram Kargaşası," *Milli Gazete*, March 8, 1997.

Index

1967 War, 49, 114–15, 125–26, 157

Abdulaziz Mecdi (Karesi), 91, 382n60
Abdulmecid II, 94
accommodationist model, 67–68; accommodationists, 76, 108, 203–4, 220; orthodox, 108; National View, 203–4, 219; religious, 76; secular, 76
acculturation, 58, 249, 273; counter-acculturation, 55, 112, 131, 152, 204, 280
Adalet ve Kalkınma Partisi. *See* Justice and Development Party
adaptive transformation, 22, 348, 354
Adil Düzen. *See* Just Order
Agudat Israel, 76, 79–81, 84, 99, 109, 113, 124, 126, 129–34, 138, 142, 149–53, 280, 372n29, 386n62
Agunot, 127
Akit, 193–94
Alevi, 175–76, 198–99, 213, 217–18, 223, 290, 294, 303, 312, 324, 365, 394n110
allegory, 58, 182
Alperen, 172–73, 391n33
Am Israel, 117, 137
Am Kadosh, 235
Anavatan Partisi. *See* Motherland Party
Arınç Bülent, 395n151
Aristotle, 34; democracy, 34–35
Aryeh Deri, 132, 149–52, 157, 231, 266, 299; effect, 266; trial, 266
Ashkenazi, 47, 82, 120–21, 128, 130, 142–45, 150, 153, 155, 232–36, 238, 254–58, 273–76, 385, 388n106; Ashkenazi chief rabbi, 83, 110, 113, 121–22, 126, 135, 240; non-

Ashkenazi, 134, 150, 153, 155; tradition, 134–35, 142, 150
Assembly of Experts, Iran, 69
Atatürk, Mustafa Kemal, 72, 90–91, 93, 98, 168, 194, 339, 378–79n14
Attiah, Ezra, 142
Avraham HaCohen Kook. *See* Kook, Avraham

Bahçeli, Devlet, 169–73, 180–81, 298, 338, 392n55, 401n42
Bainbridge, William Sims, 40, 375n26
Balıkesir Mosque talk, Atatürk, 191
Beck, Paul, 321
Ben-Gurion, 16, 84, 126
Ben Meir Yehuda, 123, 386n52
Benizri Sholomo, 153–54
Berger, Peter, 35, 39, 53
Bildung, 380n27
Birnbaum, Nathan, 74–77, 108, 131; *Confession*, 76
bivalence, 55, 91, 105, 152, 220, 337–38, 355
Bnei Akiva, 107, 118–19, 127, 383
Bobbio, Norberto, 314
Büyük Birlik Partisi. *See* Grand Union Party

Çakmak, Fevzi, 162
caliphate, 48, 82, 90, 95, 109–10; caliph, 88, 90, 95, 199, 382n51
Calvinism, 37
Campbell, James E., 245
charismatic: appeal, 25, 153, 204, 230, 237, 241–42, 293, 297–99; leadership, 37, 180, 222, 272, 299, 60; party, 49, 242, 297–98
Chaves, Mark, 54

Chief Rabbinate, 81–84, 130, 135,
  381n38
choice model, 40, 44–47, 50, 232; choice-
  centered models, 45–47, 244; politics
  of religion, 44–50, 230–33, 237, 244,
  247, 248, 251–55, 262–67, 270
Church of England, 69, 378n11
cihad, 58, 201
civil religion, 234, 287
community, 1, 10, 19, 38, 49, 56, 58,
  62; ethnic religious, 178, 226; global,
  6; Islamic, 58, 91–92, 96, 164,
  167–68, 183, 197, 224, 355, 369; political, 33, 92, 105, 112, 139, 174,
  177, 193–97, 226, 230, 289, 342,
  357, 358, 368; religious, 10, 13, 42,
  52, 83–84, 92, 134–37, 139, 156,
  167, 170, 177, 182, 189, 198, 224,
  226, 237, 326, 347, 358, 362–66; territorial religious, 224, 366
compliant dissension, 22, 135, 205, 348,
  356
Compte, Auguste, 374n10
Confession, 76, 77–78, 108, 379, 383,
  396. *See also* Birnbaum, Nathan
conflict model, 41–42, 233–35, 248,
  251–55, 264, 285–89, 325
confrontation frameworks, 5–12, 16, 19,
  22–25, 37
conservative democracy, 206–7, 210–12,
  213–25, 354–55
Constitutional Court, 15, 183, 187, 193,
  205, 391n23, 395n150
controlled dependency, 60, 71, 346
convergence approach, 5–12, 16, 19,
  22–24, 37
Coşan Esat, 185, 201
counter-acculturation, 55, 112, 131,
  204, 280
crisis: leader, 178; of stateness, 169, 184,
  334
crisis model, 25, 40, 43–47, 58, 231–33,
  235–37, 242, 258, 289–92, 319–36
  passim

Danbury Baptist Association, 66, 378n4
Dati (religious), 107, 248
dayanim, 240, 287, 381n40, 389n117
dealignment, 316, 396
Democratic Party, 87, 94, 99, 162, 178,
  286
Democratic People's Party, (DEHAP)
  316, 318, 321, 402n60

Democratic Society Party (*Demokratik
  Toplum Partisi*). *See* Democratic
  People's Party
Demokrat Parti. *See* Democratic Party
dependent autonomy, 60, 71, 346
Deri. *See* Aryeh Deri
desecularization, 27, 36, 54
dina d'malchuta dina, 113
Directorate of Religious Affairs, 49, 60,
  95–97, 192, 216–17
disenchantment, 54, 281, 307, 377n54,
  403n1
Dobbeleare, Karel, 54
Dokuz Işık. *See* Nine Lights
Don Yehiya, Eliezer, 77, 234
Druckman, Haim, 127, 386n52
Dryzek, John, 12, 301
duality, 38, 85, 284
Durkheim, Emile, 22, 36–40,
  374nn19,20; conceptualization of po-
  litical religion, 36–40, 51, 54, 374n20

Easton, David, 34
easy entrance policy, 61, 99, 350
Education Reform Act of 1988, En-
  gland, 69
Eitam Effi, 118, 126
El Ha'maayan, 145. *See also* Shas
  schools
Elbaz, Reuven, 146, 154, 399n61
Eliahu, Mordechai, 113
Enlightenment, 9, 12, 73, 116, 118, 189,
  375n26, 378n14; European, 225,
  380n28
Erbakan, Necmettin, 182, 184–91, 193,
  196–201, 203–4, 218, 298–99, 354,
  360, 367, 392n63
Erdoğan, Recep Tayyip, 187, 199–200,
  204–5, 214–22, 298–99, 338–39, 360
Eretz Yisrael (Land of Israel), 115, 122,
  384n6
Esengül, Lütfü, 181, 204
ethnic liberalization, 326
European Union, 186, 208
Euthyphro, 33
Evren Kenan, 184, 403n2

Fazilet Partisi. *See* Virtue Party
Finkelstein, Gila, 127
fundamentalism, 50–51; global, 3, 26

Geertz, Clifford, 51–52
geullah. *See* redemption

Gökalp, Ziya, 92–93
Gorny Yosef, 77, 380n27
Grand National Assembly, 90, 93–94, 193
Grand Union Party (GUP), 160, 164, 172–73, 179–80, 390n4, 392n52
Granovetter, Mark, 63
Gül, Abdullah, 186, 203, 220, 394n118
Gülle, Akif, 213, 221
Gümüşhaneevi Dergah, 200
Gush Emunim, 125, 240, 273
Guttman Report, 249

Hacıbayram Mosque, 91
Hadash, 148
Hakibbutz Hadati, 107, 273, 386n54
Halakhic, 74, 86, 95, 107–14, 117–20, 123, 126, 133–35, 138, 140, 143, 242; anti-, 153; rules, 85, 117, 249, 267; state, 79, 247, 252, tradition, 60, 109, 121, 134, 156–57
Hallel, 132–33
halutzim, 116
Halutziut, 112
Halvet der encumen, 189
Hamizrahi, 76, 81–84, 99, 380n35
Hapoel Hamizrachi, 106
Haredi (ulta-Orthodox), 120, 129–36, 140, 145–48, 153–58, 238, 248–51, 268, 272–73, 278, 381n36; blocs, 250; community, 120, 156, 158, 238, 381n36; party, 131, 136, 153, 250–51, 254–55
Hasidim, 80
headscarf, 168, 186, 330, 332–33
Hearths of Idealists. *See* Ülkü Ocakları
Hebrew culture, 79–82
Hebron, 114, 115
Heilman, Samuel, 54
heretic, 39, 49, 225
Herzl, Theodor, 72–75, 77–79, 378n14, 379nn20,25, 389n121; *Altneuland*, 74–75, 378n14; Herzlian Zionism, 79; *The Jewish State*, 73, 75, 378n14
Hess, Moses, 74, 379n17
High Court of Justice, 83
Histadrut, 124, 278
Hizmet, 170, 202
holy alliance, 163
Homo Islamicus, 340
horizontal: equality and rights, 217, 341; organizations, 344, 355–56, 359

İmam Hatip, 192, 203, 218, 347
immigration: Ethiopians, 144, 271; Falashas, 144; policies, 95, 129, 153, 255, 271–72
İnönü, İsmet, 167–68, 392n49
integrationist state, 67, 69–71, 338
internal secularization, 24, 54–55, 106, 132, 139, 155, 158, 204, 224, 272, 360–66
Iran, 69–70, 141, 184, 192
İskenderpaşa, 185
Islamist-Turkish idealism, 161, 206
istiare, 203

Jefferson, Thomas, 66, 378n4
Jewish Question, 73, 108, 380n29
Jewish State, The (Herzl), 73, 75, 378n14
Judaic: doctrine, 53; parties, 3, 11; politics, 23; tradition, 379n23
Judeah and Samariah, 264–65
Judeo-Christian tradition and parties, 9–11
Just Order, 172, 189–91, 197–99, 290–91
Justice and Development Party (JDP), 15, 17, 87, 100, 160, 164, 171, 187–88, 199–226, 232, 284–88, 308, 313–24, 326–27, 329–30, 332–35, 338–42, 353–55, 357–60, 363, 365, 394n118, 395nn147,151, 399n2, 400n10

Karo, Yosef, 141, 387n70
Kavakçı, Merve, 203, 391n23
Kedouri, Yitzhak, 274
Kemalism, 72, 82, 89, 91–92, 94, 165–69, 188–94, 196, 205, 207, 209, 212, 223–25, 285–87, 289, 293, 363–64, 382n71
Kemalist, 48, 86, 88–89, 93–94, 96–98, 161, 164–65, 167–68, 181–83, 188–89, 191, 193–95, 196, 197–99, 205, 207–9, 213, 223–24, 226, 286–87, 289, 293, 300, 305, 310, 313, 325, 337, 339, 353, 363, 393n76; nation, 97; state, 86, 164–65, 191, 195, 286, 289, 313
Kemalist nationalism, 48, 88–89, 93–94, 97, 164–65, 167, 188, 194, 205, 286; and the Justice and Development Party, 205–7; and the Nationalist Action Party, 164–70; and the National View parties, 188–94

Knesset, 14, 21, 113, 127, 129–131,
146, 153–154, 349, 386n57, 397n36,
398n37
Kook, Avraham (Avraham HaCohen
Kook), 110, 114–16, 119–20, 123–24,
136, 157, 241, 379n24, 384n6
Kook, Zvi Yehudea, 114
Köprülü, Fuat, 383n76
Kotku, Zait, 182, 189, 200
Kurds, 91, 175–77, 197, 303, 338, 365;
Kurdish identity, 176, 288, 312; Kurdish problem, 163, 197, 214–16, 290,
294, 322; Kurdish question, 197,
213–14, 363; Kurdishness, 311–12,
326
Kutan, Recai, 187–88, 194, 199,
394n118

labor, 125, 129, 152, 231, 233, 235,
238, 266–67
laïcité, 15, 67–68, 189, 305–6
laicization, 54, 95–96, 192, 204
Lasswell, Harold D., 34
Law 2004–228, France, 68
Left-Right, 248, 252–54, 258, 268, 276,
302, 304, 314–18
Leighley, Jan E., 240
Levy, Yitzhak, 125–28, 386n60
Liebman, Charles, 234
Likud, 99, 125, 129, 153, 235, 254,
277, 397nn33,36
Lithuanian schools, 149, 152; leadership,
149, 150, 152
Luz, Ehud, 77, 380n28

Ma'ayan Hahinuch Hatorani, 145–46.
See also Shas schools
Mafdal, 14, 48, 80, 82, 103, 106–69
passim, 229–90 *passim*, 326, 352–63
passim; ideology, 109–18, 125, 131,
134, 141, 157, 172, 23–37, 325, 352,
358, 362–63; leadership, 109, 121,
123, 138; supporters, 115, 251, 254,
260, 262–70
mamlakhtiyut, 278, 339
Mapai, 17, 84, 112, 236, 241, 247, 278
Masorati, 248. *See also* traditional, religious identity in Israel
mechanical societies, 38
Medina Contract, 55, 195
medreseler, 288
Meimad, 122–23
Meretz, 120, 235, 279

Miflaga Datit Le'umit. *See* Mafdal
Milhemet Tarbut (Culture War), 120, 123
military, 49, 56, 69, 86–88, 94, 120,
122–27, 133, 140, 153, 163, 178–79,
202, 302–5; coups, 182–84; Israel and
religious parties, 270; JDP and military,
205–8, 270, 331–34; Mafdal, 120–27;
NAP and military, 162–63, 178–79;
National View and military, 184–88,
331–34, 363; post modern coup, 186,
209; Shas, 127, 133, 140, 153; Shas
and military, minhag, 135, 140; Turkish parties, 182–85, 283, 305–7, 347
millet, 16, 78, 88–90, 94, 196, 305,
399n61
Milli Gazete, 192–93, 197, 199,
393n90, 394n111
Milli Görüş. *See* National View
Milliyetçi Hareket Partisi. *See* Nationalist Action Party
minhag, 135, 139
Ministry of Religious Affairs, 84, 381n41
Misak-ı Milli, 91, 165. *See also* National
Pact
Mishnah, 77, 146
Mitnaggedim, 77, 80
mitzvah, 117, 135; mitzvoth, 123, 134,
138, 249
mizrahi, 148, 275
modernity, 3–5, 9–12, 16, 19, 24, 31,
41, 97, 103–4, 157–58, 210–11, 225,
230, 251, 295, 304, 343; multiple
modernities, 9
Motherland Party, 87, 184, 201, 318
mücahid, 172, 201, 298
müftü, 192, 216
MÜSİAD (Müstakil İşadamlari Derneği),
291, 400n22

Nakshibendi, 178, 182, 189, 191,
200–201
National Order Party, 100, 182, 188
National Pact, 82, 91
National Religious Zionism Party, 126
National Salvation Party, 183, 188
National View, 48, 87, 159–60, 182–88,
194, 198–99, 218, 326, 358, 372
National View parties, 87, 159–60, 182,
188–89, 194, 218, 326, 372n30; lead-
ership, 199–204
Nationalist Action Party (NAP), 15,
160–81, 198, 203, 219, 223–26, 232,
248, 284–98, 308–42, 352, 358,

362–63, 368, 390nn4,5, 392n57, 399n2, 403n66, 404n8
Neturei Karta, 131
Nine Lights, 162, 165–66, 170
Nordau, Max, 77, 379n24
Nursi, Said, 93, 96

Or, Haim, 154
organic societies, 38. *See also* Weber, Max
Orlev, Zevulun, 121
Ottoman Muslim, 91
Ottomanism, 86, 90, 165
Ovadia, Yosef, 130–34, 136–39, 142, 147–51, 155, 157, 200, 234, 241–42, 264–66, 272–75, 279, 358, 387; ideology, 132–33; Ovadia effect, 272
Öz, Esat, 161, 390n5

Pan Turkism, 86, 164
Panebianco, Angelo, 241, 298
Parsons, Talcott, 39
Peretz, Yitzhak, 131, 151–52, 389n121
pikuach nefesh, 121, 140–41, 147, 154, 388n87
Plato, 34
plausibility structure, 39
Polat, Hanan, 127
political alienation, 25, 235–37, 287, 289, 327–28, 335, 355
Political Dimension of Religion (Arjomand), 56
political religion, 4, 35–36, 46, 52
politics, definition, 34
Politics of Mobilization, 239–42, 293, 295–98
Post-Zionist redemptive era, 118–19
Progressive Republican Party, 87, 159
Prosperity Party, 17, 87, 100, 181–82, 187–88, 224, 284–85, 288, 291, 294–98, 305, 307–16, 321–27, 332–42, 352–54, 357, 372n30, 399n2, 402n54

Quranic, 183, 186, 216, 403n2

Ravitzky, Aviezer, 85
realignment, 239, 260, 316, 338, 342
redemption, 58, 75–76, 107–9, 111–25, 131–39, 146, 154–56, 352, 363, 377n60, 379nn20–23, 383n2; auto-, 156; collective, 139; geullah, 383n3; individual, 139
redemptive Zionism, 109, 118, 240, 257

Refah Partisi. *See* Welfare Party and National View parties
religion: definition, 20, 35–38, 40, 51–53; JDP and Religious symbols, 206–21, 224; Mafdal and religious symbols, 111–26; NAP and religious symbols, 165–77, 287–89; Prosperity Party and religious symbols, 181–98; religion in state, 59–61; Shas and religious symbols, 137, 140–48; symbolic system and capacity, 19–20, 41, 50–53, 56–63; Turkish and nationalism, 92–95, 159; Zionism and religion, 74–77
religious disinvolvement, 54
religious party, 15, 18, 45, 105, 129, 148, 161, 337, 350; elites, 19, 21, 23, 62; leader, 21, 126, 160, 353; religious political parties, 2, 17–18, 34, 42, 104, 262, 366; supporters, 25–26, 45, 49, 229, 243, 245, 248, 252–58, 259, 281, 283, 293, 297, 301, 305, 311–14, 318–22, 327, 334
religious politics, 56–59
religious voluntarism, 40
religious Zionism, 79, 109–11, 115–31, 140–41, 157, 236, 384n6; national religious Zionist movement, 84; religious Zionist parties, 80, 106, 241
Republican People's Party (RPP), 17, 87, 162, 167, 182–83, 204, 286, 296, 318–19, 321, 338
Resource Mobilization Model, 45–47
responsa, 132, 155, 242, 278
return of religion, 3, 6, 26, 36, 54, 343–44, 349, 360, 366, 368–69
Rishon Letzion, 83
rites, 38
Roman Catholic Church, 67
Rome and Jerusalem, 379n17. *See also* Hess, Moses

Sabra, 256–57
sacralization 24, 55, 106, 111, 115–17, 122, 134, 155–58, 164, 178, 215, 223–24, 289, 360–366; of Mafdal, 134, 156, 158; of the secular, 55, 117
Schach, Eliezer Menahem, 149–52, 238
secularism, 6, 16–17, 23, 49, 51, 53–54, 60, 77, 82, 92, 97–99, 152, 162, 165, 167–68, 191–92, 194, 205–8, 211, 218, 220, 224, 285–88, 293, 300, 304–5, 313, 335, 341, 346–74, 352–53, 363–65, 377n54

secularization, 6, 8–10, 24, 35–36,
39–40, 42–44, 53–55, 94–97, 287,
362; cognitive, 54; desecularizarion, 3,
36, 54; internal, 24, 54, 55, 106, 132,
139, 158, 164, 204, 224, 272, 360,
361–66; paradigm, 35; of the sacred,
55; theories, 39, 40; thesis, 44
sefer der vatan, 189
Sephardi, 47, 78, 83, 113, 121–22, 125,
128–30, 134–35, 139–44, 147–50,
153, 155–57, 232–36, 248, 251,
254–58, 264–66, 271–70 *passim*,
354, 357, 368, 380n31; community,
128, 130, 135, 141, 236–38; haredi,
129; identity, 129, 141–44, 238;
rabbi, 130, 135, 150; Sephardization,
139; tradition, 139, 143
Sephardic communities, 134, 142, 147,
150, 237, 358, 368
Şeyhülislam, 93, 97
Shaki, Avner, 122
Shamir, Michal, 239, 372n31
Shapira, Avraham, 113, 126
Sharia, 305, 307–9, 341, 402n54
Shas (Hit'akhdut ha-Sephardim ha-
Olamit Shomrey Torah): approach to
religion, 259; ideology, 131–48, 232,
235–36, 357–60, 365, 368; leadership, 135, 139, 141, 144, 148–54,
241–42, 271, 279; movement, 143,
149, 272–73, 388n100; Party, rise
of, 14, 47, 121–23, 129–30; schools,
145, 275, 388nn104,106; supporters, 241–45, 248–82 *passim*,
397n30. *See also* Ma'ayan Hahinuch
Hatorani
Sheirut Leumi, 127
Shinui, 120, 267, 270
Shulkan Aruch, 141
Socrates, 33
Stark, Rodney, 40, 375n26
stateness, 65, 169, 184, 225, 334–35
statism, 191, 337
Status Quo Agreement, 81–85,
233, 346
Stern-Katan, Sarah, 127
strict separation, 9, 59, 66–67, 70, 361
survey data, 13, 25–26, 243–47, 251,
253–54, 256–57, 259–60, 262,
265–66, 270–71, 276–77, 302–4,
307–9, 312, 315, 319, 323, 331, 334,
377n54, 402n50
şuur, 193

symbolic capital, 20, 59, 61–63, 98,
103, 105–6, 277, 344, 369
syncretist-transformative identity, 233,
293

takiyye, 159–60; 220, 290n3
Tami (Movement for Tradition), 122,
129, 135–36
Tanrı, 382n71
Tanzimat, 88
Tel Aviv (Herzl), 75
territorial issues, 121, 125–26, 128, 141,
235, 254, 280
teshuvah, 55, 71, 138–40
Tocqueville, Alexis de, 1, 65, 67
traditional, religious identity in Israel,
248–52
traditional reactionary, 36
transitional domains, 145
trust, in communities, 173, 191, 291,
318–35 *passim*
türban. *See* headscarf
Türkeş, Alparslan, 162, 175, 178–79
Turkish Islamist, 198, 205
Turkish Parliament, 215, 349
Tzur Yisrael, 85

Ülkü Ocakları, 167, 171, 181, 392n55
Ülkücü, 162, 170–73, 179–180, 290,
356, 391n33, 392n55
Ulus, 94, 193
ummah, 26, 58, 166, 172, 174, 196–99,
377n60
United Torah Judaism, 27, 48, 278, 352,
386n62

vakf, 182
value rationalism, 37
vernacularization, 11, 19
Virtue Party, 168, 187–88, 315, 372n30

Wall of Separation: history, 66; permeable walls, 67, 68, 69, 83–85, 98
Weber, Max, 22, 36, 37, 40, 54, 55, 56,
62, 230, 348, 373n3, 374n12, 403n1;
political religion, 36–39, 54–55, 62,
374n20, 377n54
Welfare Party, 15, 184–88, 197, 283,
312, 391n45, 393n74, 404n6
West, 165, 176, 184, 186, 190, 206, 208

Yahnici, Bülent, 176
Yazıcıoğlu, Muhsin, 179–80, 392n54

Yeshiva education, 150, 272, 275
Yeshivat Porat, 142
Yishau, Eli, 151–53, 360, 389n115
Yishuv, 77, 81, 83, 107, 150
Yosef. *See* Ovadia, Yosef
Yusufiyye Medrasha, 163

Zait Kotku. *See* Kotku
Zeev, Nissim, 129, 149, 273
Zion, 74, 76–77, 136, 379n22
Zionism, 72–80, 82–86, 89–92, 98, 107–26, 130–36, 140–41, 154–57, 229, 231–35, 238–39, 252, 257, 266–67, 271, 273, 280, 293, 362, 364, 370, 379nn17,25, 380n27; Ashkenazi, 136; Herzlian, 79, 89; Israeli, 234; labor, 238, 252, 267, 293; Labor Zionism, 238, 252, 266–67, 293; Mafdal's Zionism, 119–28; Mapai, 236; religious, 79, 109–11, 115, 118–19, 126, 131, 140–41, 157, 236, 384n6; Sephardi, 155
Zionist Congress, 74, 81, 84, 378n14
Zohar Zvi, 139, 387n70